MARVEL KNIGHT

#1

DONNY CATES
Writer

TRAVEL FOREMAN
Penciler

DEREK FRIDOLFS
Inker

MATT MILLA
Color Artist

#2 & #5

MATTHEW ROSENBERG & DONNY CATES
Story

MATTHEW ROSENBERG
Script

NIKO HENRICHON
Artist & Colors

LAURENT GROSSAT
Color Assistant

#3

TINI HOWARD & DONNY CATES
Story

TINI HOWARD
Script

DAMIAN COUCEIRO
Artist

MATT MILLA
Color Artist

#4

VITA AYALA & DONNY CATES
Story

VITA AYALA
Script

JOSHUA CASSARA
Artist

MATT MILLA
Color Artist

#6

DONNY CATES
Writer

KIM JACINTO & TRAVEL FOREMAN
Pencilers

KIM JACINTO & RICHARD FRIEND
Inkers

MATT MILLA
Color Artist

VC'S CORY PETIT
Letterer

GEOFF SHAW & RAIN BEREDO
Cover Art

ALANNA SMITH
Associate Editor

TOM BREVOORT
Custodian

JOE QUESADA & JIMMY PALMIOTTI
Editors Emeriti

Collection Editor **JENNIFER GRÜN**
Assistant Editor **CAITLIN O'CON**
Associate Managing Editor **KATERI W**
Editor, Special Projects **MARK D. BE**

Editor In Chief **C.B. CEBULSKI**
Chief Creative Officer **JOE QUESADA**
President **DAN BUCKLEY**
Executive Producer **ALAN FINE**

MARVEL KNIGHTS 20TH. Contains material originally ... 574-9. Published by MARVEL WORLDWIDE, INC., a subsidiary of MARVEL ENTERTAINMENT, LLC. OFFICE OF PUBLICATI... names, characters, persons, and/or institutions in this magazine with those of any living or dead person or institution is inte... purely coincidental. **Printed in the U.S.A.** DAN BUCKLEY, President, Marvel Entertainment; JOHN NEE, Publisher; JOE QUESADA, Chief Creative Officer; TOM BREVOORT, SVP of Publishing; DAVID BOGART, Associate Publisher & SVP of Talent Affairs; DAVID GABRIEL, SVP of Sales & Marketing, Publishing; JEFF YOUNGQUIST, VP of Production & Special Projects; DAN CARR, Executive Director of Publishing Technology; ALEX MORALES, Director of Publishing Operations; DAN EDINGTON, Managing Editor; SUSAN CRESPI, Production Manager; STAN LEE, Chairman Emeritus. For information regarding advertising in Marvel Comics or on Marvel.com, please contact Vit DeBellis, Custom Solutions & Integrated Advertising Manager, at vdebellis@marvel.com. For Marvel subscription inquiries, please call 888-511-5480. **Manufactured between 3/1/2019 and 4/2/2019 by LSC COMMUNICATIONS INC., KENDALLVILLE, IN, USA.**

10 9 8 7 6 5 4 3 2 1

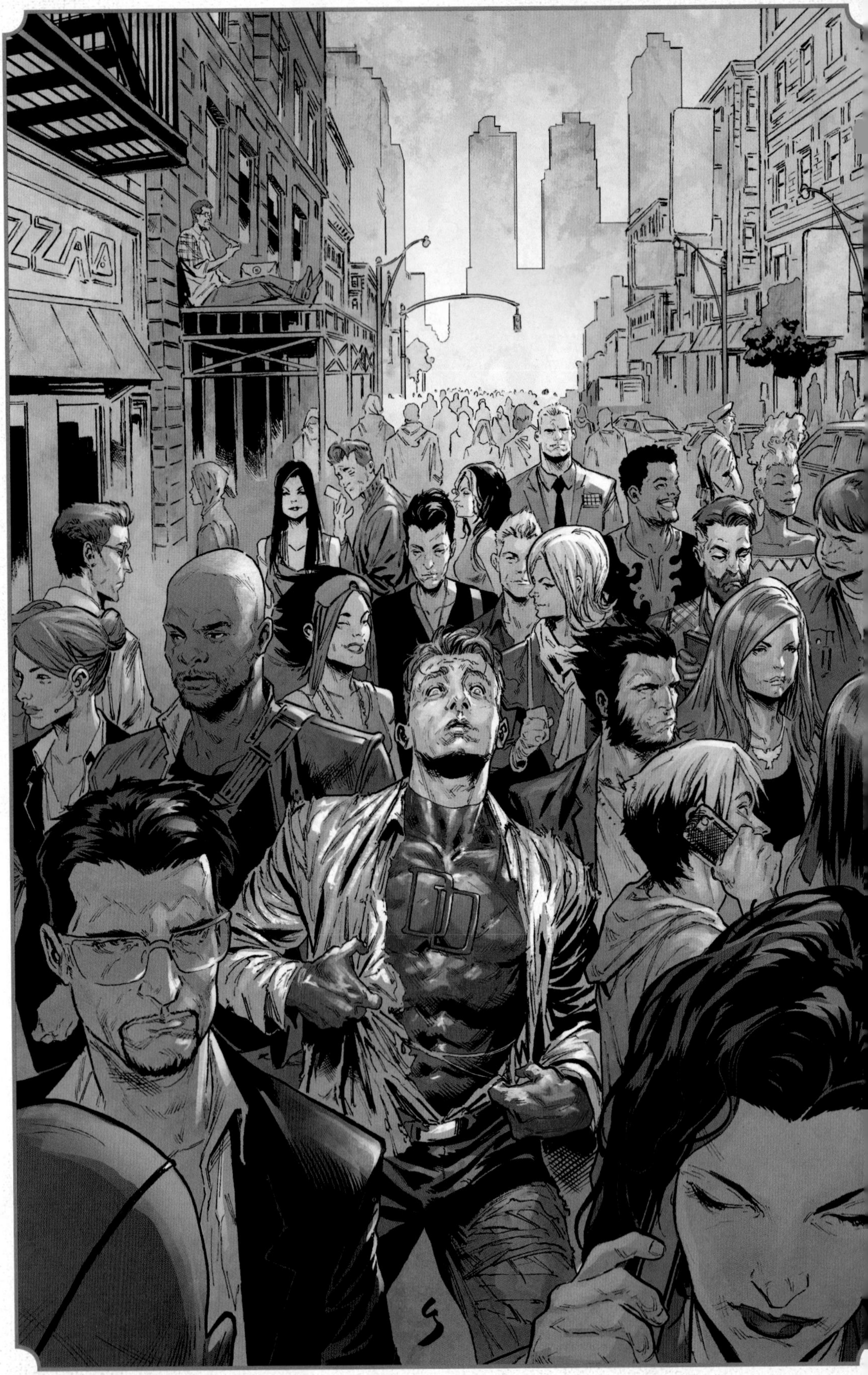

1

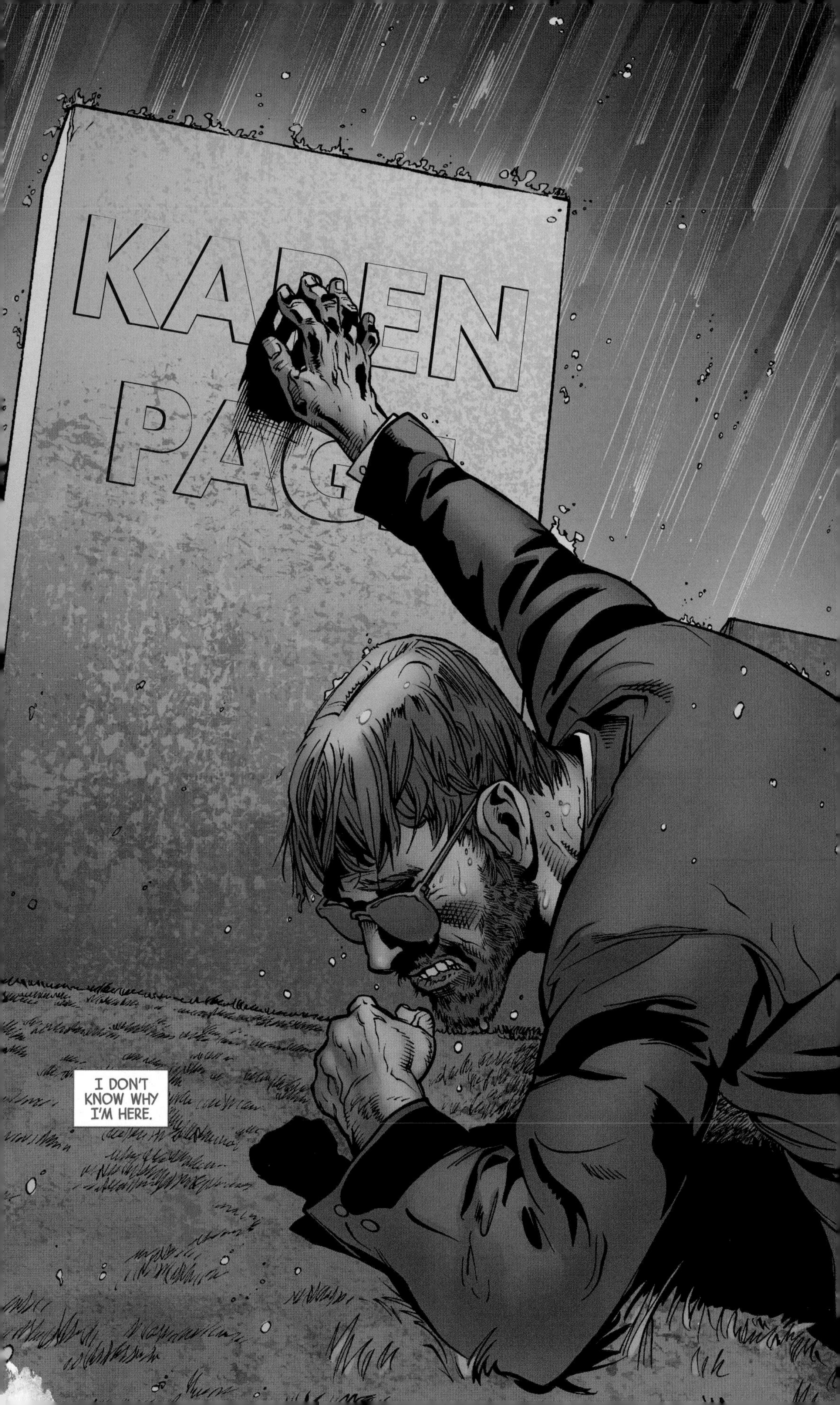
KAREN
PAGE
I DON'T KNOW WHY I'M HERE.

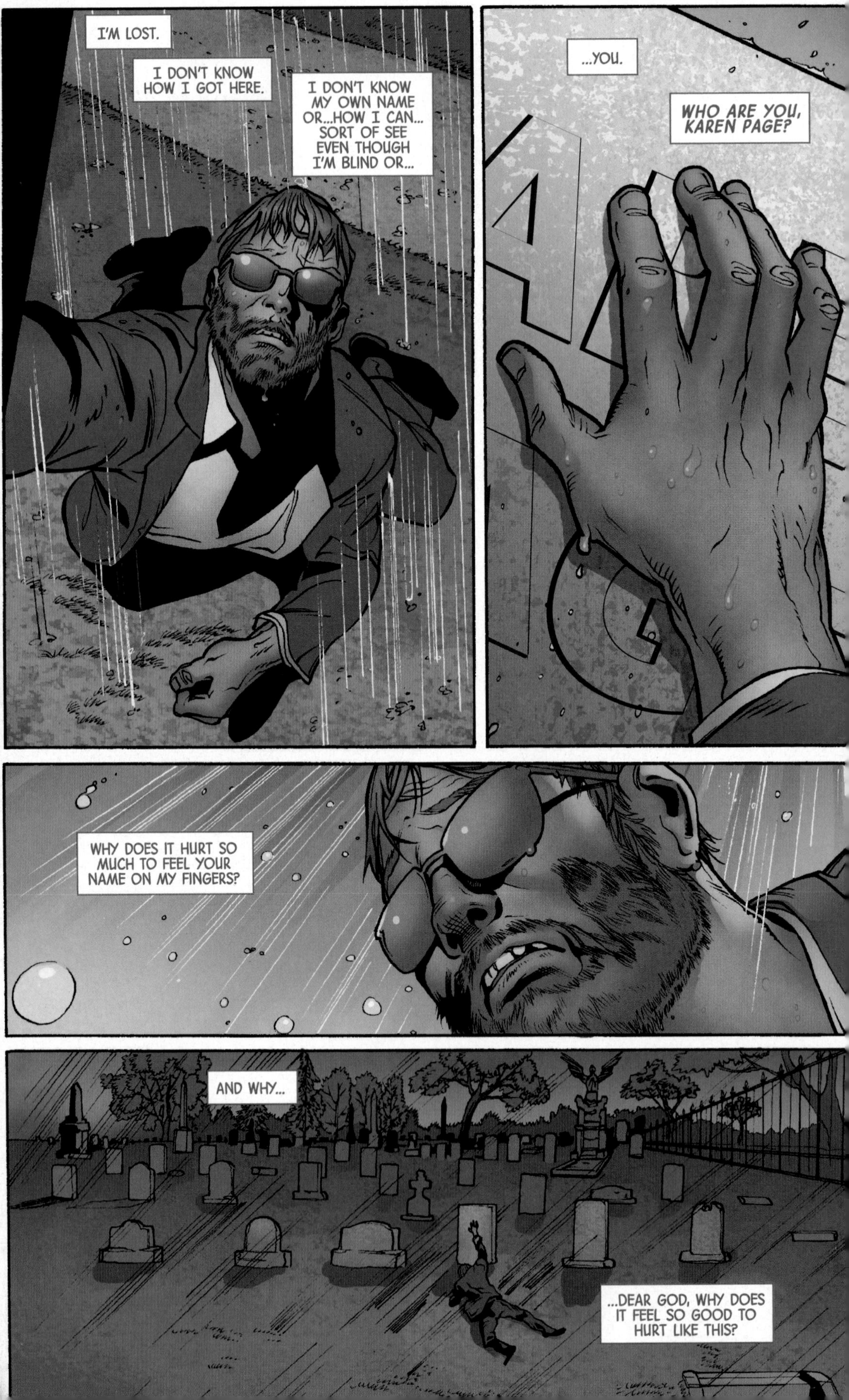

I'M LOST.
I DON'T KNOW HOW I GOT HERE.
I DON'T KNOW MY OWN NAME OR...HOW I CAN... SORT OF SEE EVEN THOUGH I'M BLIND OR...
...YOU.
WHO ARE YOU, KAREN PAGE?
WHY DOES IT HURT SO MUCH TO FEEL YOUR NAME ON MY FINGERS?
AND WHY...
...DEAR GOD, WHY DOES IT FEEL SO GOOD TO HURT LIKE THIS?

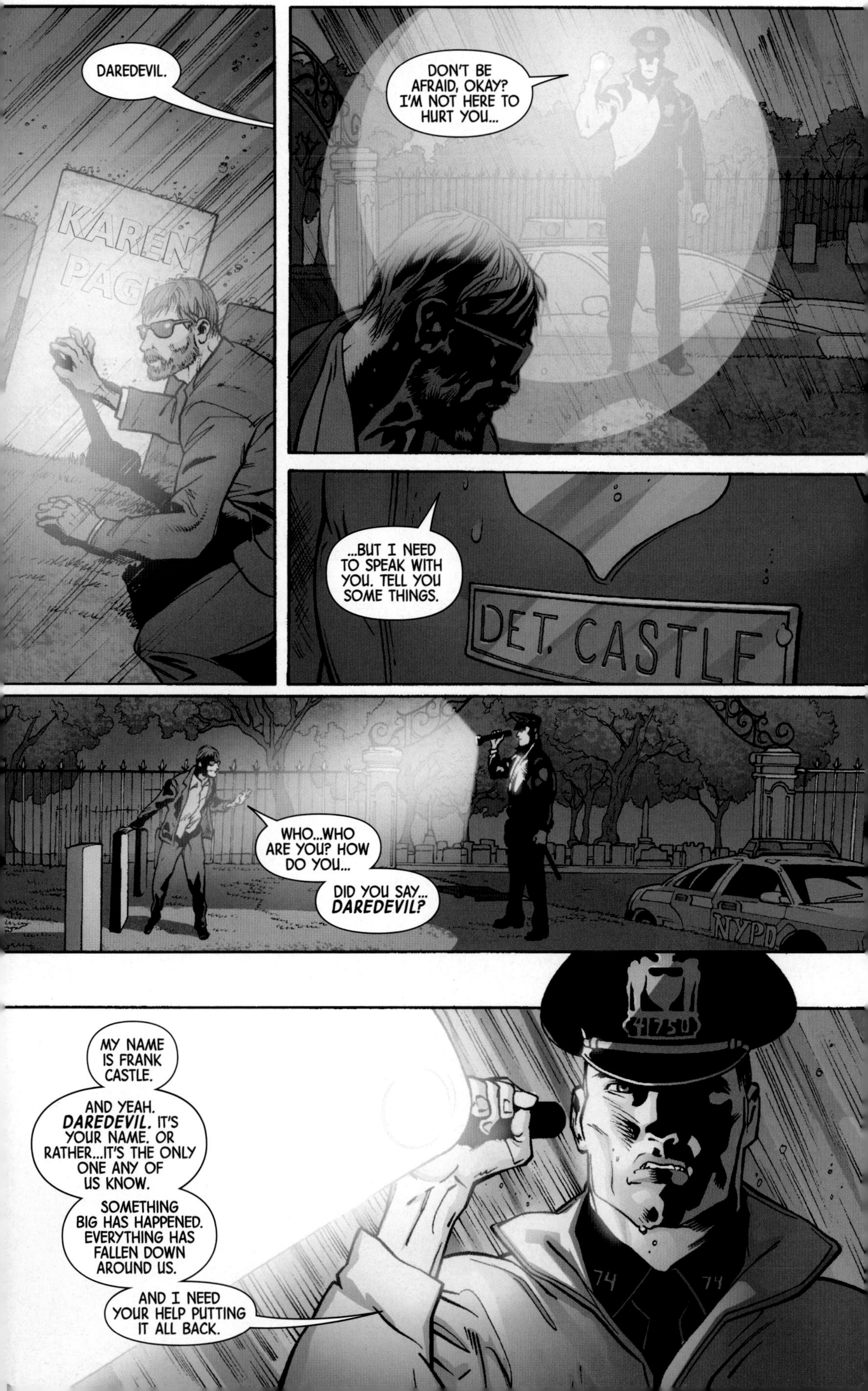
DAREDEVIL.
KAREN PAGE
DON'T BE AFRAID, OKAY? I'M NOT HERE TO HURT YOU...
...BUT I NEED TO SPEAK WITH YOU. TELL YOU SOME THINGS.
DET. CASTLE
WHO...WHO ARE YOU? HOW DO YOU...
DID YOU SAY... DAREDEVIL?
NYPD
MY NAME IS FRANK CASTLE.
AND YEAH. DAREDEVIL. IT'S YOUR NAME. OR RATHER...IT'S THE ONLY ONE ANY OF US KNOW.
SOMETHING BIG HAS HAPPENED. EVERYTHING HAS FALLEN DOWN AROUND US.
AND I NEED YOUR HELP PUTTING IT ALL BACK.

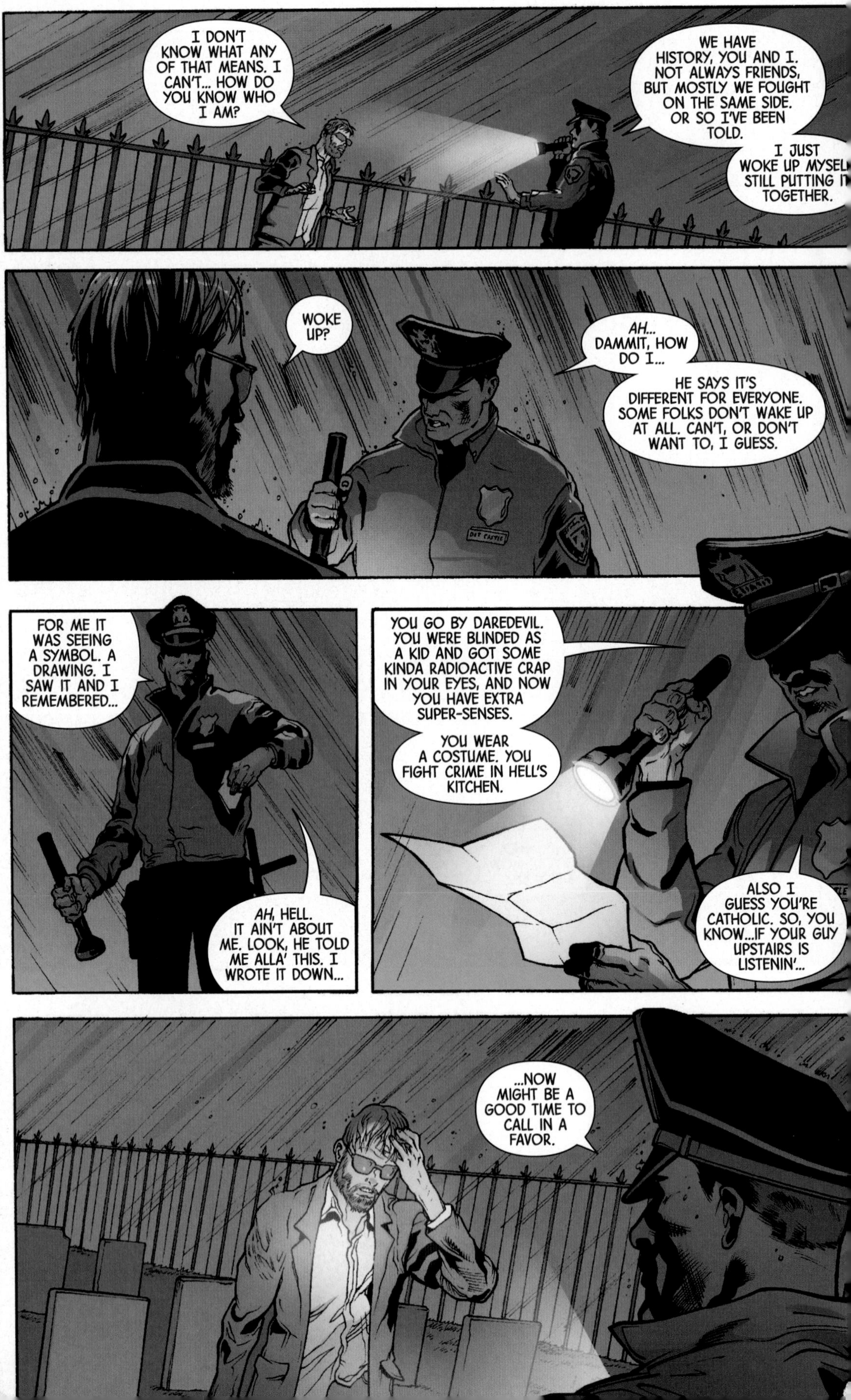
I DON'T KNOW WHAT ANY OF THAT MEANS. I CAN'T... HOW DO YOU KNOW WHO I AM?
WE HAVE HISTORY, YOU AND I. NOT ALWAYS FRIENDS, BUT MOSTLY WE FOUGHT ON THE SAME SIDE. OR SO I'VE BEEN TOLD.
I JUST WOKE UP MYSEL STILL PUTTING I TOGETHER.
WOKE UP?
AH... DAMMIT, HOW DO I...
HE SAYS IT'S DIFFERENT FOR EVERYONE. SOME FOLKS DON'T WAKE UP AT ALL. CAN'T, OR DON'T WANT TO, I GUESS.
FOR ME IT WAS SEEING A SYMBOL. A DRAWING. I SAW IT AND I REMEMBERED...
AH, HELL. IT AIN'T ABOUT ME. LOOK, HE TOLD ME ALLA' THIS. I WROTE IT DOWN...
YOU GO BY DAREDEVIL. YOU WERE BLINDED AS A KID AND GOT SOME KINDA RADIOACTIVE CRAP IN YOUR EYES, AND NOW YOU HAVE EXTRA SUPER-SENSES.
YOU WEAR A COSTUME. YOU FIGHT CRIME IN HELL'S KITCHEN.
ALSO I GUESS YOU'RE CATHOLIC. SO, YOU KNOW...IF YOUR GUY UPSTAIRS IS LISTENIN'...
...NOW MIGHT BE A GOOD TIME TO CALL IN A FAVOR.

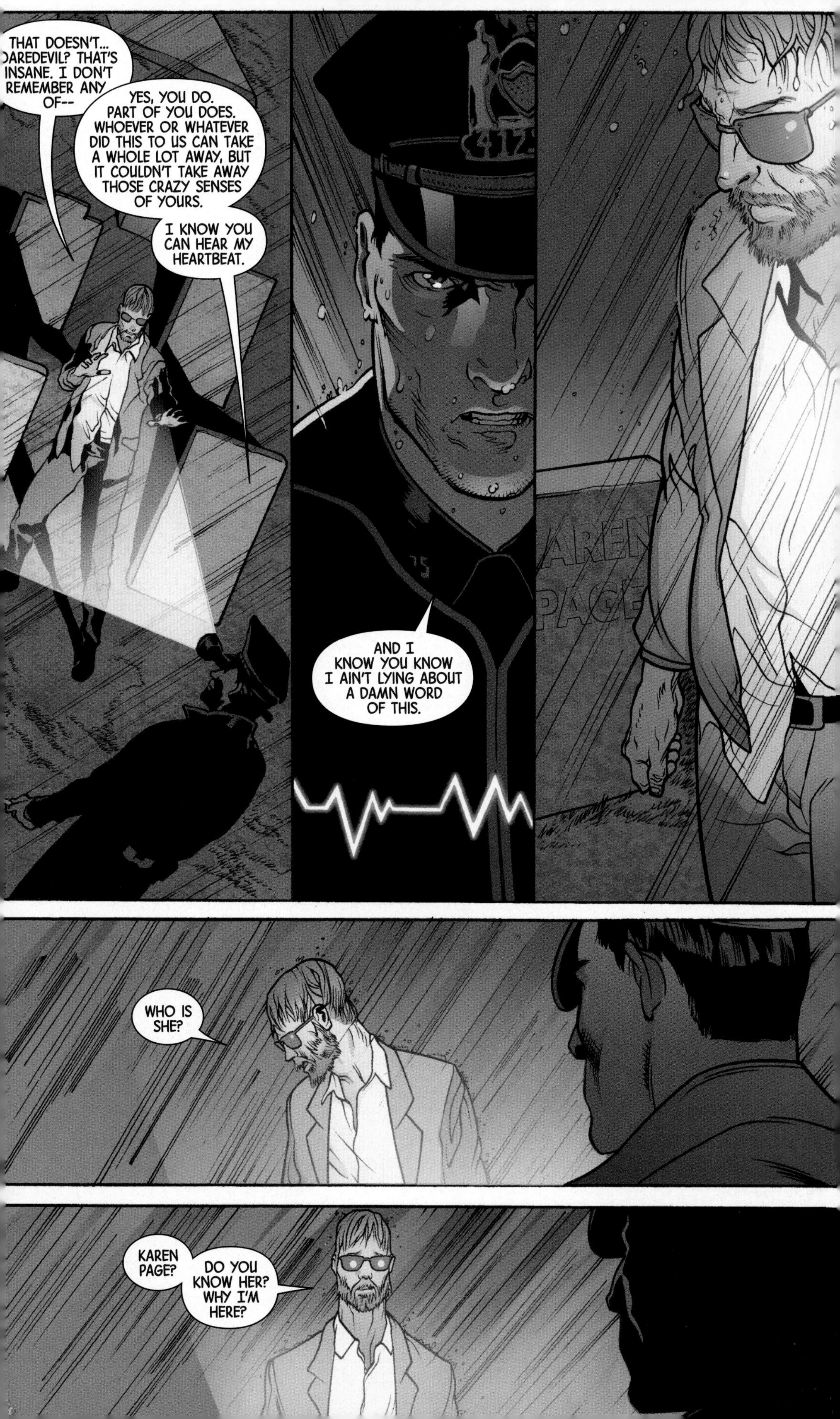
THAT DOESN'T... DAREDEVIL? THAT'S INSANE. I DON'T REMEMBER ANY OF--
YES, YOU DO. PART OF YOU DOES. WHOEVER OR WHATEVER DID THIS TO US CAN TAKE A WHOLE LOT AWAY, BUT IT COULDN'T TAKE AWAY THOSE CRAZY SENSES OF YOURS.
I KNOW YOU CAN HEAR MY HEARTBEAT.
AND I KNOW YOU KNOW I AIN'T LYING ABOUT A DAMN WORD OF THIS.
KAREN PAGE
WHO IS SHE?
KAREN PAGE?
DO YOU KNOW HER? WHY I'M HERE?

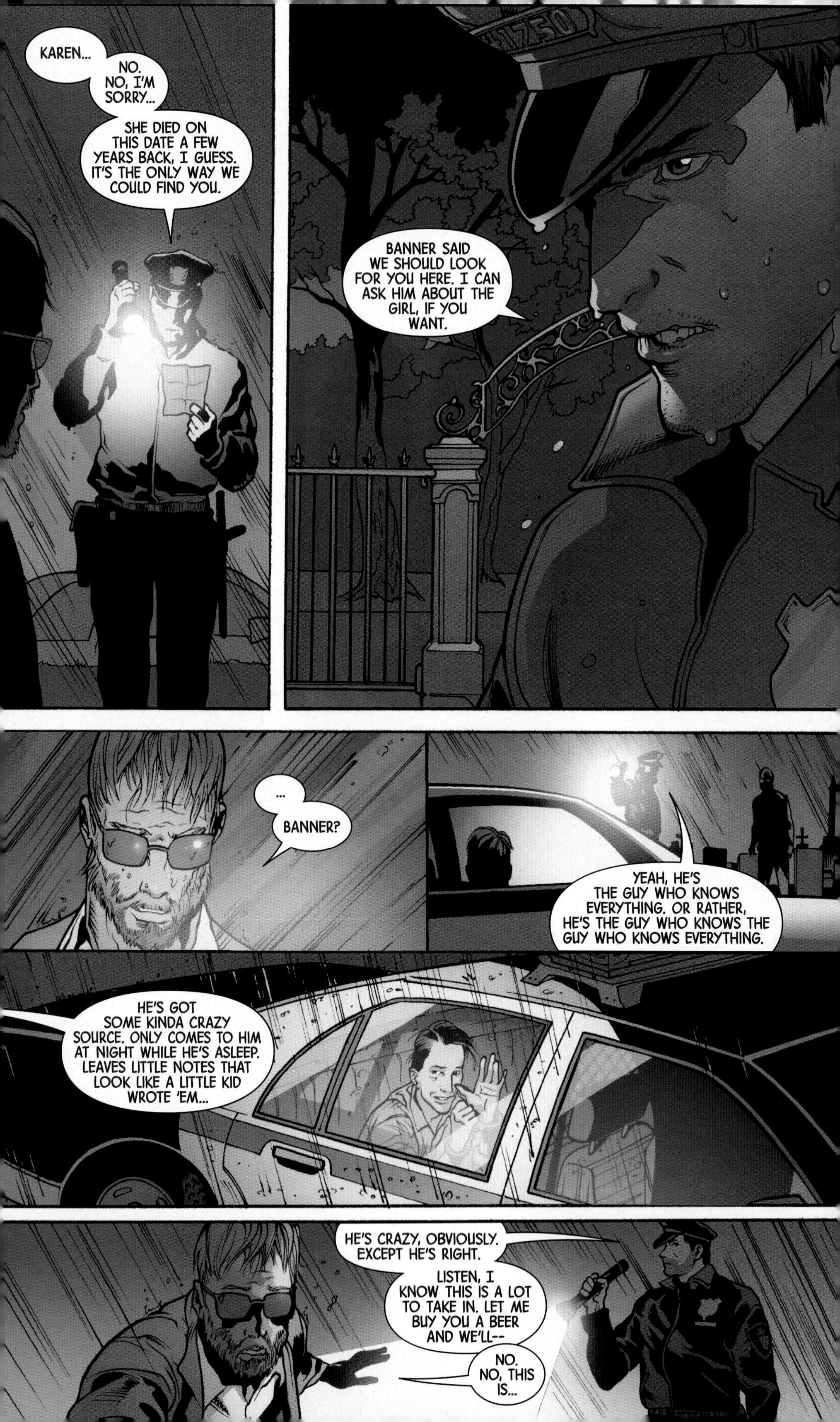
KAREN...
NO. NO, I'M SORRY...
SHE DIED ON THIS DATE A FEW YEARS BACK, I GUESS. IT'S THE ONLY WAY WE COULD FIND YOU.
BANNER SAID WE SHOULD LOOK FOR YOU HERE. I CAN ASK HIM ABOUT THE GIRL, IF YOU WANT.
...
BANNER?
YEAH, HE'S THE GUY WHO KNOWS EVERYTHING. OR RATHER, HE'S THE GUY WHO KNOWS THE GUY WHO KNOWS EVERYTHING.
HE'S GOT SOME KINDA CRAZY SOURCE. ONLY COMES TO HIM AT NIGHT WHILE HE'S ASLEEP. LEAVES LITTLE NOTES THAT LOOK LIKE A LITTLE KID WROTE 'EM...
HE'S CRAZY, OBVIOUSLY. EXCEPT HE'S RIGHT.
LISTEN, I KNOW THIS IS A LOT TO TAKE IN. LET ME BUY YOU A BEER AND WE'LL--
NO. NO, THIS IS...

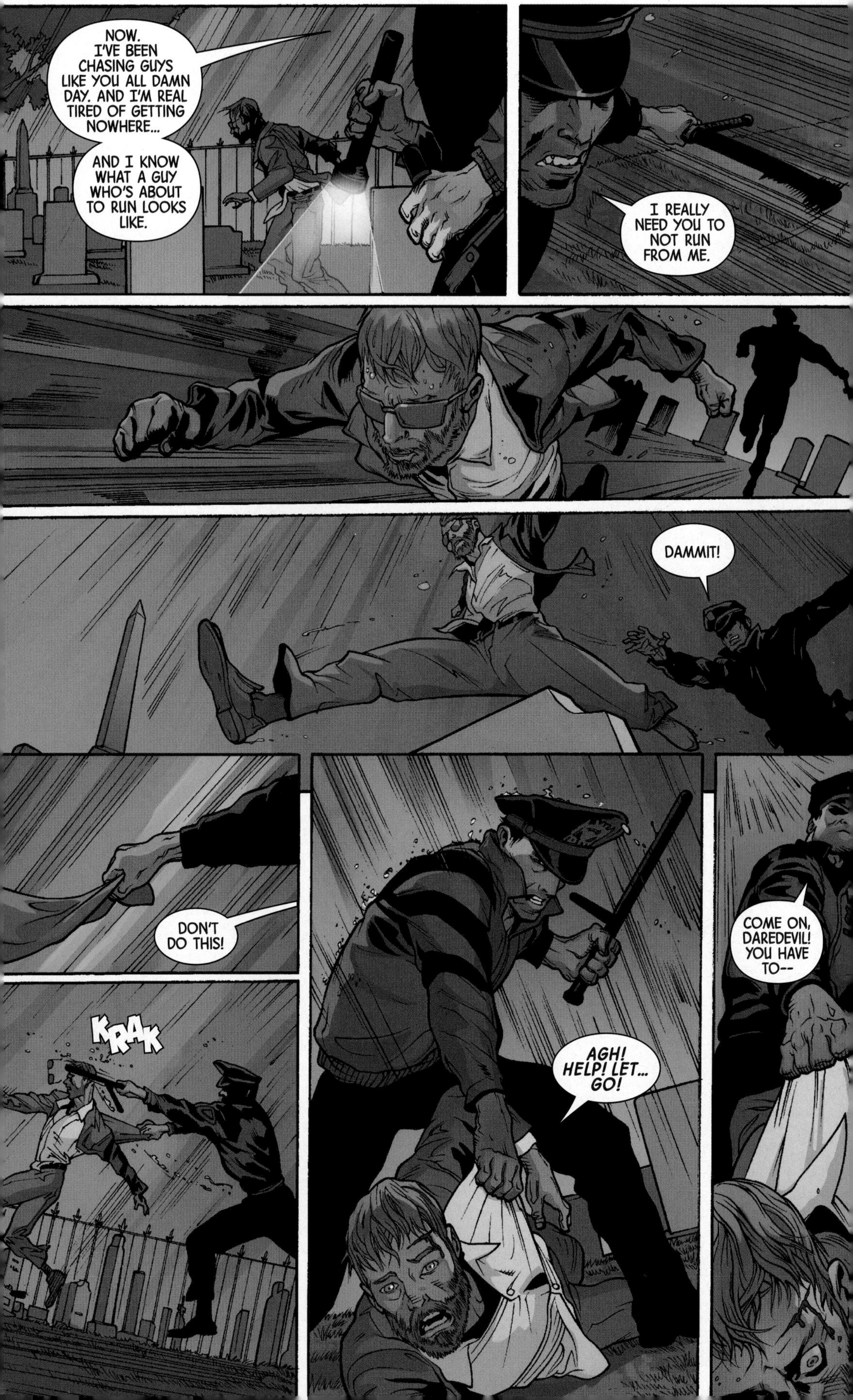
NOW. I'VE BEEN CHASING GUYS LIKE YOU ALL DAMN DAY. AND I'M REAL TIRED OF GETTING NOWHERE...
AND I KNOW WHAT A GUY WHO'S ABOUT TO RUN LOOKS LIKE.
I REALLY NEED YOU TO NOT RUN FROM ME.
DAMMIT!
DON'T DO THIS!
KRAK
AGH! HELP! LET... GO!
COME ON, DAREDEVIL! YOU HAVE TO--

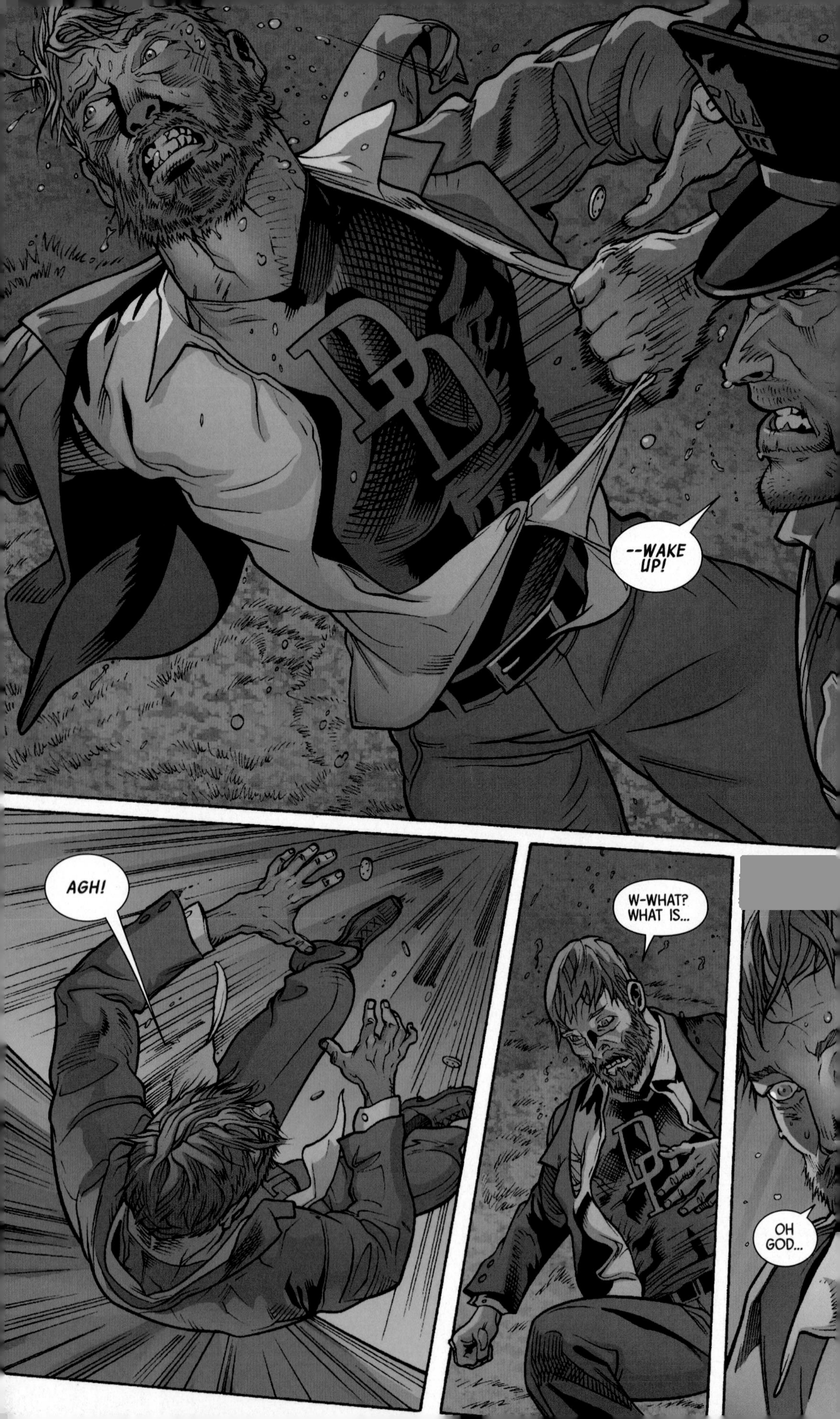
--WAKE UP!
AGH!
W-WHAT? WHAT IS...
OH GOD...

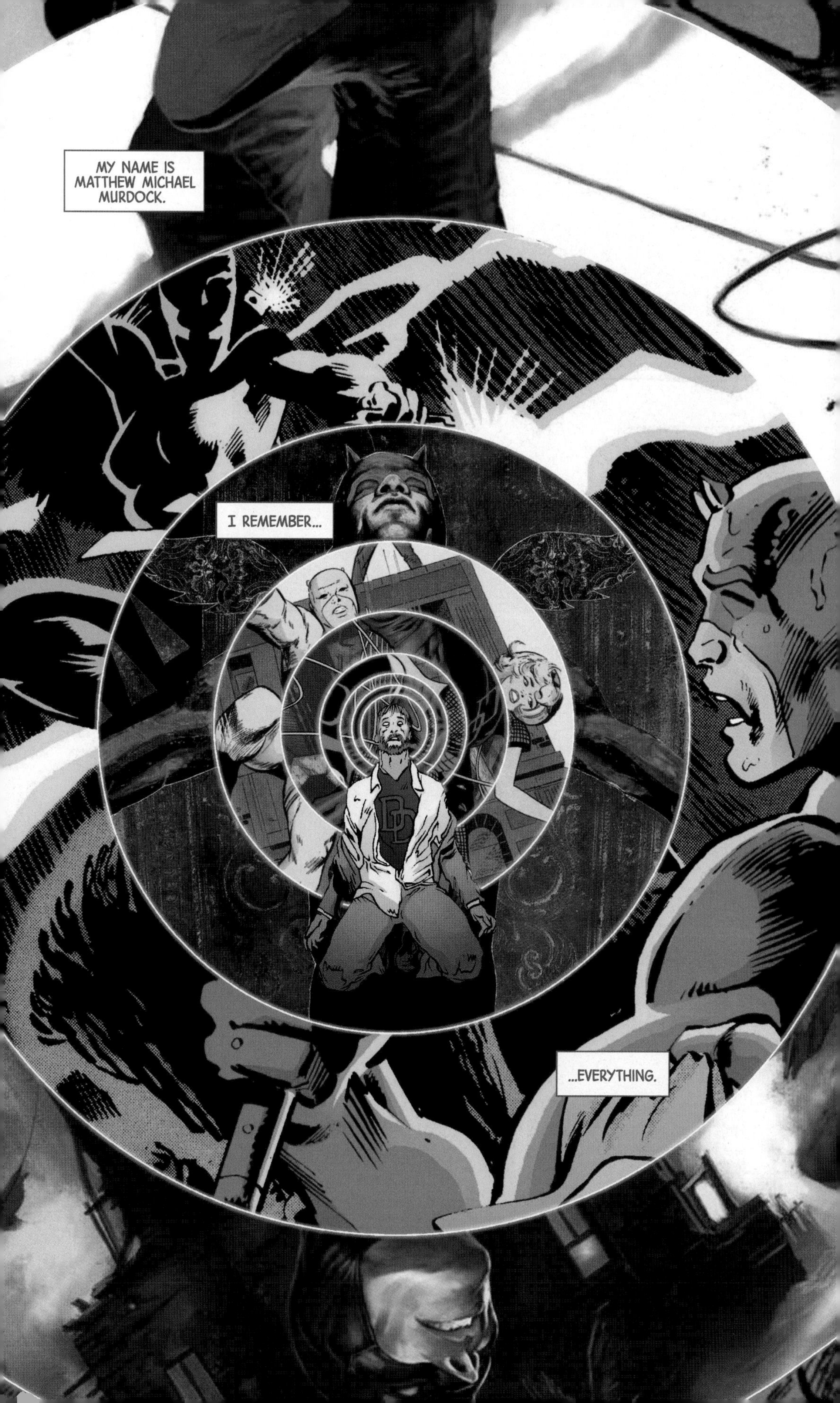
MY NAME IS MATTHEW MICHAEL MURDOCK.
I REMEMBER...
...EVERYTHING.

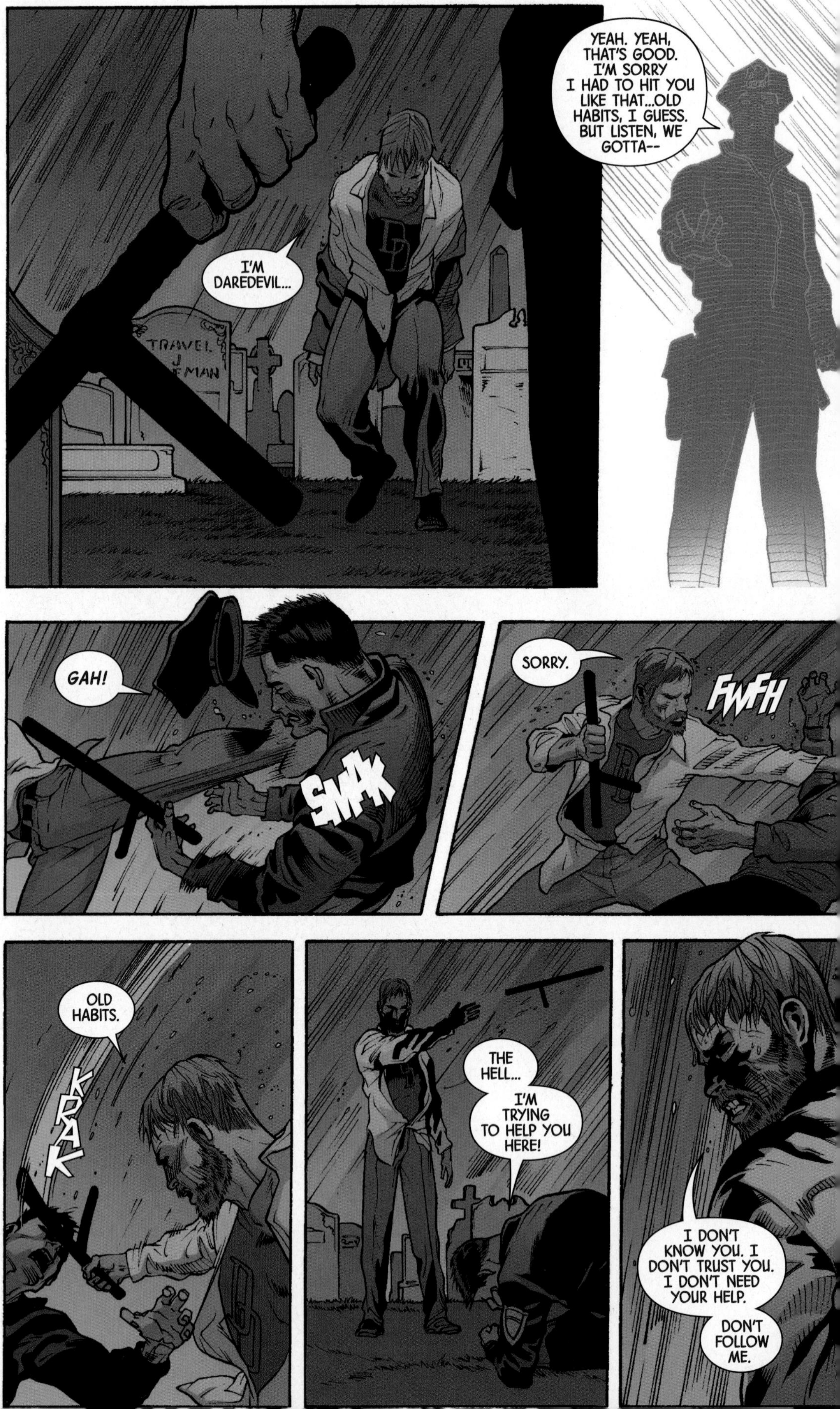
I'M DAREDEVIL...
TRAVEL J MAN
YEAH. YEAH, THAT'S GOOD. I'M SORRY I HAD TO HIT YOU LIKE THAT...OLD HABITS, I GUESS. BUT LISTEN, WE GOTTA--
GAH!
SMAK
SORRY.
FWFH
OLD HABITS.
KRAK
THE HELL...
I'M TRYING TO HELP YOU HERE!
I DON'T KNOW YOU. I DON'T TRUST YOU. I DON'T NEED YOUR HELP.
DON'T FOLLOW ME.

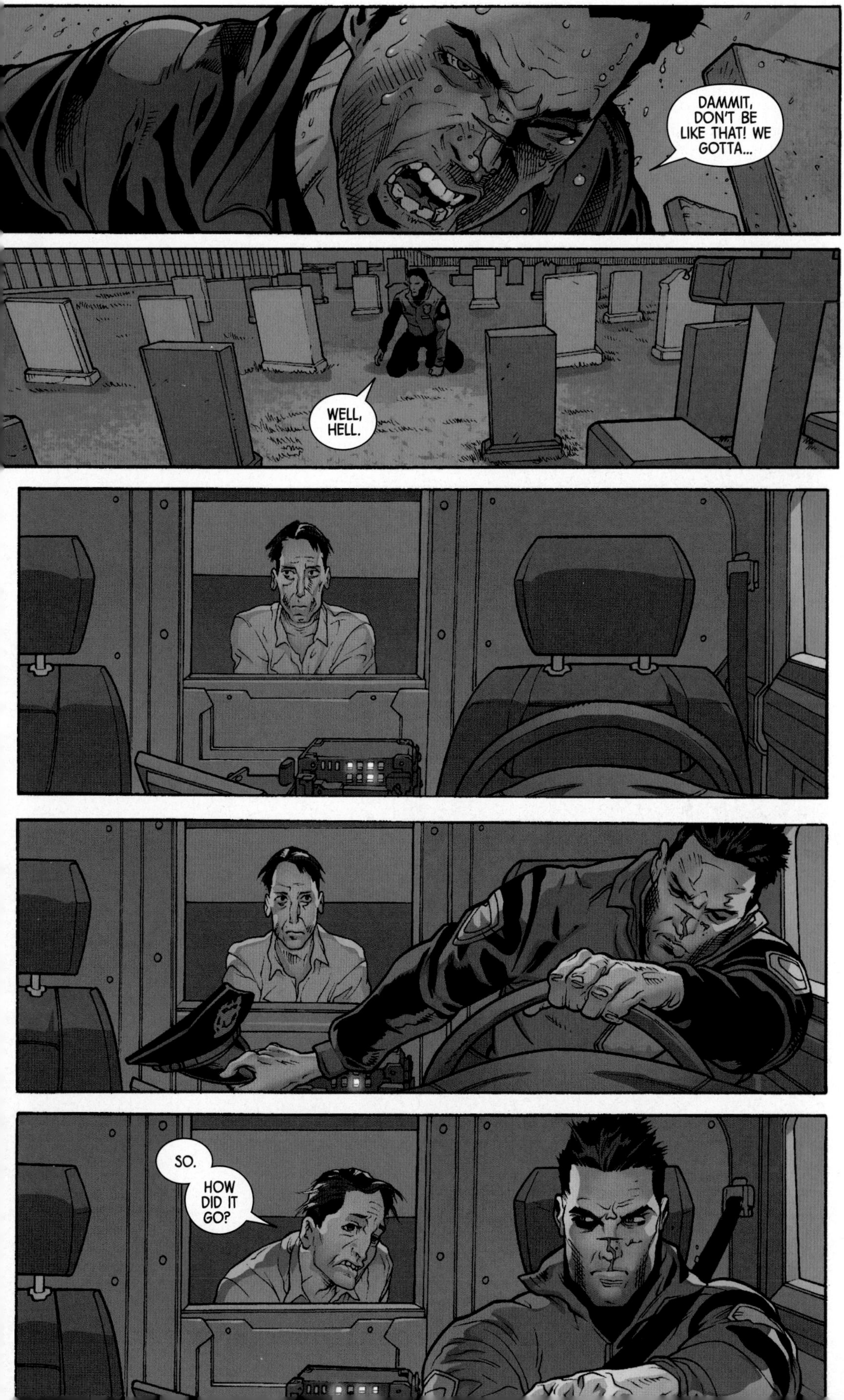
DAMMIT, DON'T BE LIKE THAT! WE GOTTA...
WELL, HELL.
SO.
HOW DID IT GO?

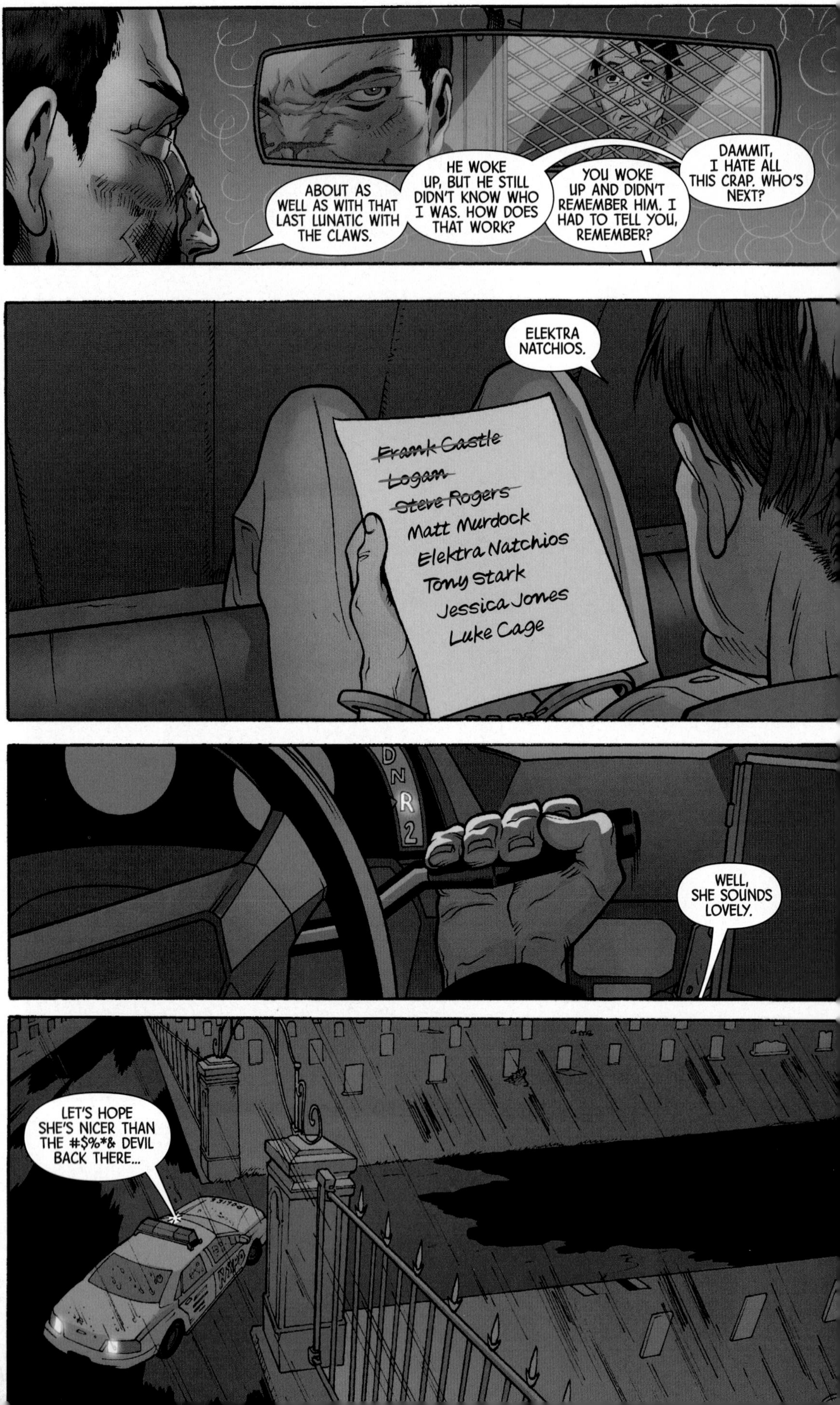
ABOUT AS WELL AS WITH THAT LAST LUNATIC WITH THE CLAWS.
HE WOKE UP, BUT HE STILL DIDN'T KNOW WHO I WAS. HOW DOES THAT WORK?
YOU WOKE UP AND DIDN'T REMEMBER HIM. I HAD TO TELL YOU, REMEMBER?
DAMMIT, I HATE ALL THIS CRAP. WHO'S NEXT?
ELEKTRA NATCHIOS.
Frank Castle
Logan
Steve Rogers
Matt Murdock
Elektra Natchios
Tony Stark
Jessica Jones
Luke Cage
WELL, SHE SOUNDS LOVELY.
LET'S HOPE SHE'S NICER THAN THE #$%*& DEVIL BACK THERE...

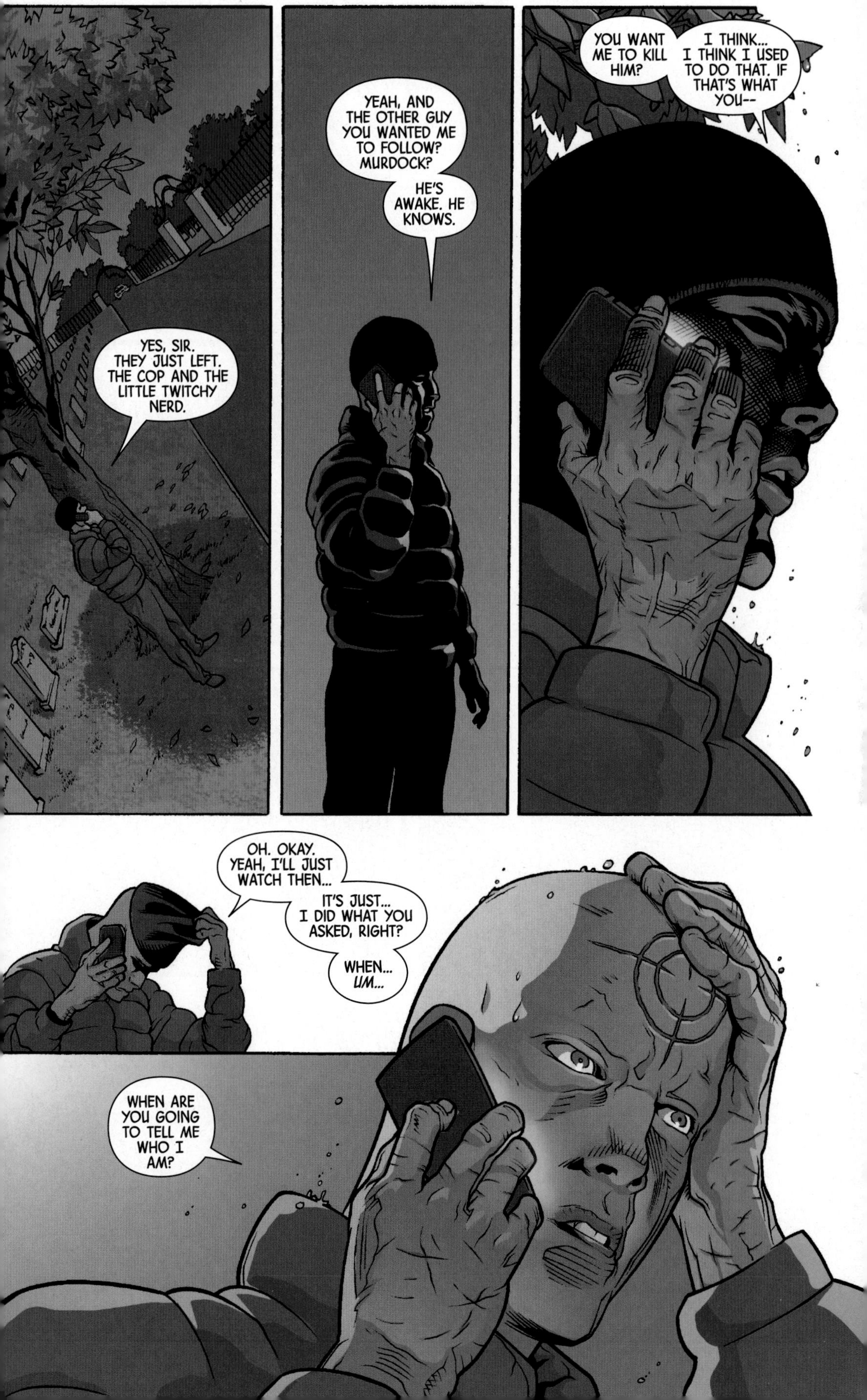

YES, SIR. THEY JUST LEFT. THE COP AND THE LITTLE TWITCHY NERD.
YEAH, AND THE OTHER GUY YOU WANTED ME TO FOLLOW? MURDOCK?
HE'S AWAKE. HE KNOWS.
YOU WANT ME TO KILL HIM?
I THINK... I THINK I USED TO DO THAT. IF THAT'S WHAT YOU--
OH. OKAY. YEAH, I'LL JUST WATCH THEN...
IT'S JUST... I DID WHAT YOU ASKED, RIGHT?
WHEN... *UM...*
WHEN ARE YOU GOING TO TELL ME WHO I AM?

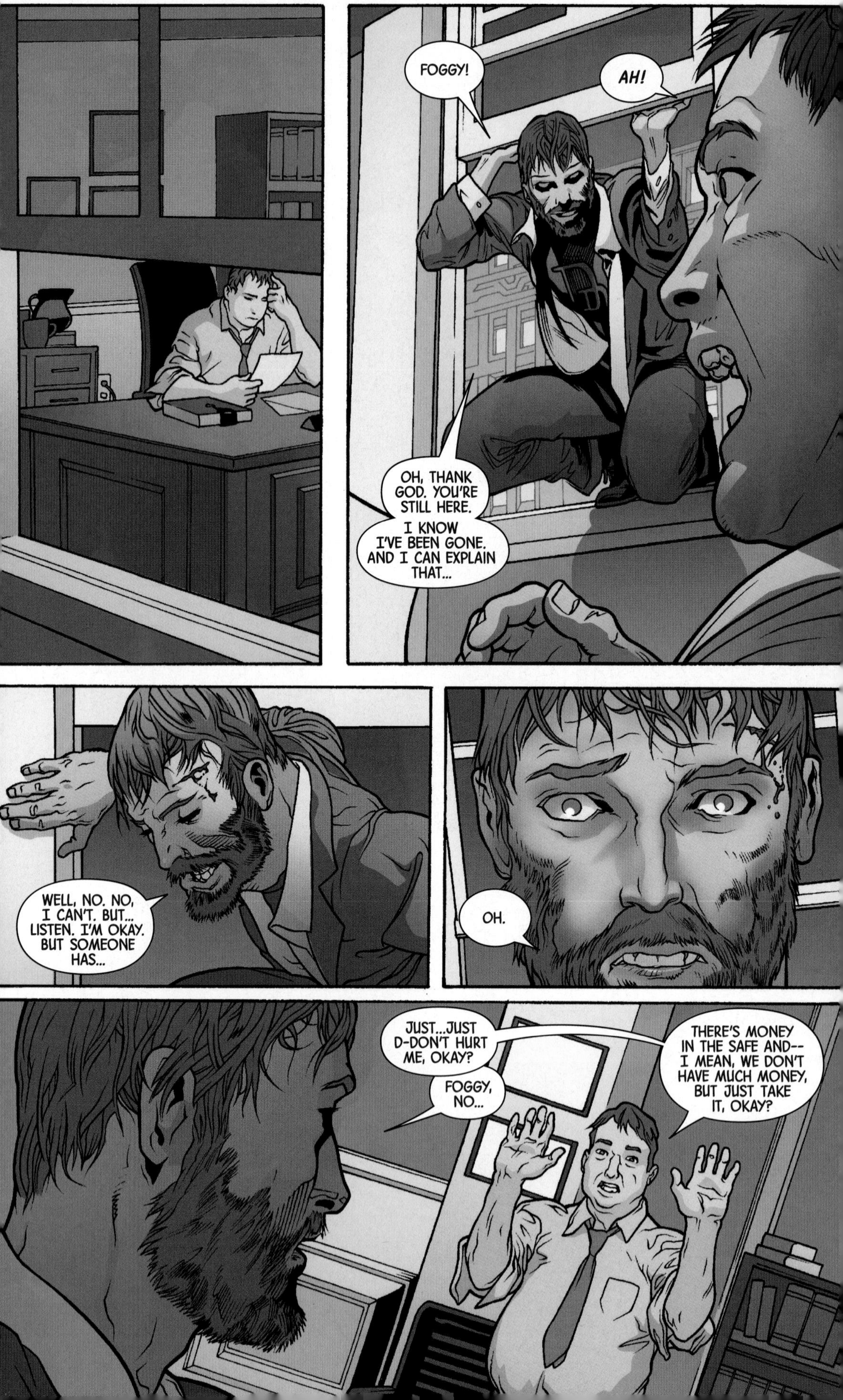

FOGGY!
AH!
OH, THANK GOD. YOU'RE STILL HERE.
I KNOW I'VE BEEN GONE. AND I CAN EXPLAIN THAT...
WELL, NO. NO, I CAN'T. BUT... LISTEN. I'M OKAY. BUT SOMEONE HAS...
OH.
JUST...JUST D-DON'T HURT ME, OKAY?
THERE'S MONEY IN THE SAFE AND-- I MEAN, WE DON'T HAVE MUCH MONEY, BUT JUST TAKE IT, OKAY?
FOGGY, NO...

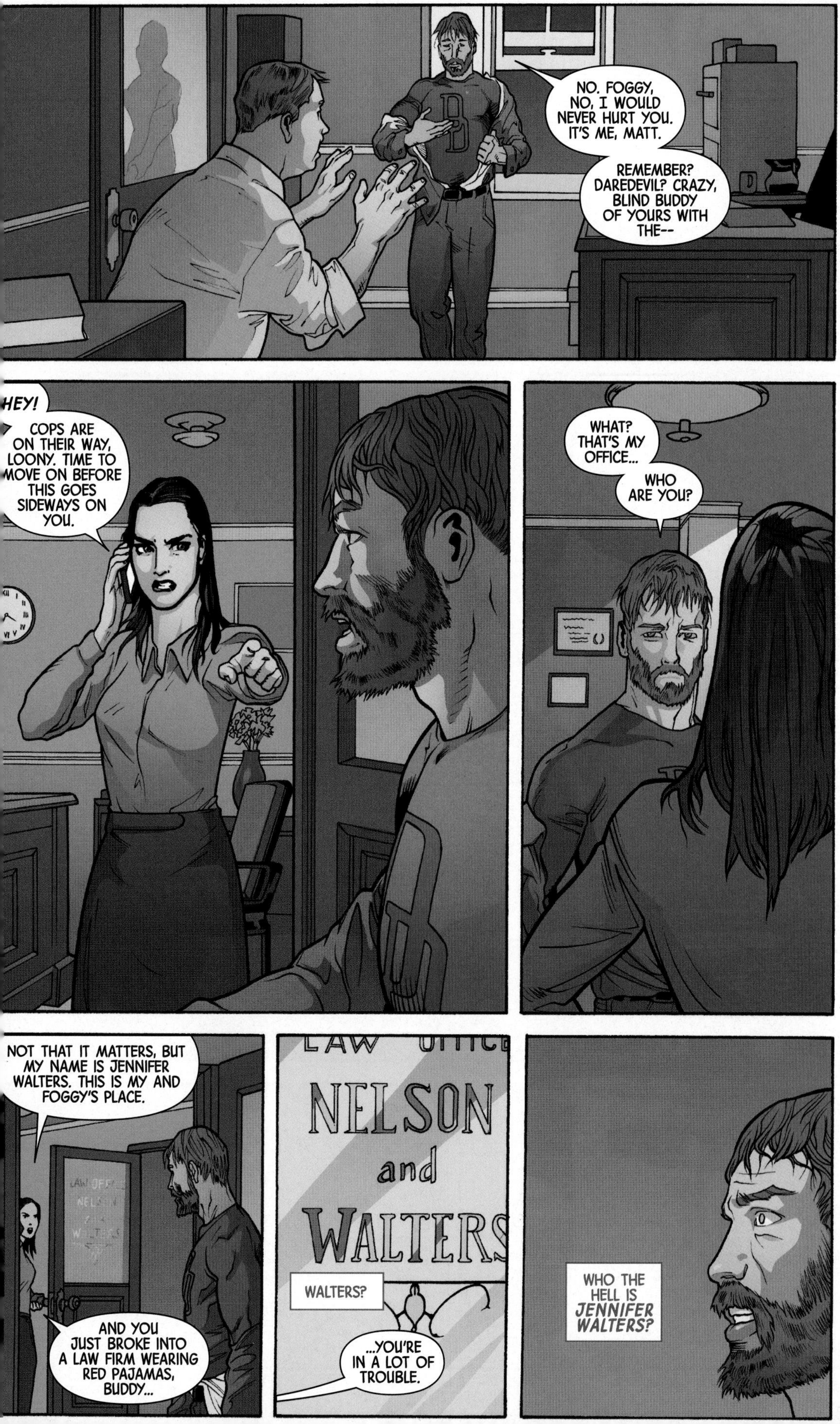
NO. FOGGY, NO, I WOULD NEVER HURT YOU. IT'S ME, MATT.
REMEMBER? DAREDEVIL? CRAZY, BLIND BUDDY OF YOURS WITH THE--
HEY!
COPS ARE ON THEIR WAY, LOONY. TIME TO MOVE ON BEFORE THIS GOES SIDEWAYS ON YOU.
WHAT? THAT'S MY OFFICE...
WHO ARE YOU?
NOT THAT IT MATTERS, BUT MY NAME IS JENNIFER WALTERS. THIS IS MY AND FOGGY'S PLACE.
AND YOU JUST BROKE INTO A LAW FIRM WEARING RED PAJAMAS, BUDDY...
NELSON and WALTERS
WALTERS?
...YOU'RE IN A LOT OF TROUBLE.
WHO THE HELL IS *JENNIFER WALTERS?*

LEAVE. NOW. DON'T MAKE ME ANGRY...

JUST... PLEASE. JUST... HOLD ON.

HEY! HANDS WHERE WE CAN SEE THEM!

NO. JUST WAIT. I HAVE MY...

LOOK. I CAN PROVE IT. I WORK HERE, LOOK I HAVE MY--

FWAP

WOW. YOU ARE STRONG.

FOGGY, PULL THIS GUY'S I.D.

NEW YORK STATE BAR ASSOCIATION

MATTHEW MURDOCK
STATUS: ACTIVE
I.D. NUMBER: ||||||||
ISSUED: ||||||

JEN...

HE'S...

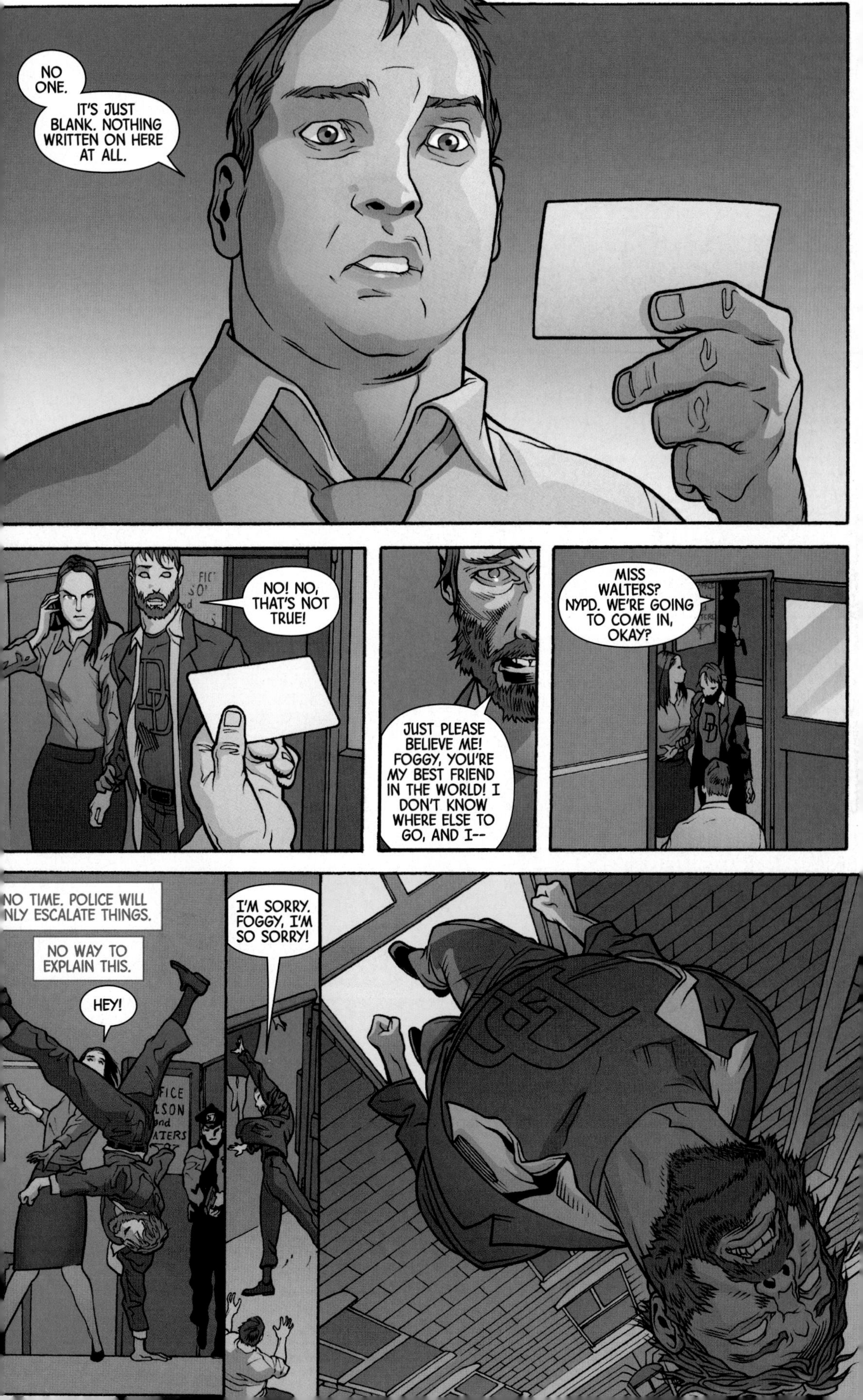

NO ONE.
IT'S JUST BLANK. NOTHING WRITTEN ON HERE AT ALL.
NO! NO, THAT'S NOT TRUE!
JUST PLEASE BELIEVE ME! FOGGY, YOU'RE MY BEST FRIEND IN THE WORLD! I DON'T KNOW WHERE ELSE TO GO, AND I--
MISS WALTERS? NYPD. WE'RE GOING TO COME IN, OKAY?
NO TIME. POLICE WILL NLY ESCALATE THINGS.
NO WAY TO EXPLAIN THIS.
HEY!
I'M SORRY. FOGGY, I'M SO SORRY!

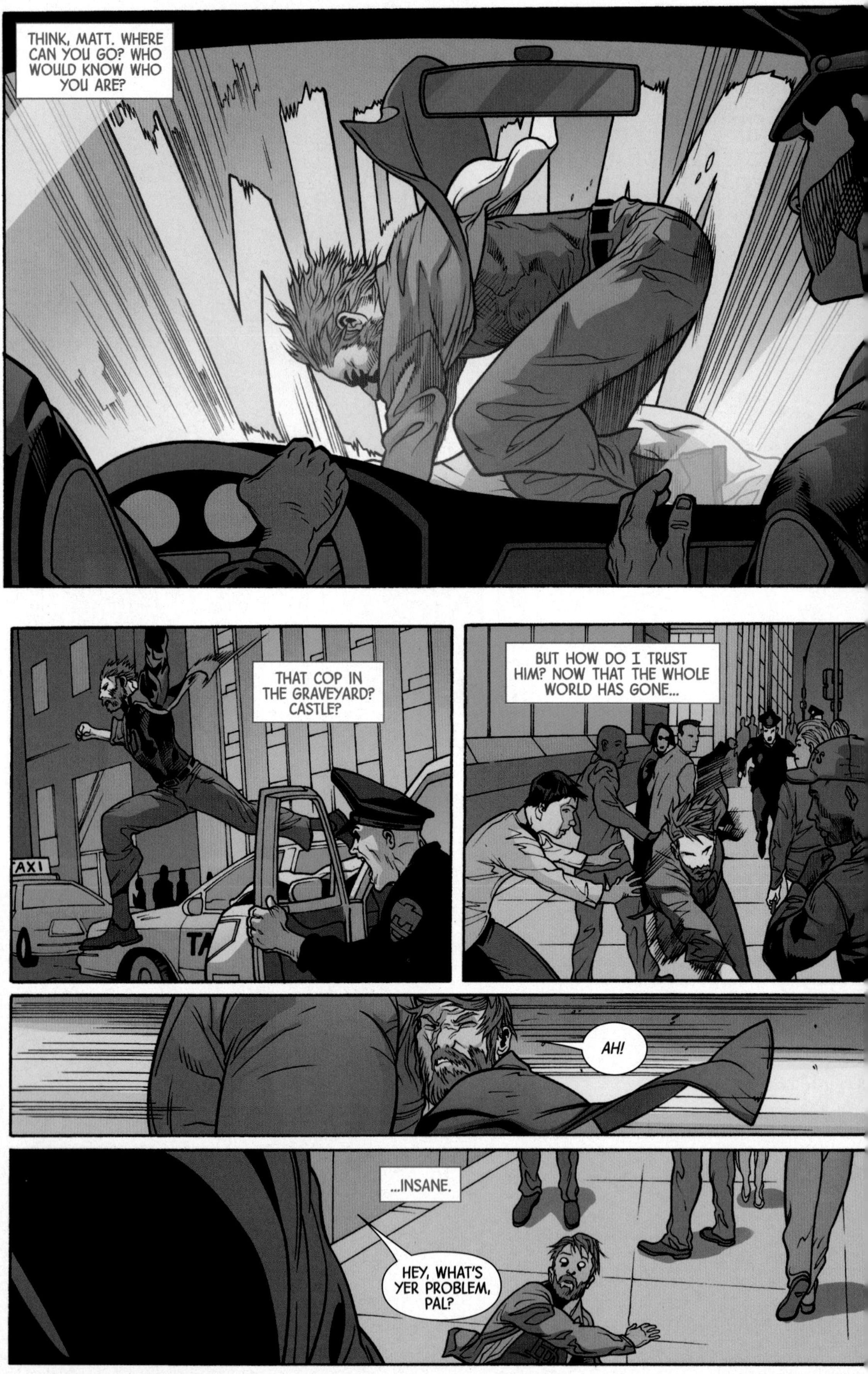
THINK, MATT. WHERE CAN YOU GO? WHO WOULD KNOW WHO YOU ARE?
THAT COP IN THE GRAVEYARD? CASTLE?
TAXI
BUT HOW DO I TRUST HIM? NOW THAT THE WHOLE WORLD HAS GONE...
AH!
...INSANE.
HEY, WHAT'S YER PROBLEM, PAL?

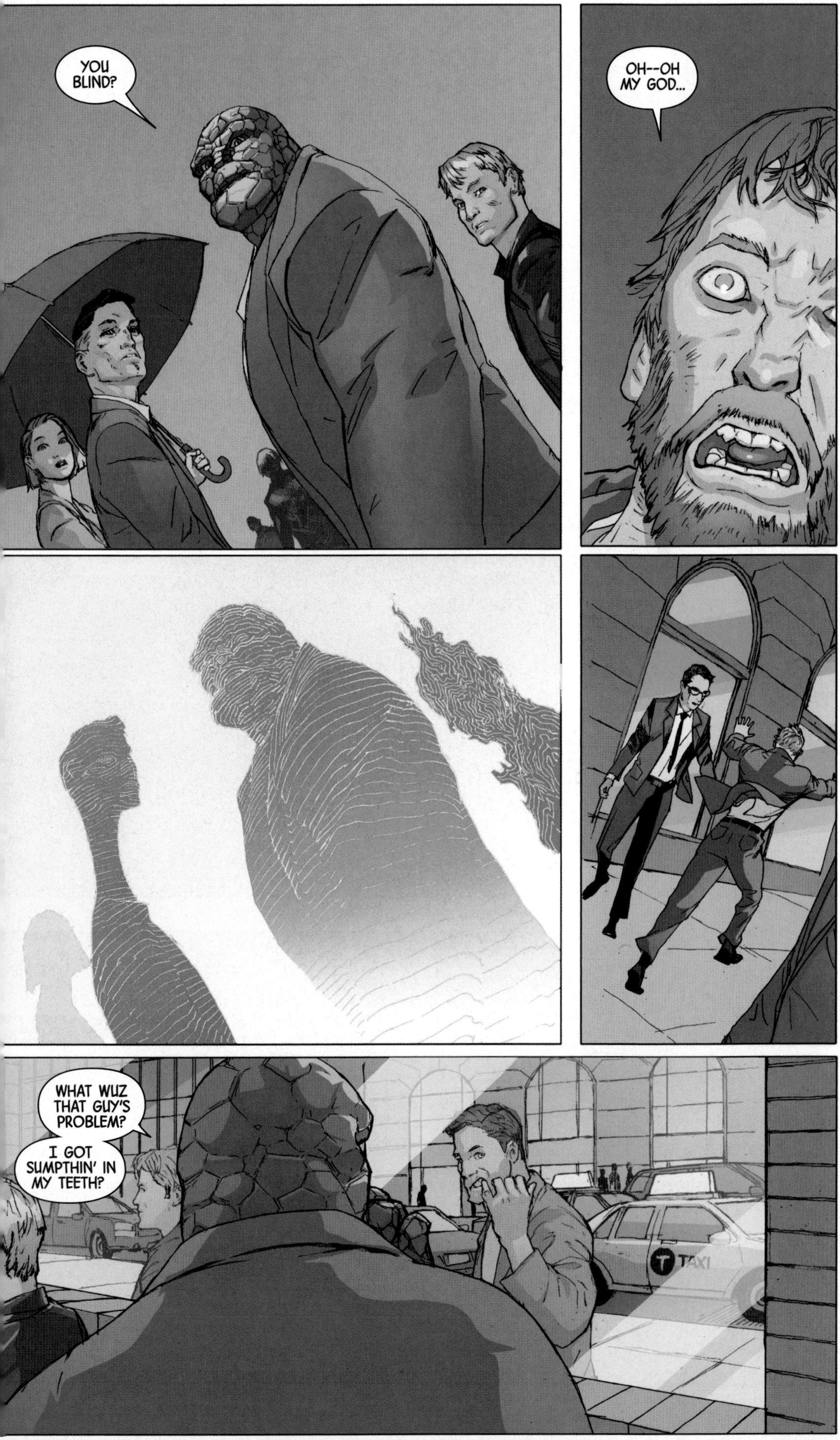
YOU BLIND?
OH--OH MY GOD...
WHAT WUZ THAT GUY'S PROBLEM?
I GOT SUMPTHIN' IN MY TEETH?
TAXI

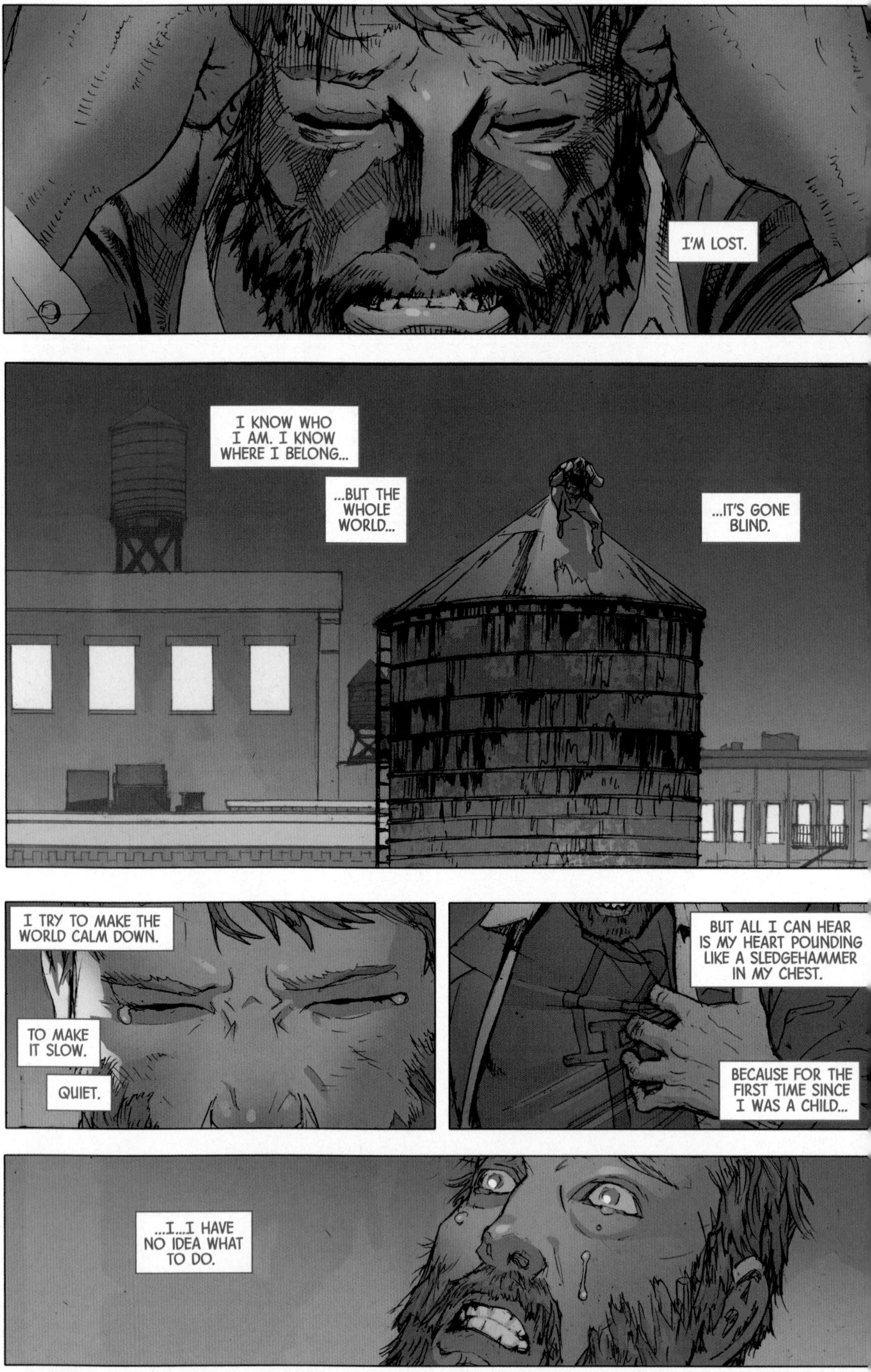
I'M LOST.
I KNOW WHO I AM. I KNOW WHERE I BELONG...
...BUT THE WHOLE WORLD...
...IT'S GONE BLIND.
I TRY TO MAKE THE WORLD CALM DOWN.
TO MAKE IT SLOW.
QUIET.
BUT ALL I CAN HEAR IS MY HEART POUNDING LIKE A SLEDGEHAMMER IN MY CHEST.
BECAUSE FOR THE FIRST TIME SINCE I WAS A CHILD...
...I...I HAVE NO IDEA WHAT TO DO.

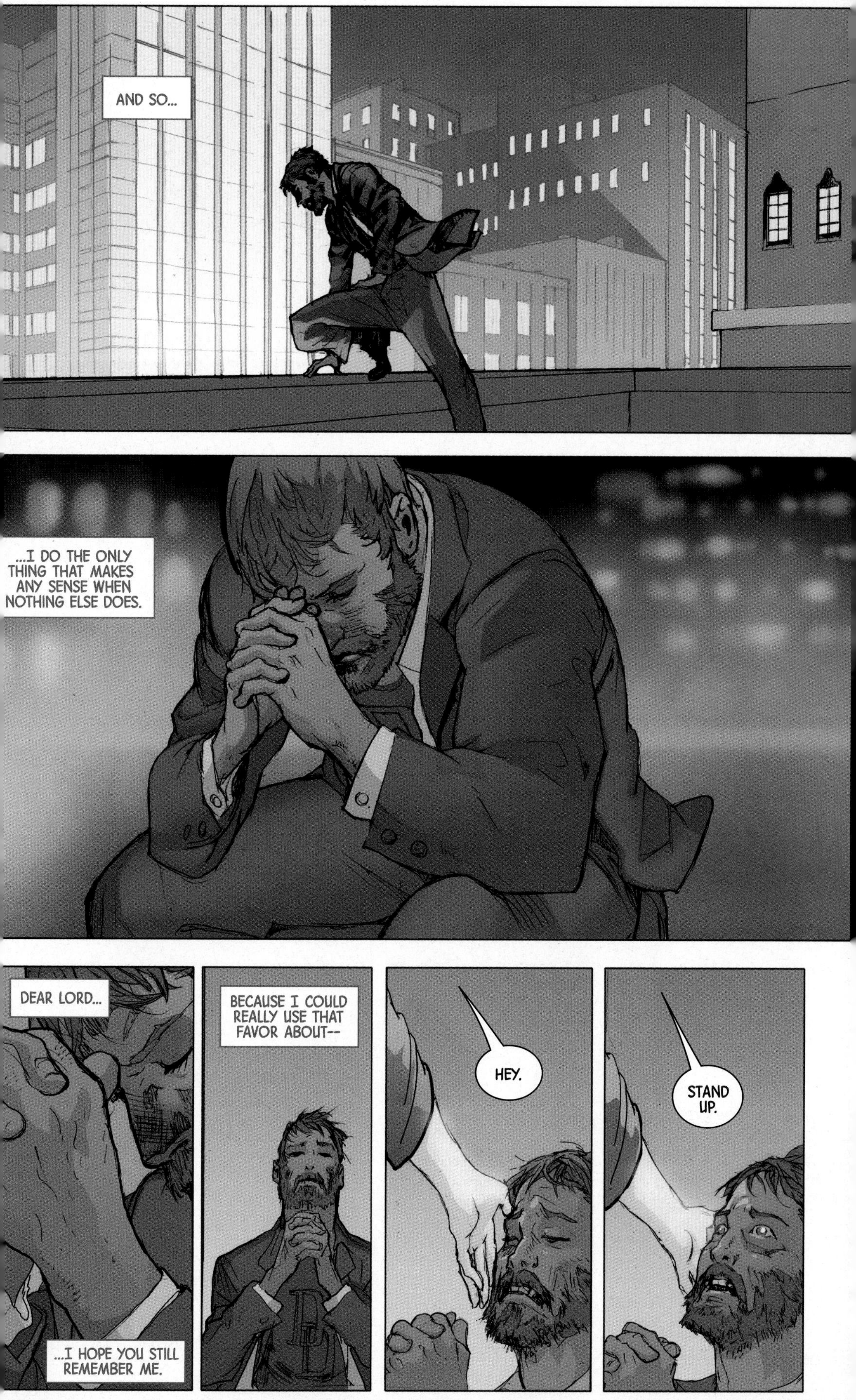
AND SO...
...I DO THE ONLY THING THAT MAKES ANY SENSE WHEN NOTHING ELSE DOES.
DEAR LORD...
...I HOPE YOU STILL REMEMBER ME.
BECAUSE I COULD REALLY USE THAT FAVOR ABOUT--
HEY.
STAND UP.

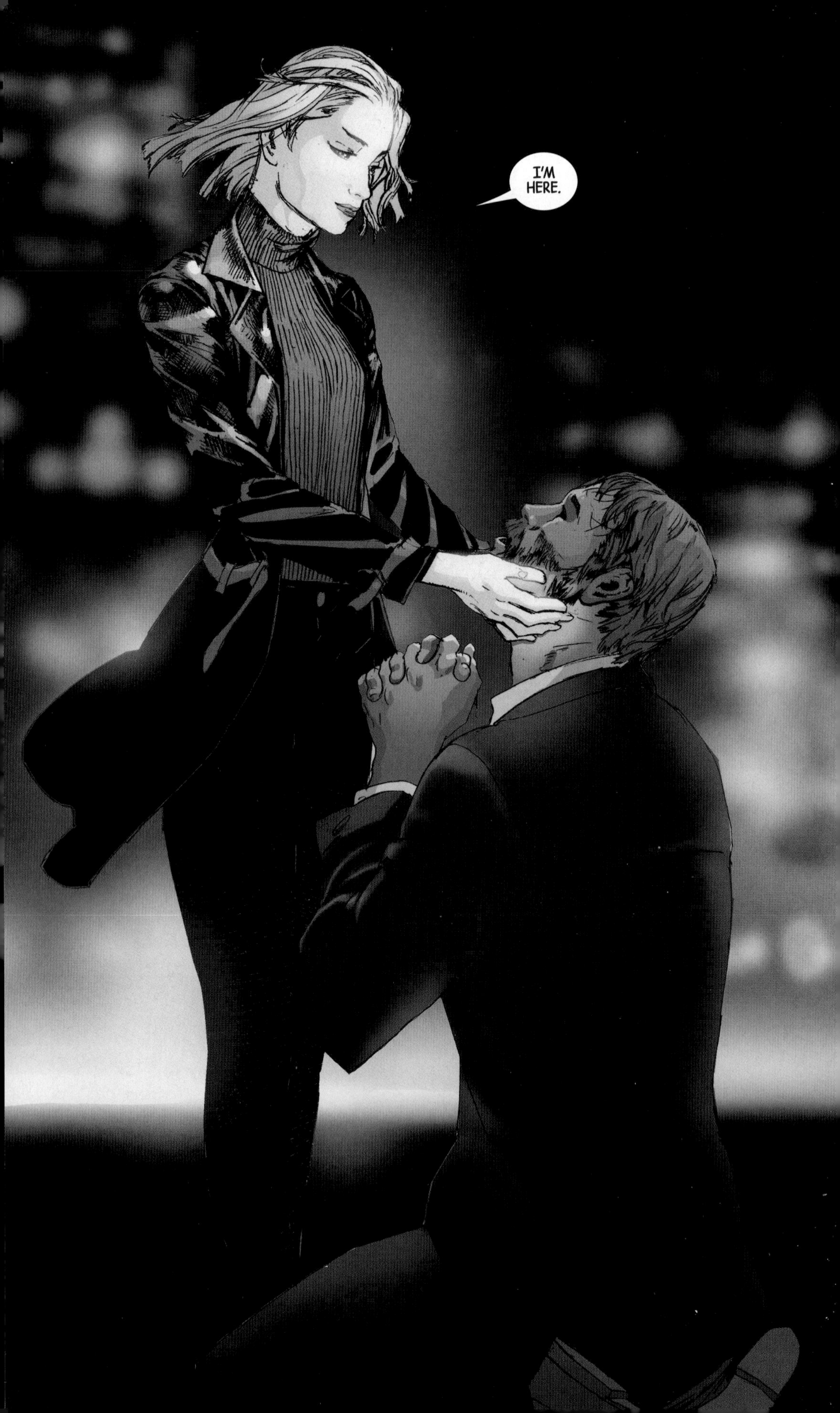
I'M HERE.

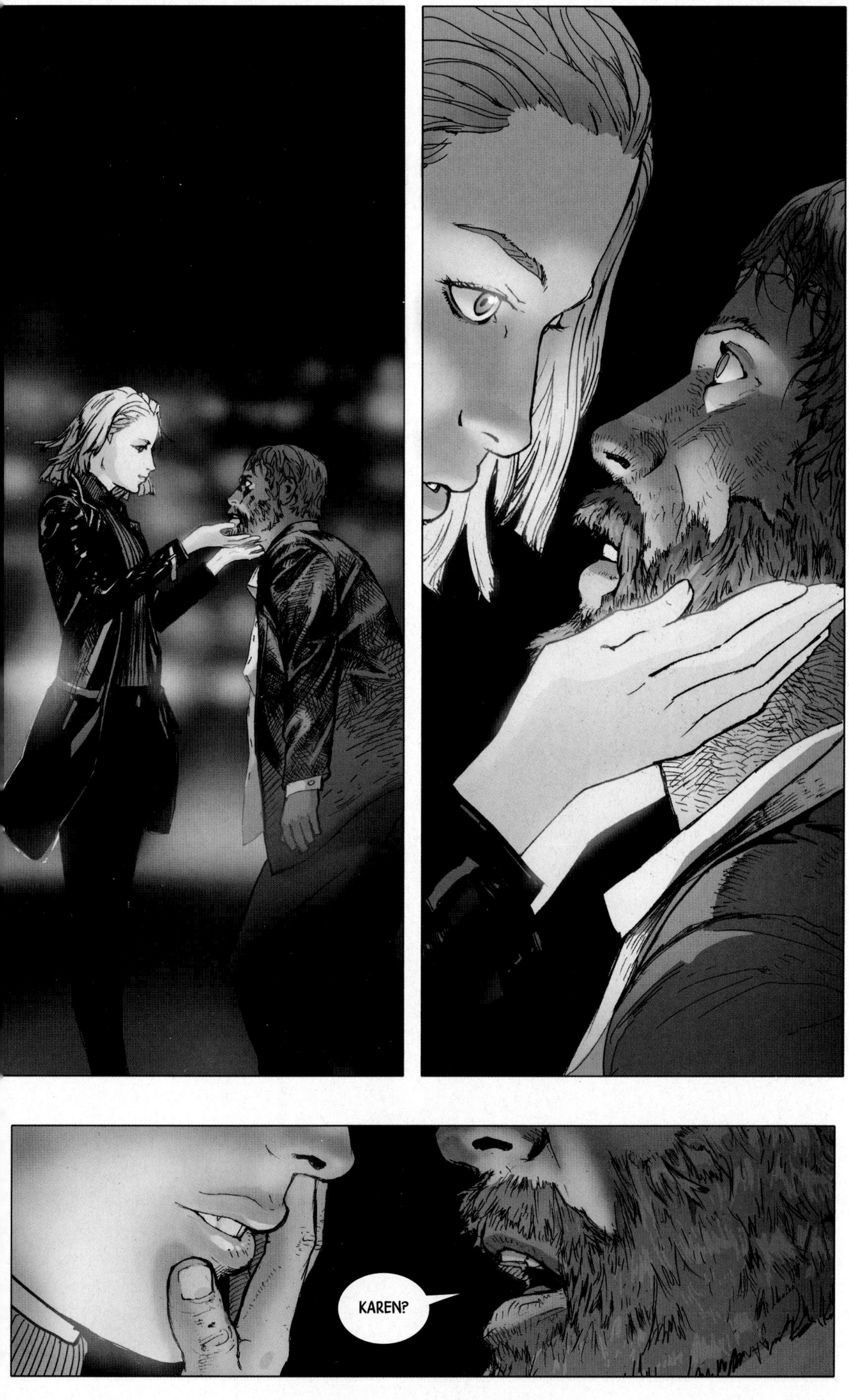
KAREN?

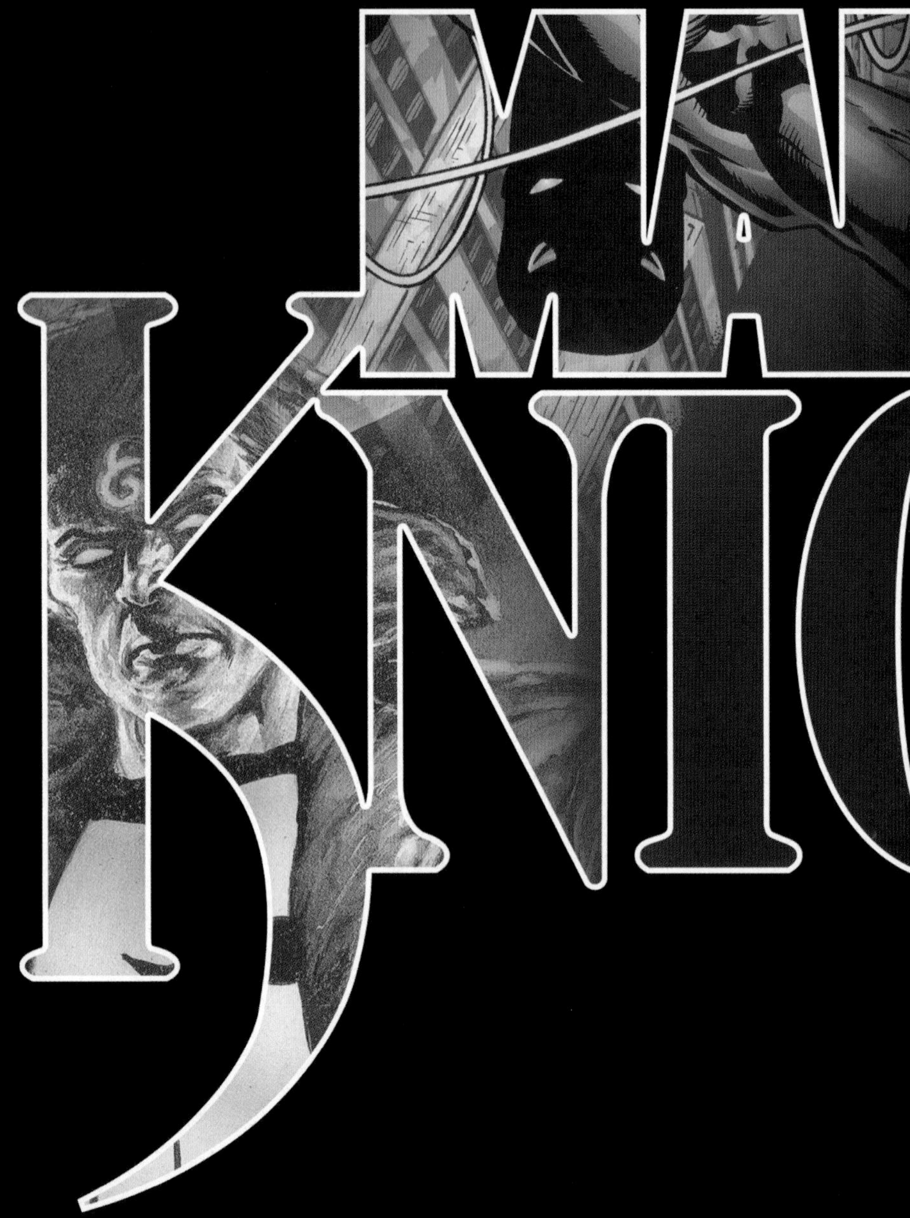

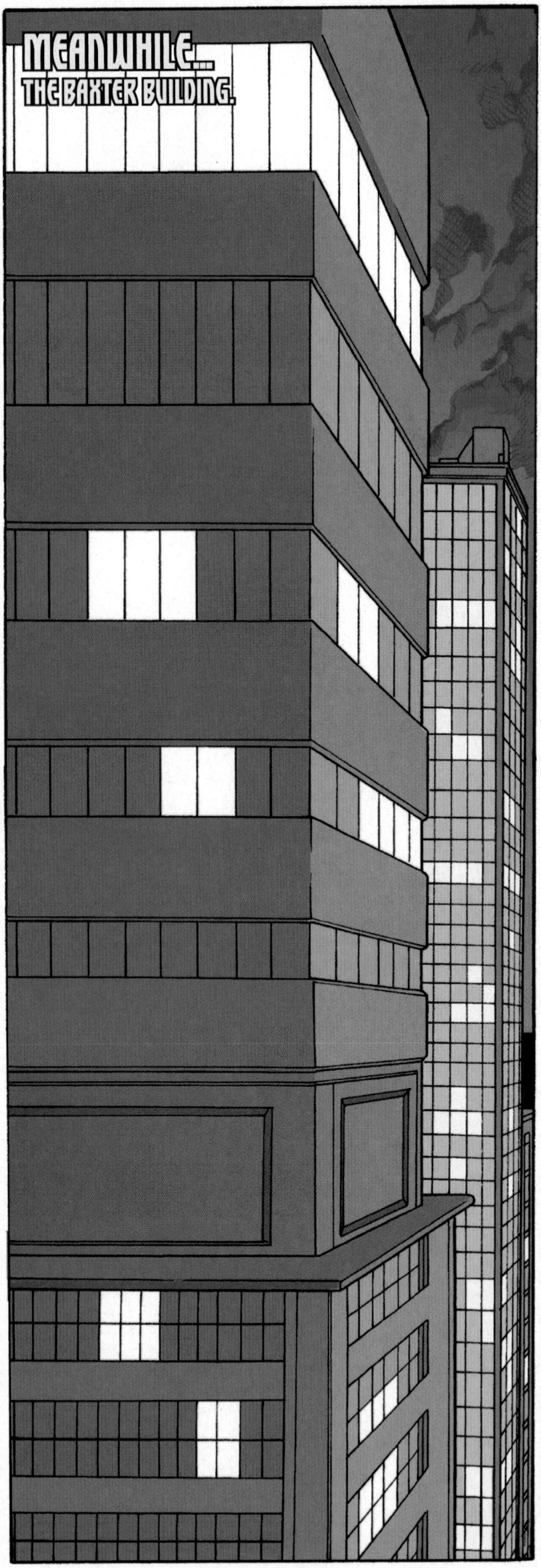
MEANWHILE...
THE BAXTER BUILDING.

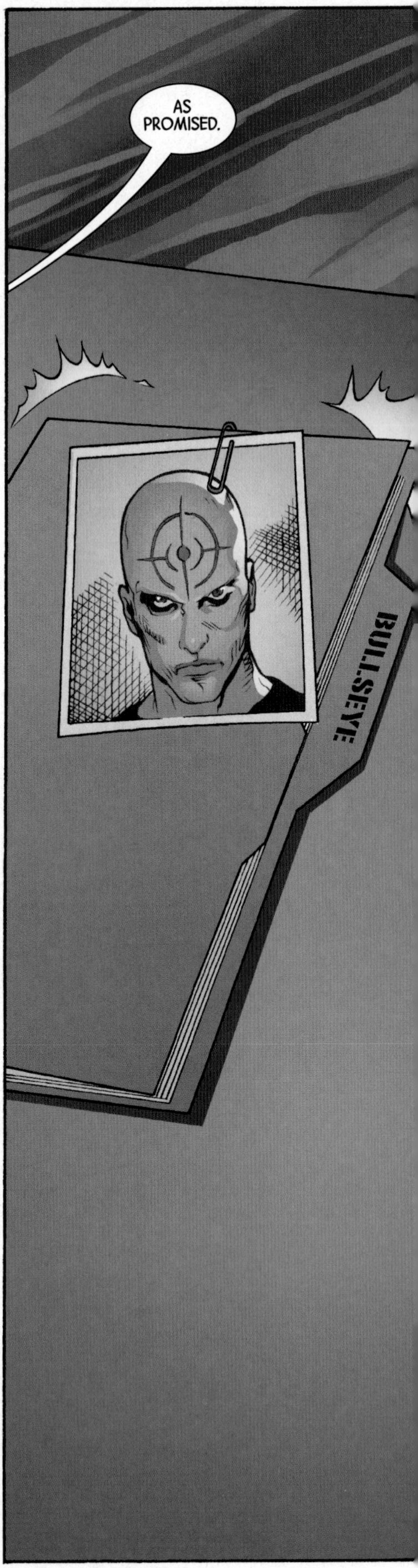
AS PROMISED.
BULLSEYE

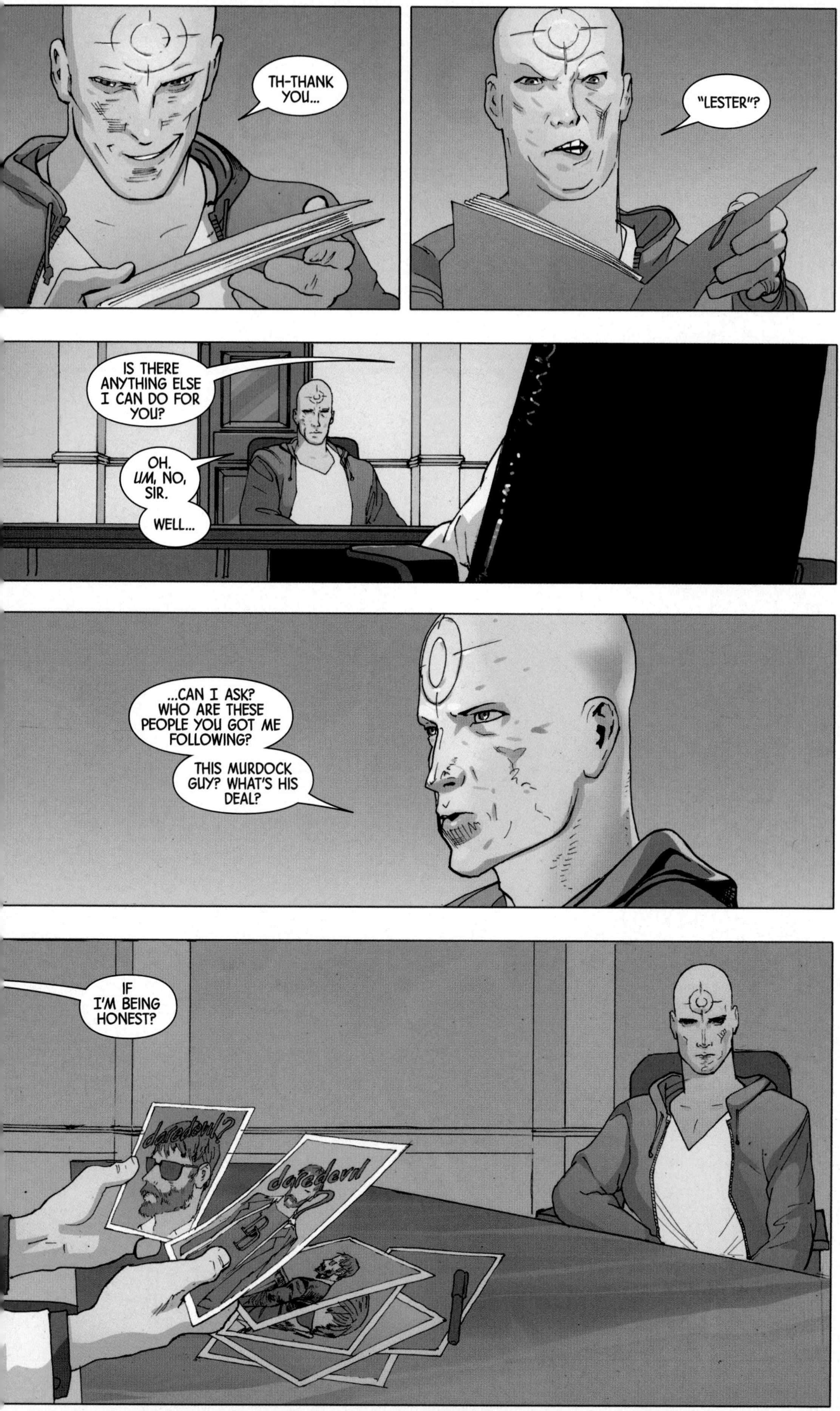
TH-THANK YOU...
"LESTER"?
IS THERE ANYTHING ELSE I CAN DO FOR YOU?
OH. UM, NO, SIR.
WELL...
...CAN I ASK? WHO ARE THESE PEOPLE YOU GOT ME FOLLOWING?
THIS MURDOCK GUY? WHAT'S HIS DEAL?
IF I'M BEING HONEST?
daredevil?
daredevil

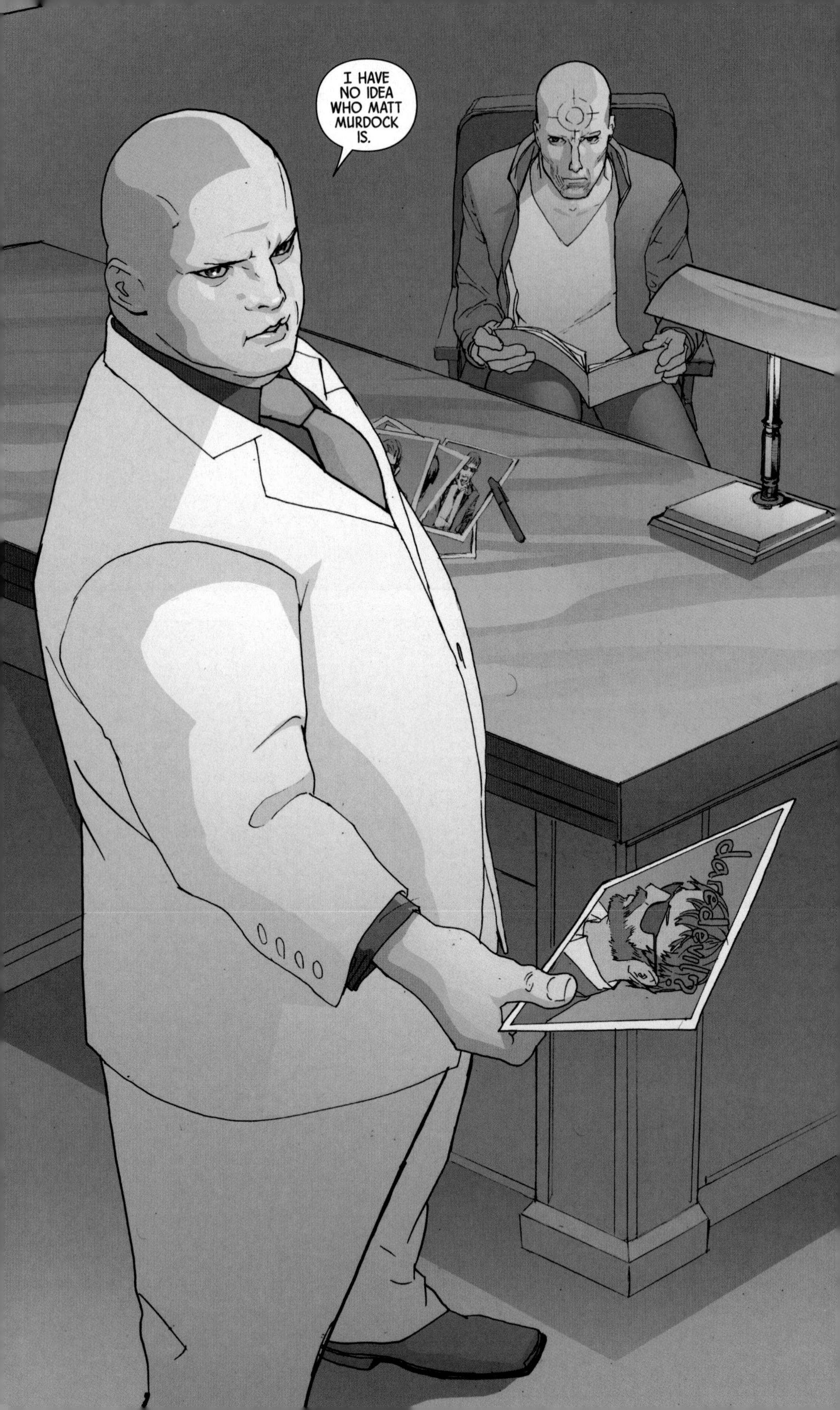
I HAVE NO IDEA WHO MATT MURDOCK IS.

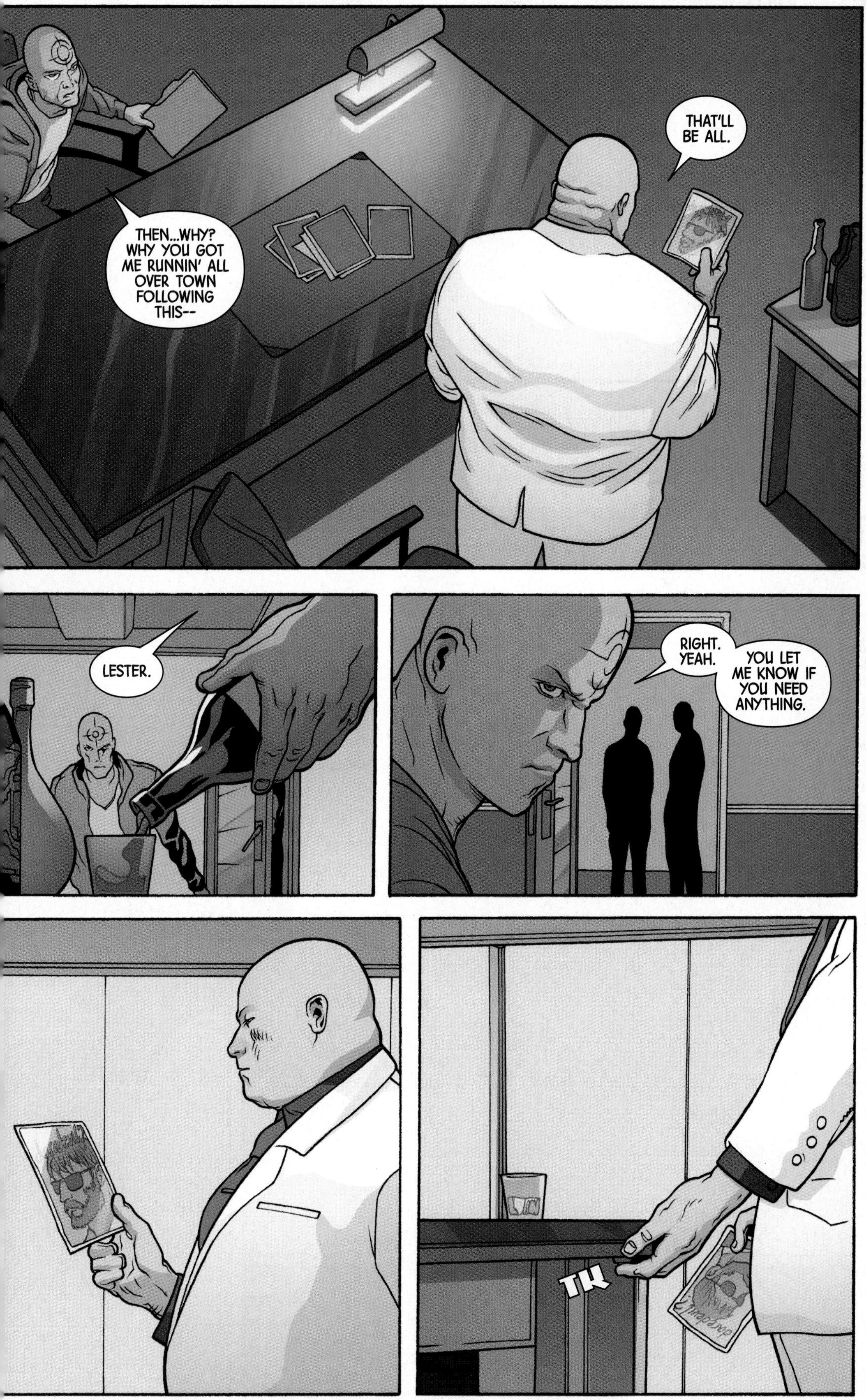
THEN...WHY? WHY YOU GOT ME RUNNIN' ALL OVER TOWN FOLLOWING THIS--
THAT'LL BE ALL.
LESTER.
RIGHT. YEAH.
YOU LET ME KNOW IF YOU NEED ANYTHING.
TK

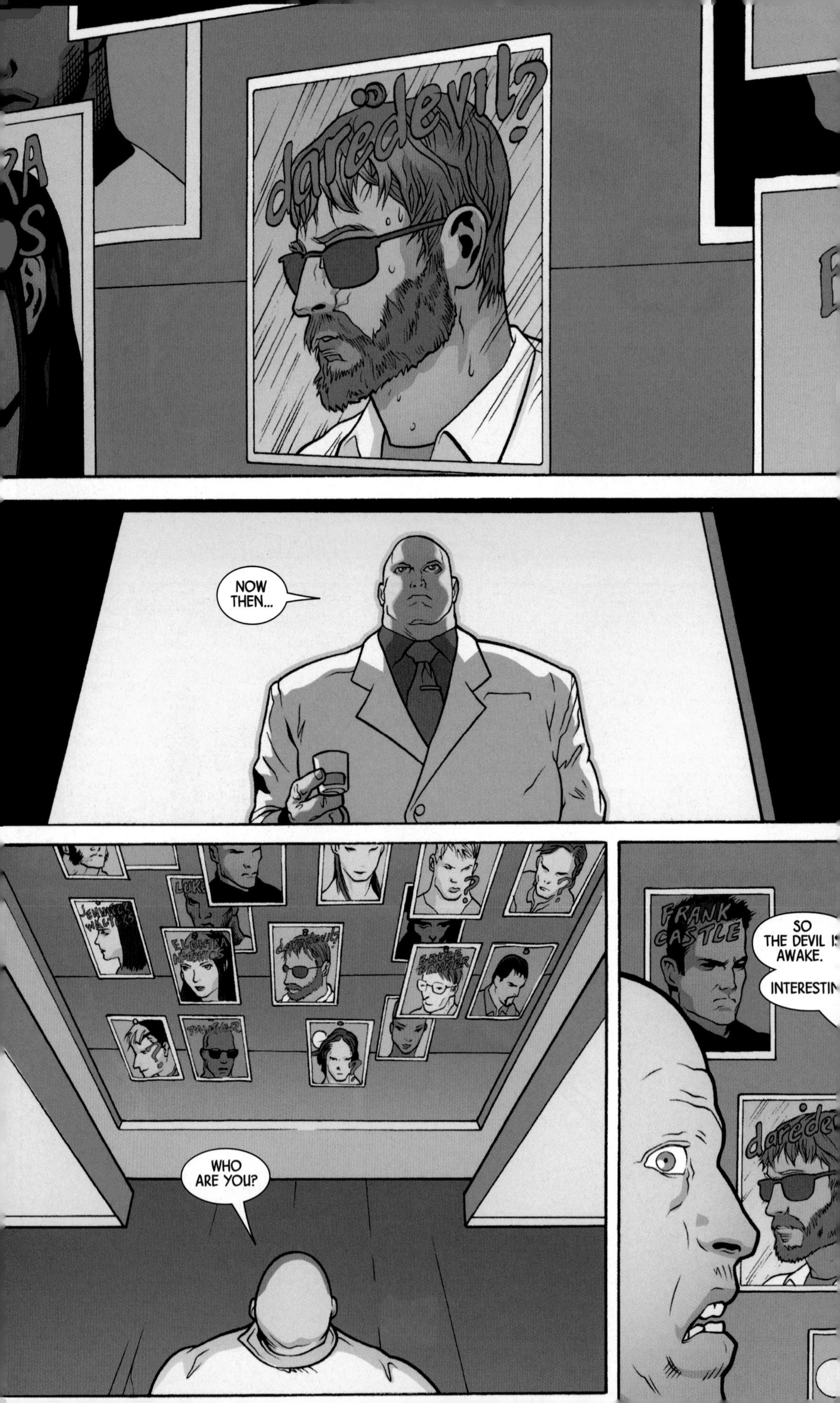
daredevil?
NOW THEN...
WHO ARE YOU?
SO THE DEVIL IS AWAKE.
INTERESTIN
FRANK CASTLE

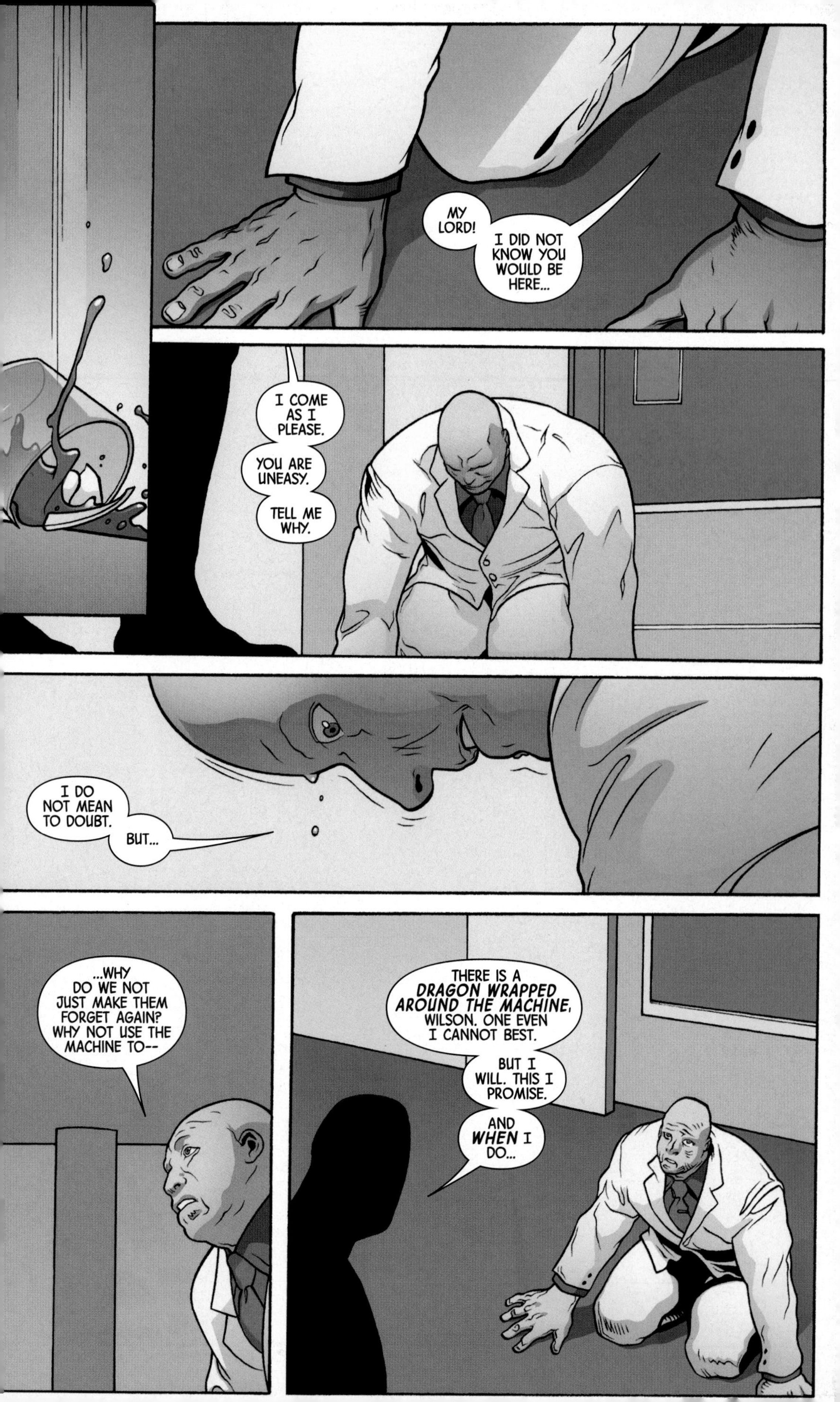

MY LORD!
I DID NOT KNOW YOU WOULD BE HERE...
I COME AS I PLEASE.
YOU ARE UNEASY.
TELL ME WHY.
I DO NOT MEAN TO DOUBT.
BUT...
...WHY DO WE NOT JUST MAKE THEM FORGET AGAIN? WHY NOT USE THE MACHINE TO--
THERE IS A DRAGON WRAPPED AROUND THE MACHINE, WILSON. ONE EVEN I CANNOT BEST.
BUT I WILL. THIS I PROMISE.
AND WHEN I DO...

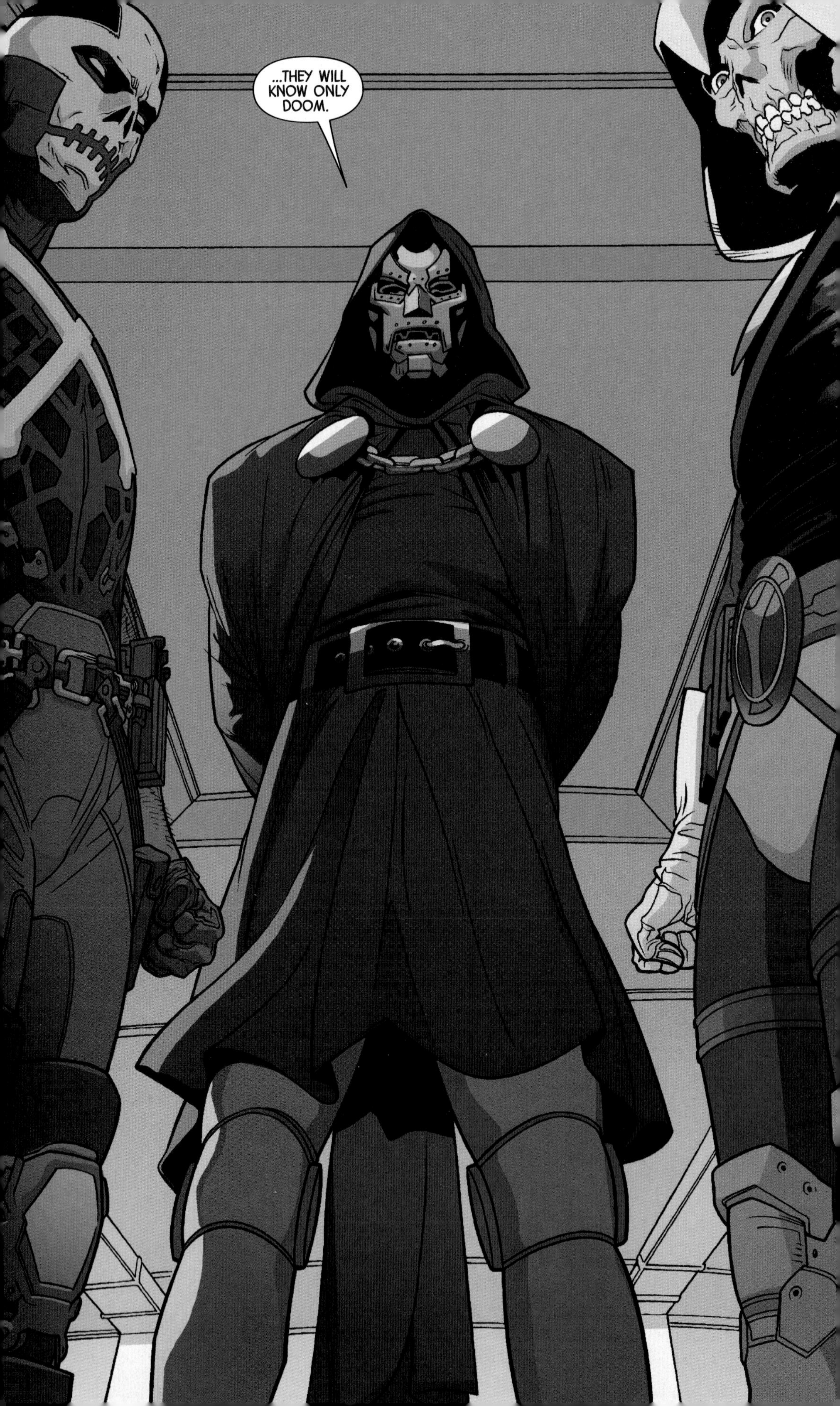
...THEY WILL KNOW ONLY DOOM.

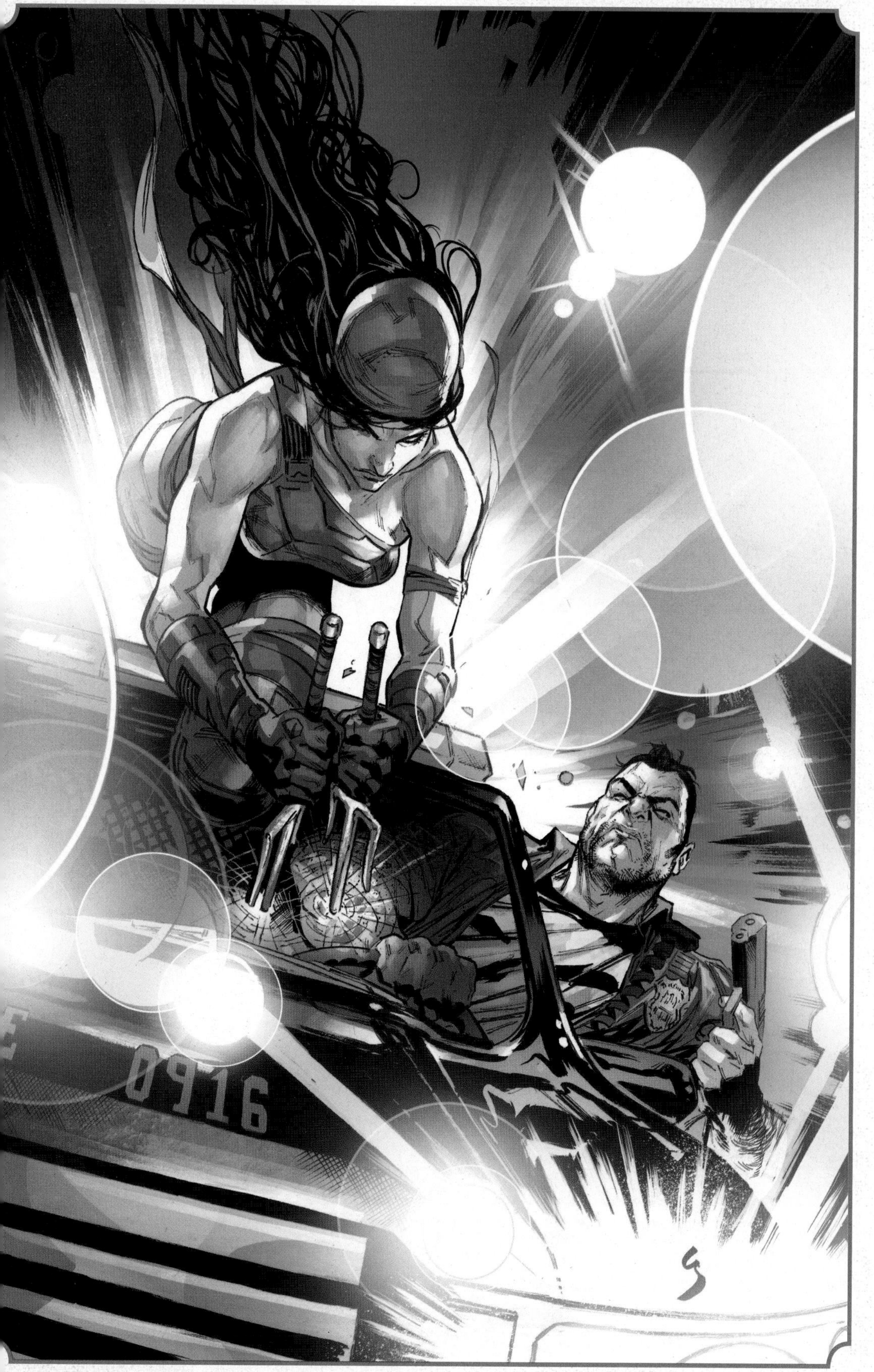
0916

2

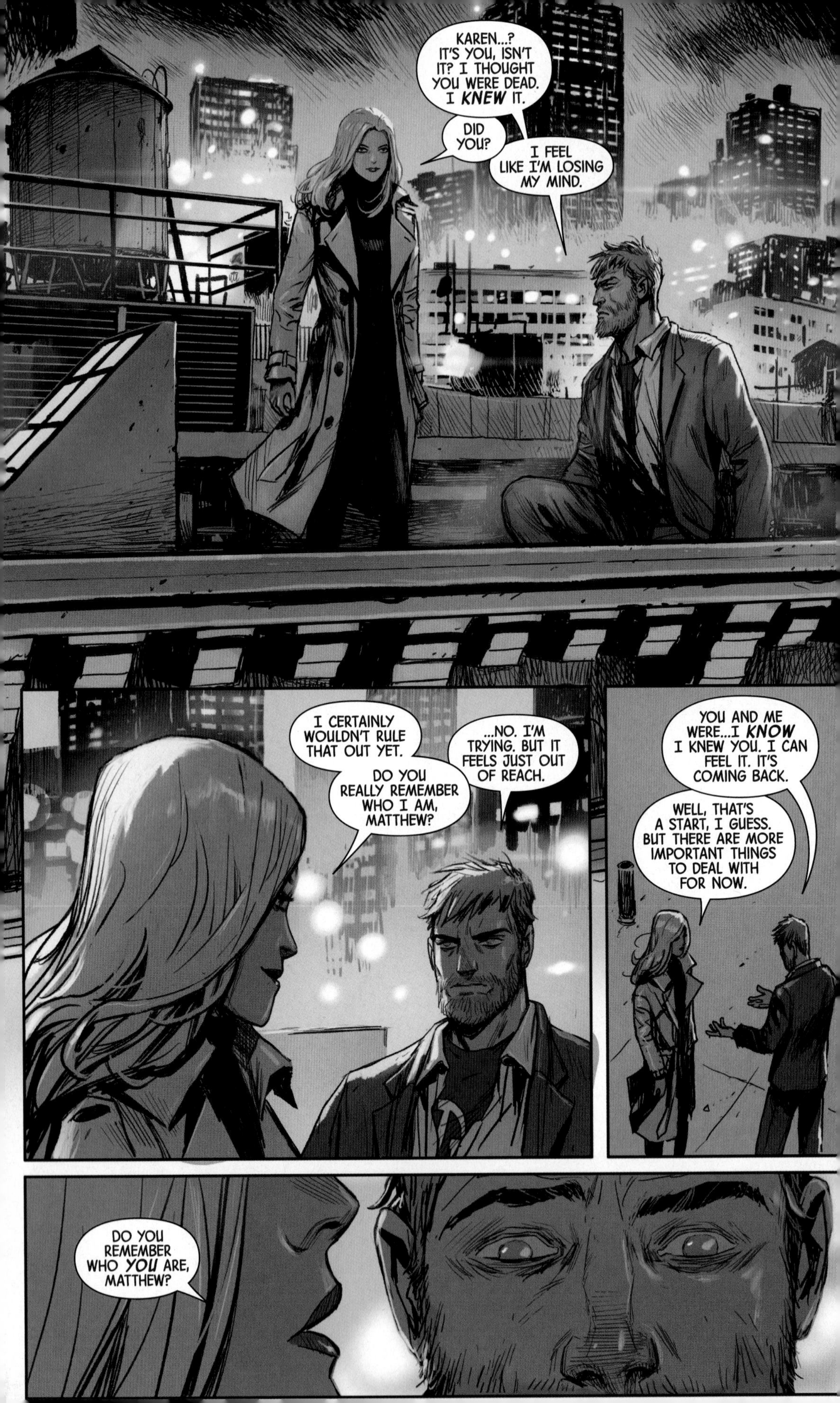
KAREN...? IT'S YOU, ISN'T IT? I THOUGHT YOU WERE DEAD. I *KNEW* IT.
DID YOU?
I FEEL LIKE I'M LOSING MY MIND.
I CERTAINLY WOULDN'T RULE THAT OUT YET.
DO YOU REALLY REMEMBER WHO I AM, MATTHEW?
...NO. I'M TRYING. BUT IT FEELS JUST OUT OF REACH.
YOU AND ME WERE...I *KNOW* I KNEW YOU. I CAN FEEL IT. IT'S COMING BACK.
WELL, THAT'S A START, I GUESS. BUT THERE ARE MORE IMPORTANT THINGS TO DEAL WITH FOR NOW.
DO YOU REMEMBER WHO *YOU* ARE, MATTHEW?

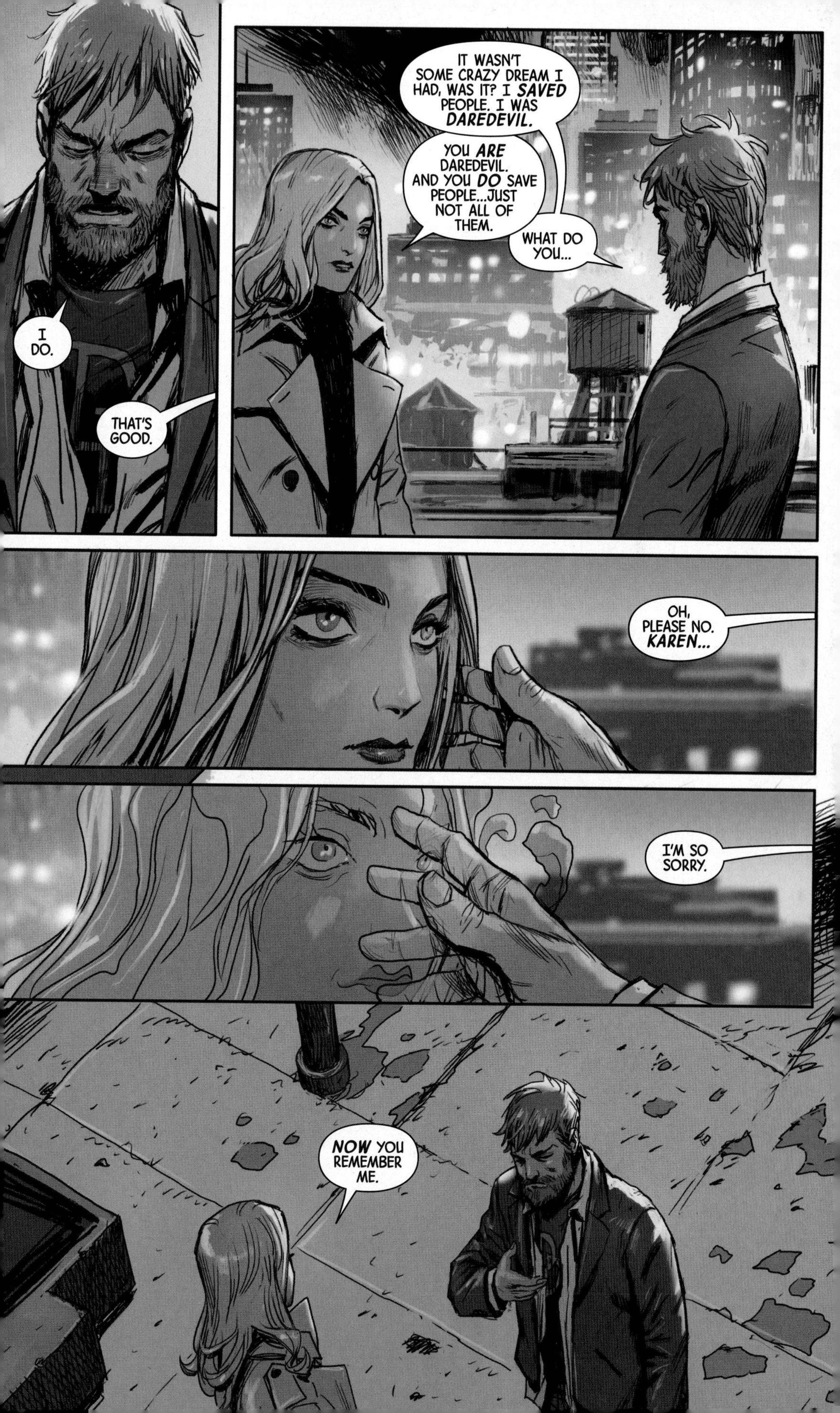
I DO.
THAT'S GOOD.
IT WASN'T SOME CRAZY DREAM I HAD, WAS IT? I SAVED PEOPLE. I WAS DAREDEVIL.
YOU ARE DAREDEVIL. AND YOU DO SAVE PEOPLE...JUST NOT ALL OF THEM.
WHAT DO YOU...
OH, PLEASE NO. KAREN...
I'M SO SORRY.
NOW YOU REMEMBER ME.

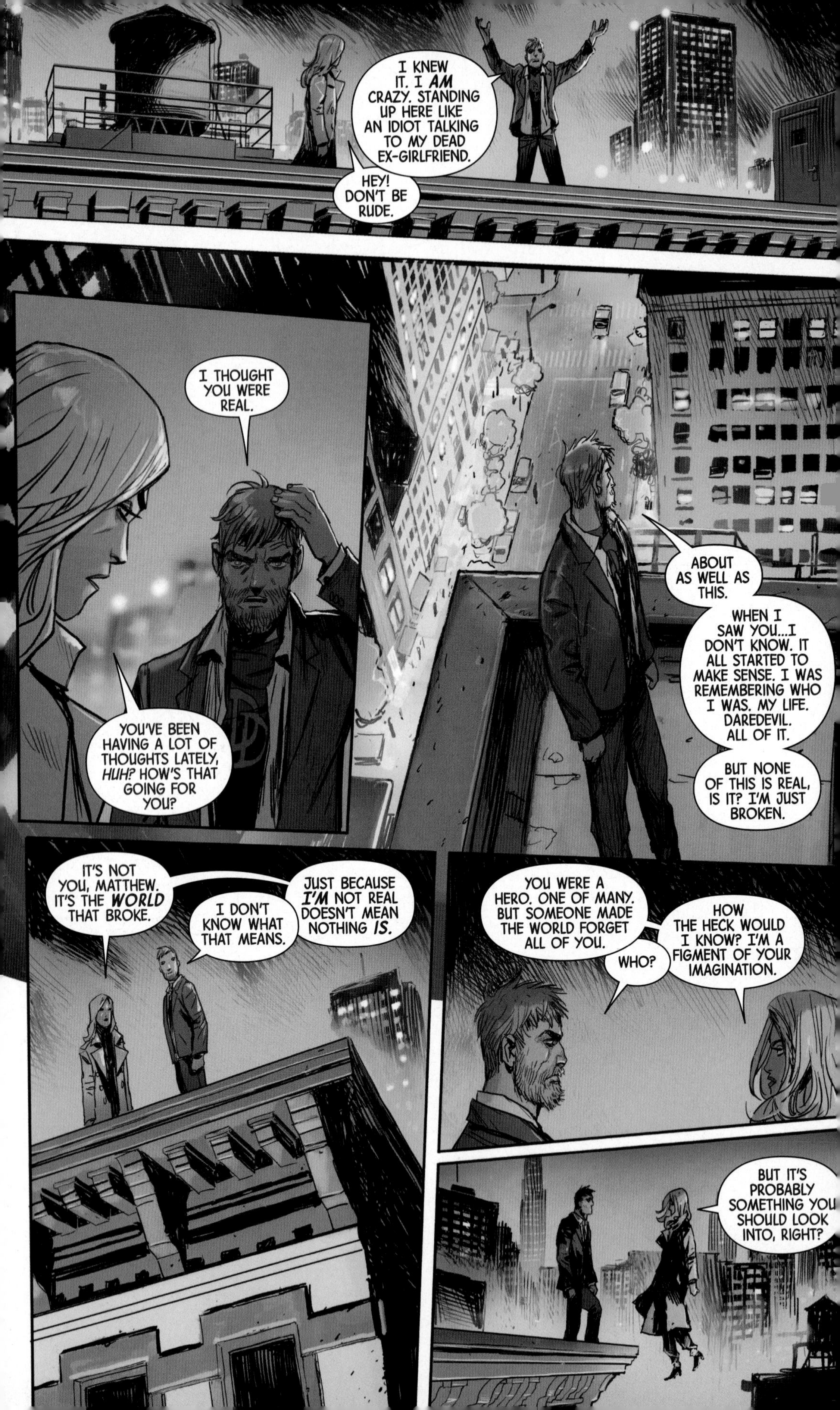
I KNEW IT. I *AM* CRAZY. STANDING UP HERE LIKE AN IDIOT TALKING TO MY DEAD EX-GIRLFRIEND.
HEY! DON'T BE RUDE.
I THOUGHT YOU WERE REAL.
YOU'VE BEEN HAVING A LOT OF THOUGHTS LATELY, *HUH?* HOW'S THAT GOING FOR YOU?
ABOUT AS WELL AS THIS.
WHEN I SAW YOU...I DON'T KNOW. IT ALL STARTED TO MAKE SENSE. I WAS REMEMBERING WHO I WAS. MY LIFE. DAREDEVIL. ALL OF IT.
BUT NONE OF THIS IS REAL, IS IT? I'M JUST BROKEN.
IT'S NOT YOU, MATTHEW. IT'S THE *WORLD* THAT BROKE.
I DON'T KNOW WHAT THAT MEANS.
JUST BECAUSE *I'M* NOT REAL DOESN'T MEAN NOTHING *IS.*
YOU WERE A HERO. ONE OF MANY. BUT SOMEONE MADE THE WORLD FORGET ALL OF YOU.
WHO?
HOW THE HECK WOULD I KNOW? I'M A FIGMENT OF YOUR IMAGINATION.
BUT IT'S PROBABLY SOMETHING YOU SHOULD LOOK INTO, RIGHT?

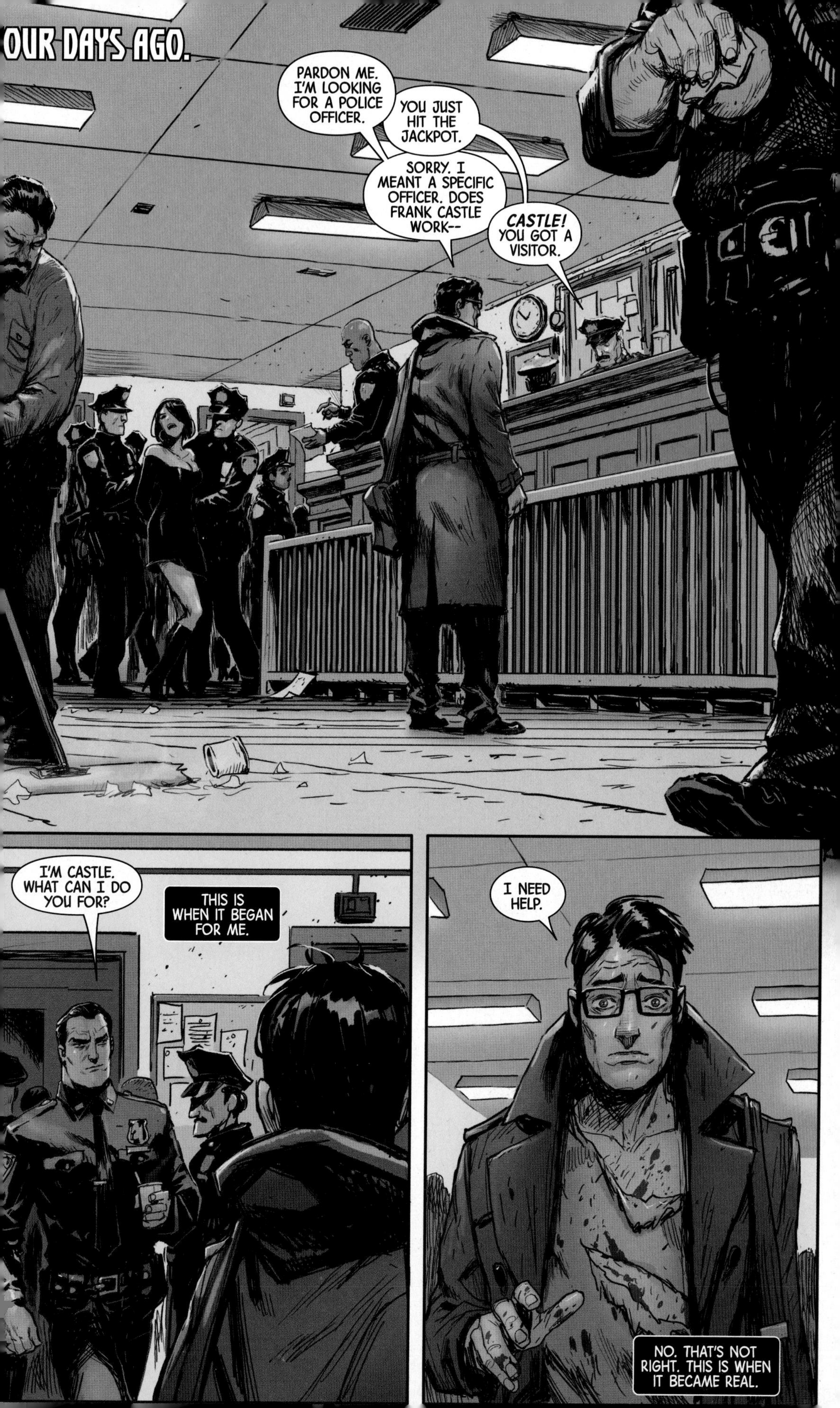
OUR DAYS AGO.
PARDON ME. I'M LOOKING FOR A POLICE OFFICER.
YOU JUST HIT THE JACKPOT.
SORRY. I MEANT A SPECIFIC OFFICER. DOES FRANK CASTLE WORK--
CASTLE! YOU GOT A VISITOR.
I'M CASTLE. WHAT CAN I DO YOU FOR?
THIS IS WHEN IT BEGAN FOR ME.
I NEED HELP.
NO. THAT'S NOT RIGHT. THIS IS WHEN IT BECAME REAL.

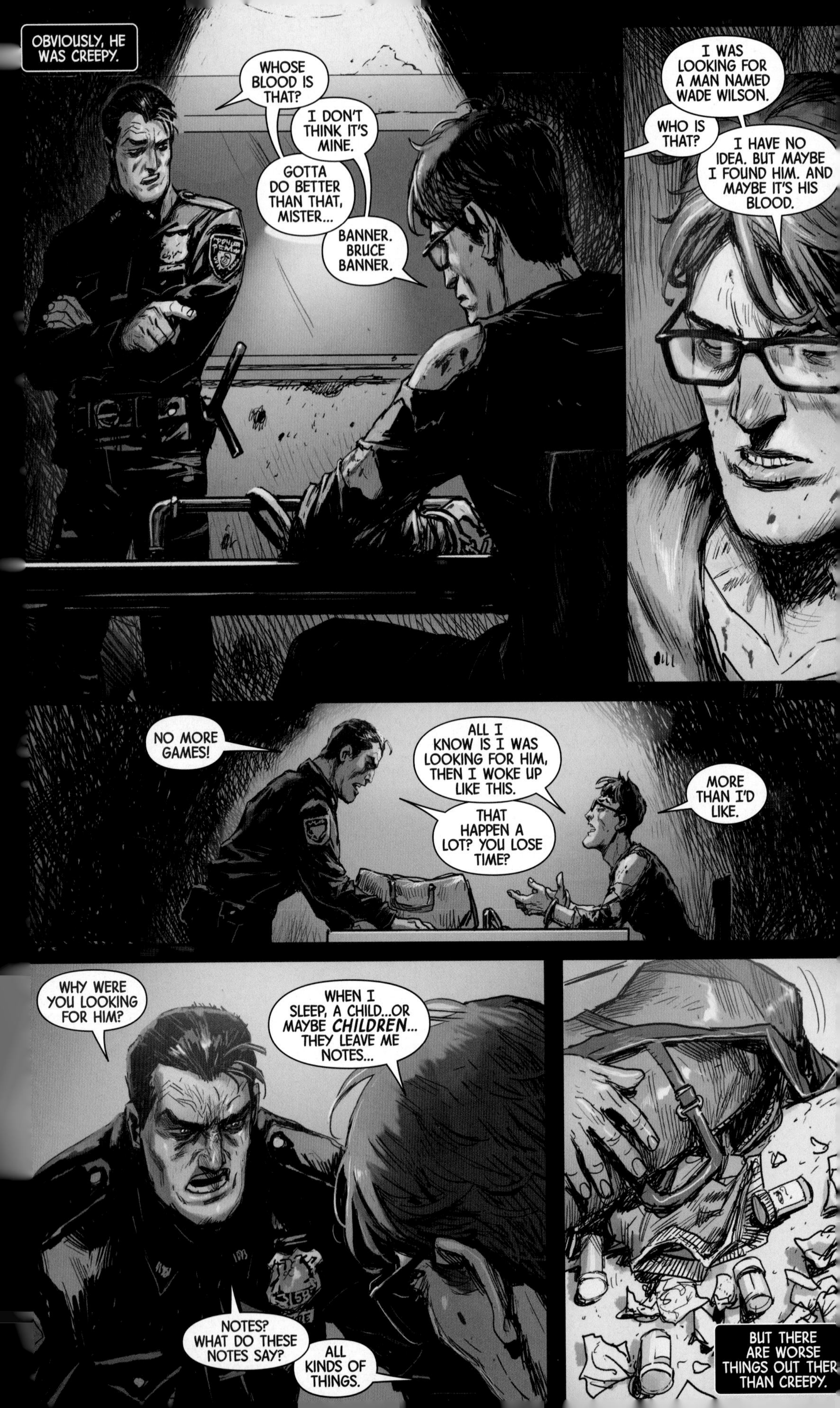
OBVIOUSLY, HE WAS CREEPY.
WHOSE BLOOD IS THAT?
I DON'T THINK IT'S MINE.
GOTTA DO BETTER THAN THAT, MISTER...
BANNER. BRUCE BANNER.
I WAS LOOKING FOR A MAN NAMED WADE WILSON.
WHO IS THAT?
I HAVE NO IDEA. BUT MAYBE I FOUND HIM. AND MAYBE IT'S HIS BLOOD.
NO MORE GAMES!
ALL I KNOW IS I WAS LOOKING FOR HIM, THEN I WOKE UP LIKE THIS.
THAT HAPPEN A LOT? YOU LOSE TIME?
MORE THAN I'D LIKE.
WHY WERE YOU LOOKING FOR HIM?
WHEN I SLEEP, A CHILD...OR MAYBE CHILDREN... THEY LEAVE ME NOTES...
NOTES? WHAT DO THESE NOTES SAY?
ALL KINDS OF THINGS.
BUT THERE ARE WORSE THINGS OUT THER THAN CREEPY.

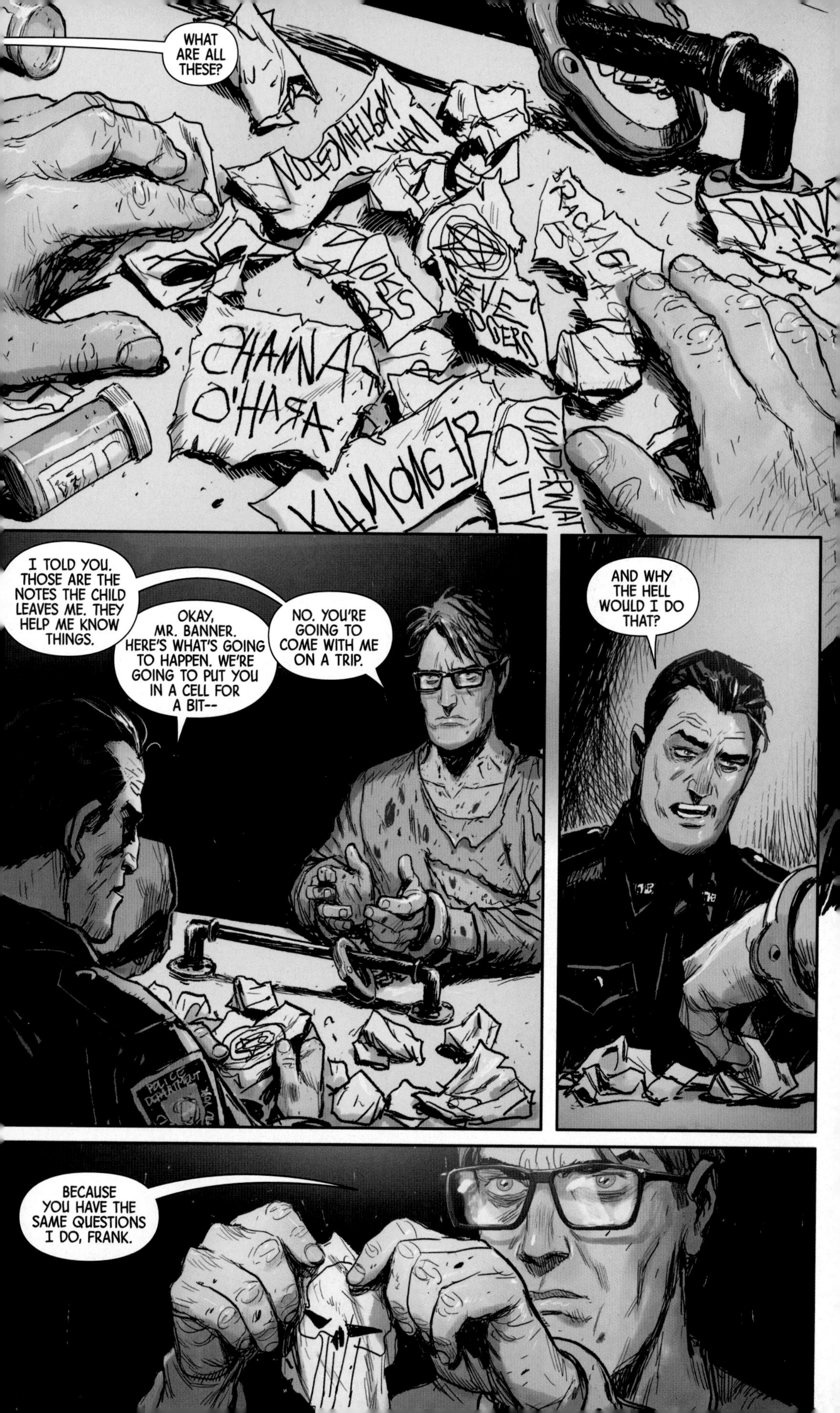
WHAT ARE ALL THESE?
I TOLD YOU. THOSE ARE THE NOTES THE CHILD LEAVES ME. THEY HELP ME KNOW THINGS.
OKAY, MR. BANNER. HERE'S WHAT'S GOING TO HAPPEN. WE'RE GOING TO PUT YOU IN A CELL FOR A BIT--
NO. YOU'RE GOING TO COME WITH ME ON A TRIP.
AND WHY THE HELL WOULD I DO THAT?
BECAUSE YOU HAVE THE SAME QUESTIONS I DO, FRANK.

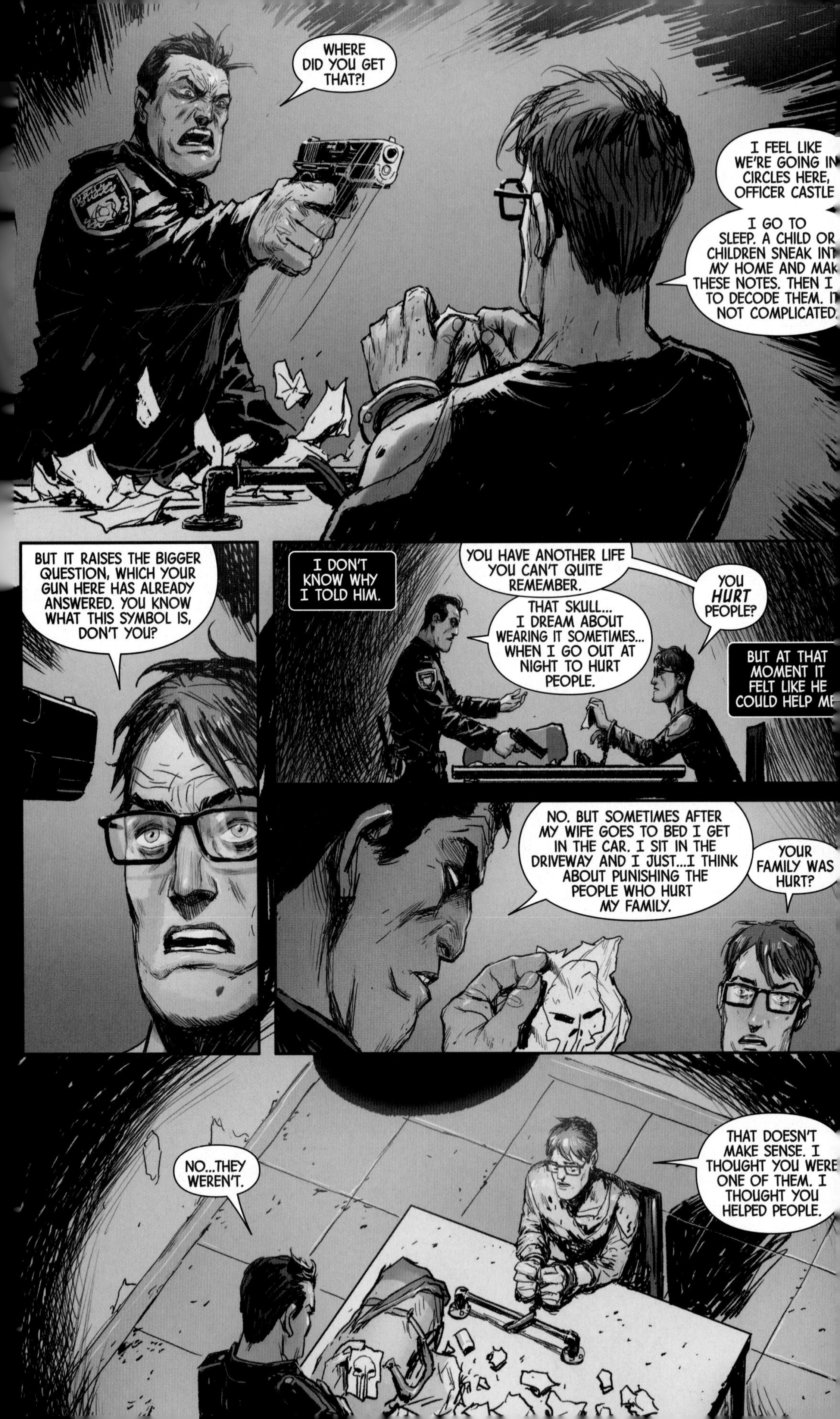
WHERE DID YOU GET THAT?!
I FEEL LIKE WE'RE GOING IN CIRCLES HERE, OFFICER CASTLE
I GO TO SLEEP. A CHILD OR CHILDREN SNEAK INT MY HOME AND MAK THESE NOTES. THEN I TO DECODE THEM. IT NOT COMPLICATED.
BUT IT RAISES THE BIGGER QUESTION, WHICH YOUR GUN HERE HAS ALREADY ANSWERED. YOU KNOW WHAT THIS SYMBOL IS, DON'T YOU?
I DON'T KNOW WHY I TOLD HIM.
YOU HAVE ANOTHER LIFE YOU CAN'T QUITE REMEMBER.
THAT SKULL... I DREAM ABOUT WEARING IT SOMETIMES... WHEN I GO OUT AT NIGHT TO HURT PEOPLE.
YOU HURT PEOPLE?
BUT AT THAT MOMENT IT FELT LIKE HE COULD HELP ME
NO. BUT SOMETIMES AFTER MY WIFE GOES TO BED I GET IN THE CAR. I SIT IN THE DRIVEWAY AND I JUST...I THINK ABOUT PUNISHING THE PEOPLE WHO HURT MY FAMILY.
YOUR FAMILY WAS HURT?
NO...THEY WEREN'T.
THAT DOESN'T MAKE SENSE. I THOUGHT YOU WERE ONE OF THEM. I THOUGHT YOU HELPED PEOPLE.

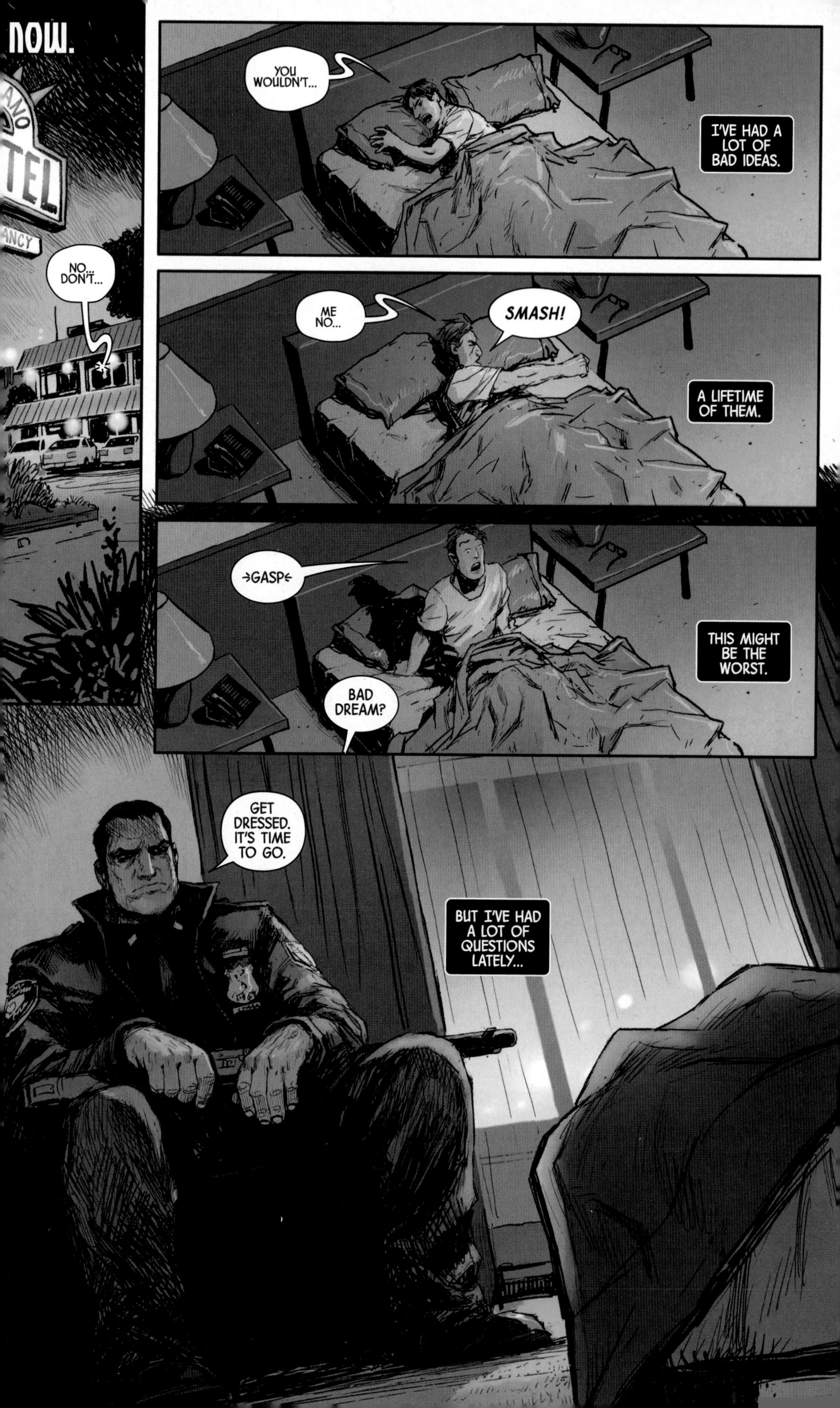
NOW.
YOU WOULDN'T...
I'VE HAD A LOT OF BAD IDEAS.
NO... DON'T...
ME NO...
SMASH!
A LIFETIME OF THEM.
GASP
THIS MIGHT BE THE WORST.
BAD DREAM?
GET DRESSED. IT'S TIME TO GO.
BUT I'VE HAD A LOT OF QUESTIONS LATELY...

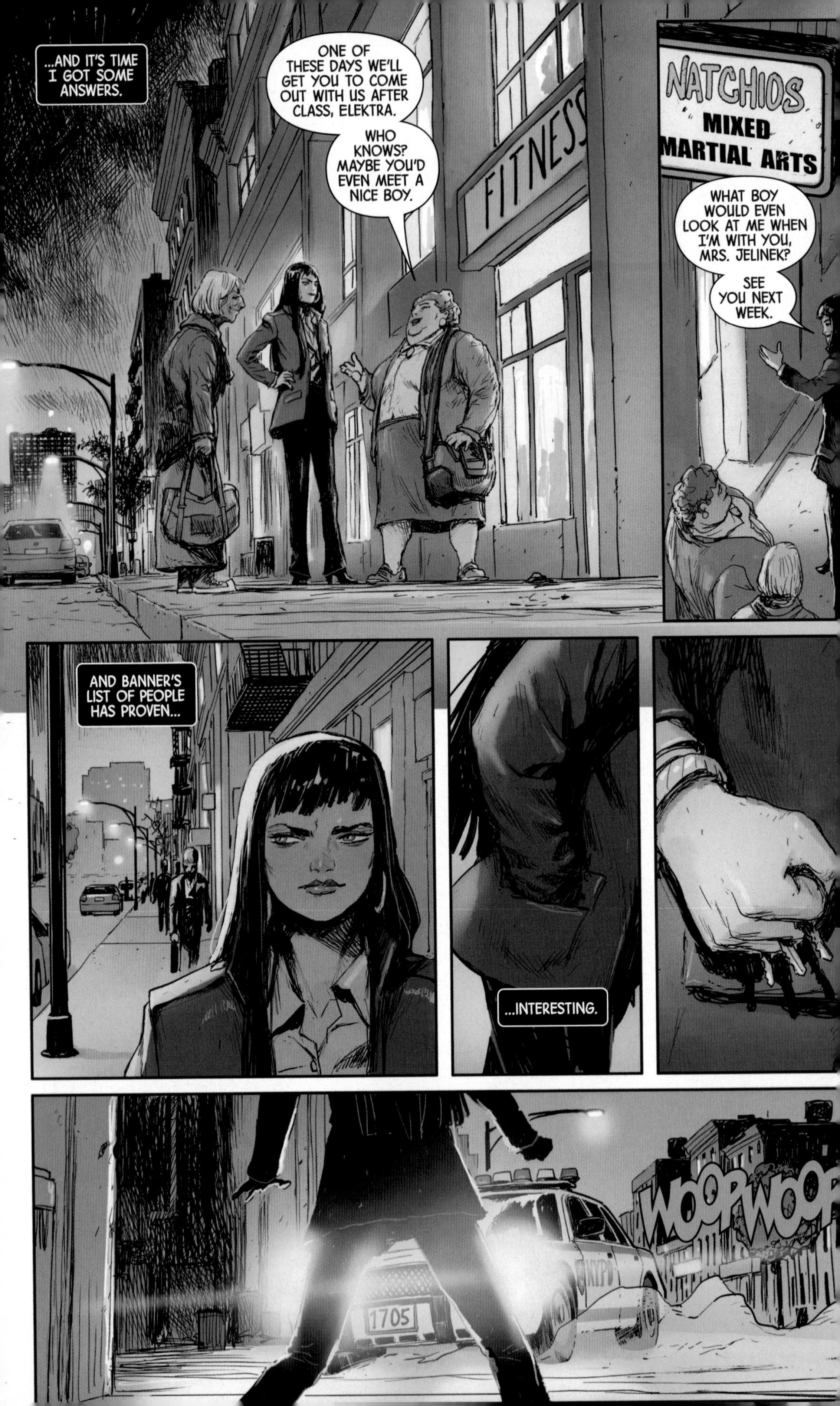

...AND IT'S TIME I GOT SOME ANSWERS.
ONE OF THESE DAYS WE'LL GET YOU TO COME OUT WITH US AFTER CLASS, ELEKTRA.
WHO KNOWS? MAYBE YOU'D EVEN MEET A NICE BOY.
FITNESS
NATCHIOS MIXED MARTIAL ARTS
WHAT BOY WOULD EVEN LOOK AT ME WHEN I'M WITH YOU, MRS. JELINEK?
SEE YOU NEXT WEEK.
AND BANNER'S LIST OF PEOPLE HAS PROVEN...
...INTERESTING.
WOOPWOOP
NYPD
1705

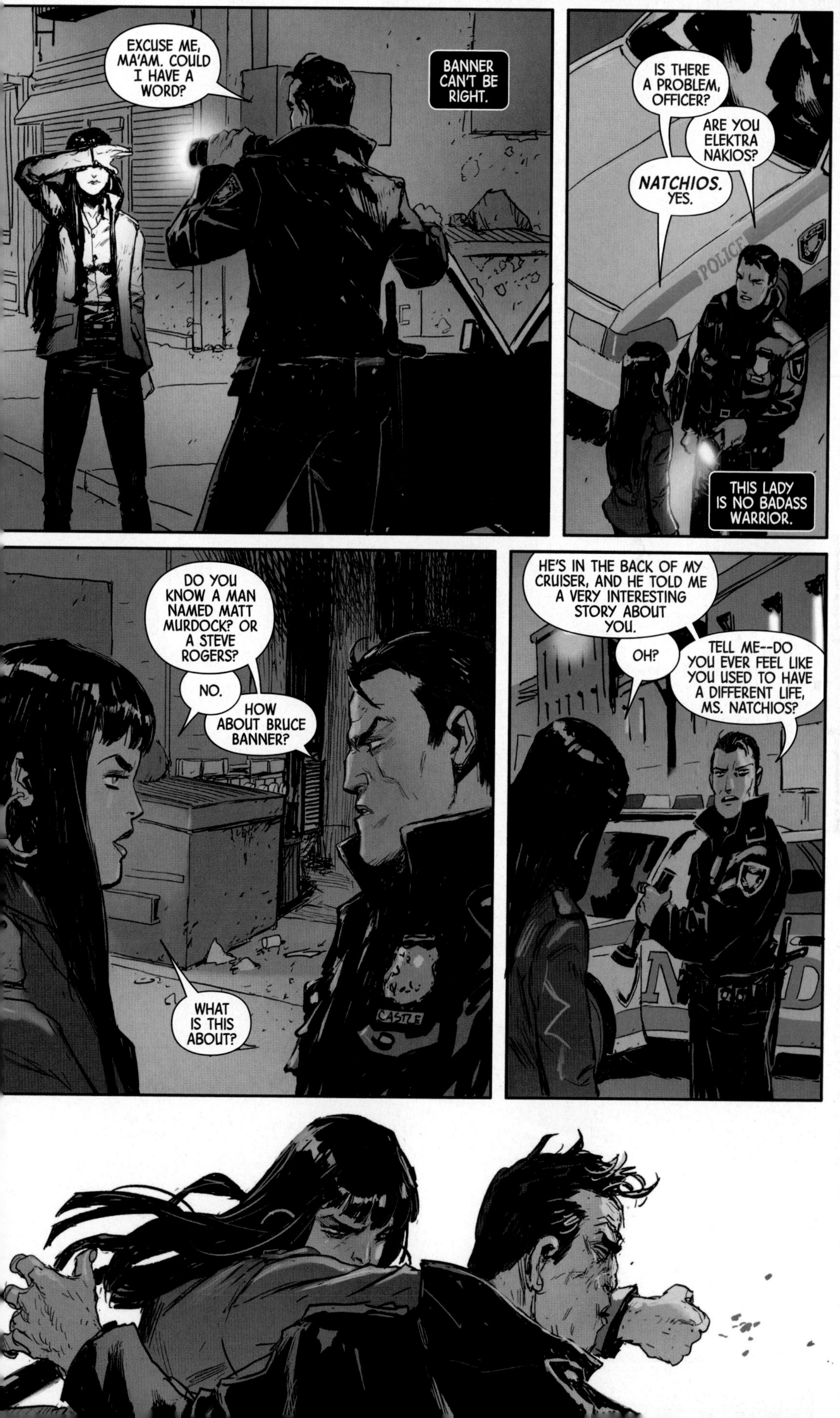
EXCUSE ME, MA'AM. COULD I HAVE A WORD?
BANNER CAN'T BE RIGHT.
IS THERE A PROBLEM, OFFICER?
ARE YOU ELEKTRA NAKIOS?
NATCHIOS. YES.
THIS LADY IS NO BADASS WARRIOR.
DO YOU KNOW A MAN NAMED MATT MURDOCK? OR A STEVE ROGERS?
NO.
HOW ABOUT BRUCE BANNER?
WHAT IS THIS ABOUT?
HE'S IN THE BACK OF MY CRUISER, AND HE TOLD ME A VERY INTERESTING STORY ABOUT YOU.
OH?
TELL ME--DO YOU EVER FEEL LIKE YOU USED TO HAVE A DIFFERENT LIFE, MS. NATCHIOS?

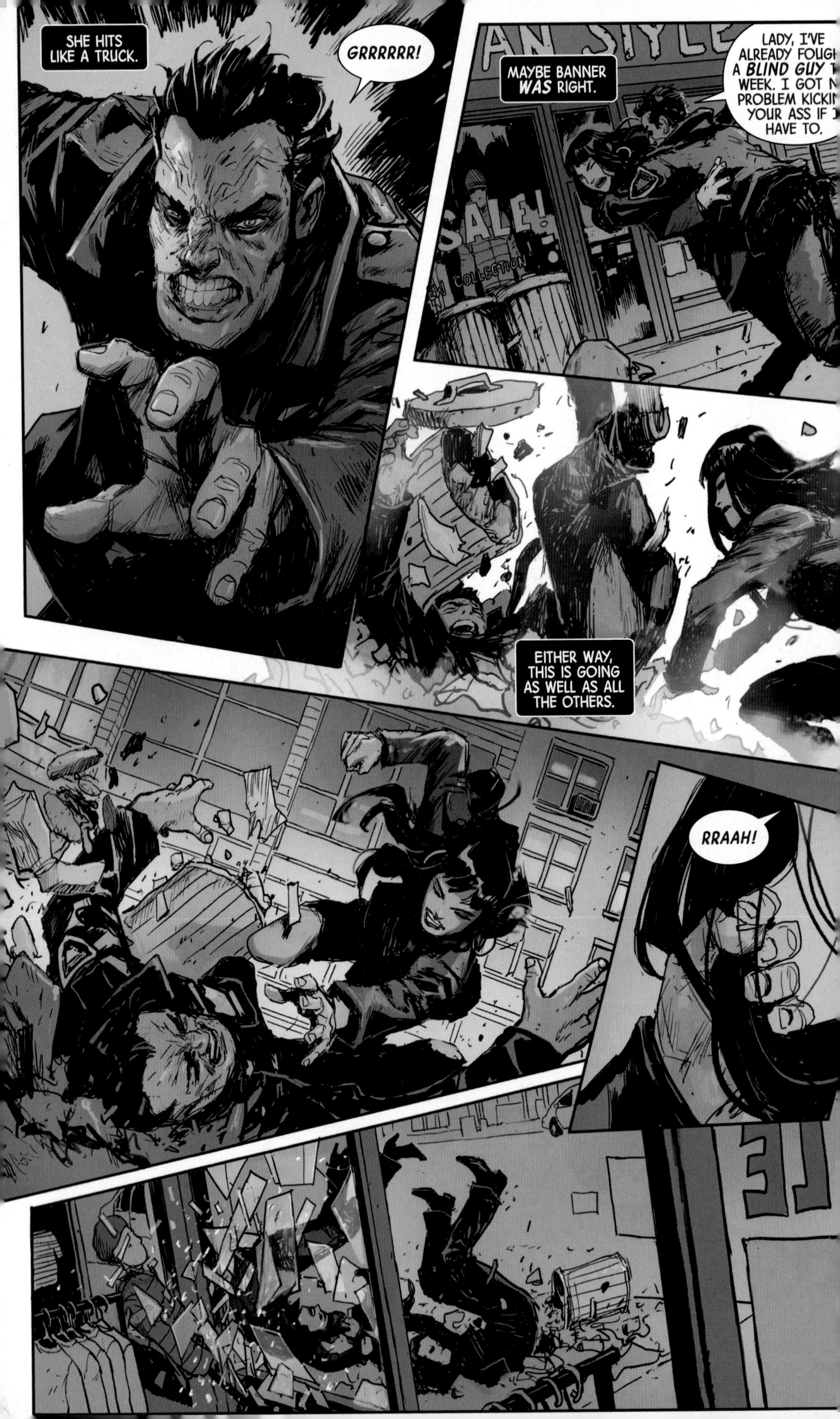
SHE HITS LIKE A TRUCK.
GRRRRRR!
MAYBE BANNER *WAS* RIGHT.
LADY, I'VE ALREADY FOUG A *BLIND GUY* WEEK. I GOT PROBLEM KICKI YOUR ASS IF HAVE TO.
SALE!
EITHER WAY, THIS IS GOING AS WELL AS ALL THE OTHERS.
RRAAH!

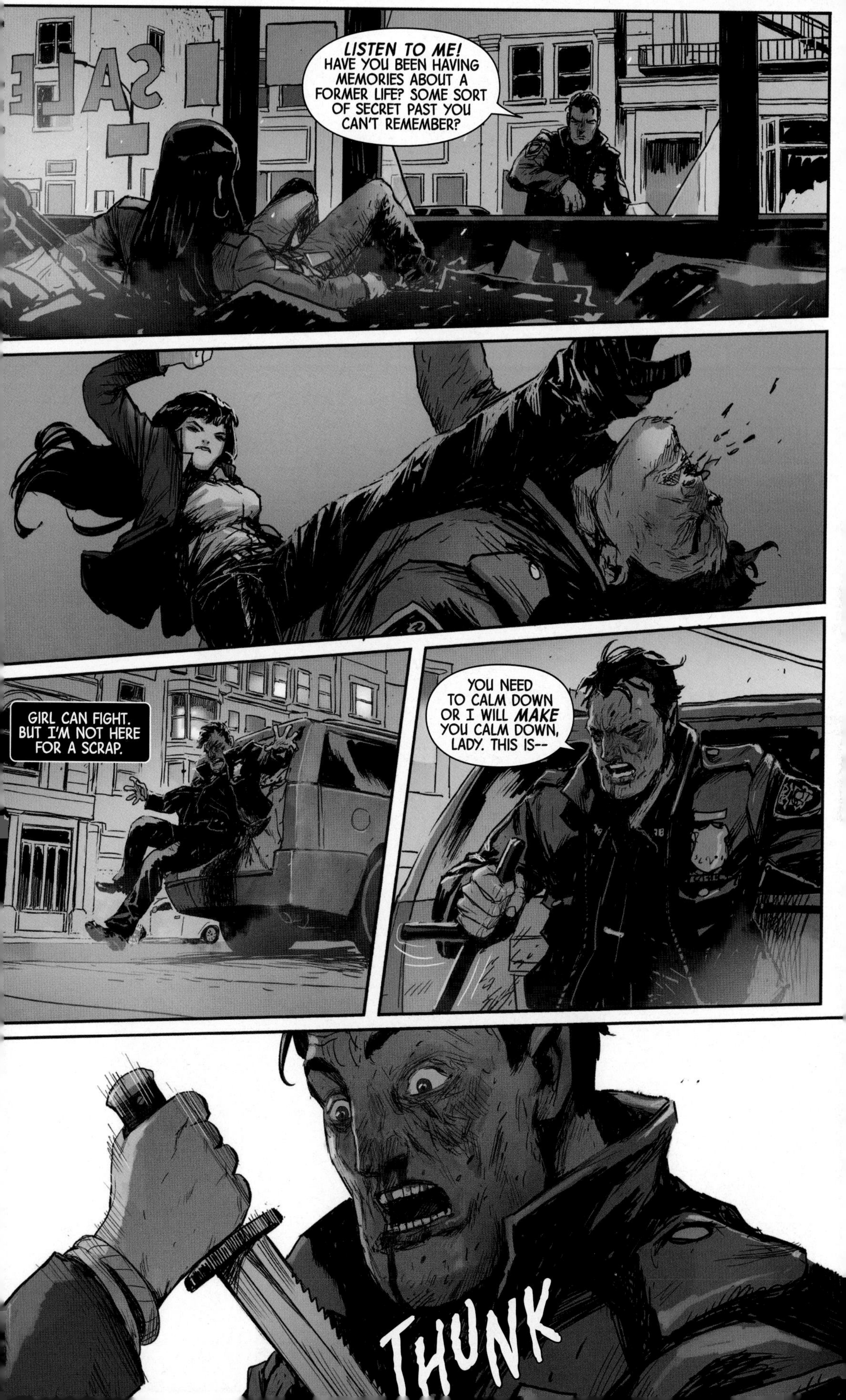
SALE
LISTEN TO ME! HAVE YOU BEEN HAVING MEMORIES ABOUT A FORMER LIFE? SOME SORT OF SECRET PAST YOU CAN'T REMEMBER?
GIRL CAN FIGHT. BUT I'M NOT HERE FOR A SCRAP.
YOU NEED TO CALM DOWN OR I WILL MAKE YOU CALM DOWN, LADY. THIS IS--
THUNK

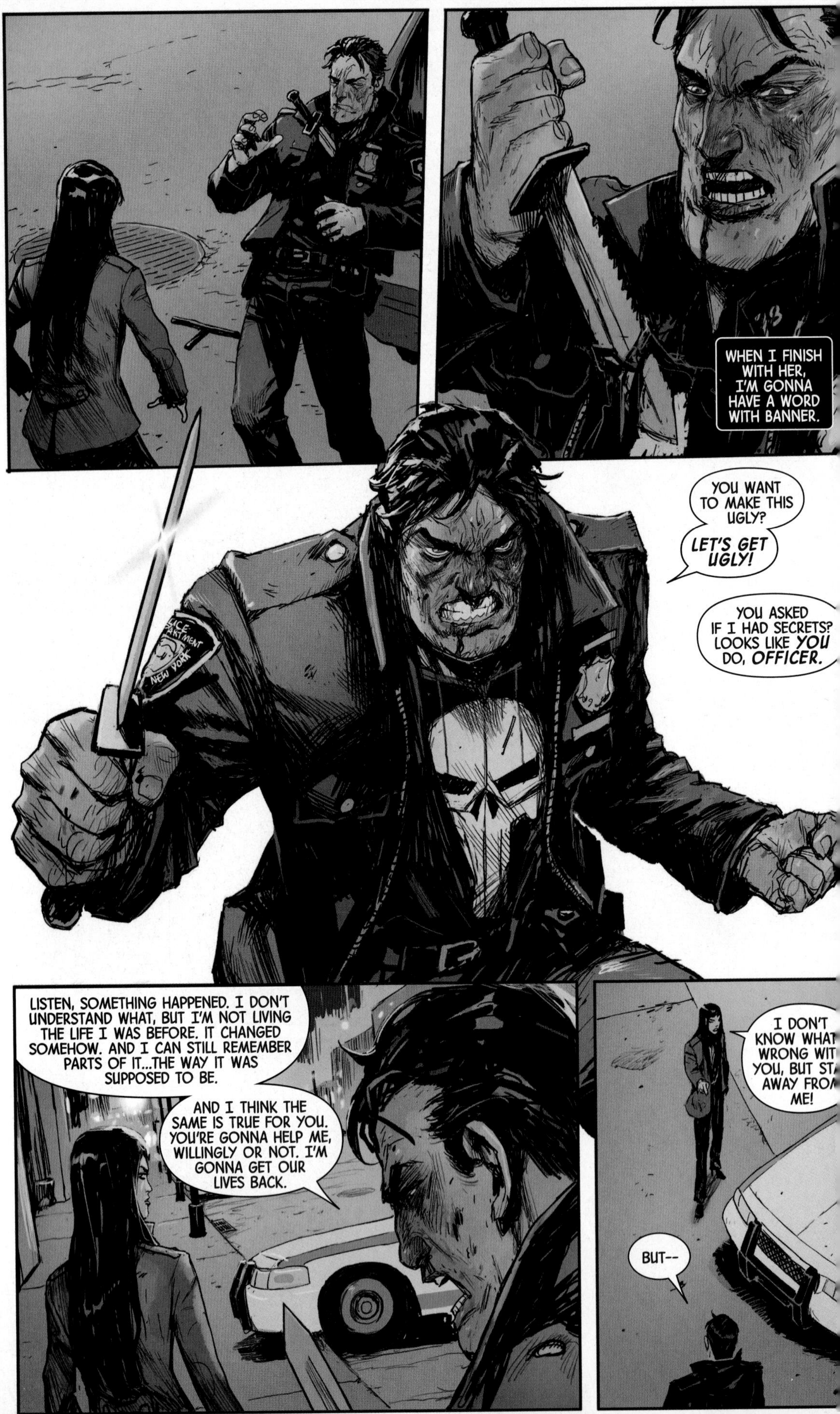
WHEN I FINISH WITH HER, I'M GONNA HAVE A WORD WITH BANNER.
YOU WANT TO MAKE THIS UGLY?
LET'S GET UGLY!
YOU ASKED IF I HAD SECRETS? LOOKS LIKE *YOU* DO, *OFFICER.*
LISTEN, SOMETHING HAPPENED. I DON'T UNDERSTAND WHAT, BUT I'M NOT LIVING THE LIFE I WAS BEFORE. IT CHANGED SOMEHOW. AND I CAN STILL REMEMBER PARTS OF IT...THE WAY IT WAS SUPPOSED TO BE.
AND I THINK THE SAME IS TRUE FOR YOU. YOU'RE GONNA HELP ME, WILLINGLY OR NOT. I'M GONNA GET OUR LIVES BACK.
I DON'T KNOW WHAT WRONG WIT YOU, BUT ST AWAY FRO ME!
BUT--

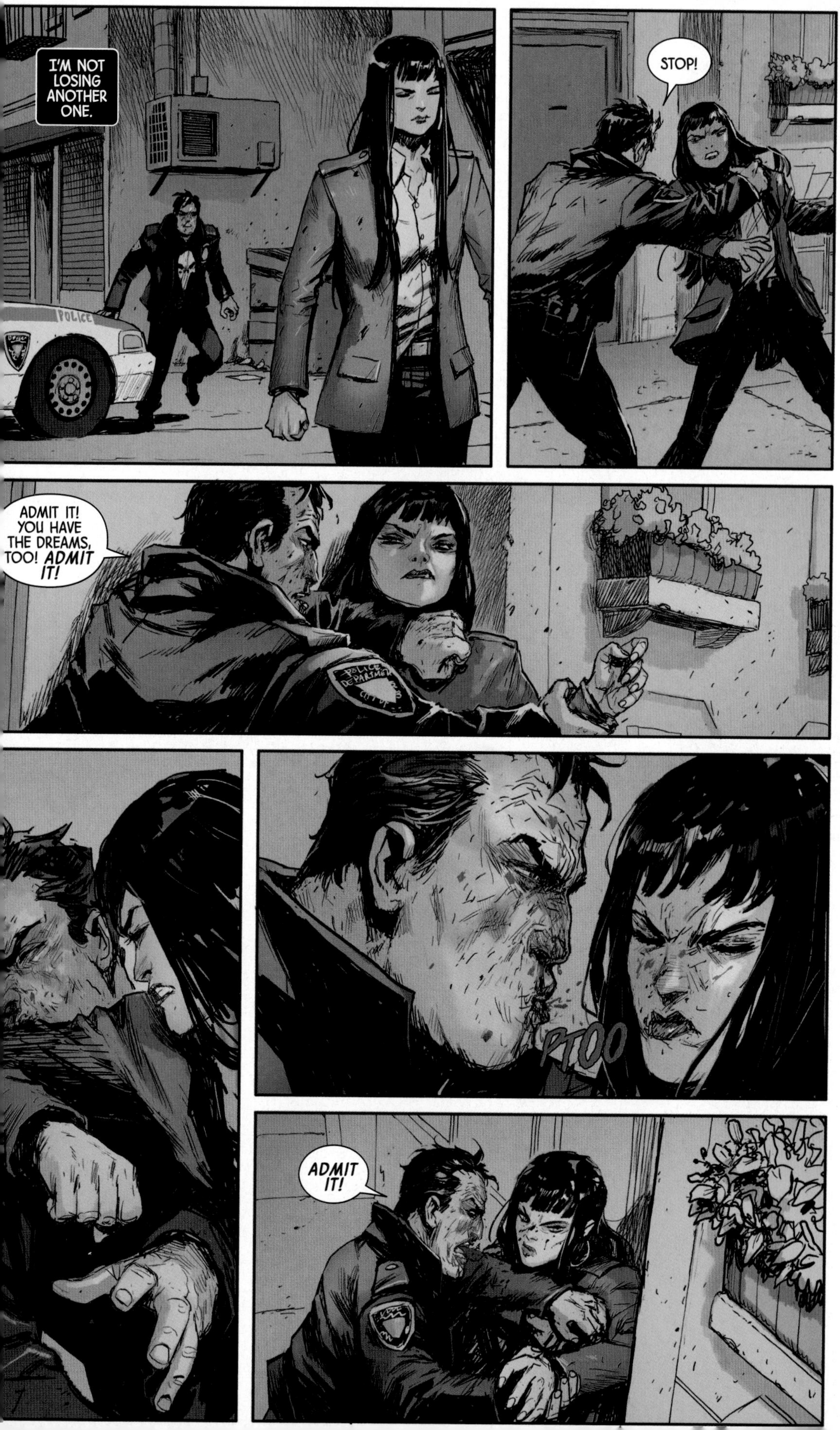

I'M NOT LOSING ANOTHER ONE.
POLICE
STOP!
ADMIT IT! YOU HAVE THE DREAMS, TOO! *ADMIT IT!*
PTOO
ADMIT IT!

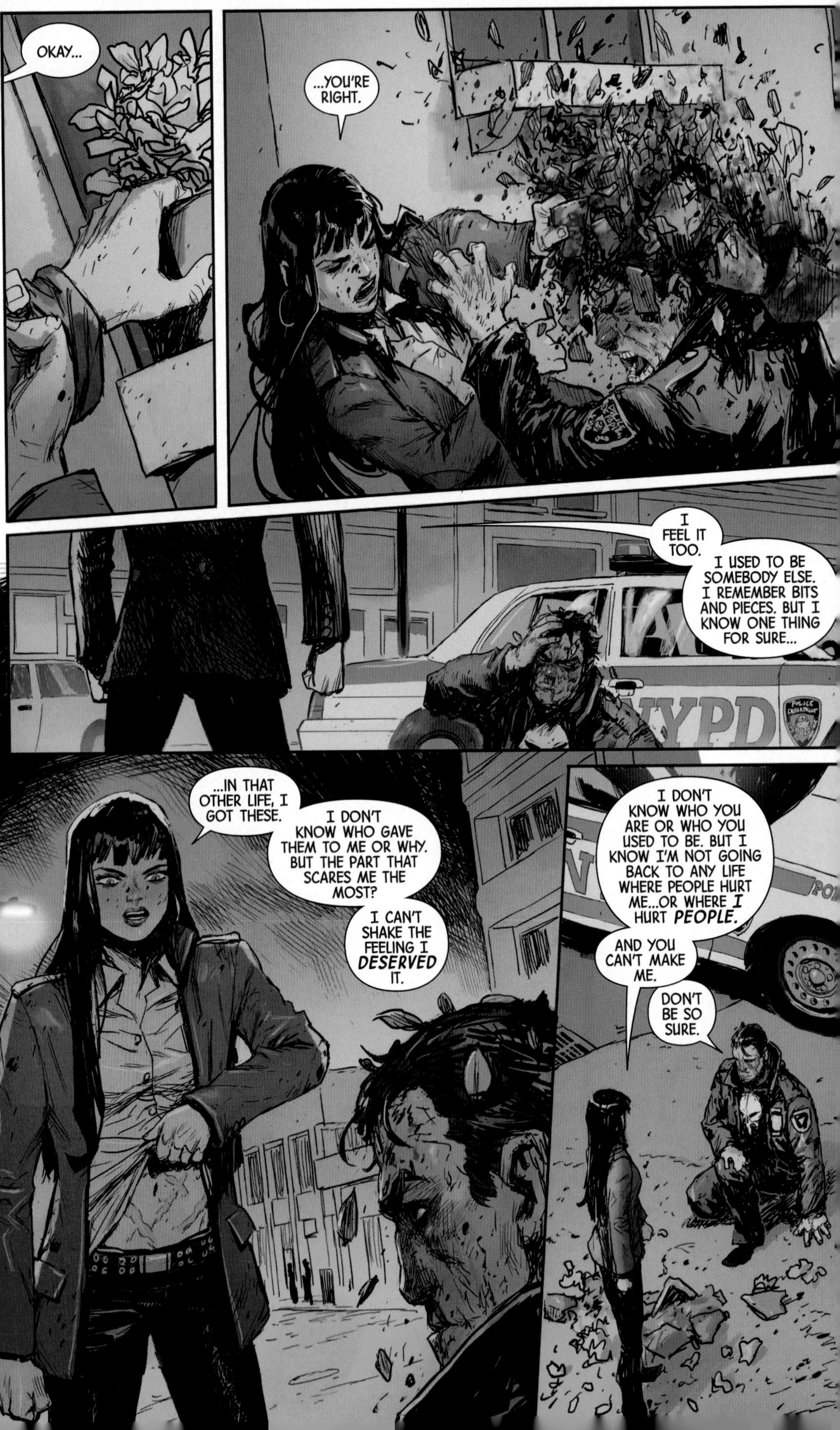
OKAY...
...YOU'RE RIGHT.
I FEEL IT TOO.
I USED TO BE SOMEBODY ELSE. I REMEMBER BITS AND PIECES. BUT I KNOW ONE THING FOR SURE...
NYPD
...IN THAT OTHER LIFE, I GOT THESE.
I DON'T KNOW WHO GAVE THEM TO ME OR WHY. BUT THE PART THAT SCARES ME THE MOST?
I CAN'T SHAKE THE FEELING I DESERVED IT.
I DON'T KNOW WHO YOU ARE OR WHO YOU USED TO BE. BUT I KNOW I'M NOT GOING BACK TO ANY LIFE WHERE PEOPLE HURT ME...OR WHERE I HURT PEOPLE.
AND YOU CAN'T MAKE ME.
DON'T BE SO SURE.

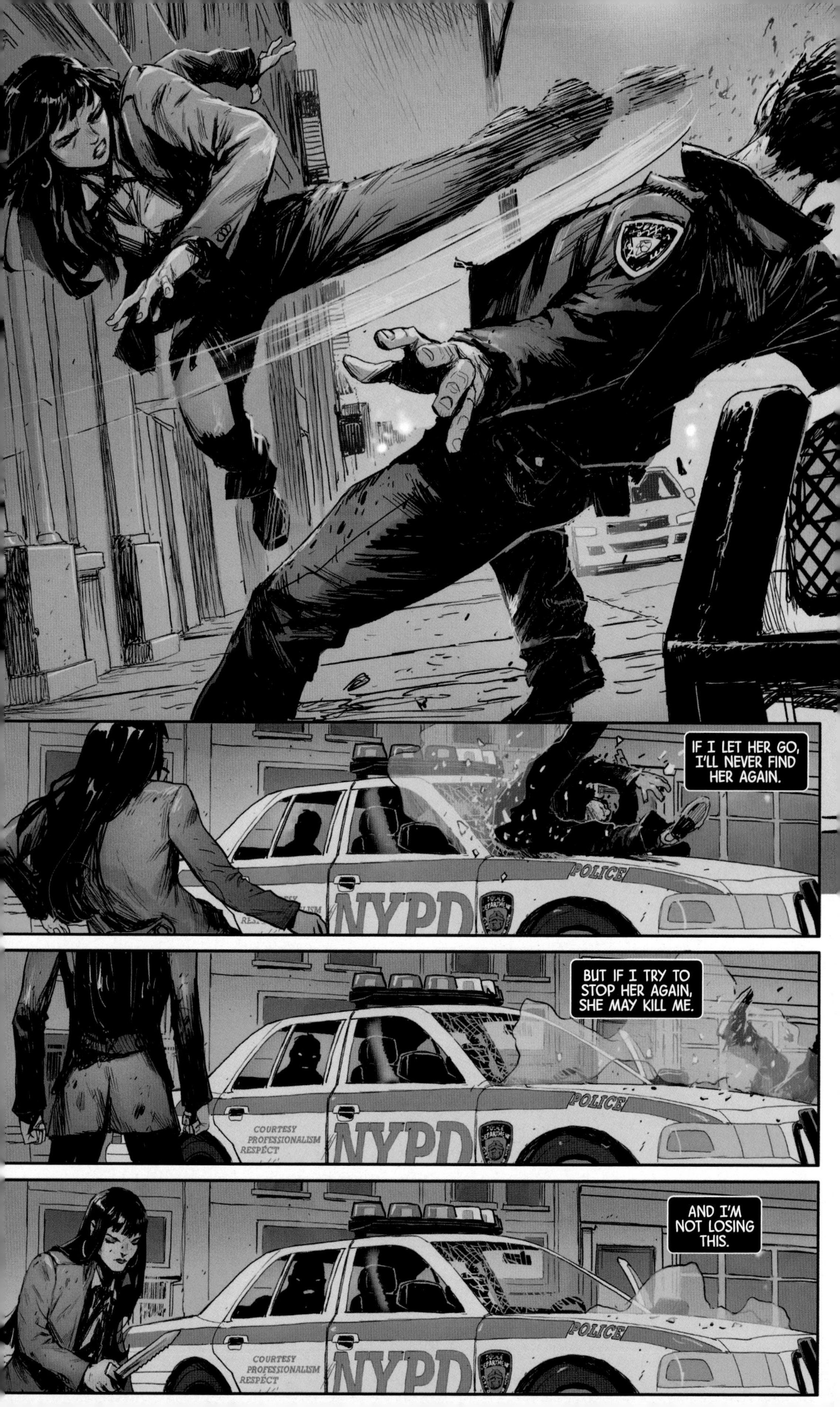
IF I LET HER GO, I'LL NEVER FIND HER AGAIN.
POLICE
NYPD
BUT IF I TRY TO STOP HER AGAIN, SHE MAY KILL ME.
COURTESY PROFESSIONALISM RESPECT
POLICE
NYPD
AND I'M NOT LOSING THIS.
COURTESY PROFESSIONALISM RESPECT
POLICE
NYPD

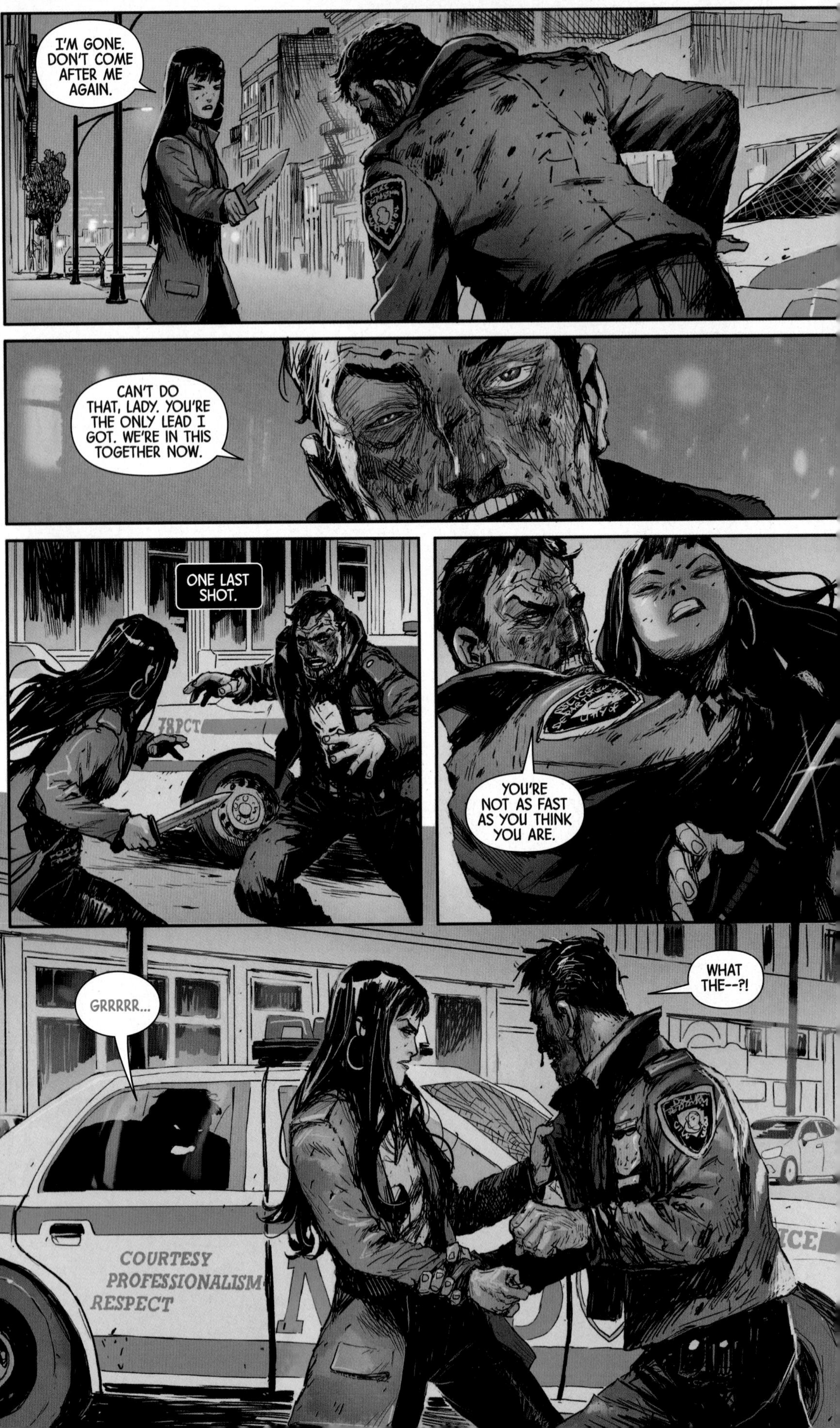
I'M GONE. DON'T COME AFTER ME AGAIN.
CAN'T DO THAT, LADY. YOU'RE THE ONLY LEAD I GOT. WE'RE IN THIS TOGETHER NOW.
ONE LAST SHOT.
78PCT
YOU'RE NOT AS FAST AS YOU THINK YOU ARE.
GRRRRR...
WHAT THE--?!
COURTESY
PROFESSIONALISM
RESPECT

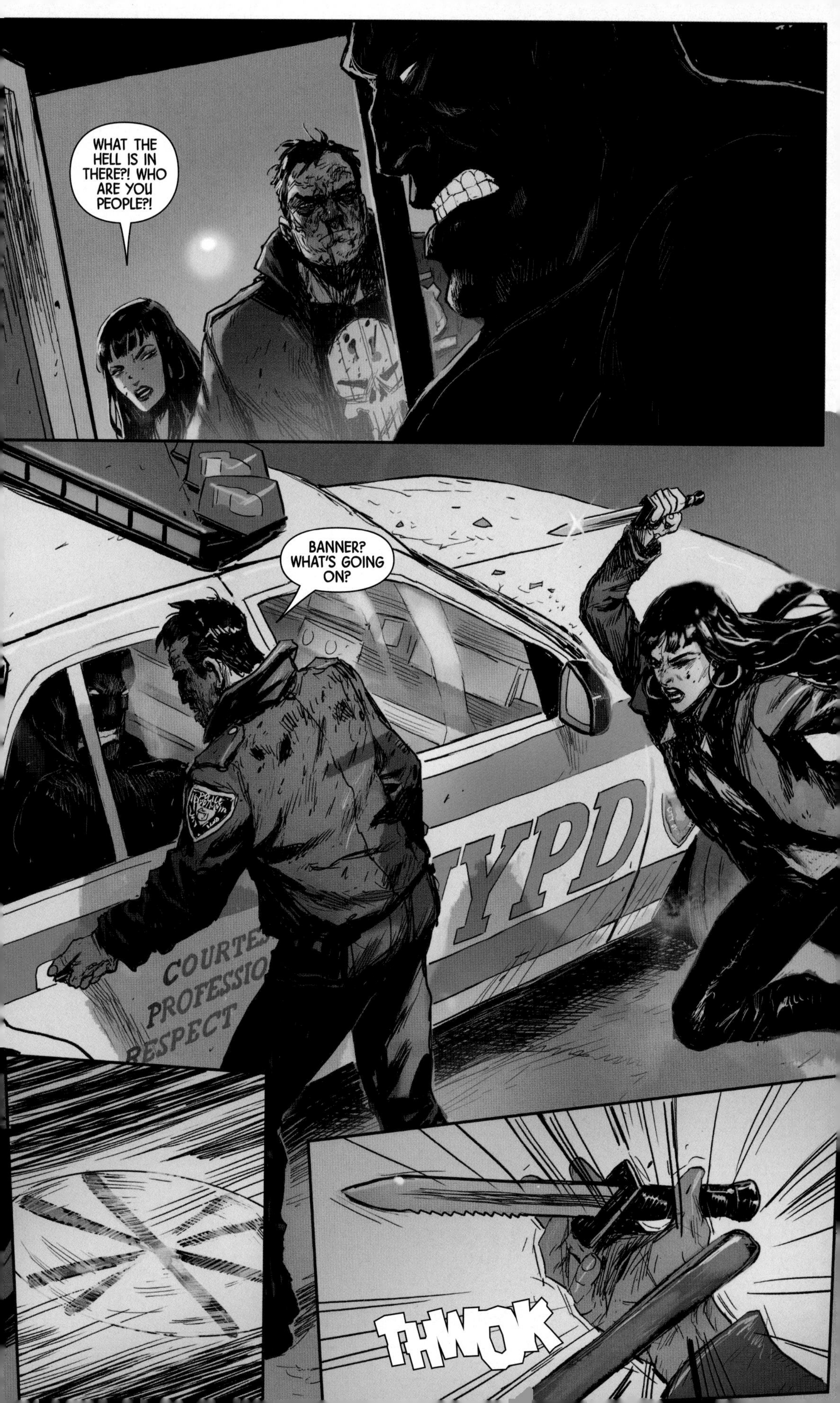
WHAT THE HELL IS IN THERE?! WHO ARE YOU PEOPLE?!
BANNER? WHAT'S GOING ON?
NYPD
COURTES
PROFESSIO
RESPECT
THWOK

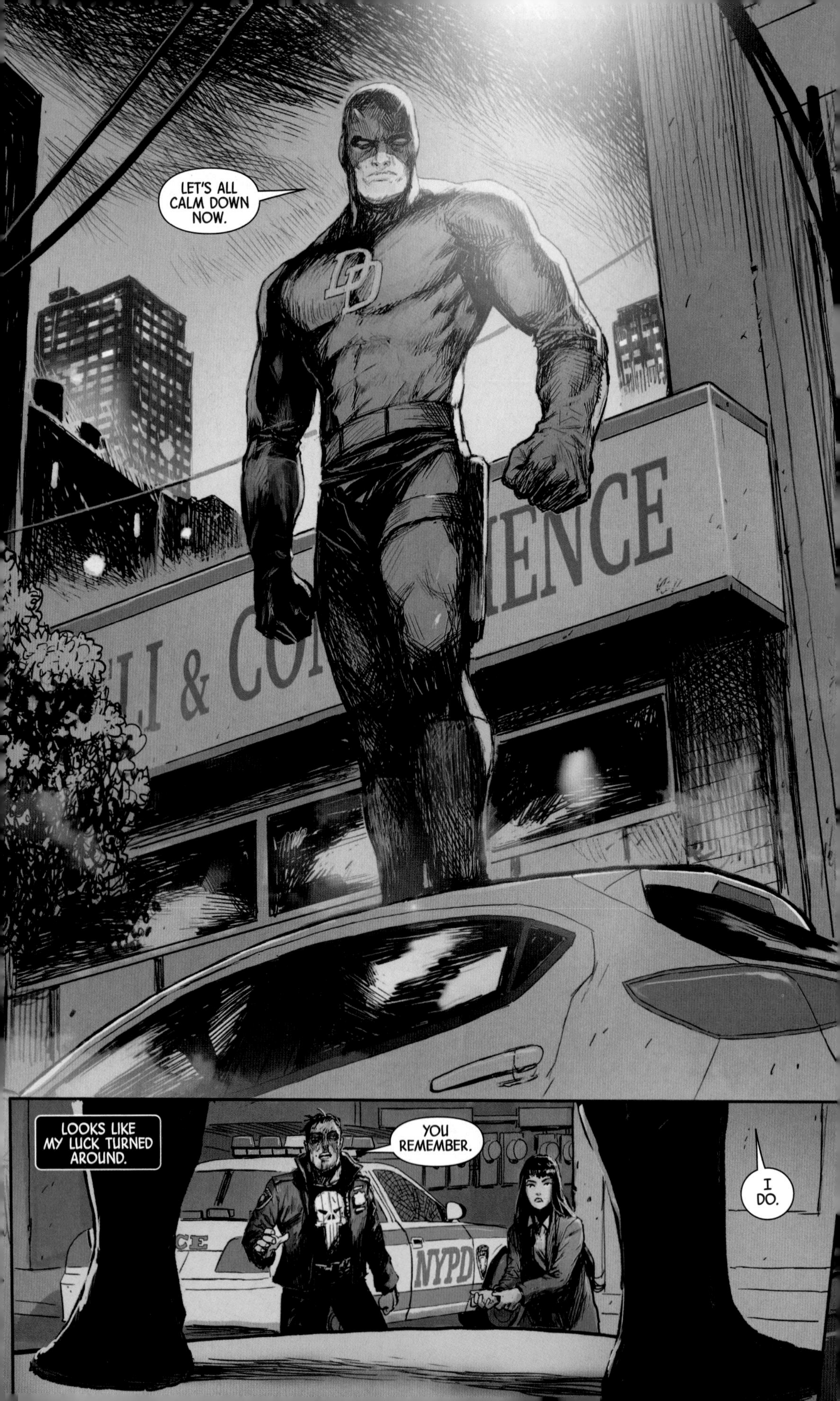
LET'S ALL CALM DOWN NOW.
LI & CO IENCE
LOOKS LIKE MY LUCK TURNED AROUND.
YOU REMEMBER.
I DO.
NYPD

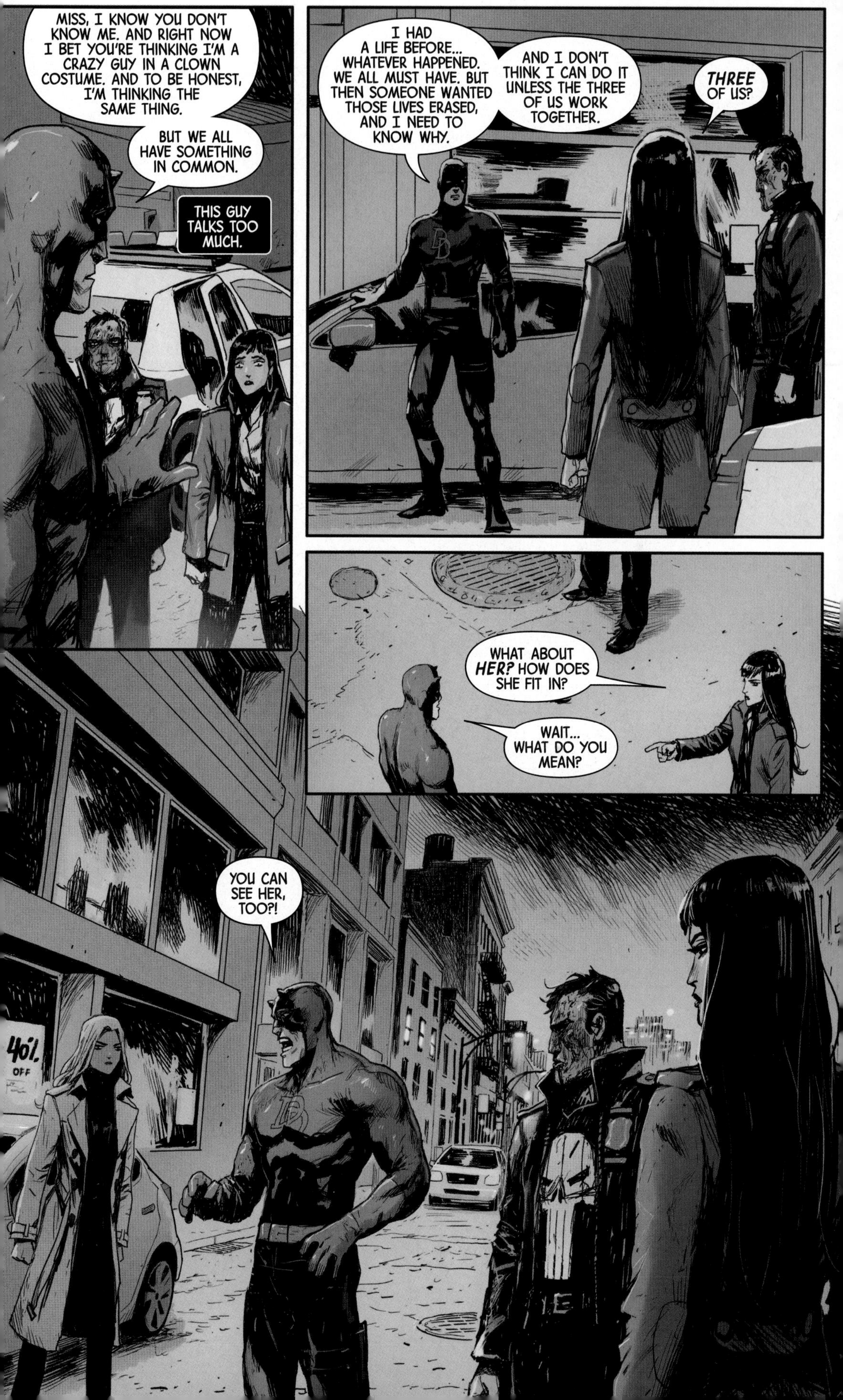
MISS, I KNOW YOU DON'T KNOW ME. AND RIGHT NOW I BET YOU'RE THINKING I'M A CRAZY GUY IN A CLOWN COSTUME. AND TO BE HONEST, I'M THINKING THE SAME THING.
BUT WE ALL HAVE SOMETHING IN COMMON.
THIS GUY TALKS TOO MUCH.
I HAD A LIFE BEFORE... WHATEVER HAPPENED. WE ALL MUST HAVE. BUT THEN SOMEONE WANTED THOSE LIVES ERASED, AND I NEED TO KNOW WHY.
AND I DON'T THINK I CAN DO IT UNLESS THE THREE OF US WORK TOGETHER.
THREE OF US?
WHAT ABOUT HER? HOW DOES SHE FIT IN?
WAIT... WHAT DO YOU MEAN?
YOU CAN SEE HER, TOO?!
40% OFF

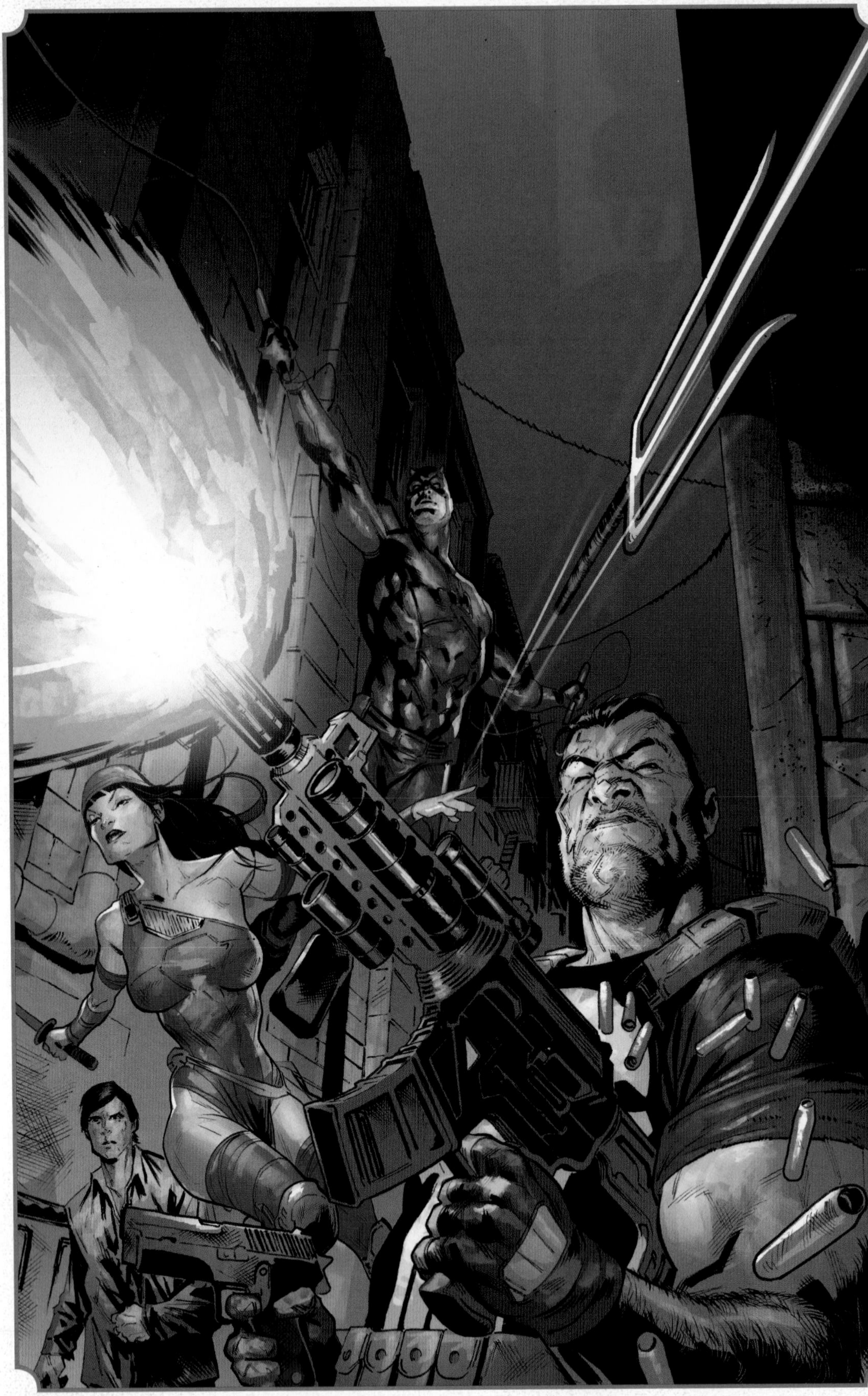

3

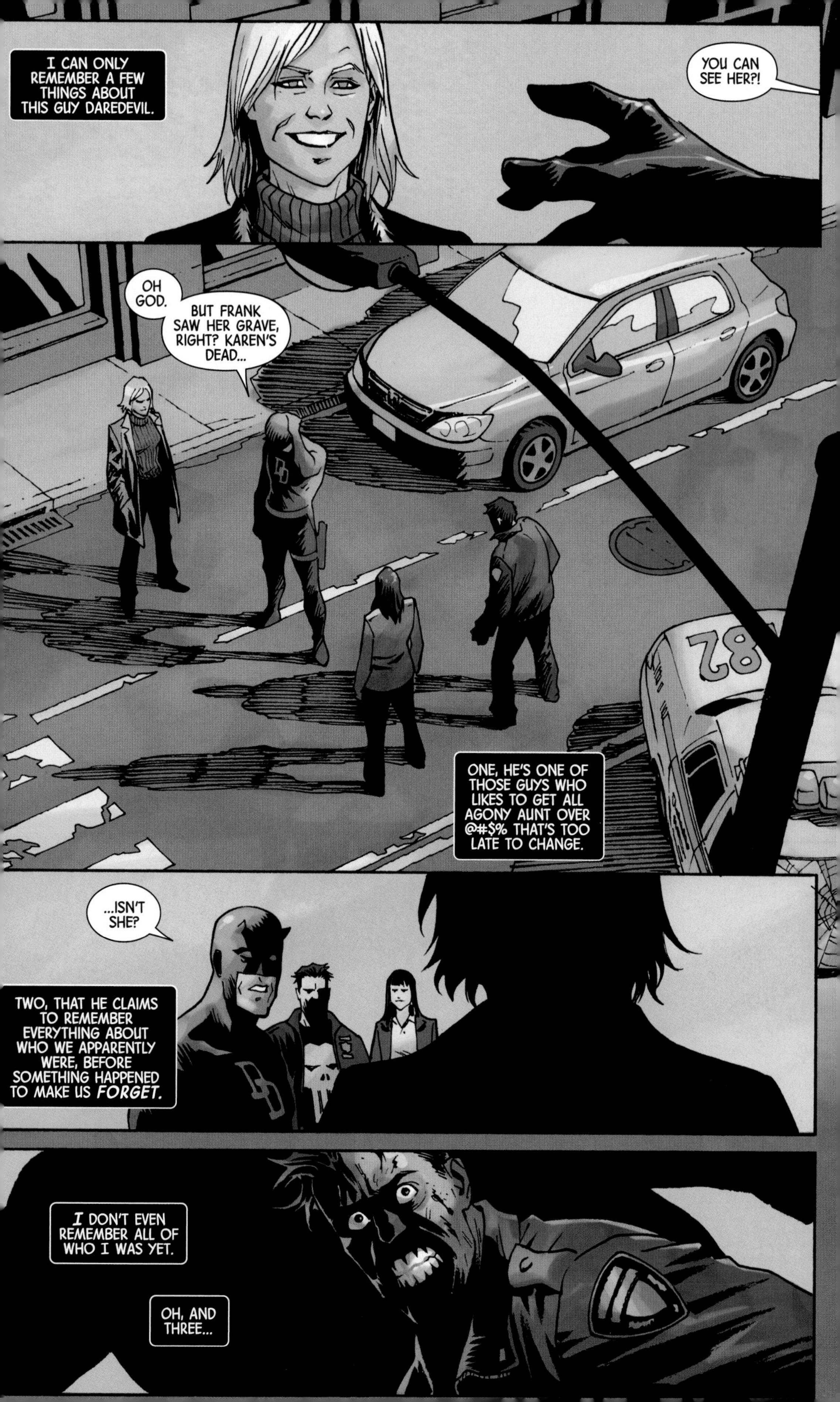
I CAN ONLY REMEMBER A FEW THINGS ABOUT THIS GUY DAREDEVIL.
YOU CAN SEE HER?!
OH GOD.
BUT FRANK SAW HER GRAVE, RIGHT? KAREN'S DEAD...
ONE, HE'S ONE OF THOSE GUYS WHO LIKES TO GET ALL AGONY AUNT OVER @#$% THAT'S TOO LATE TO CHANGE.
...ISN'T SHE?
TWO, THAT HE CLAIMS TO REMEMBER EVERYTHING ABOUT WHO WE APPARENTLY WERE, BEFORE SOMETHING HAPPENED TO MAKE US *FORGET.*
I DON'T EVEN REMEMBER ALL OF WHO I WAS YET.
OH, AND THREE...

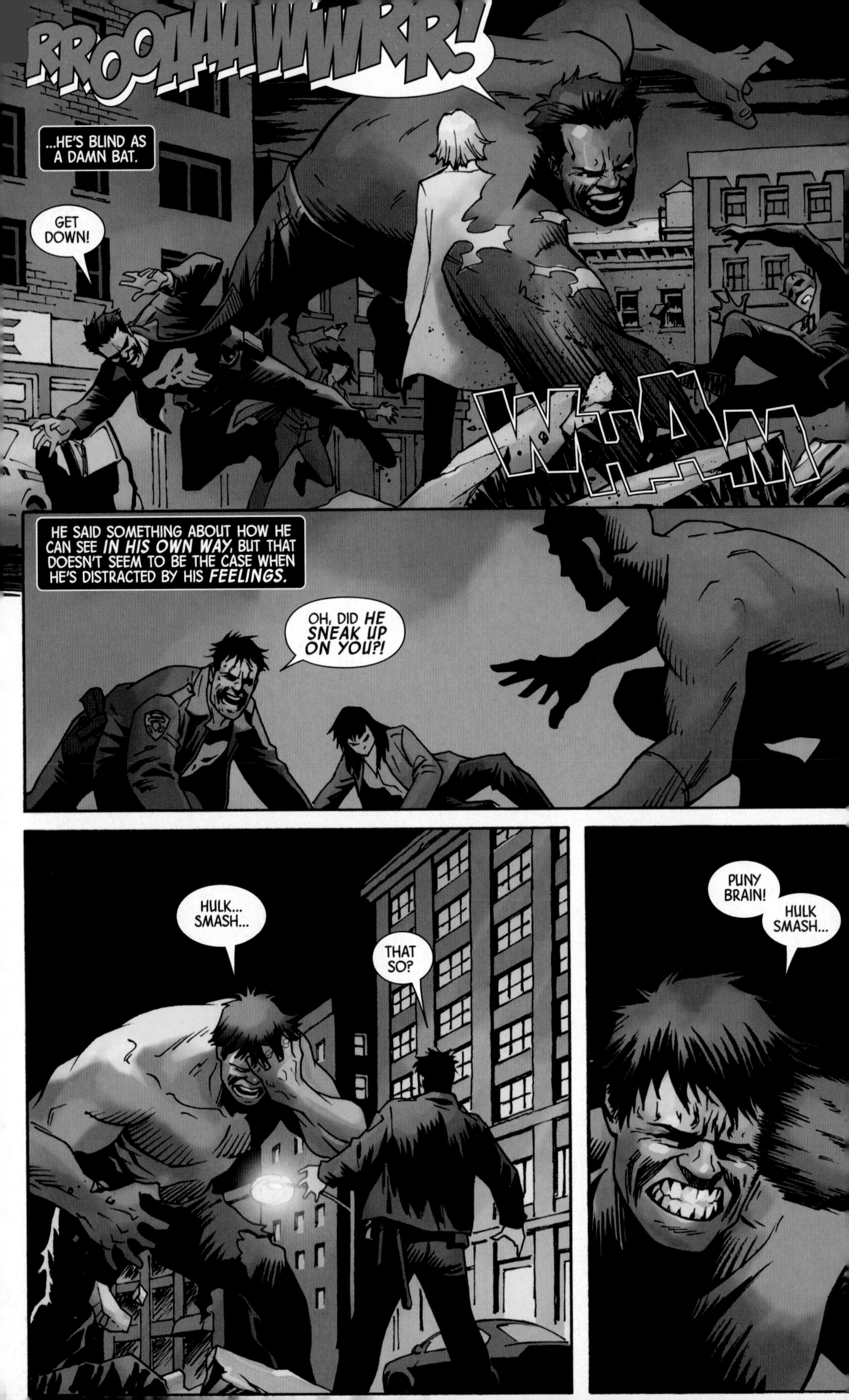

RROOAAAWWRR!
...HE'S BLIND AS A DAMN BAT.
GET DOWN!
WHAM
HE SAID SOMETHING ABOUT HOW HE CAN SEE IN HIS OWN WAY, BUT THAT DOESN'T SEEM TO BE THE CASE WHEN HE'S DISTRACTED BY HIS FEELINGS.
OH, DID HE SNEAK UP ON YOU?!
HULK... SMASH...
THAT SO?
PUNY BRAIN!
HULK SMASH...

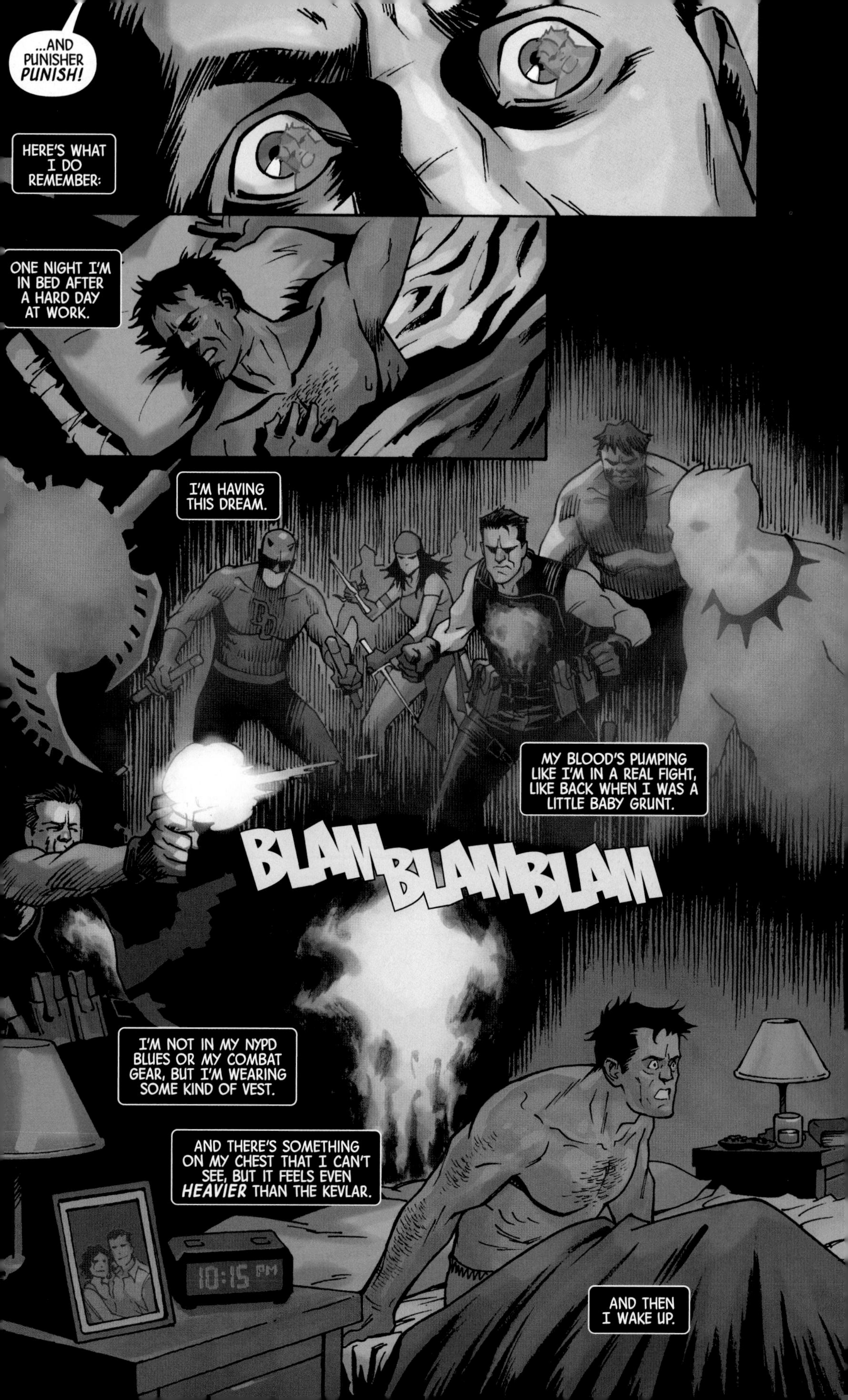
...AND PUNISHER PUNISH!
HERE'S WHAT I DO REMEMBER:
ONE NIGHT I'M IN BED AFTER A HARD DAY AT WORK.
I'M HAVING THIS DREAM.
MY BLOOD'S PUMPING LIKE I'M IN A REAL FIGHT, LIKE BACK WHEN I WAS A LITTLE BABY GRUNT.
BLAM BLAM BLAM
I'M NOT IN MY NYPD BLUES OR MY COMBAT GEAR, BUT I'M WEARING SOME KIND OF VEST.
AND THERE'S SOMETHING ON MY CHEST THAT I CAN'T SEE, BUT IT FEELS EVEN HEAVIER THAN THE KEVLAR.
10:15 PM
AND THEN I WAKE UP.

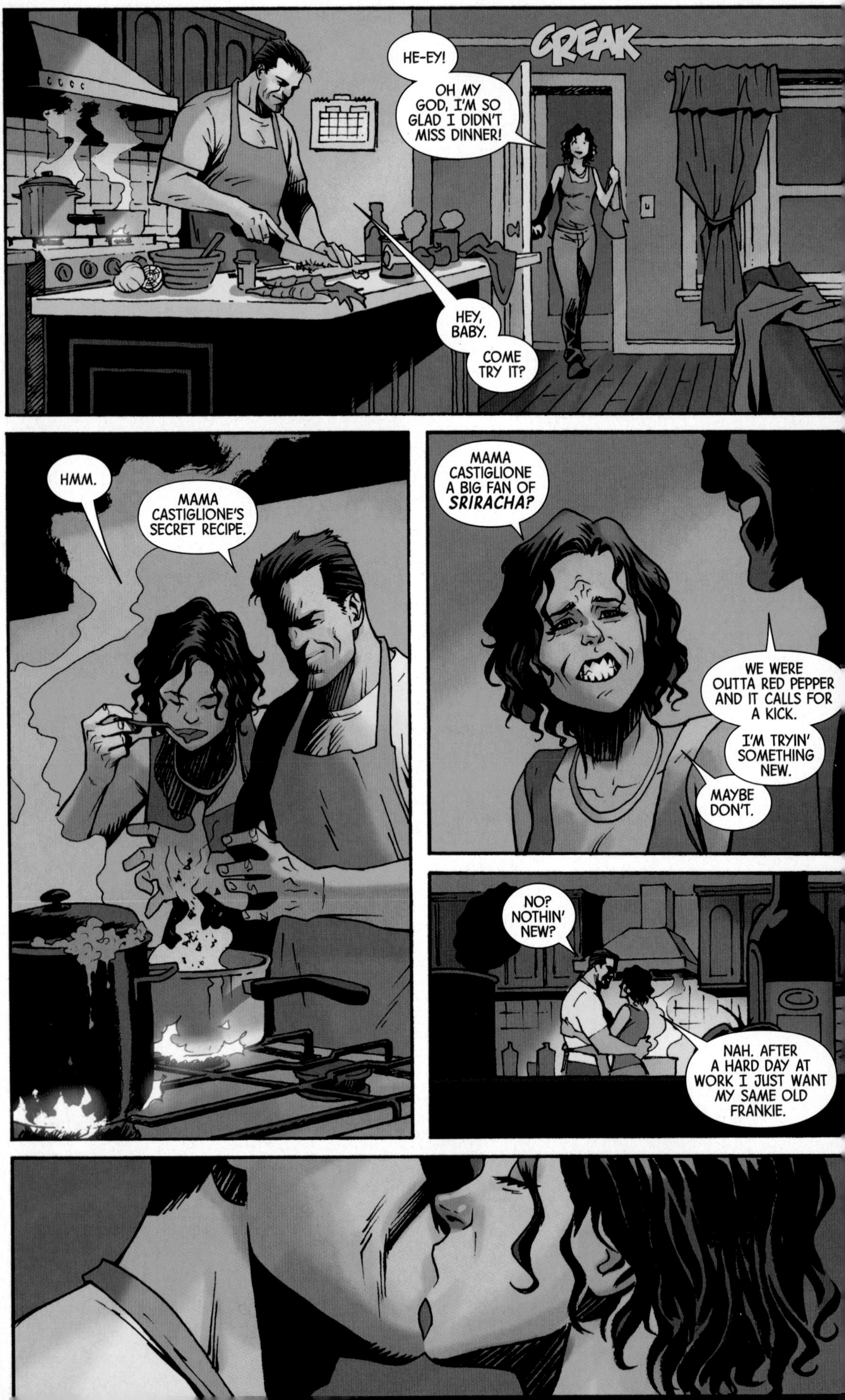

CREAK
HE-EY!
OH MY GOD, I'M SO GLAD I DIDN'T MISS DINNER!
HEY, BABY.
COME TRY IT?
HMM.
MAMA CASTIGLIONE'S SECRET RECIPE.
MAMA CASTIGLIONE A BIG FAN OF *SRIRACHA?*
WE WERE OUTTA RED PEPPER AND IT CALLS FOR A KICK.
I'M TRYIN' SOMETHING NEW.
MAYBE DON'T.
NO? NOTHIN' NEW?
NAH. AFTER A HARD DAY AT WORK I JUST WANT MY SAME OLD FRANKIE.

I'M FRANK CASTLE.

I WAS A MARINE CORPS GRUNT JUST LIKE MY OLD MAN, AND NOW I'M AN NYPD BEAT COP.

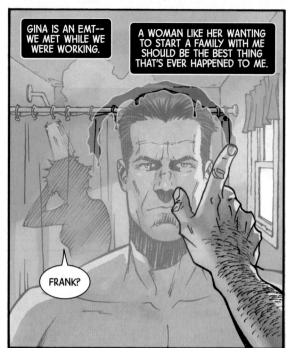

GINA IS AN EMT-- WE MET WHILE WE WERE WORKING.

A WOMAN LIKE HER WANTING TO START A FAMILY WITH ME SHOULD BE THE BEST THING THAT'S EVER HAPPENED TO ME.

FRANK?

SO WHY'S IT FEEL LIKE SOMETHING'S HOLDING ME BACK?

WHY'S IT FEEL LIKE I'M *SPITTING ON SOMEONE'S GRAVE?*

YOU GETTIN' IN?

YEAH.

THEN THIS BANNER PSYCHO SHOWS UP AT THE PRECINCT ONE DAY, TELLING STORIES THAT SOUND AS DESPERATE AS I FEEL...

MAYBE I HELP PEOPLE *BY* HURTING THEM, BANNER.

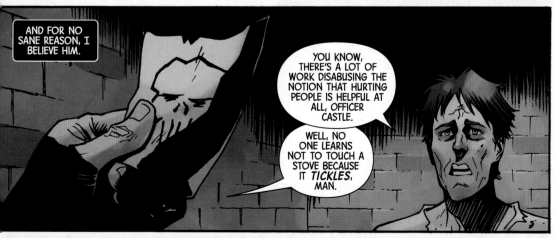

AND FOR NO SANE REASON, I BELIEVE HIM.

YOU KNOW, THERE'S A LOT OF WORK DISABUSING THE NOTION THAT HURTING PEOPLE IS HELPFUL AT ALL, OFFICER CASTLE.

WELL, NO ONE LEARNS NOT TO TOUCH A STOVE BECAUSE IT *TICKLES,* MAN.

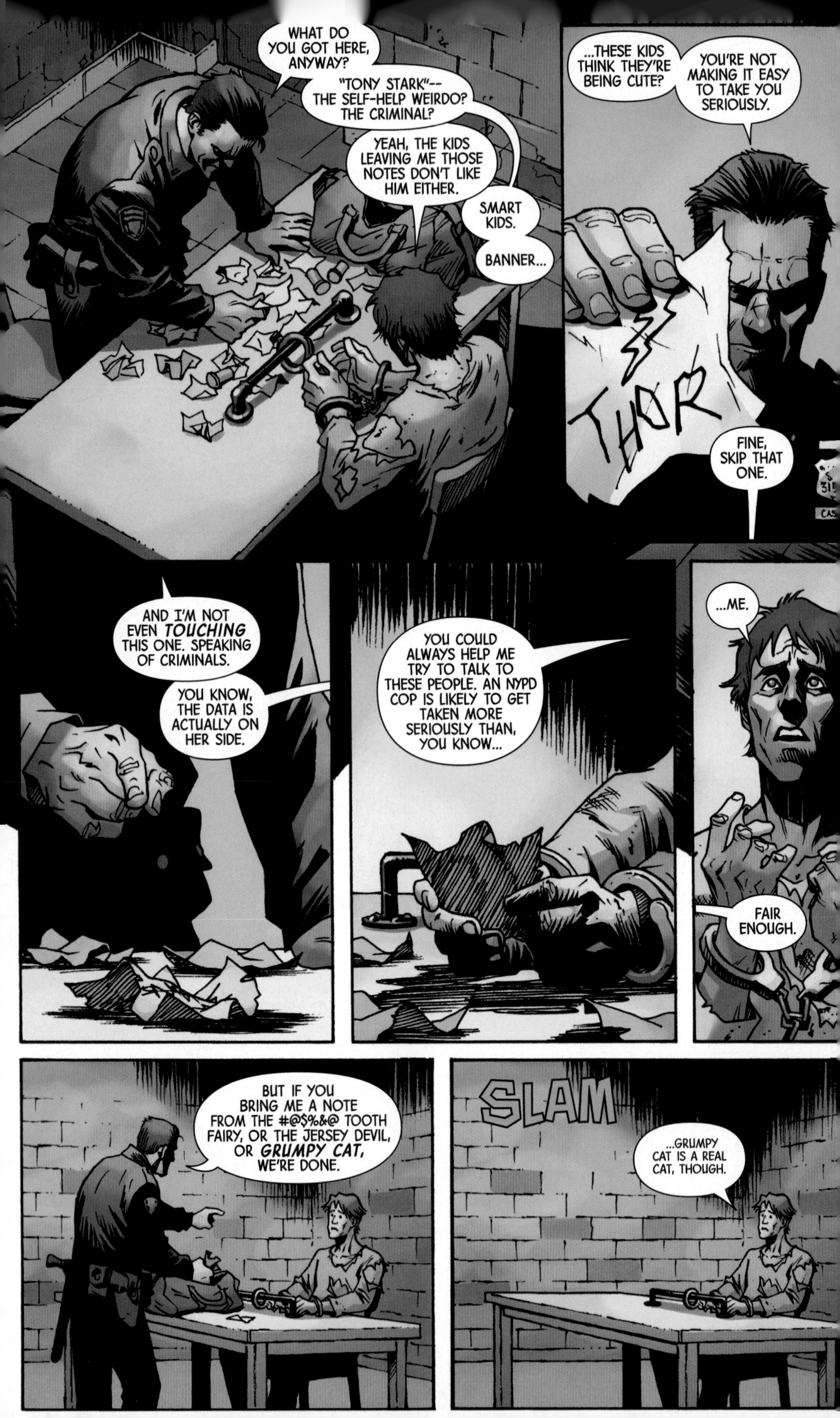
WHAT DO YOU GOT HERE, ANYWAY?
"TONY STARK"-- THE SELF-HELP WEIRDO? THE CRIMINAL?
YEAH, THE KIDS LEAVING ME THOSE NOTES DON'T LIKE HIM EITHER.
SMART KIDS.
BANNER...
...THESE KIDS THINK THEY'RE BEING CUTE?
YOU'RE NOT MAKING IT EASY TO TAKE YOU SERIOUSLY.
THOR
FINE, SKIP THAT ONE.
AND I'M NOT EVEN TOUCHING THIS ONE. SPEAKING OF CRIMINALS.
YOU KNOW, THE DATA IS ACTUALLY ON HER SIDE.
YOU COULD ALWAYS HELP ME TRY TO TALK TO THESE PEOPLE. AN NYPD COP IS LIKELY TO GET TAKEN MORE SERIOUSLY THAN, YOU KNOW...
...ME.
FAIR ENOUGH.
BUT IF YOU BRING ME A NOTE FROM THE #@$%&@ TOOTH FAIRY, OR THE JERSEY DEVIL, OR GRUMPY CAT, WE'RE DONE.
SLAM
...GRUMPY CAT IS A REAL CAT, THOUGH.

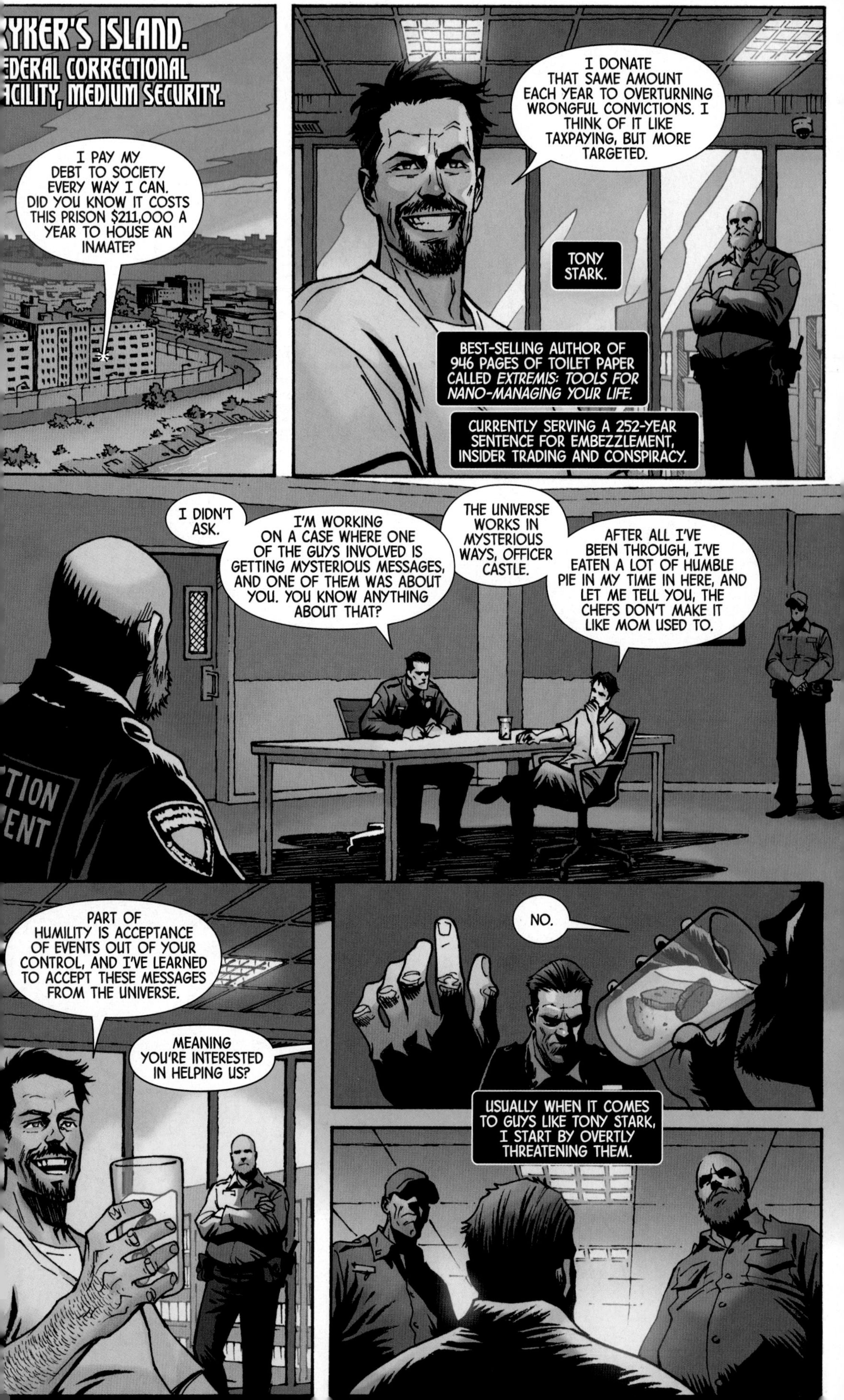
YKER'S ISLAND.
EDERAL CORRECTIONAL
ACILITY, MEDIUM SECURITY.
I PAY MY DEBT TO SOCIETY EVERY WAY I CAN. DID YOU KNOW IT COSTS THIS PRISON $211,000 A YEAR TO HOUSE AN INMATE?
I DONATE THAT SAME AMOUNT EACH YEAR TO OVERTURNING WRONGFUL CONVICTIONS. I THINK OF IT LIKE TAXPAYING, BUT MORE TARGETED.
TONY STARK.
BEST-SELLING AUTHOR OF 946 PAGES OF TOILET PAPER CALLED EXTREMIS: TOOLS FOR NANO-MANAGING YOUR LIFE.
CURRENTLY SERVING A 252-YEAR SENTENCE FOR EMBEZZLEMENT, INSIDER TRADING AND CONSPIRACY.
I DIDN'T ASK.
I'M WORKING ON A CASE WHERE ONE OF THE GUYS INVOLVED IS GETTING MYSTERIOUS MESSAGES, AND ONE OF THEM WAS ABOUT YOU. YOU KNOW ANYTHING ABOUT THAT?
THE UNIVERSE WORKS IN MYSTERIOUS WAYS, OFFICER CASTLE.
AFTER ALL I'VE BEEN THROUGH, I'VE EATEN A LOT OF HUMBLE PIE IN MY TIME IN HERE, AND LET ME TELL YOU, THE CHEFS DON'T MAKE IT LIKE MOM USED TO.
PART OF HUMILITY IS ACCEPTANCE OF EVENTS OUT OF YOUR CONTROL, AND I'VE LEARNED TO ACCEPT THESE MESSAGES FROM THE UNIVERSE.
MEANING YOU'RE INTERESTED IN HELPING US?
NO.
USUALLY WHEN IT COMES TO GUYS LIKE TONY STARK, I START BY OVERTLY THREATENING THEM.

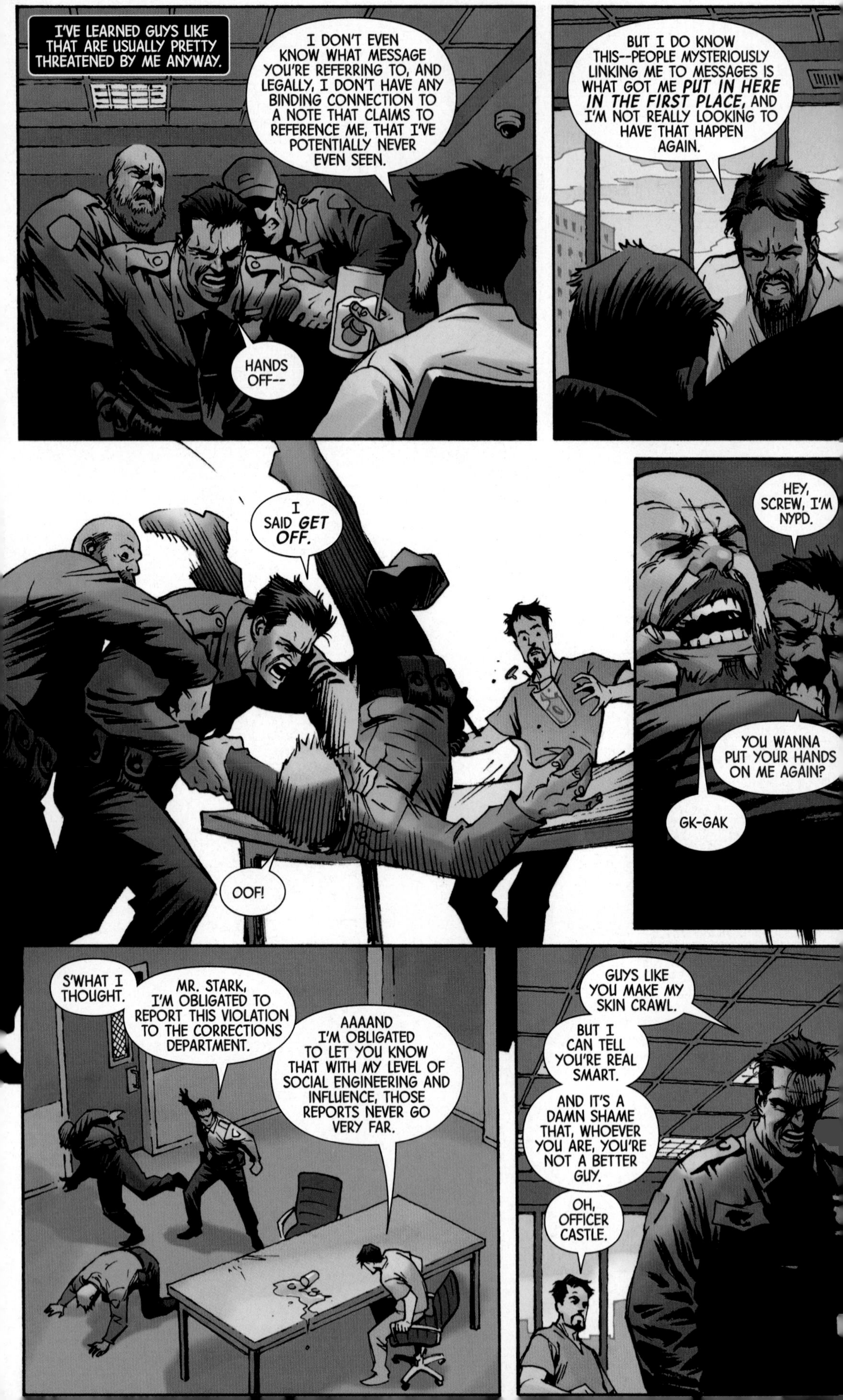

I'VE LEARNED GUYS LIKE THAT ARE USUALLY PRETTY THREATENED BY ME ANYWAY.
I DON'T EVEN KNOW WHAT MESSAGE YOU'RE REFERRING TO, AND LEGALLY, I DON'T HAVE ANY BINDING CONNECTION TO A NOTE THAT CLAIMS TO REFERENCE ME, THAT I'VE POTENTIALLY NEVER EVEN SEEN.
HANDS OFF--
BUT I DO KNOW THIS--PEOPLE MYSTERIOUSLY LINKING ME TO MESSAGES IS WHAT GOT ME PUT IN HERE IN THE FIRST PLACE, AND I'M NOT REALLY LOOKING TO HAVE THAT HAPPEN AGAIN.
I SAID GET OFF.
OOF!
HEY, SCREW, I'M NYPD.
YOU WANNA PUT YOUR HANDS ON ME AGAIN?
GK-GAK
S'WHAT I THOUGHT.
MR. STARK, I'M OBLIGATED TO REPORT THIS VIOLATION TO THE CORRECTIONS DEPARTMENT.
AAAAND I'M OBLIGATED TO LET YOU KNOW THAT WITH MY LEVEL OF SOCIAL ENGINEERING AND INFLUENCE, THOSE REPORTS NEVER GO VERY FAR.
GUYS LIKE YOU MAKE MY SKIN CRAWL.
BUT I CAN TELL YOU'RE REAL SMART.
AND IT'S A DAMN SHAME THAT, WHOEVER YOU ARE, YOU'RE NOT A BETTER GUY.
OH, OFFICER CASTLE.

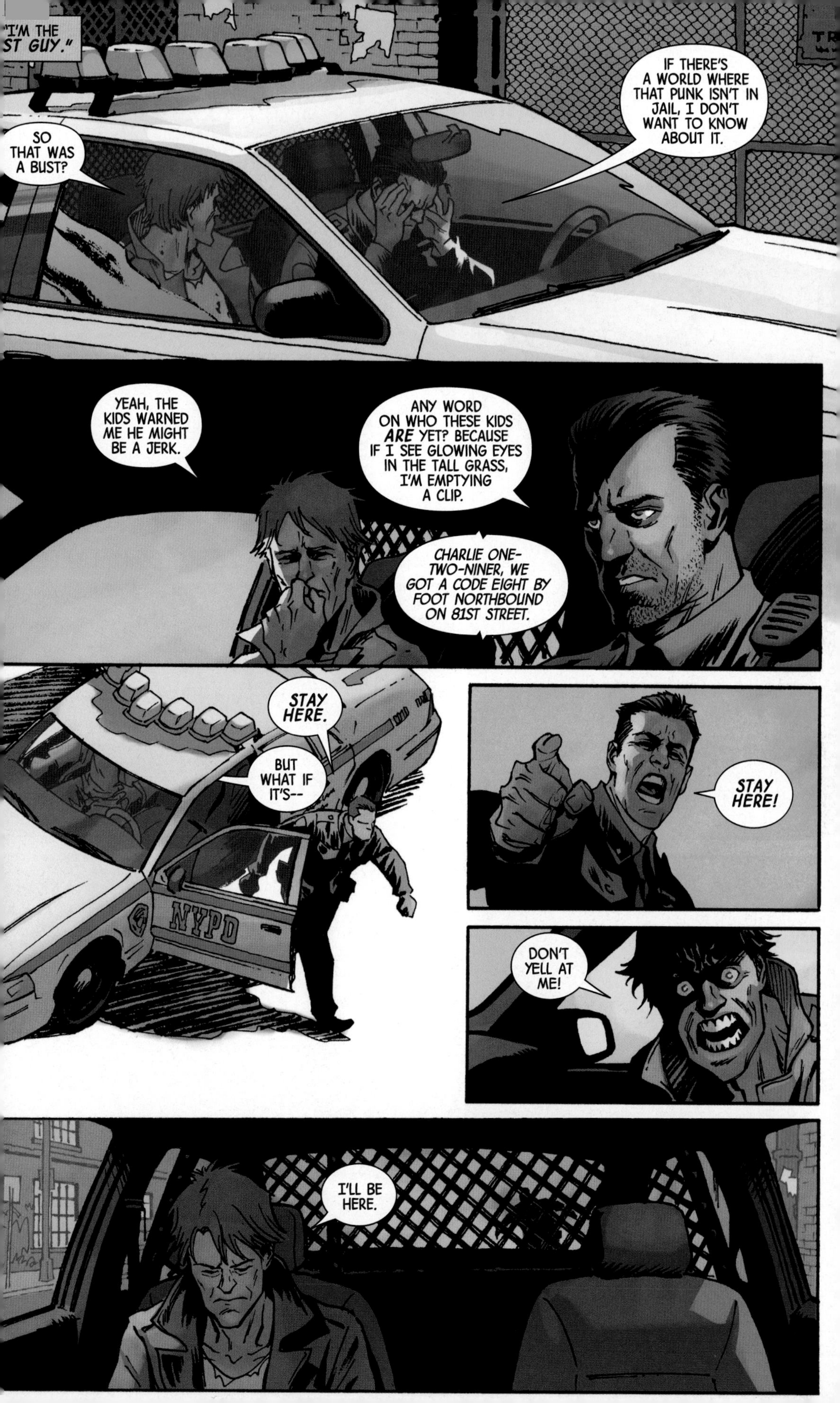
"I'M THE
ST GUY."
SO THAT WAS A BUST?
IF THERE'S A WORLD WHERE THAT PUNK ISN'T IN JAIL, I DON'T WANT TO KNOW ABOUT IT.
YEAH, THE KIDS WARNED ME HE MIGHT BE A JERK.
ANY WORD ON WHO THESE KIDS ARE YET? BECAUSE IF I SEE GLOWING EYES IN THE TALL GRASS, I'M EMPTYING A CLIP.
CHARLIE ONE-TWO-NINER, WE GOT A CODE EIGHT BY FOOT NORTHBOUND ON 81ST STREET.
STAY HERE.
BUT WHAT IF IT'S--
NYPD
STAY HERE!
DON'T YELL AT ME!
I'LL BE HERE.

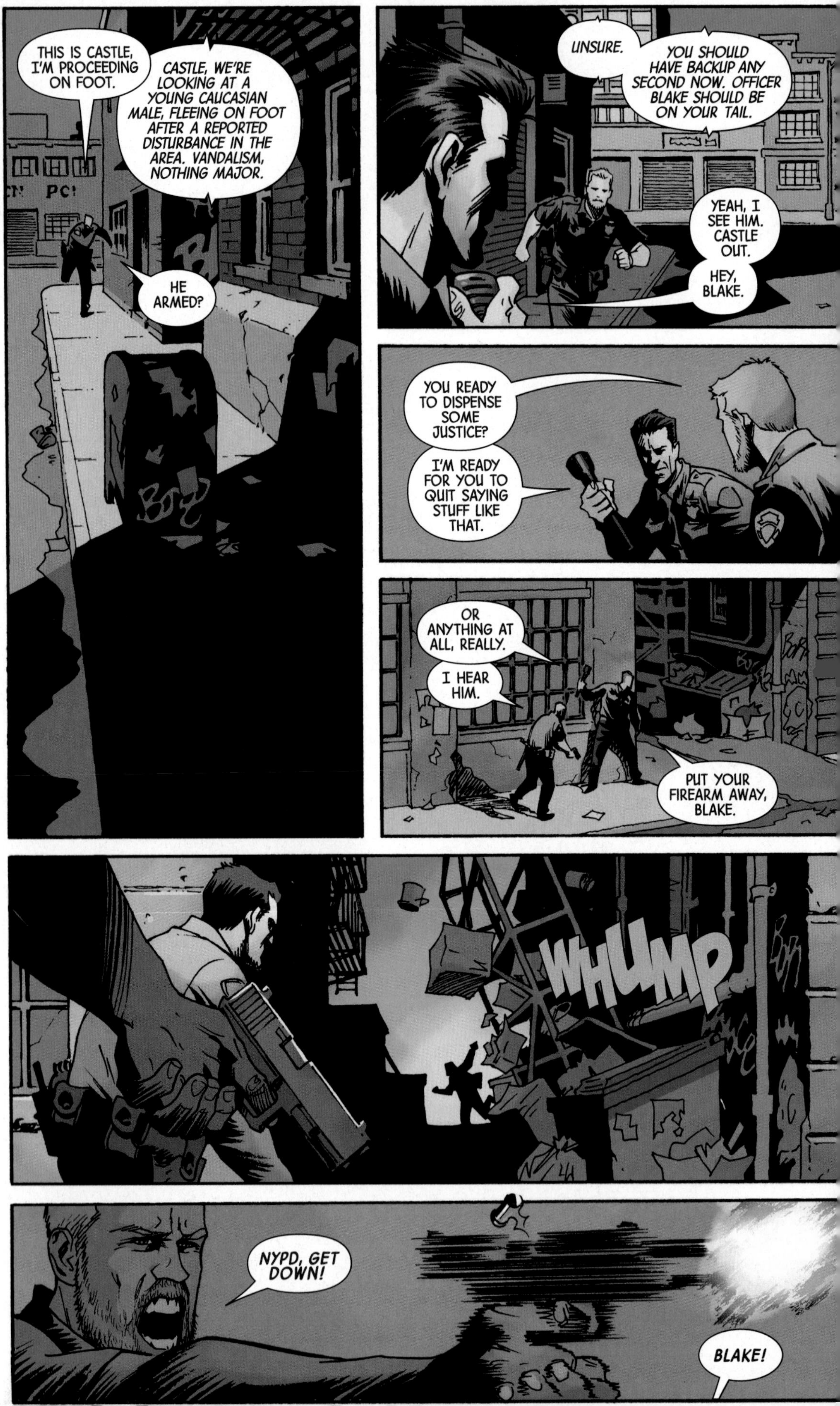
THIS IS CASTLE, I'M PROCEEDING ON FOOT.
CASTLE, WE'RE LOOKING AT A YOUNG CAUCASIAN MALE, FLEEING ON FOOT AFTER A REPORTED DISTURBANCE IN THE AREA. VANDALISM, NOTHING MAJOR.
HE ARMED?
UNSURE.
YOU SHOULD HAVE BACKUP ANY SECOND NOW. OFFICER BLAKE SHOULD BE ON YOUR TAIL.
YEAH, I SEE HIM. CASTLE OUT.
HEY, BLAKE.
YOU READY TO DISPENSE SOME JUSTICE?
I'M READY FOR YOU TO QUIT SAYING STUFF LIKE THAT.
OR ANYTHING AT ALL, REALLY.
I HEAR HIM.
PUT YOUR FIREARM AWAY, BLAKE.
WHUMP
NYPD, GET DOWN!
BLAKE!

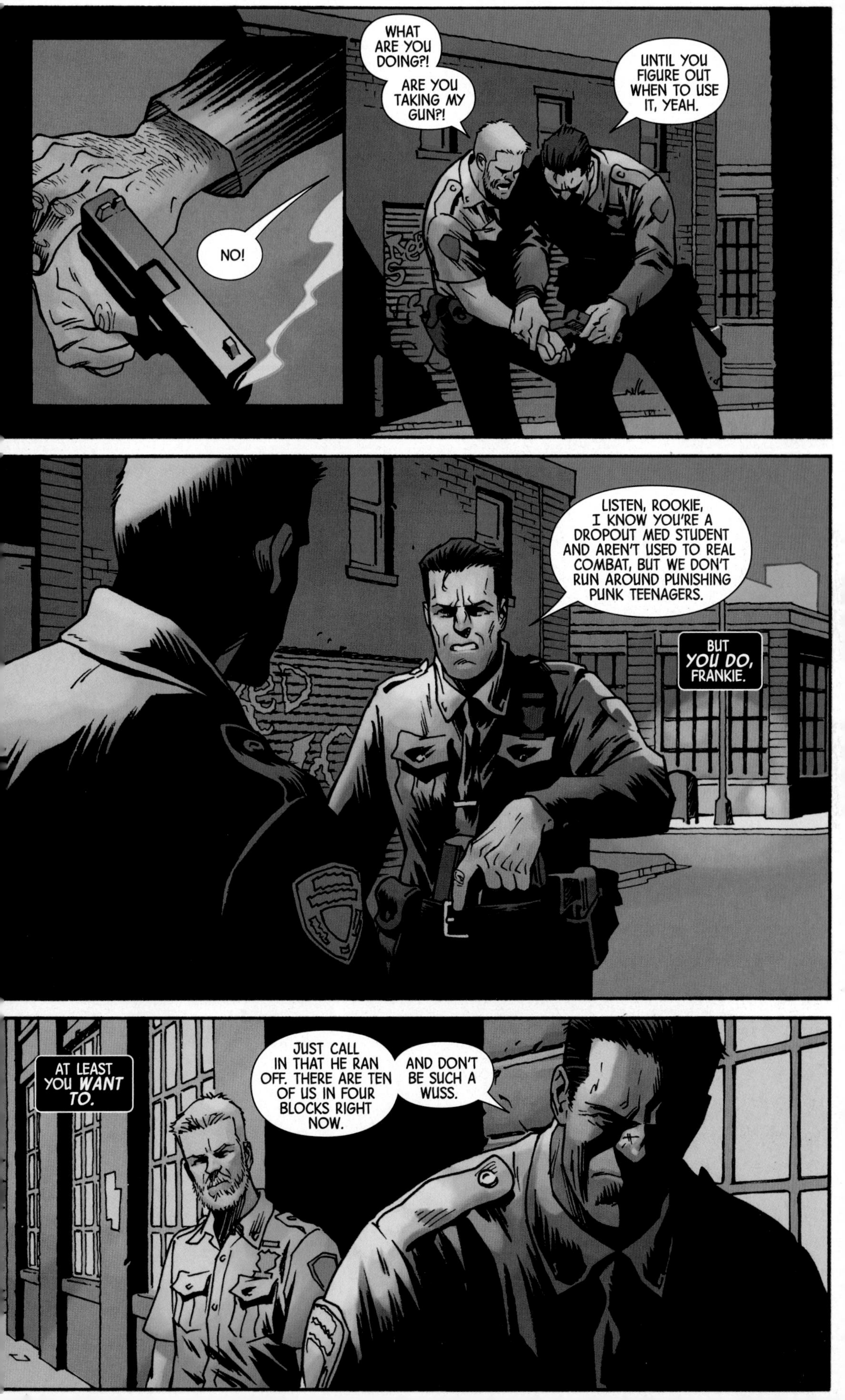
WHAT ARE YOU DOING?!
ARE YOU TAKING MY GUN?!
UNTIL YOU FIGURE OUT WHEN TO USE IT, YEAH.
NO!
LISTEN, ROOKIE, I KNOW YOU'RE A DROPOUT MED STUDENT AND AREN'T USED TO REAL COMBAT, BUT WE DON'T RUN AROUND PUNISHING PUNK TEENAGERS.
BUT YOU DO, FRANKIE.
AT LEAST YOU WANT TO.
JUST CALL IN THAT HE RAN OFF. THERE ARE TEN OF US IN FOUR BLOCKS RIGHT NOW.
AND DON'T BE SUCH A WUSS.

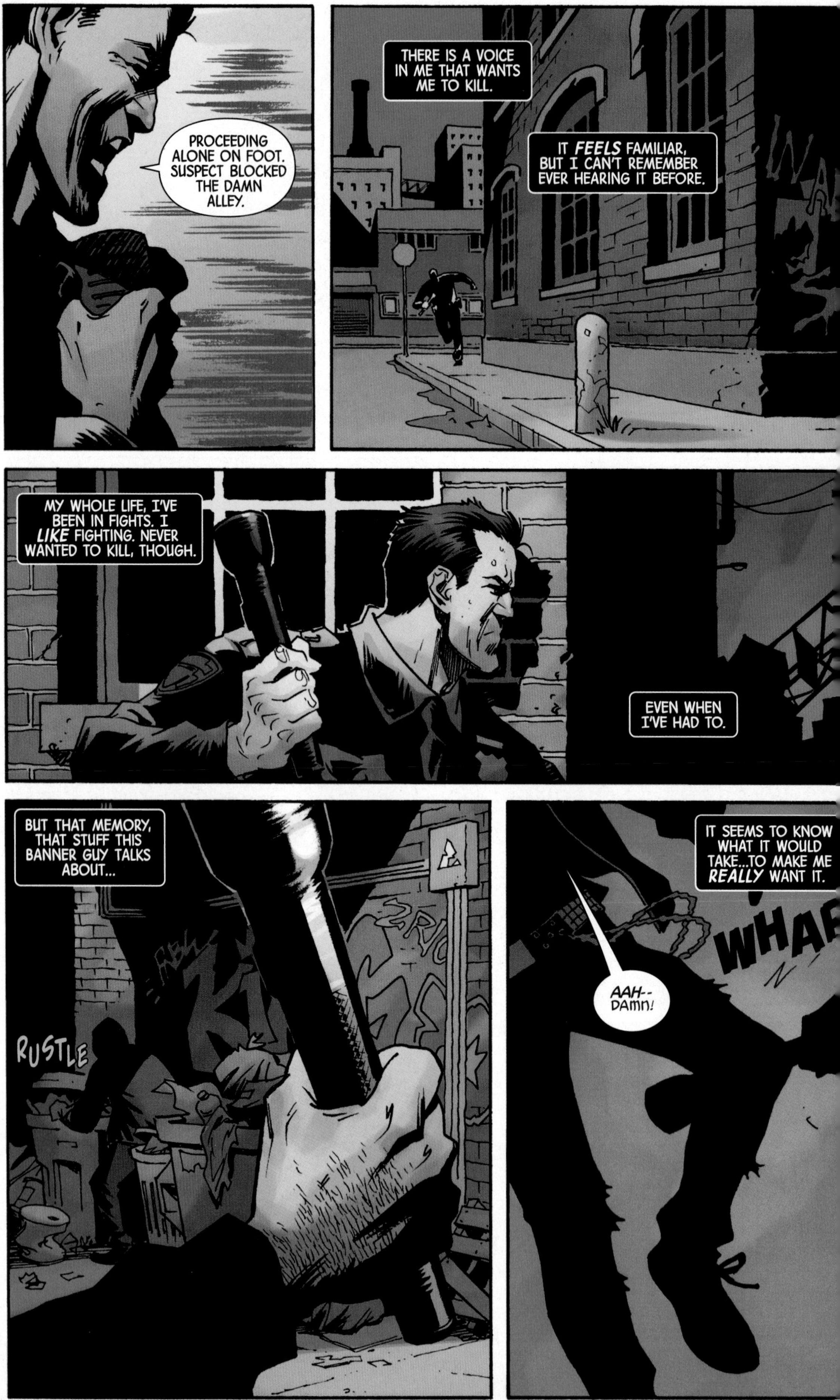
PROCEEDING ALONE ON FOOT. SUSPECT BLOCKED THE DAMN ALLEY.
THERE IS A VOICE IN ME THAT WANTS ME TO KILL.
IT FEELS FAMILIAR, BUT I CAN'T REMEMBER EVER HEARING IT BEFORE.
MY WHOLE LIFE, I'VE BEEN IN FIGHTS. I LIKE FIGHTING. NEVER WANTED TO KILL, THOUGH.
EVEN WHEN I'VE HAD TO.
BUT THAT MEMORY, THAT STUFF THIS BANNER GUY TALKS ABOUT...
RUSTLE
IT SEEMS TO KNOW WHAT IT WOULD TAKE...TO MAKE ME REALLY WANT IT.
AAH-- DAMN!

IDIOT MORTAL-- WAS TRYING TO LURE THE *OTHER* ONE, NOT *YOU.*

YOU LECTURE HIM ABOUT RESTRAINT AND THEN BASH ME LIKE I'M A SNAKE IN A GARDEN?

GOOD NEWS, THEN--YOU'LL BE RIDING WITH OFFICER BLAKE IN THE CRUISER BACK TO THE STATION. YOU TWO CAN CHAT THERE.

THIS IS A WASTE OF TIME. I HAVE THINGS TO TELL MY BROTHER'S MORTAL ONCE-HOST. I CAN EXERCISE MY MAGICS IF NECESSARY--

SAY "MORTAL" ONE MORE TIME AND I TASE YOU, WACKO.

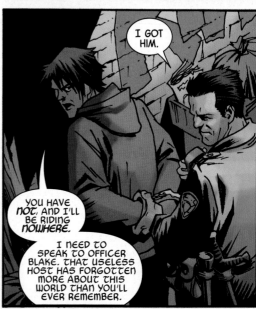

I GOT HIM.

YOU HAVE *NOT,* AND I'LL BE RIDING *NOWHERE.*

I NEED TO SPEAK TO OFFICER BLAKE. THAT USELESS HOST HAS FORGOTTEN MORE ABOUT THIS WORLD THAN YOU'LL EVER REMEMBER.

YOU GOT ANYTHING IN YOUR POCKETS I NEED TO KNOW ABOUT?

I HAVE A GREAT MANY THINGS A MORTAL LIKE YOU OUGHT TO KNOW ABOUT, FRANK CASTLE.

AND NONE OF THEM ARE WITHIN MY POCKETS.

WHAT'D I TELL YOU ABOUT CRAZY TALK--

ZZZT-ZZTT

THERE IT WAS, THE VIOLENT STIRRING AGAIN.

KRAK KRAK

MOSTLY I JUST THOUGHT I WANTED TO PUNCH HIM...

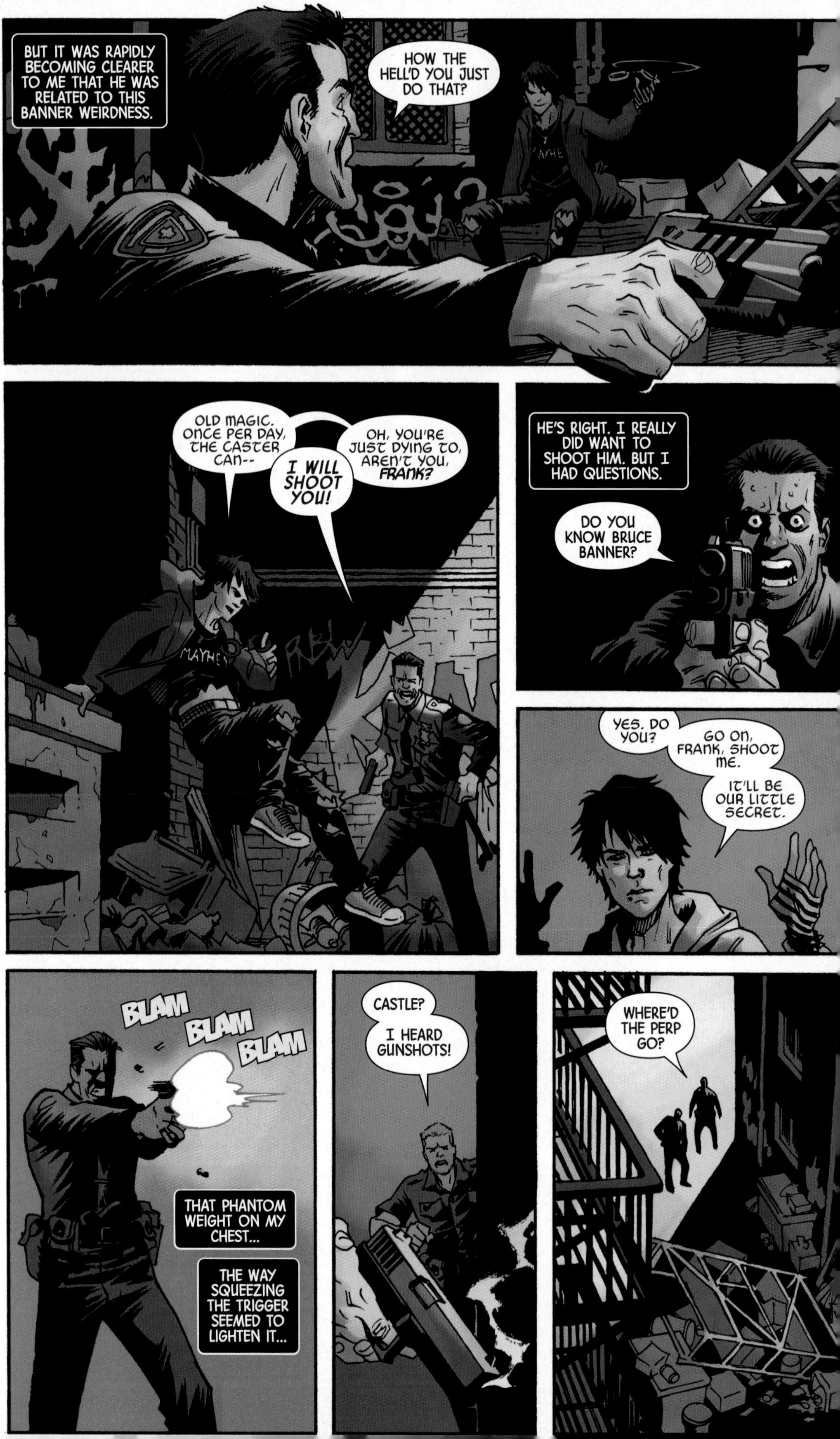
BUT IT WAS RAPIDLY BECOMING CLEARER TO ME THAT HE WAS RELATED TO THIS BANNER WEIRDNESS.
HOW THE HELL'D YOU JUST DO THAT?
OLD MAGIC. ONCE PER DAY, THE CASTER CAN--
I WILL SHOOT YOU!
OH, YOU'RE JUST DYING TO, AREN'T YOU, FRANK?
MAYHEM
HE'S RIGHT. I REALLY DID WANT TO SHOOT HIM. BUT I HAD QUESTIONS.
DO YOU KNOW BRUCE BANNER?
YES. DO YOU?
GO ON, FRANK, SHOOT ME.
IT'LL BE OUR LITTLE SECRET.
BLAM
BLAM
BLAM
THAT PHANTOM WEIGHT ON MY CHEST...
THE WAY SQUEEZING THE TRIGGER SEEMED TO LIGHTEN IT...
CASTLE?
I HEARD GUNSHOTS!
WHERE'D THE PERP GO?

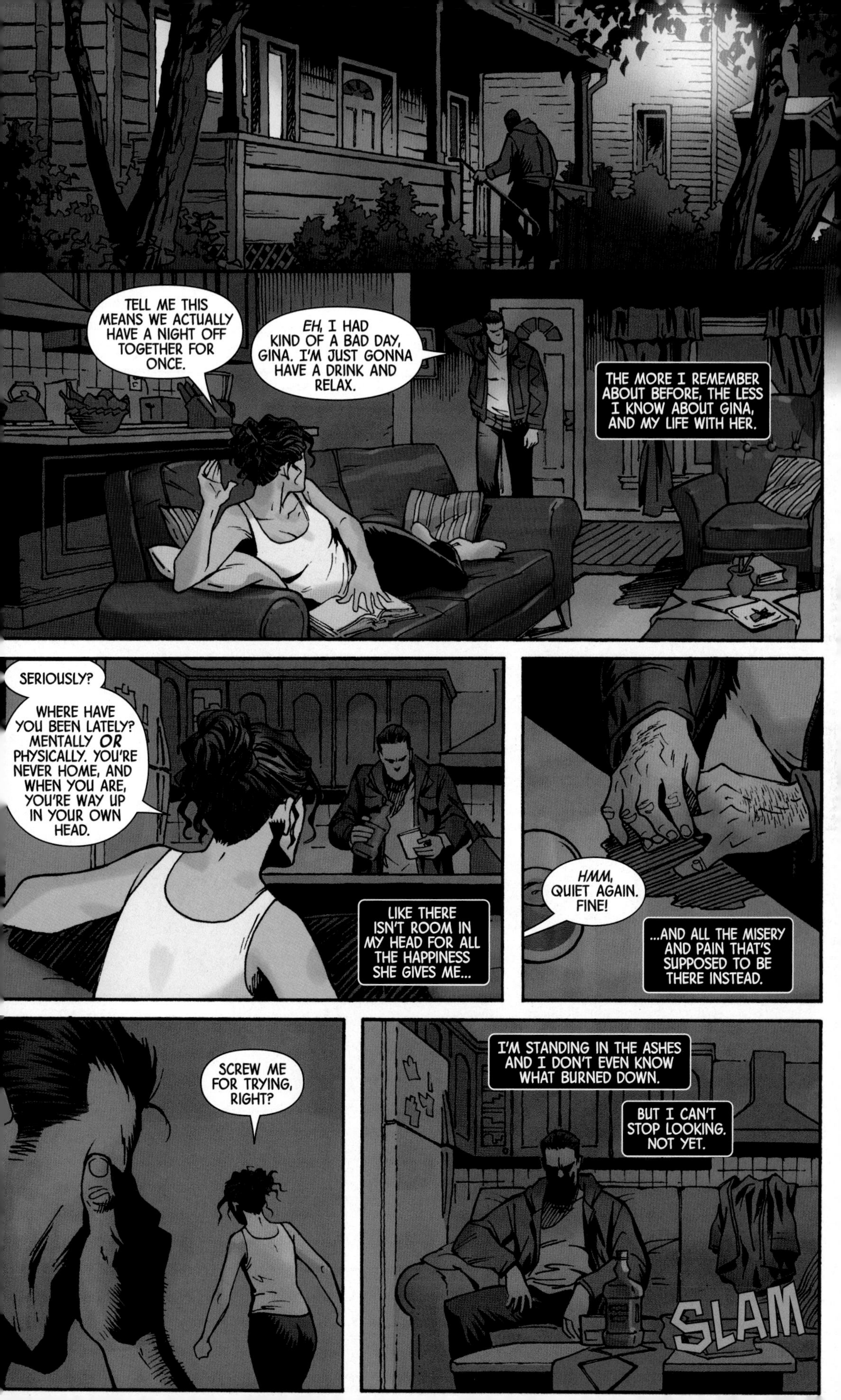
TELL ME THIS MEANS WE ACTUALLY HAVE A NIGHT OFF TOGETHER FOR ONCE.
EH, I HAD KIND OF A BAD DAY, GINA. I'M JUST GONNA HAVE A DRINK AND RELAX.
THE MORE I REMEMBER ABOUT BEFORE, THE LESS I KNOW ABOUT GINA, AND MY LIFE WITH HER.
SERIOUSLY?
WHERE HAVE YOU BEEN LATELY? MENTALLY OR PHYSICALLY. YOU'RE NEVER HOME, AND WHEN YOU ARE, YOU'RE WAY UP IN YOUR OWN HEAD.
LIKE THERE ISN'T ROOM IN MY HEAD FOR ALL THE HAPPINESS SHE GIVES ME...
HMM, QUIET AGAIN. FINE!
...AND ALL THE MISERY AND PAIN THAT'S SUPPOSED TO BE THERE INSTEAD.
SCREW ME FOR TRYING, RIGHT?
I'M STANDING IN THE ASHES AND I DON'T EVEN KNOW WHAT BURNED DOWN.
BUT I CAN'T STOP LOOKING. NOT YET.
SLAM

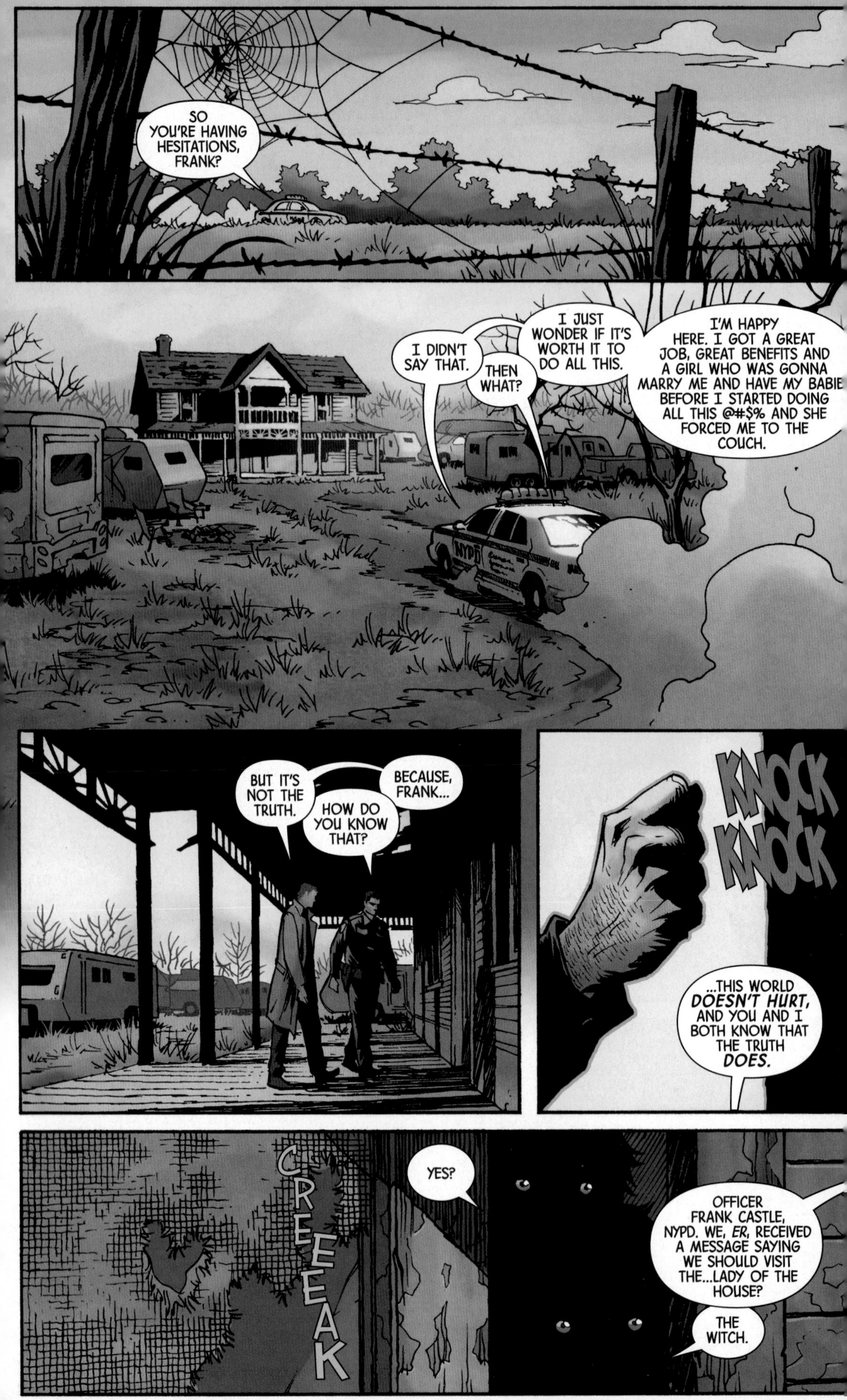
SO YOU'RE HAVING HESITATIONS, FRANK?
I DIDN'T SAY THAT.
THEN WHAT?
I JUST WONDER IF IT'S WORTH IT TO DO ALL THIS.
I'M HAPPY HERE. I GOT A GREAT JOB, GREAT BENEFITS AND A GIRL WHO WAS GONNA MARRY ME AND HAVE MY BABIE BEFORE I STARTED DOING ALL THIS @#$% AND SHE FORCED ME TO THE COUCH.
BUT IT'S NOT THE TRUTH.
HOW DO YOU KNOW THAT?
BECAUSE, FRANK...
KNOCK KNOCK
...THIS WORLD DOESN'T HURT, AND YOU AND I BOTH KNOW THAT THE TRUTH DOES.
CREEAK
YES?
OFFICER FRANK CASTLE, NYPD. WE, ER, RECEIVED A MESSAGE SAYING WE SHOULD VISIT THE...LADY OF THE HOUSE?
THE WITCH.

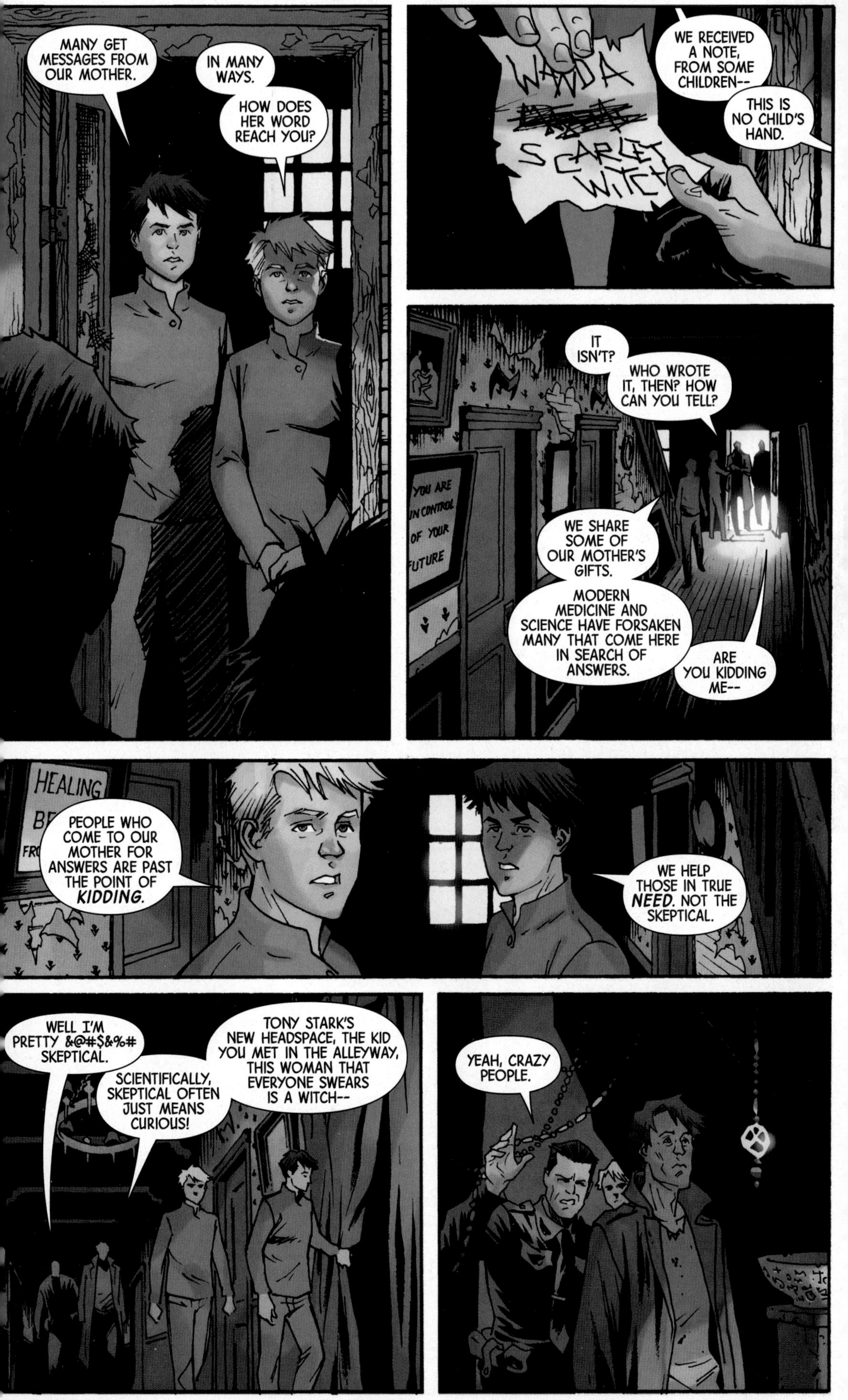
MANY GET MESSAGES FROM OUR MOTHER.
IN MANY WAYS.
HOW DOES HER WORD REACH YOU?
WANDA
SCARLET WITCH
WE RECEIVED A NOTE, FROM SOME CHILDREN--
THIS IS NO CHILD'S HAND.
IT ISN'T?
WHO WROTE IT, THEN? HOW CAN YOU TELL?
YOU ARE IN CONTROL OF YOUR FUTURE
WE SHARE SOME OF OUR MOTHER'S GIFTS.
MODERN MEDICINE AND SCIENCE HAVE FORSAKEN MANY THAT COME HERE IN SEARCH OF ANSWERS.
ARE YOU KIDDING ME--
HEALING
PEOPLE WHO COME TO OUR MOTHER FOR ANSWERS ARE PAST THE POINT OF ***KIDDING***.
WE HELP THOSE IN TRUE ***NEED***. NOT THE SKEPTICAL.
WELL I'M PRETTY &@#$&%# SKEPTICAL.
SCIENTIFICALLY, SKEPTICAL OFTEN JUST MEANS CURIOUS!
TONY STARK'S NEW HEADSPACE, THE KID YOU MET IN THE ALLEYWAY, THIS WOMAN THAT EVERYONE SWEARS IS A WITCH--
YEAH, CRAZY PEOPLE.

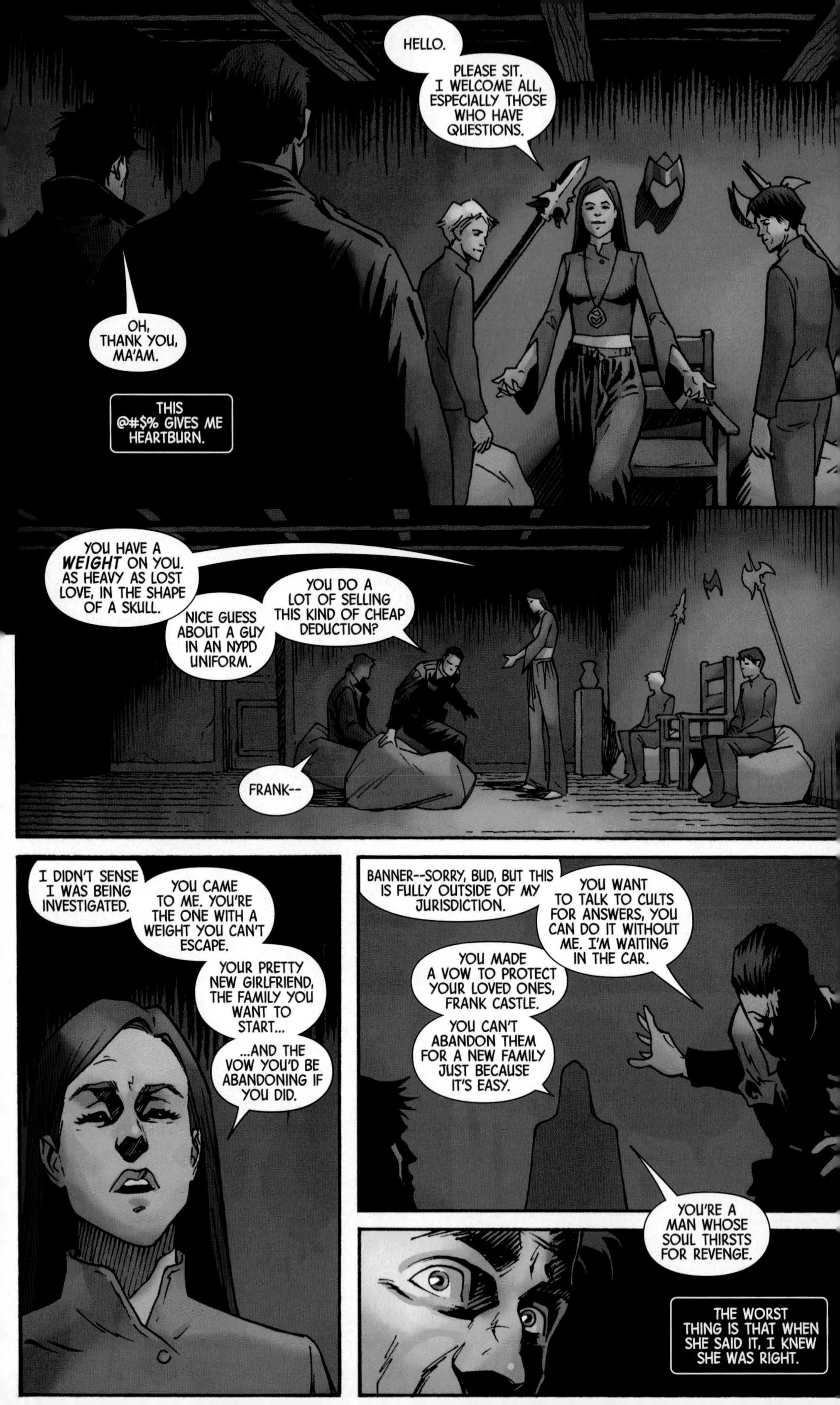
HELLO.
PLEASE SIT. I WELCOME ALL, ESPECIALLY THOSE WHO HAVE QUESTIONS.
OH, THANK YOU, MA'AM.
THIS @#$% GIVES ME HEARTBURN.
YOU HAVE A WEIGHT ON YOU. AS HEAVY AS LOST LOVE, IN THE SHAPE OF A SKULL.
NICE GUESS ABOUT A GUY IN AN NYPD UNIFORM.
YOU DO A LOT OF SELLING THIS KIND OF CHEAP DEDUCTION?
FRANK--
I DIDN'T SENSE I WAS BEING INVESTIGATED.
YOU CAME TO ME. YOU'RE THE ONE WITH A WEIGHT YOU CAN'T ESCAPE.
YOUR PRETTY NEW GIRLFRIEND, THE FAMILY YOU WANT TO START...
...AND THE VOW YOU'D BE ABANDONING IF YOU DID.
BANNER--SORRY, BUD, BUT THIS IS FULLY OUTSIDE OF MY JURISDICTION.
YOU WANT TO TALK TO CULTS FOR ANSWERS, YOU CAN DO IT WITHOUT ME. I'M WAITING IN THE CAR.
YOU MADE A VOW TO PROTECT YOUR LOVED ONES, FRANK CASTLE.
YOU CAN'T ABANDON THEM FOR A NEW FAMILY JUST BECAUSE IT'S EASY.
YOU'RE A MAN WHOSE SOUL THIRSTS FOR REVENGE.
THE WORST THING IS THAT WHEN SHE SAID IT, I KNEW SHE WAS RIGHT.

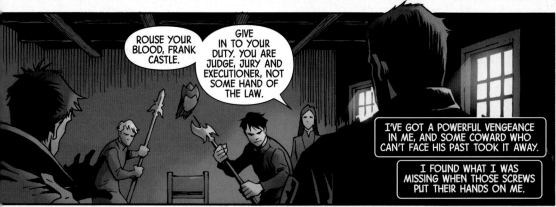

ROUSE YOUR BLOOD, FRANK CASTLE.

GIVE IN TO YOUR DUTY. YOU ARE JUDGE, JURY AND EXECUTIONER, NOT SOME HAND OF THE LAW.

I'VE GOT A POWERFUL VENGEANCE IN ME, AND SOME COWARD WHO CAN'T FACE HIS PAST TOOK IT AWAY.

I FOUND WHAT I WAS MISSING WHEN THOSE SCREWS PUT THEIR HANDS ON ME.

THAT PAIN-IN-THE-ASS KID IN THE ALLEY.

YES, FRANK CASTLE!

THE TRUTH CAN BE OBSCURED FROM OTHERS, BUT NOT FROM YOU! THESE THINGS I SEE, THESE MAGICS CANNOT BE UNMADE BY ANY HAND!

WHEN BLAKE RAISED THAT GUN.

YOU ARE FORSETI, SYDYK AND MARDUK BEFORE YOU!

YOU ARE THE MYTHIC GREAT HAND OF JUSTICE, AND SOMEONE HAS STOLEN YOUR REVENGE! STOLEN YOUR VERY NATURE!

I HATE TO ADMIT IT, BUT SHE AIN'T WRONG.

SORRY I BEAT THE @#%$ OUT OF YOUR BABY BOYS.

THEY ARE WARRIORS, LIKE YOU. YOU MUSTN'T ACCEPT COMFORT IN TRADE FOR ABSOLUTION.

THERE ARE WORLDS OUTSIDE THIS ONE, CASTLE. THEY CAN BE SHAPED WITH A SENTENCE.

OR WITH A *MACHINE*.

A MACHINE? WHAT KIND OF MACHINE?

I'M A LITTLE INSULTED THAT THE ANSWER IS POTENTIALLY SCIENTIFIC IN NATURE AND I HAD TO LEARN IT FROM A *WITCH*.

YEAH....BUT A *MACHINE* IS SOMETHING I CAN *BREAK*.

WHICH BRINGS US BACK TO...

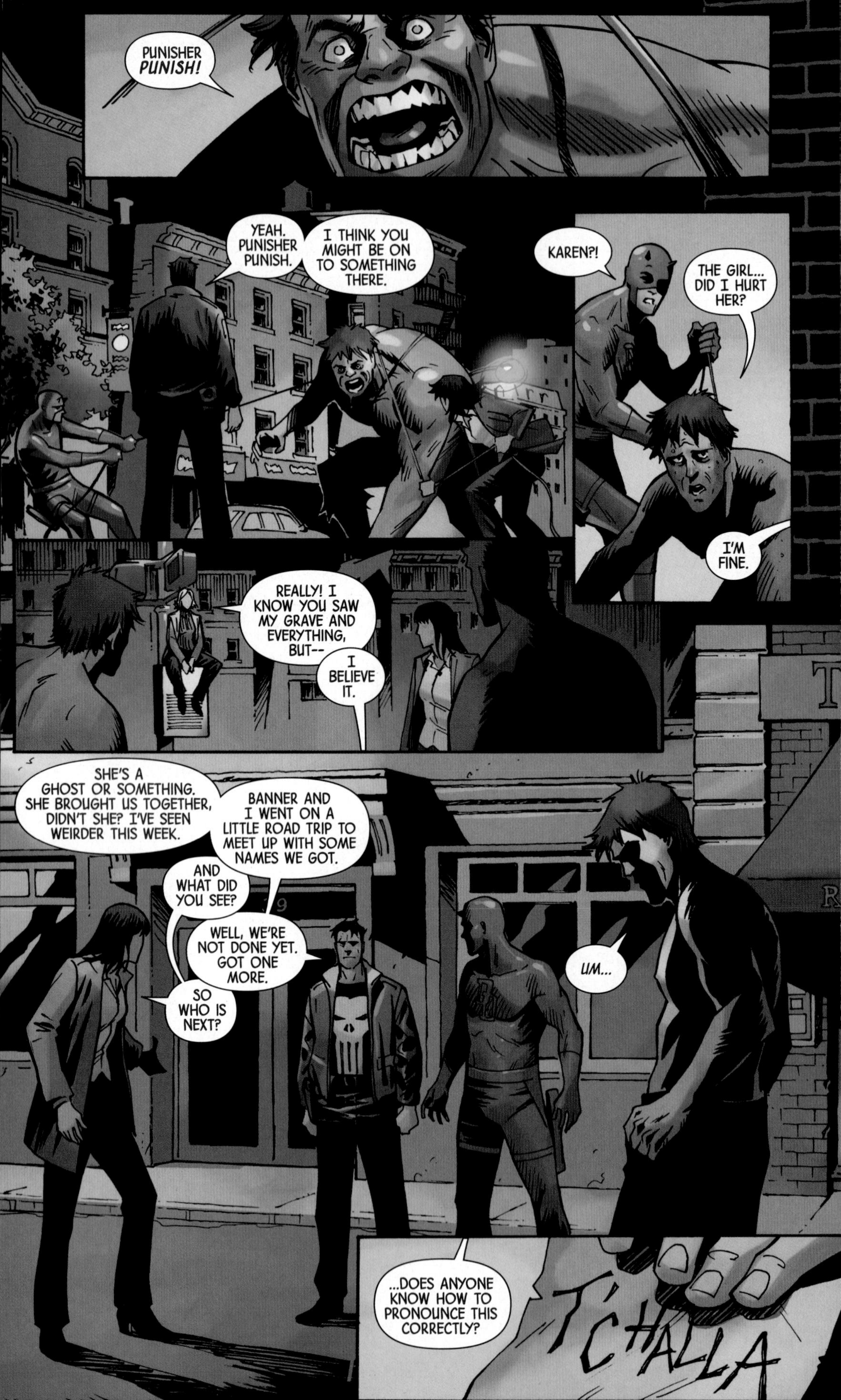
PUNISHER PUNISH!
YEAH. PUNISHER PUNISH.
I THINK YOU MIGHT BE ON TO SOMETHING THERE.
KAREN?!
THE GIRL... DID I HURT HER?
I'M FINE.
REALLY! I KNOW YOU SAW MY GRAVE AND EVERYTHING, BUT--
I BELIEVE IT.
SHE'S A GHOST OR SOMETHING. SHE BROUGHT US TOGETHER, DIDN'T SHE? I'VE SEEN WEIRDER THIS WEEK.
BANNER AND I WENT ON A LITTLE ROAD TRIP TO MEET UP WITH SOME NAMES WE GOT.
AND WHAT DID YOU SEE?
WELL, WE'RE NOT DONE YET. GOT ONE MORE.
SO WHO IS NEXT?
UM...
...DOES ANYONE KNOW HOW TO PRONOUNCE THIS CORRECTLY?
T'CHALLA

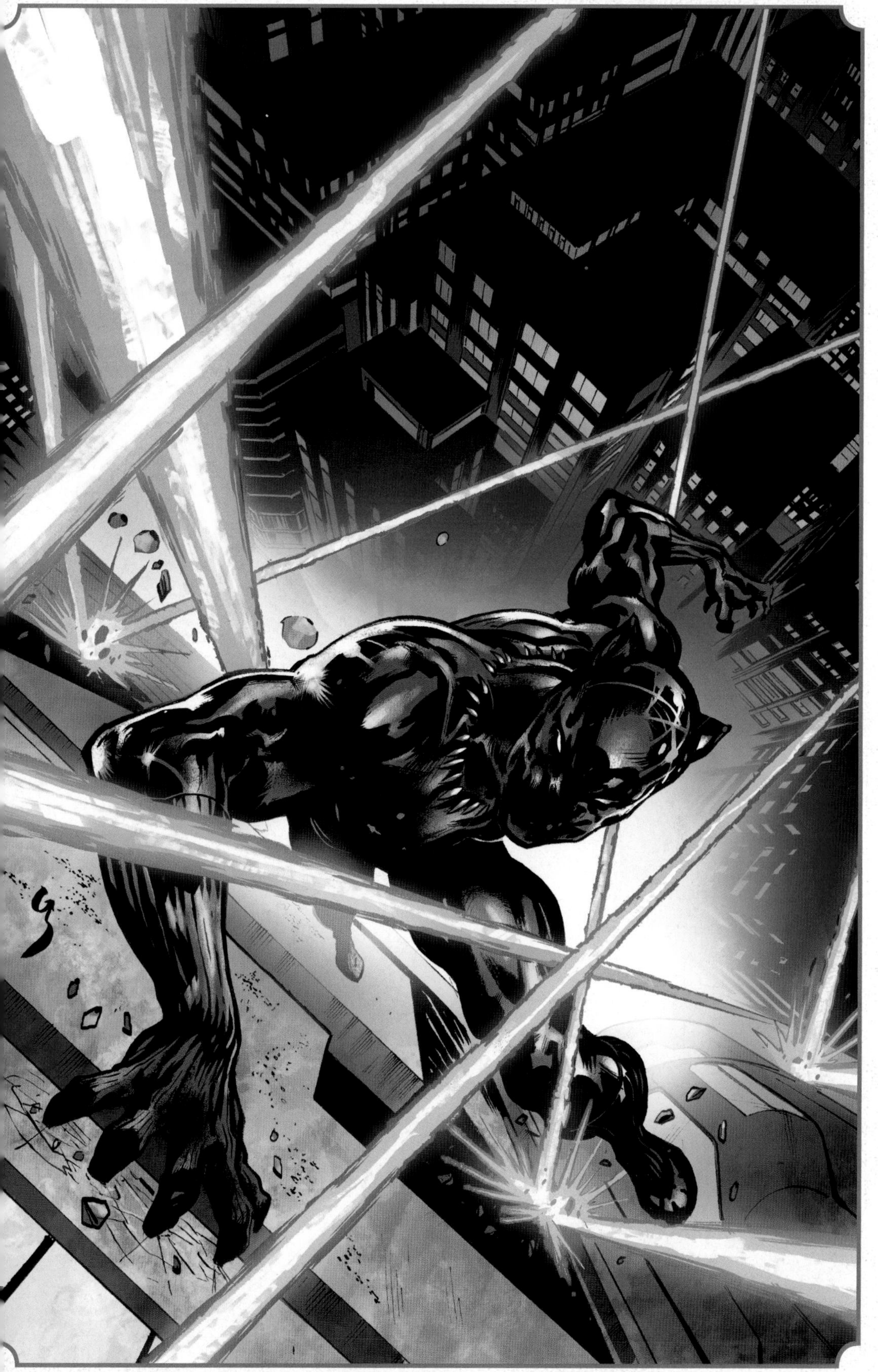

4

THIS IS THE MACHINE THAT CAUSES YOU SUCH STRIFE?

I THOUGHT IT WOULD BE... **BIGGER.**

THIS MACHINE ERASES **ALL KNOWLEDGE AND TRACE** OF PEOPLE FROM THE WORLD.

IT MAKES OTHERS UNABLE TO **PERCEIVE** ANYTHING HAVING TO DO WITH THE TARGET.

THEY COULD BE STANDING **RIGHT IN FRONT OF YOU** AND YOUR MIND WOULD KEEP YOU FROM SEEING THEM.

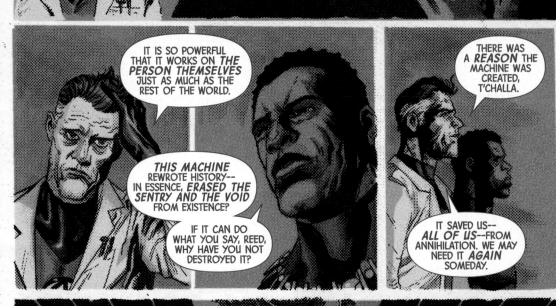

IT IS SO POWERFUL THAT IT WORKS ON **THE PERSON THEMSELVES** JUST AS MUCH AS THE REST OF THE WORLD.

THIS MACHINE REWROTE HISTORY-- IN ESSENCE, **ERASED THE SENTRY AND THE VOID** FROM EXISTENCE?

IF IT CAN DO WHAT YOU SAY, REED, WHY HAVE YOU NOT DESTROYED IT?

THERE WAS A **REASON** THE MACHINE WAS CREATED, T'CHALLA.

IT SAVED US-- **ALL OF US**--FROM ANNIHILATION. WE MAY NEED IT **AGAIN** SOMEDAY.

UNTIL THEN, IT MUST BE KEPT OUT OF THE WRONG HANDS.

I CALLED YOU HERE BECAUSE THERE IS ONLY **ONE PLACE** I CAN THINK OF THAT IS SECURE ENOUGH TO STORE SOMETHING SO **VULNERABLE AND DANGEROUS.**

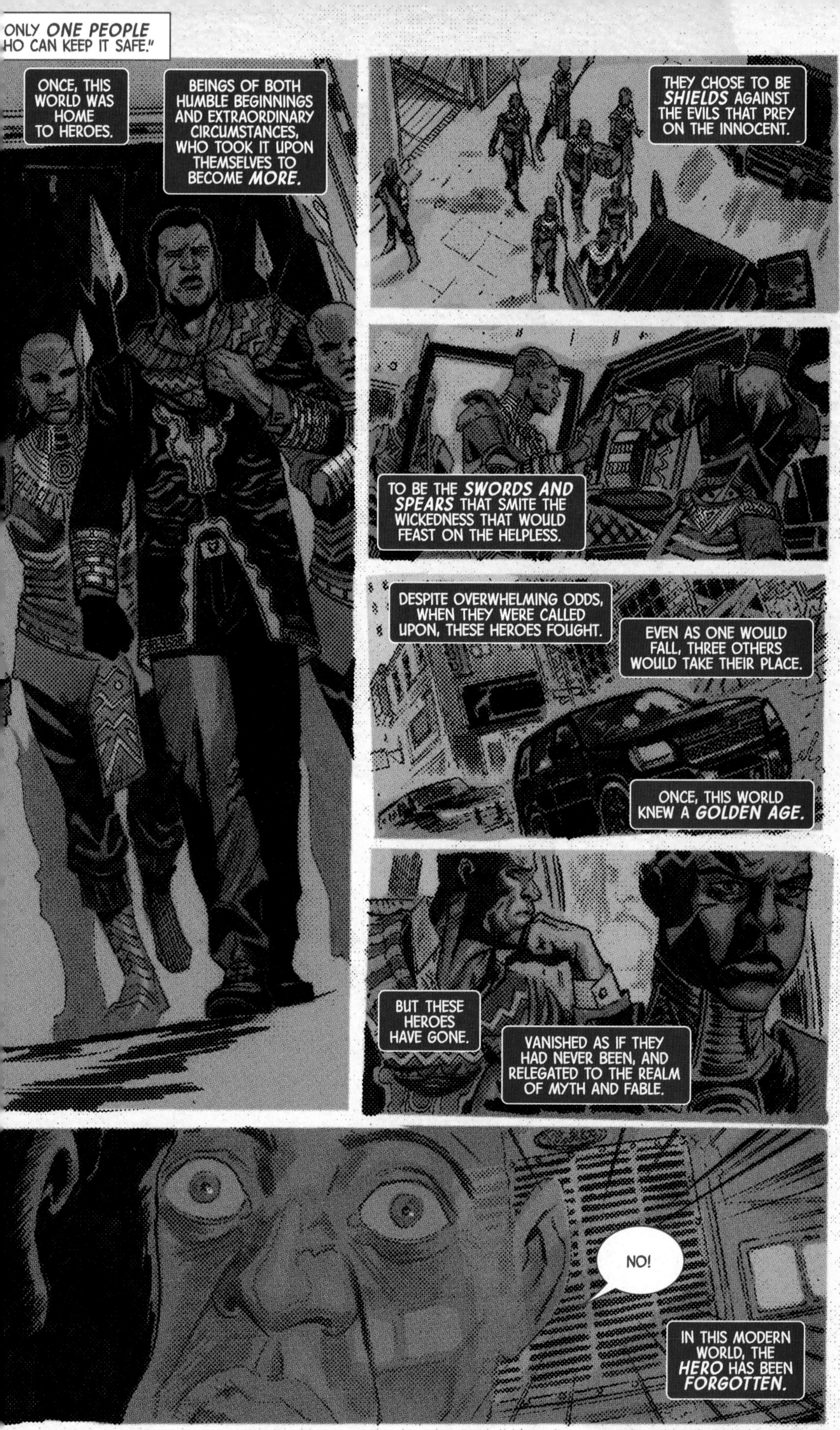
ONLY ONE PEOPLE
HO CAN KEEP IT SAFE."
ONCE, THIS WORLD WAS HOME TO HEROES.
BEINGS OF BOTH HUMBLE BEGINNINGS AND EXTRAORDINARY CIRCUMSTANCES, WHO TOOK IT UPON THEMSELVES TO BECOME MORE.
THEY CHOSE TO BE SHIELDS AGAINST THE EVILS THAT PREY ON THE INNOCENT.
TO BE THE SWORDS AND SPEARS THAT SMITE THE WICKEDNESS THAT WOULD FEAST ON THE HELPLESS.
DESPITE OVERWHELMING ODDS, WHEN THEY WERE CALLED UPON, THESE HEROES FOUGHT.
EVEN AS ONE WOULD FALL, THREE OTHERS WOULD TAKE THEIR PLACE.
ONCE, THIS WORLD KNEW A GOLDEN AGE.
BUT THESE HEROES HAVE GONE.
VANISHED AS IF THEY HAD NEVER BEEN, AND RELEGATED TO THE REALM OF MYTH AND FABLE.
NO!
IN THIS MODERN WORLD, THE HERO HAS BEEN FORGOTTEN.

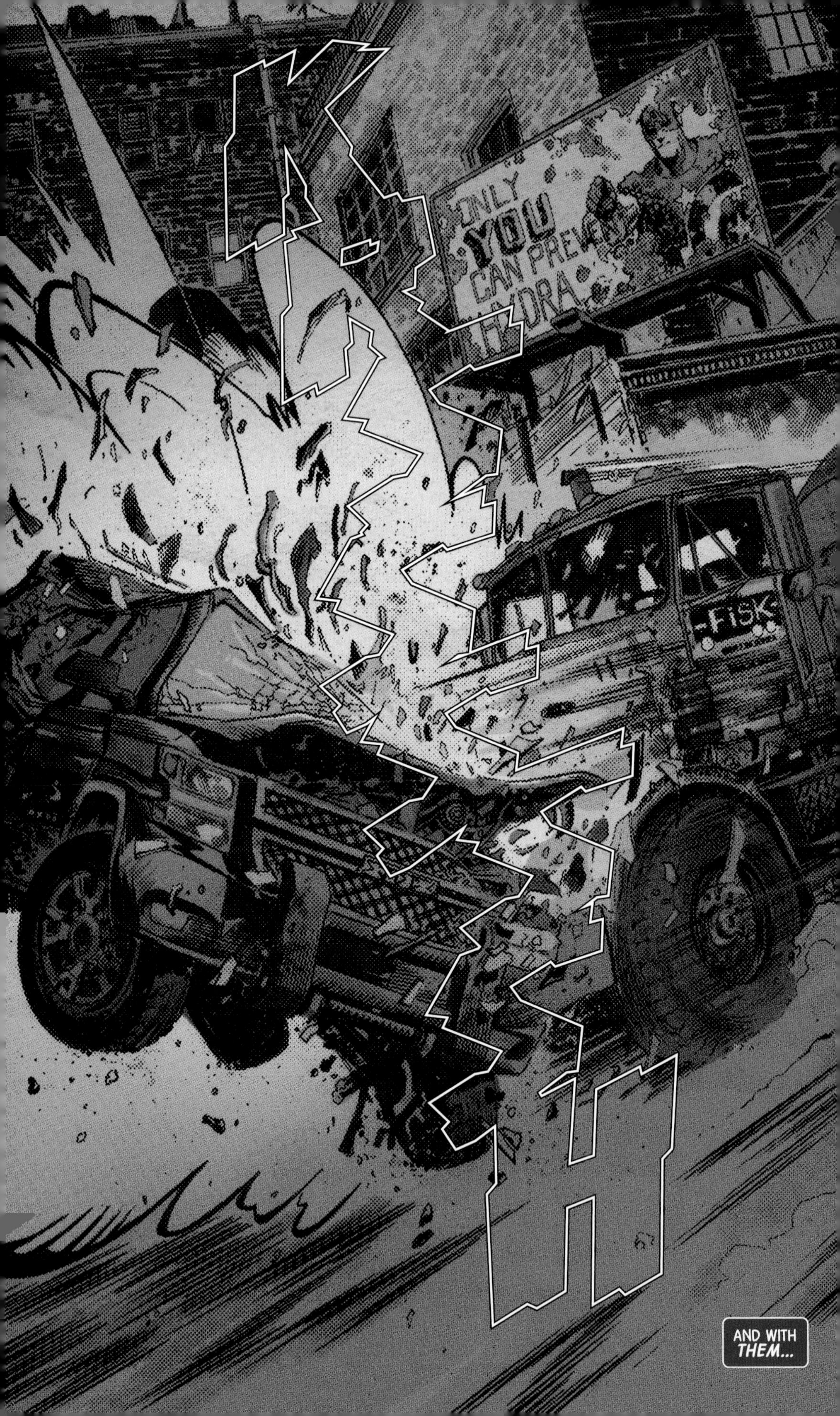
ONLY
YOU
CAN
FISK
AND WITH THEM...

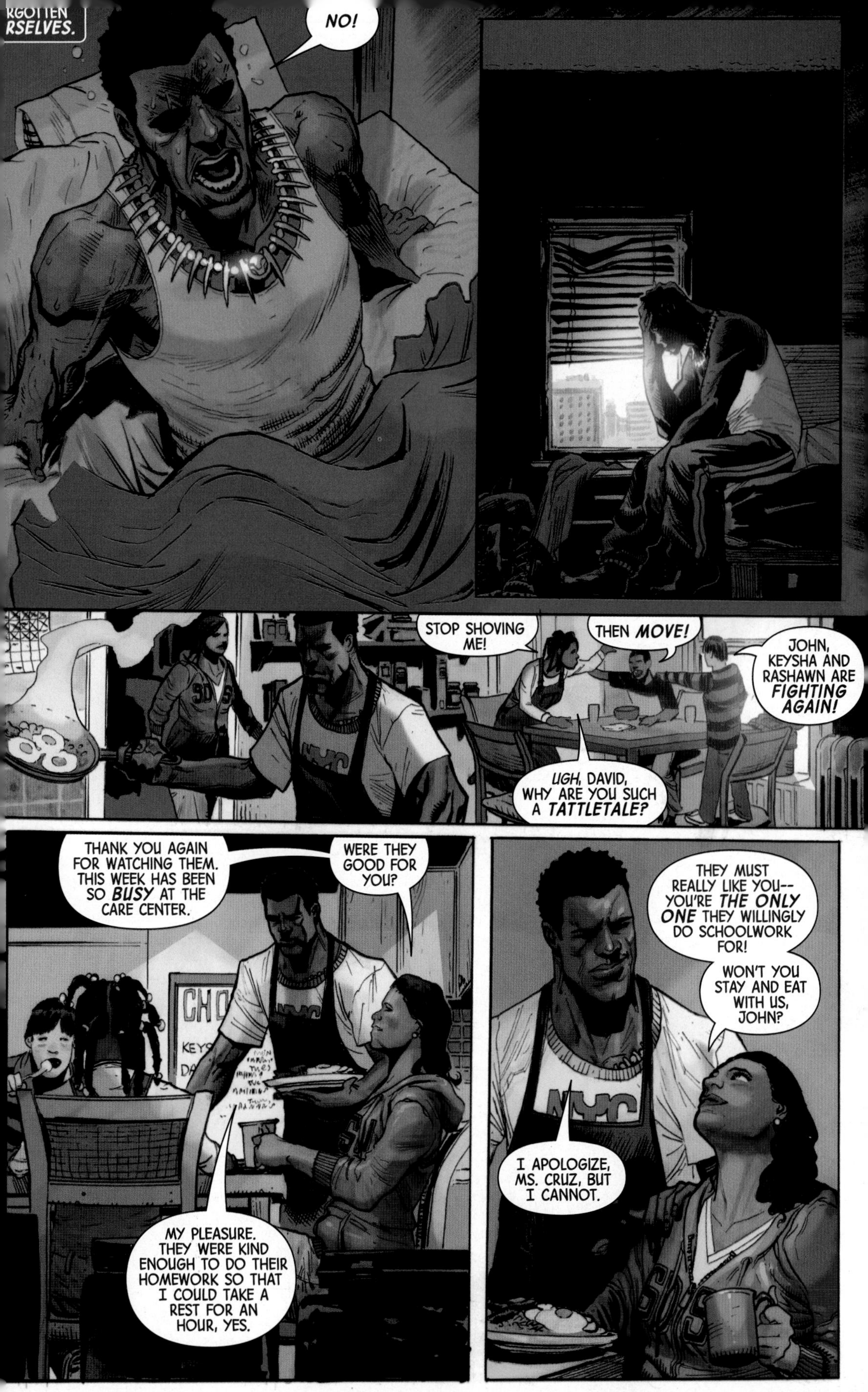
RGOTTEN
RSELVES.
NO!
STOP SHOVING ME!
THEN MOVE!
JOHN, KEYSHA AND RASHAWN ARE FIGHTING AGAIN!
UGH, DAVID, WHY ARE YOU SUCH A TATTLETALE?
THANK YOU AGAIN FOR WATCHING THEM. THIS WEEK HAS BEEN SO BUSY AT THE CARE CENTER.
WERE THEY GOOD FOR YOU?
MY PLEASURE. THEY WERE KIND ENOUGH TO DO THEIR HOMEWORK SO THAT I COULD TAKE A REST FOR AN HOUR, YES.
THEY MUST REALLY LIKE YOU-- YOU'RE THE ONLY ONE THEY WILLINGLY DO SCHOOLWORK FOR!
WON'T YOU STAY AND EAT WITH US, JOHN?
I APOLOGIZE, MS. CRUZ, BUT I CANNOT.

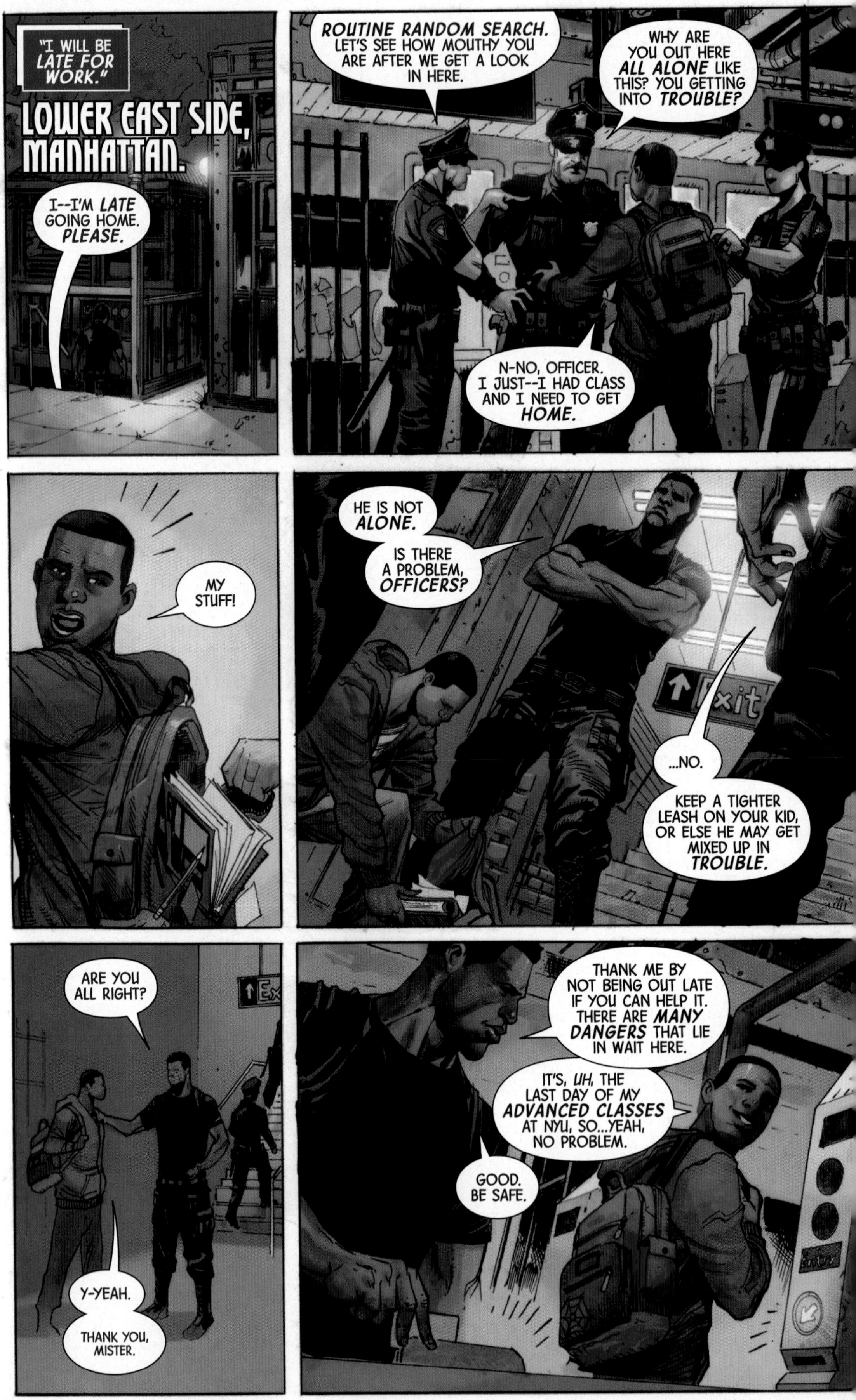
"I WILL BE LATE FOR WORK."
LOWER EAST SIDE, MANHATTAN.
I--I'M LATE GOING HOME. PLEASE.
ROUTINE RANDOM SEARCH. LET'S SEE HOW MOUTHY YOU ARE AFTER WE GET A LOOK IN HERE.
WHY ARE YOU OUT HERE ALL ALONE LIKE THIS? YOU GETTING INTO TROUBLE?
N-NO, OFFICER. I JUST--I HAD CLASS AND I NEED TO GET HOME.
MY STUFF!
HE IS NOT ALONE.
IS THERE A PROBLEM, OFFICERS?
...NO.
KEEP A TIGHTER LEASH ON YOUR KID, OR ELSE HE MAY GET MIXED UP IN TROUBLE.
ARE YOU ALL RIGHT?
Y-YEAH.
THANK YOU, MISTER.
THANK ME BY NOT BEING OUT LATE IF YOU CAN HELP IT. THERE ARE MANY DANGERS THAT LIE IN WAIT HERE.
IT'S, UH, THE LAST DAY OF MY ADVANCED CLASSES AT NYU, SO...YEAH, NO PROBLEM.
GOOD. BE SAFE.

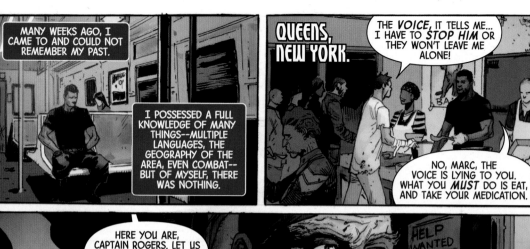

MANY WEEKS AGO, I CAME TO AND COULD NOT REMEMBER MY PAST.

I POSSESSED A FULL KNOWLEDGE OF MANY THINGS--MULTIPLE LANGUAGES, THE GEOGRAPHY OF THE AREA, EVEN COMBAT-- BUT OF MYSELF, THERE WAS NOTHING.

QUEENS, NEW YORK.

THE *VOICE*, IT TELLS ME... I HAVE TO *STOP HIM* OR THEY WON'T LEAVE ME ALONE!

NO, MARC, THE VOICE IS LYING TO YOU. WHAT YOU *MUST* DO IS EAT, AND TAKE YOUR MEDICATION.

HERE YOU ARE, CAPTAIN ROGERS. LET US SEE IF YOU CAN MANAGE TO EAT IT WHILE IT IS STILL WARM, *EH?*

I CAME TO WITH AS MANY SCARS AND OLD BROKEN BONES AS I DID SKILLS.

SOMETIMES, I WONDER ABOUT THE MAN I WAS BEFORE.

NOT *HUNGRY* TODAY?

PERHAPS TOMORROW, *EH?*

ARE THESE THE MARKS OF A *GOOD MAN?* OR ARE THEY THE *BRANDS* OF WICKEDNESS?

SEE YOU TOMORROW, JOHN.

SEE YOU TOMORROW, CAPTAIN ROGERS, SAM.

AND PLEASE, IN THE FUTURE, LEAVE THE BIRDS OUTSIDE--IT IS AGAINST THE HEALTH CODE TO BRING THEM IN HERE.

YOU ACT LIKE THEY LISTEN WHEN I TALK, HA HA!

WHAT KIND OF *MAN* WAS I?

DOES IT *MATTER?*

NO, AUSTIN, DON'T...IT'S *FINE.*

NAH, IT'S *NOT FINE.*

YOU GOT A LOT OF MOUTH WHEN YOU'RE TALKING TO SOMEONE'S *BACK.* HOW ABOUT YOU SAY THAT AGAIN TO MY *FACE?*

MIKE, GET YOUR CAMERA! HE'S *THREATENING ME.*

WHO MISSES ME NOW THAT I AM NOT THERE?

AFTER WHAT YOU SAID TO HER, YOU THINK A *CAMERA* IS GONNA SAVE YOU?

WHATEVER, MAN, IT WAS A *COMPLIMENT!* WHY'RE YOU SO *SENSITIVE?*

IF THE SELF IS A MIXTURE OF LIVED EXPERIENCE AND MENTAL STATES, WHAT AM I *NOW?*

COME ON, IT'S *NOT WORTH IT.*

AM I A MAN? A GHOST?

THINK ABOUT *THIS* THE NEXT TIME YOU WANNA GET DISRESPECTFUL.

WAIT.

IS IT BETTE THAT I HA BEEN LOST

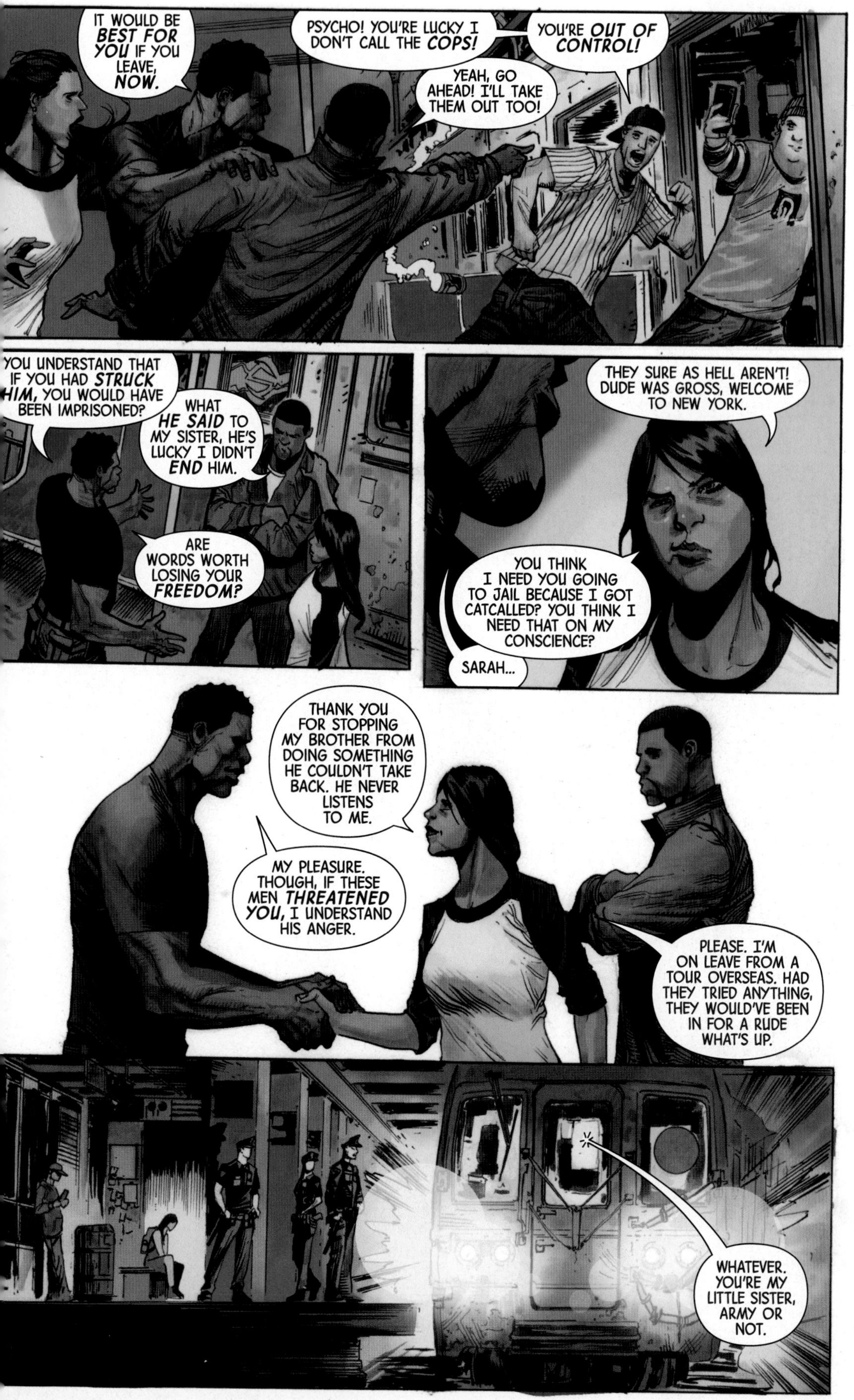
IT WOULD BE BEST FOR YOU IF YOU LEAVE, NOW.
PSYCHO! YOU'RE LUCKY I DON'T CALL THE COPS!
YOU'RE OUT OF CONTROL!
YEAH, GO AHEAD! I'LL TAKE THEM OUT TOO!
YOU UNDERSTAND THAT IF YOU HAD STRUCK HIM, YOU WOULD HAVE BEEN IMPRISONED?
WHAT HE SAID TO MY SISTER, HE'S LUCKY I DIDN'T END HIM.
ARE WORDS WORTH LOSING YOUR FREEDOM?
THEY SURE AS HELL AREN'T! DUDE WAS GROSS, WELCOME TO NEW YORK.
YOU THINK I NEED YOU GOING TO JAIL BECAUSE I GOT CATCALLED? YOU THINK I NEED THAT ON MY CONSCIENCE?
SARAH...
THANK YOU FOR STOPPING MY BROTHER FROM DOING SOMETHING HE COULDN'T TAKE BACK. HE NEVER LISTENS TO ME.
MY PLEASURE. THOUGH, IF THESE MEN THREATENED YOU, I UNDERSTAND HIS ANGER.
PLEASE. I'M ON LEAVE FROM A TOUR OVERSEAS. HAD THEY TRIED ANYTHING, THEY WOULD'VE BEEN IN FOR A RUDE WHAT'S UP.
WHATEVER. YOU'RE MY LITTLE SISTER, ARMY OR NOT.

WE GOT A CALL ABOUT A **SUSPECT** THREATENING PASSENGERS.

YOU LIKE TO START TROUBLE, DON'T YOU, **BIG MAN?**

LOOK, OFFICER, THAT GUY WAS A DIRT-BAG. HE--

NO **THREATS** WERE MADE. ONLY A **REQUEST** THAT A VERY RUDE PERSON **REMOVE** HIMSELF FROM A SITUATION.

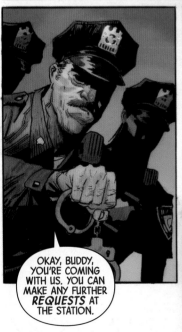

OKAY, BUDDY, YOU'RE COMING WITH US. YOU CAN MAKE ANY FURTHER **REQUESTS** AT THE STATION.

WAIT, YOU THINK--

PLEASE, **TAKE YOUR SISTER AND GO.**

BUT--

I WILL BE **FINE.** BUT YOU MUST GO. **NOW.**

I HAVE NO IDENTIFICATION, VERY LITTLE MONEY AND NO KIN.

MAN OR GHOST, RIGHT NOW, I CANNOT AFFORD TO BE AT THE **MERCY** OF PEOPLE SUCH AS THESE.

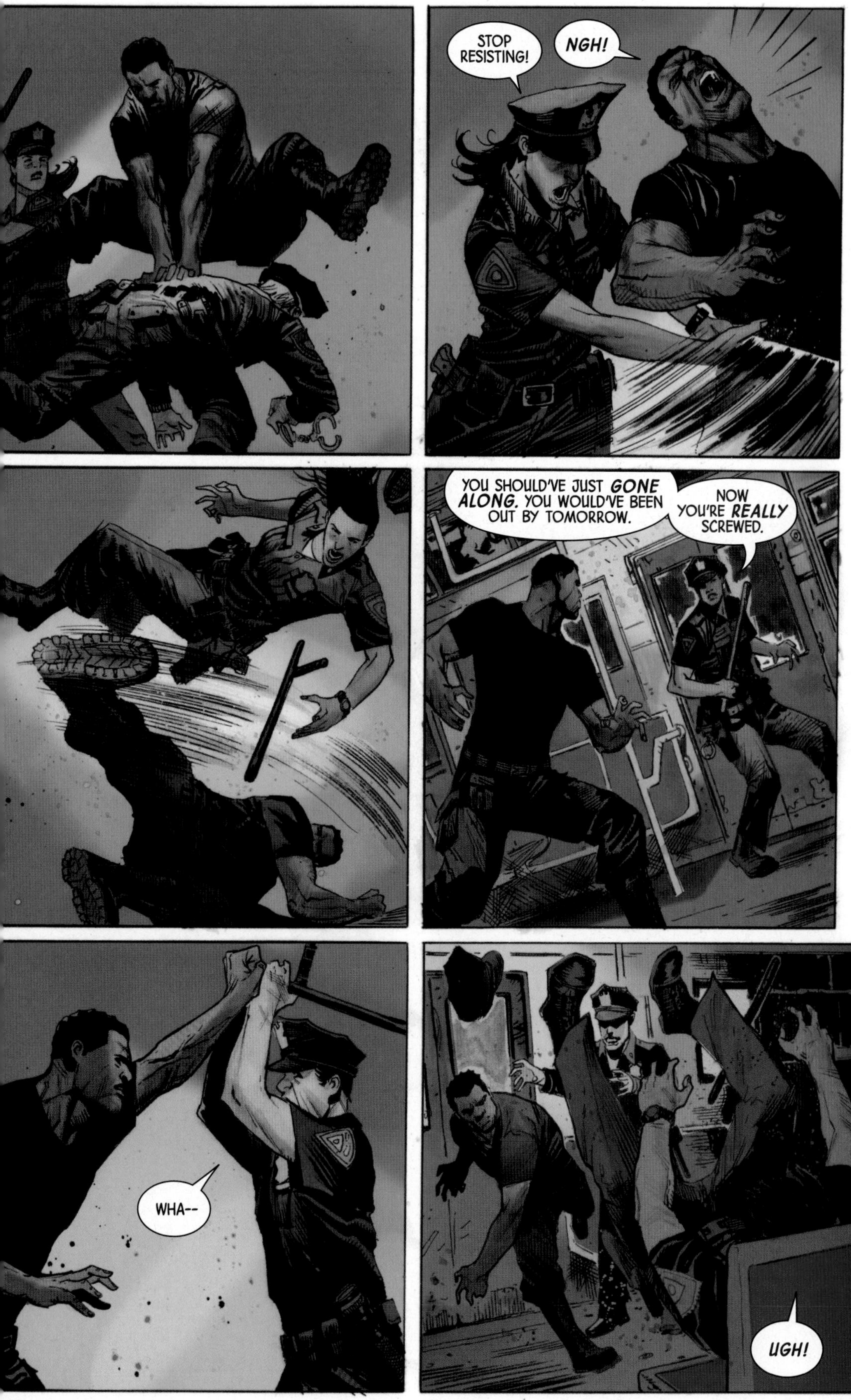
STOP RESISTING!
NGH!
YOU SHOULD'VE JUST GONE ALONG. YOU WOULD'VE BEEN OUT BY TOMORROW.
NOW YOU'RE REALLY SCREWED.
WHA--
UGH!

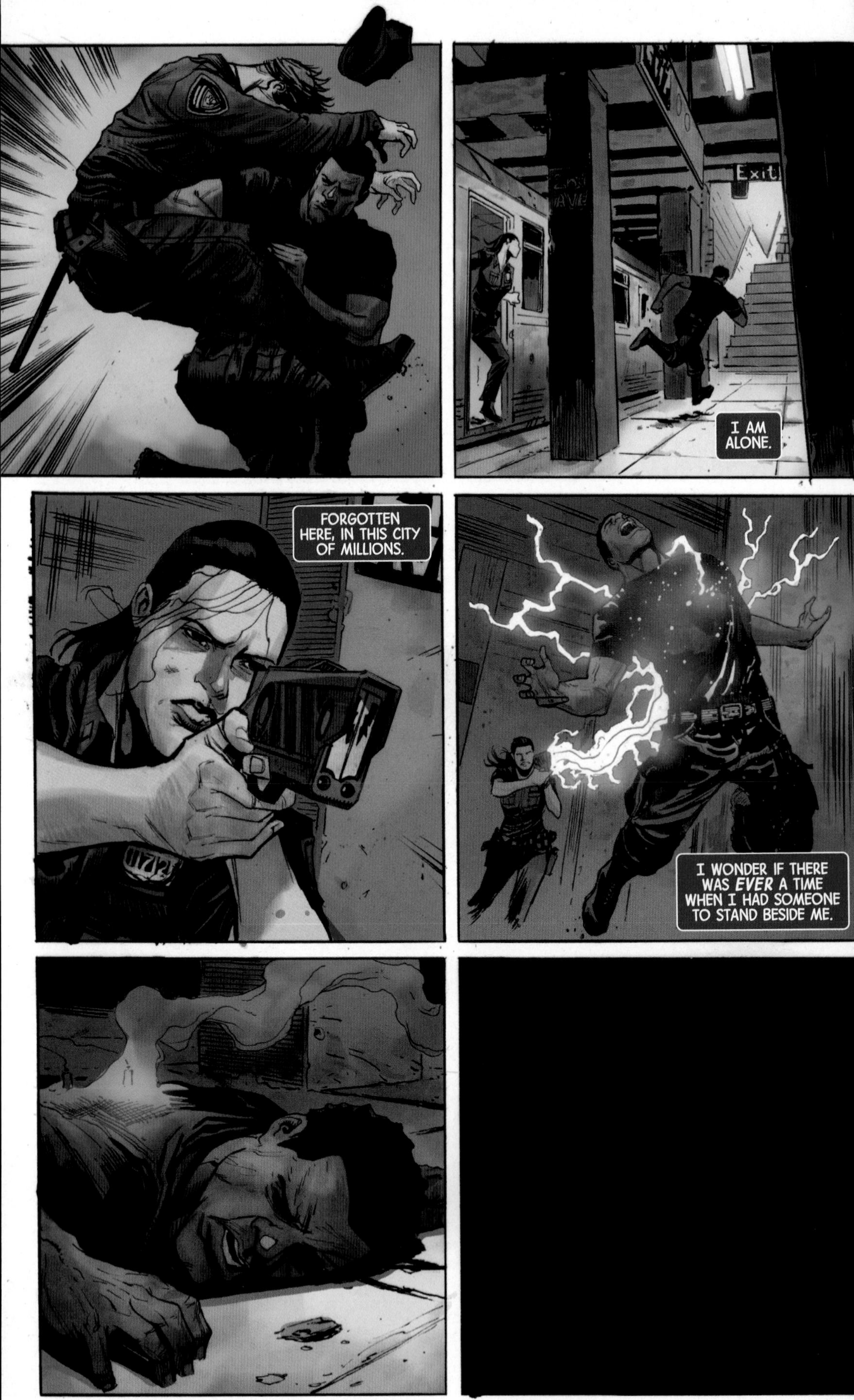
Exit
I AM ALONE.
FORGOTTEN HERE, IN THIS CITY OF MILLIONS.
I WONDER IF THERE WAS *EVER* A TIME WHEN I HAD SOMEONE TO STAND BESIDE ME.

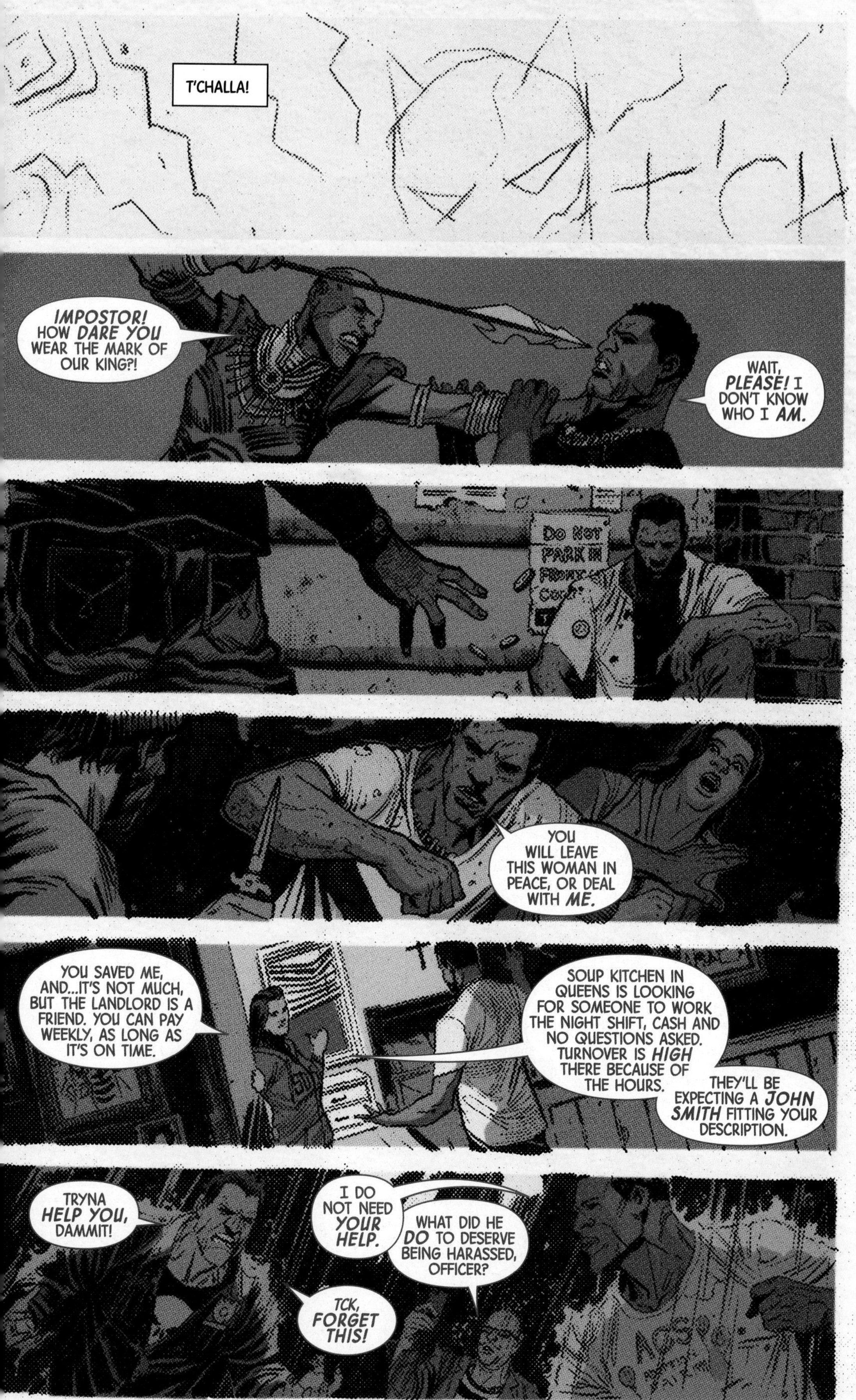
T'CHALLA!
IMPOSTOR! HOW DARE YOU WEAR THE MARK OF OUR KING?!
WAIT, PLEASE! I DON'T KNOW WHO I AM.
YOU WILL LEAVE THIS WOMAN IN PEACE, OR DEAL WITH ME.
YOU SAVED ME, AND...IT'S NOT MUCH, BUT THE LANDLORD IS A FRIEND. YOU CAN PAY WEEKLY, AS LONG AS IT'S ON TIME.
SOUP KITCHEN IN QUEENS IS LOOKING FOR SOMEONE TO WORK THE NIGHT SHIFT, CASH AND NO QUESTIONS ASKED. TURNOVER IS HIGH THERE BECAUSE OF THE HOURS.
THEY'LL BE EXPECTING A JOHN SMITH FITTING YOUR DESCRIPTION.
TRYNA HELP YOU, DAMMIT!
I DO NOT NEED YOUR HELP.
WHAT DID HE DO TO DESERVE BEING HARASSED, OFFICER?
TCK, FORGET THIS!

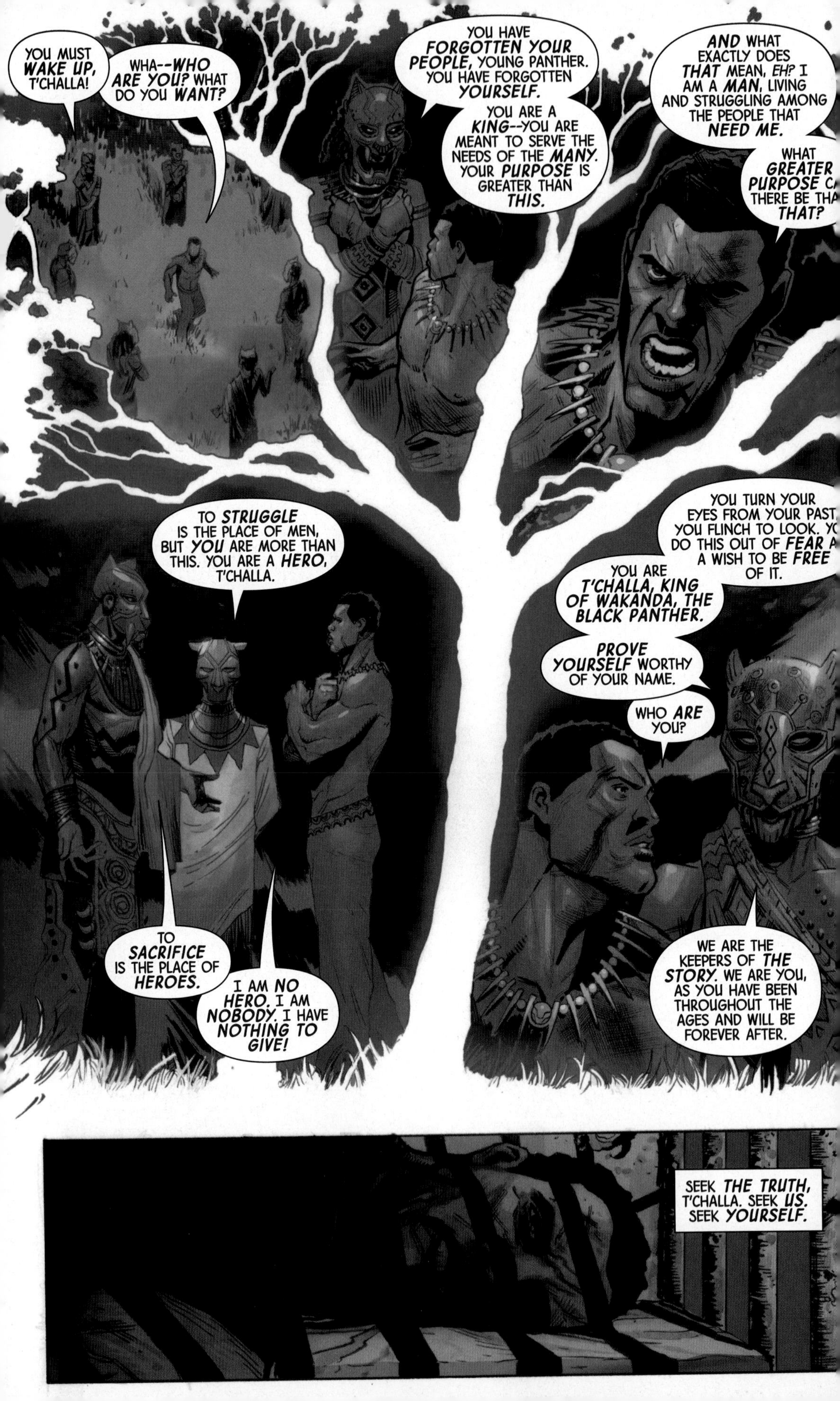
YOU MUST WAKE UP, T'CHALLA!
WHA--WHO ARE YOU? WHAT DO YOU WANT?
YOU HAVE FORGOTTEN YOUR PEOPLE, YOUNG PANTHER. YOU HAVE FORGOTTEN YOURSELF.
YOU ARE A KING--YOU ARE MEANT TO SERVE THE NEEDS OF THE MANY. YOUR PURPOSE IS GREATER THAN THIS.
AND WHAT EXACTLY DOES THAT MEAN, EH? I AM A MAN, LIVING AND STRUGGLING AMONG THE PEOPLE THAT NEED ME.
WHAT GREATER PURPOSE C THERE BE THA THAT?
TO STRUGGLE IS THE PLACE OF MEN, BUT YOU ARE MORE THAN THIS. YOU ARE A HERO, T'CHALLA.
TO SACRIFICE IS THE PLACE OF HEROES.
I AM NO HERO. I AM NOBODY. I HAVE NOTHING TO GIVE!
YOU TURN YOUR EYES FROM YOUR PAST, YOU FLINCH TO LOOK. Y DO THIS OUT OF FEAR A A WISH TO BE FREE OF IT.
YOU ARE T'CHALLA, KING OF WAKANDA, THE BLACK PANTHER.
PROVE YOURSELF WORTHY OF YOUR NAME.
WHO ARE YOU?
WE ARE THE KEEPERS OF THE STORY. WE ARE YOU, AS YOU HAVE BEEN THROUGHOUT THE AGES AND WILL BE FOREVER AFTER.
SEEK THE TRUTH, T'CHALLA. SEEK US. SEEK YOURSELF.

YOU'RE IN A BIT OF A TOUGH SPOT, SON.

ATTACKING POLICE OFFICERS? IN *PUBLIC?* YOU'RE LUCKY TO BE ALIVE.

SEEMS LIKE THIS ISN'T THE FIRST TIME YOU'VE CAUSED A STIR, THOUGH IT LOOKS LIKE YOU'VE MANAGED TO SLIP AWAY THUS FAR.

STILL, IT'S THE 21ST CENTURY, AND EVERYONE HAS A CAMERA.

THEY'VE BEEN ABLE TO LINK YOU TO RANDOM ACTS OF VIOLENCE GOING BACK OVER THE LAST FEW MONTHS.

RANDOM ACTS OF *VIOLENCE?* THOSE PEOPLE WERE TRYING TO *VICTIMIZE* OTHERS.

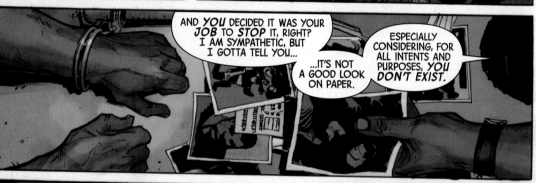

AND *YOU* DECIDED IT WAS YOUR *JOB* TO *STOP* IT, RIGHT? I AM SYMPATHETIC, BUT I GOTTA TELL YOU...

...IT'S NOT A GOOD LOOK ON PAPER.

ESPECIALLY CONSIDERING, FOR ALL INTENTS AND PURPOSES, *YOU DON'T EXIST.*

THEY HAVE YOU DEAD TO RIGHTS ASSAULTING AN OFFICER OF THE LAW ON CAMERA. THERE IS NO ARGUING AGAINST THAT.

NOW, I *KNOW THESE GUYS.* I KNOW THERE IS MORE TO THE *STORY* THAN YOU ATTACKING THEM. BUT THAT CAN'T BE *PROVEN.*

YOU ARE IN A *VERY* PRECARIOUS POSITION.

WHAT EXACTLY ARE YOU SAYING?

THAT THEY WILL KEEP ME LOCKED UP INDEFINITELY WITHOUT SEEING TO MY CONSTITUTIONAL RIGHTS?

SON, YOUR ACCENT CLOCKS YOU AS A FOREIGNER. ONE WITHOUT A RECORD OF ENTRY INTO THE COUNTRY, TO BOOT.

LET'S BE REAL HERE. AS FAR AS THEY'RE CONCERNED, YOU *DON'T HAVE* ANY RIGHTS. THAT'S WHERE *I* COME IN.

AND *WHO ARE YOU*, EXACTLY?

MY NAME IS BEN--BEN DONOVAN--AND I'M A LAWYER.

NOW, I'VE ALREADY SPOKEN TO THE OFFICERS INVOLVED. THERE WERE APPARENTLY TWO WITNESSES TO THE EVENT LAST NIGHT.

THERE'S ALREADY A FACEBOOK GROUP DEDICATED TO MAKING SURE YOU DON'T DISAPPEAR.

WHATEVER ENEMIES YOU'VE MADE, YOU'VE MADE AS MANY FRIENDS.

ELSA CRUZ-- THE SOCIAL WORKER FROM ALPHABET CITY? SHE'S GOT A FUNDTHIS GOING TO COVER YOUR BAIL. THERE ARE *EYES* ON THIS.

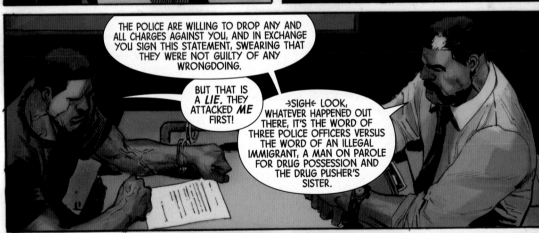

THE POLICE ARE WILLING TO DROP ANY AND ALL CHARGES AGAINST YOU, AND IN EXCHANGE YOU SIGN THIS STATEMENT, SWEARING THAT THEY WERE NOT GUILTY OF ANY WRONGDOING.

BUT THAT IS A *LIE*. THEY ATTACKED *ME* FIRST!

→SIGH← LOOK, WHATEVER HAPPENED OUT THERE, IT'S THE WORD OF THREE POLICE OFFICERS VERSUS THE WORD OF AN ILLEGAL IMMIGRANT, A MAN ON PAROLE FOR DRUG POSSESSION AND THE DRUG PUSHER'S SISTER.

YOU SIGN THIS AND KEEP OUT OF THE WAY, AND THE COPS WILL LEAVE YOU ALONE.

THINK OF MS. CRUZ AND HER KIDS.

WHO WILL LOOK OUT FOR THEM, IF NOT *YOU?*

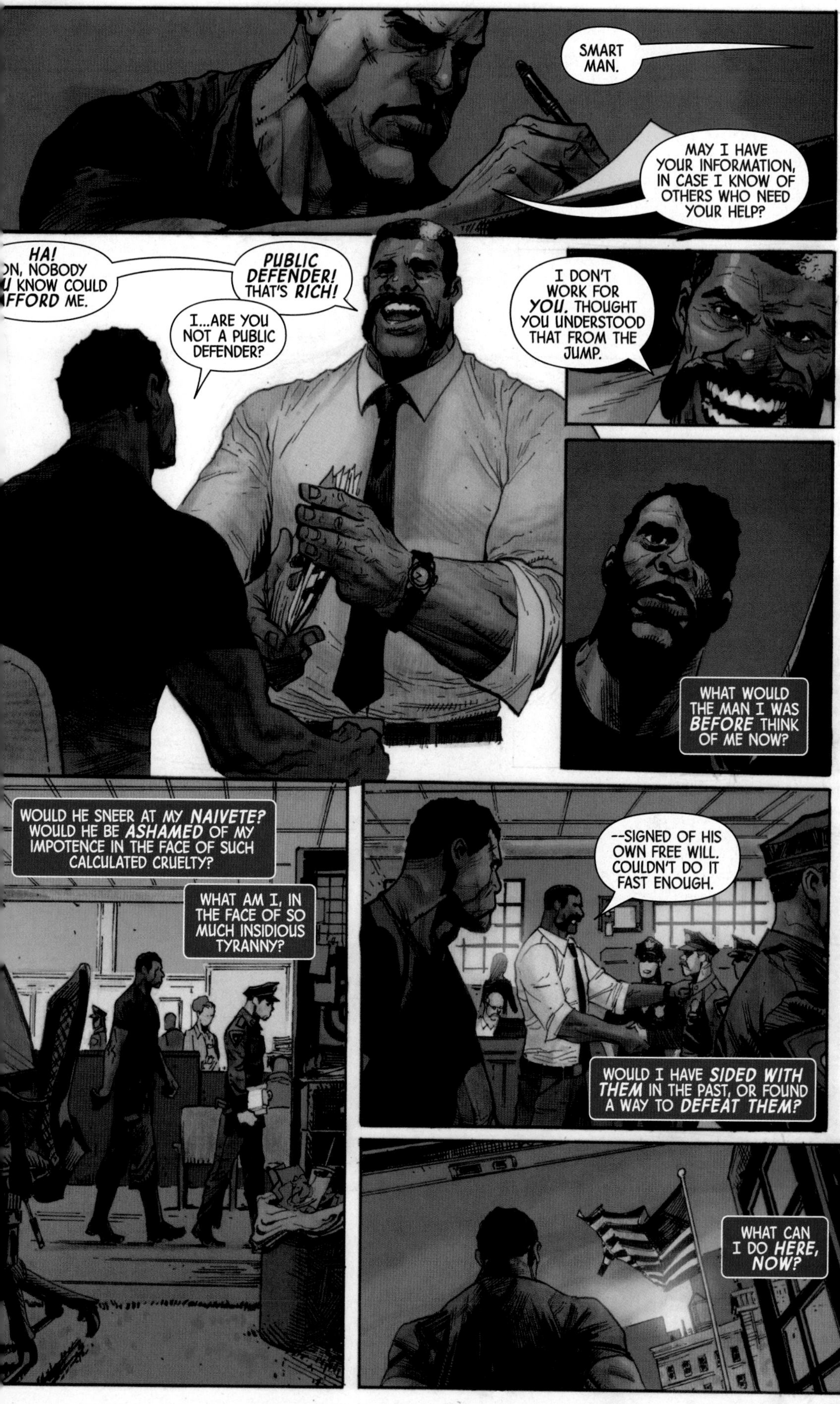
SMART MAN.
MAY I HAVE YOUR INFORMATION, IN CASE I KNOW OF OTHERS WHO NEED YOUR HELP?
PUBLIC DEFENDER! THAT'S RICH!
HA! N, NOBODY U KNOW COULD FFORD ME.
I...ARE YOU NOT A PUBLIC DEFENDER?
I DON'T WORK FOR YOU. THOUGHT YOU UNDERSTOOD THAT FROM THE JUMP.
WHAT WOULD THE MAN I WAS BEFORE THINK OF ME NOW?
WOULD HE SNEER AT MY NAIVETE? WOULD HE BE ASHAMED OF MY IMPOTENCE IN THE FACE OF SUCH CALCULATED CRUELTY?
WHAT AM I, IN THE FACE OF SO MUCH INSIDIOUS TYRANNY?
--SIGNED OF HIS OWN FREE WILL. COULDN'T DO IT FAST ENOUGH.
WOULD I HAVE SIDED WITH THEM IN THE PAST, OR FOUND A WAY TO DEFEAT THEM?
WHAT CAN I DO HERE, NOW?

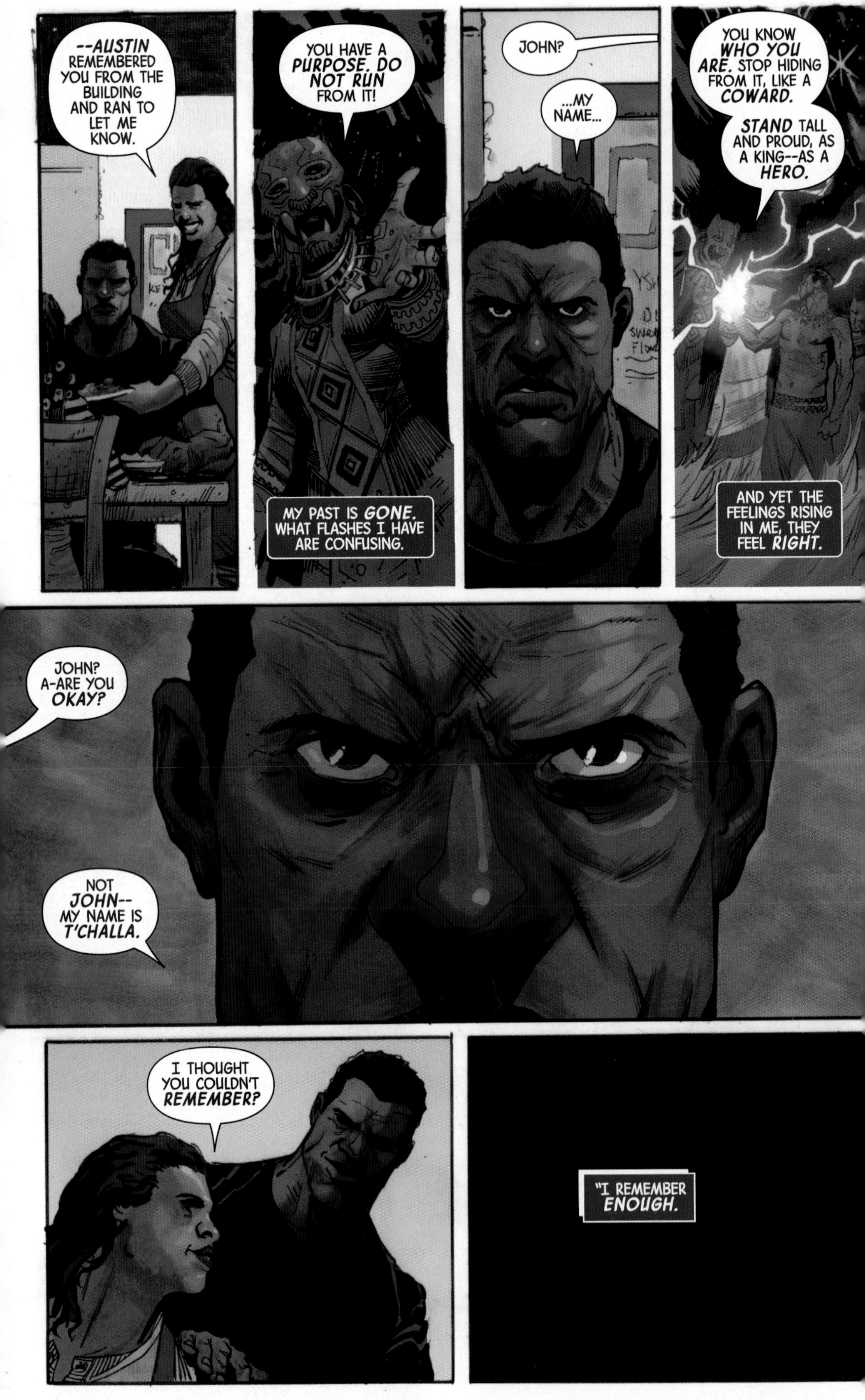
--AUSTIN REMEMBERED YOU FROM THE BUILDING AND RAN TO LET ME KNOW.
YOU HAVE A PURPOSE. DO NOT RUN FROM IT!
MY PAST IS GONE. WHAT FLASHES I HAVE ARE CONFUSING.
JOHN?
...MY NAME...
YOU KNOW WHO YOU ARE. STOP HIDING FROM IT, LIKE A COWARD.
STAND TALL AND PROUD, AS A KING--AS A HERO.
AND YET THE FEELINGS RISING IN ME, THEY FEEL RIGHT.
JOHN? A-ARE YOU OKAY?
NOT JOHN-- MY NAME IS T'CHALLA.
I THOUGHT YOU COULDN'T REMEMBER?
"I REMEMBER ENOUGH.

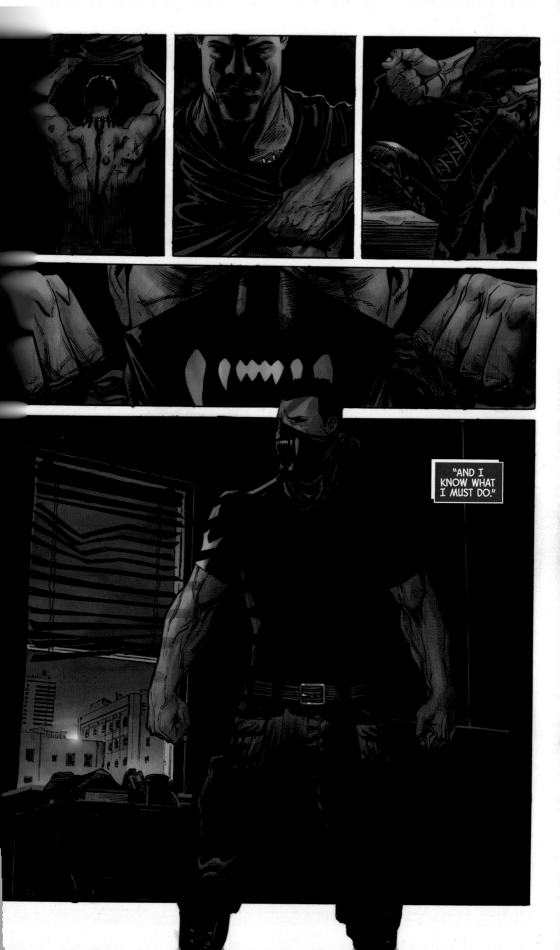

"AND I KNOW WHAT I MUST DO."

THIS MAN, BEN DONOVAN. HE *PREYS* ON THE VULNERABILITY OF THE ALREADY POWERLESS.

HE IS NOT A GOOD MAN.

HE DOES NOT KNOW WHO HE IS, BUT *THAT* DOES NOT MATTER.

HEY, PAUL, HOW GOES?

YEAH, HERE TO SEE MR. FISK...30TH FLOOR?

MY MEMORIES DO NOT RETURN TO ME ALL AT ONCE LIKE *A FLOOD*, BUT RATHER IN FLASHES AND DRIPS, LIKE A LIGHT SUMMER *RAIN*.

NAMES, SENSATIONS, FACES. THEY TAP OUT THE STORY OF MY LIFE INSIDE MY HEAD.

THEY TELL ME THAT IF I DO NOT *FIND* THIS MAN, MAKE SURE I *STOP* HIM, I WILL HAVE *FAILED* MY PURPOSE.

KSSSHHHH

I AM T'CHALLA, KING OF WAKANDA.

I AM THE *HERO* ONCE KNOWN AS THE *BLACK PANTHER.*

I CAME AS SOON AS THEY PASSED THE MESSAGE THAT YOU WANTED ME...

DANGER BEYOND THIS POINT HAZARDOUS

AND EVE FORGOT I WILL D MY DU

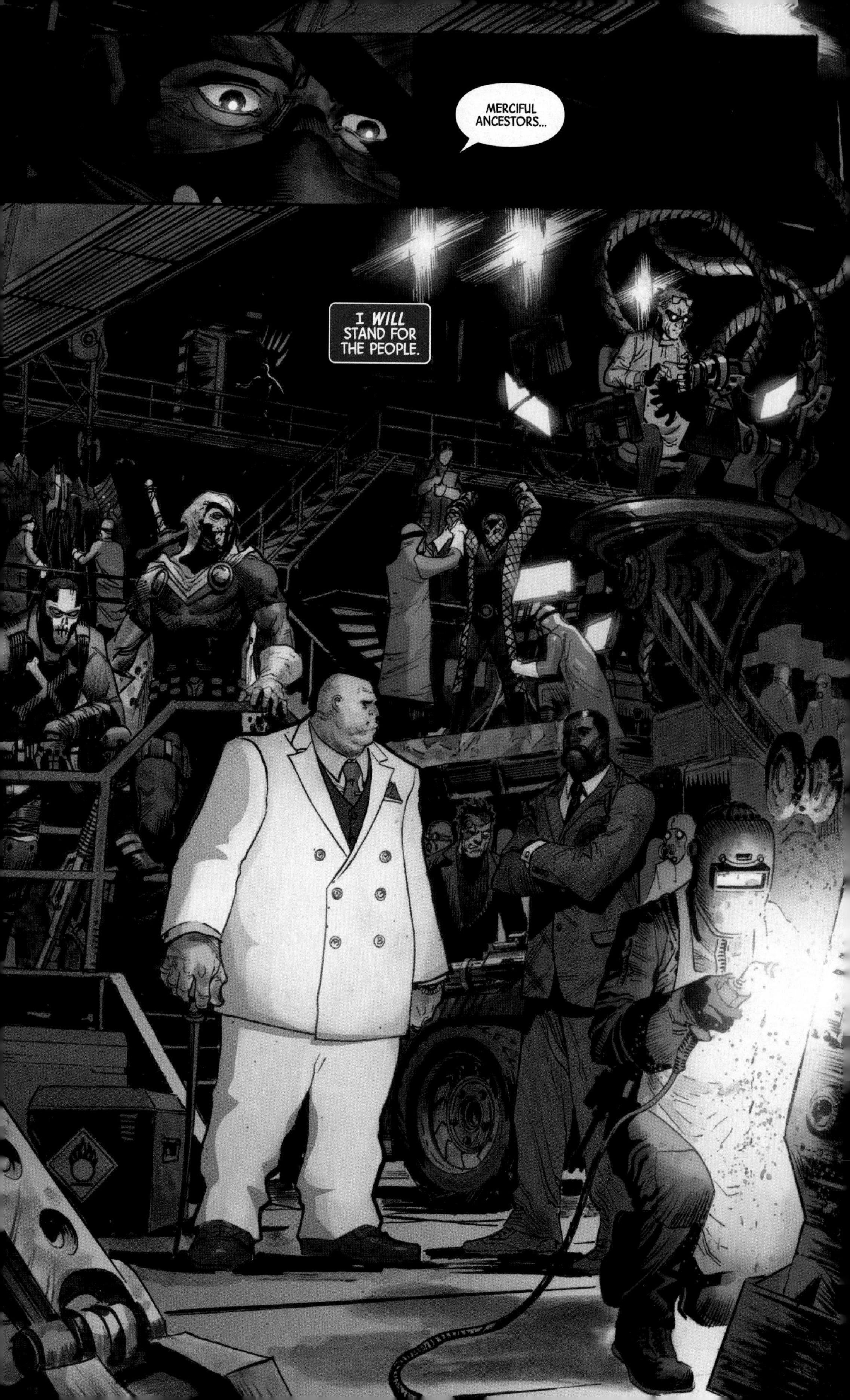
MERCIFUL ANCESTORS...
I *WILL* STAND FOR THE PEOPLE.

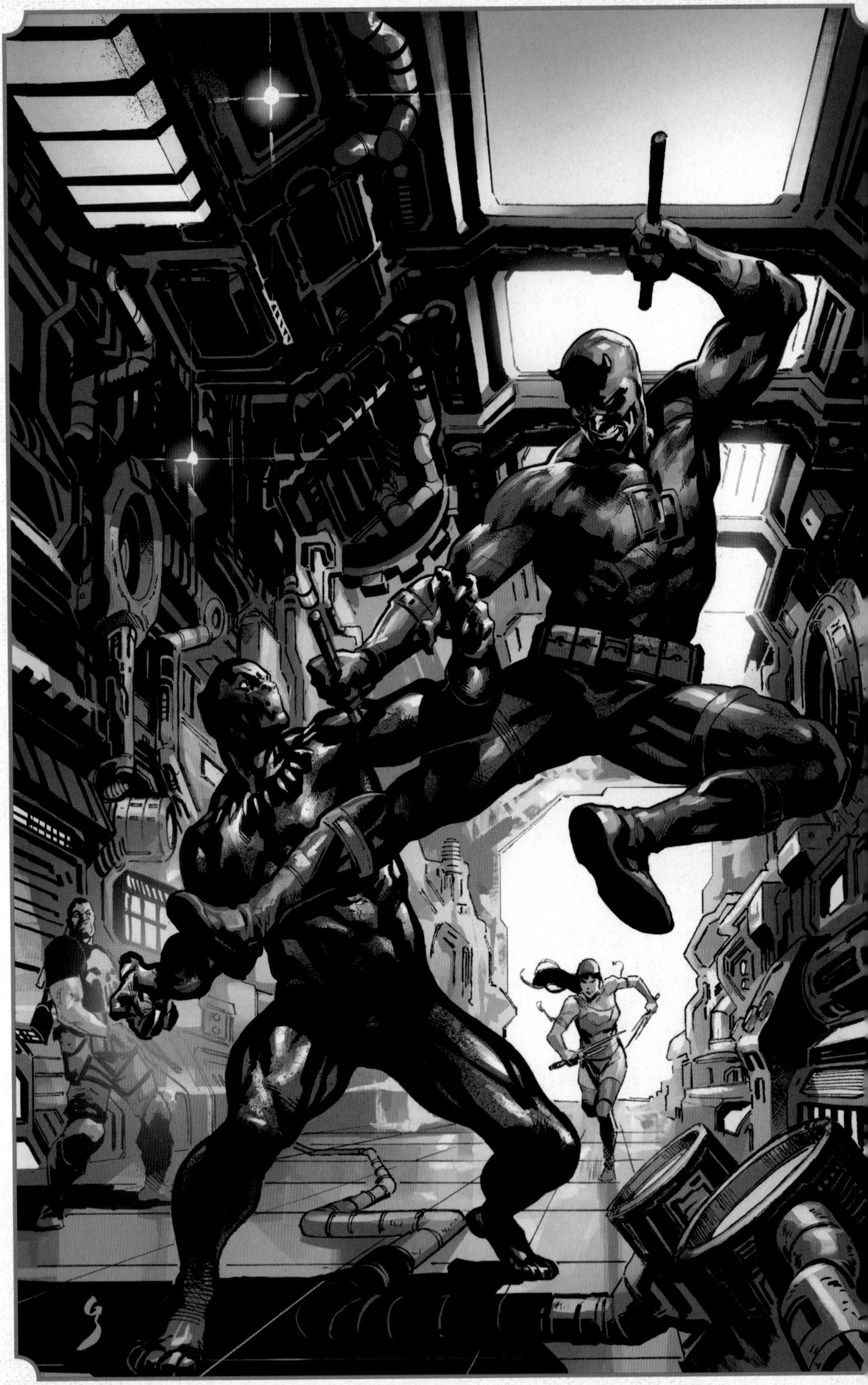

5

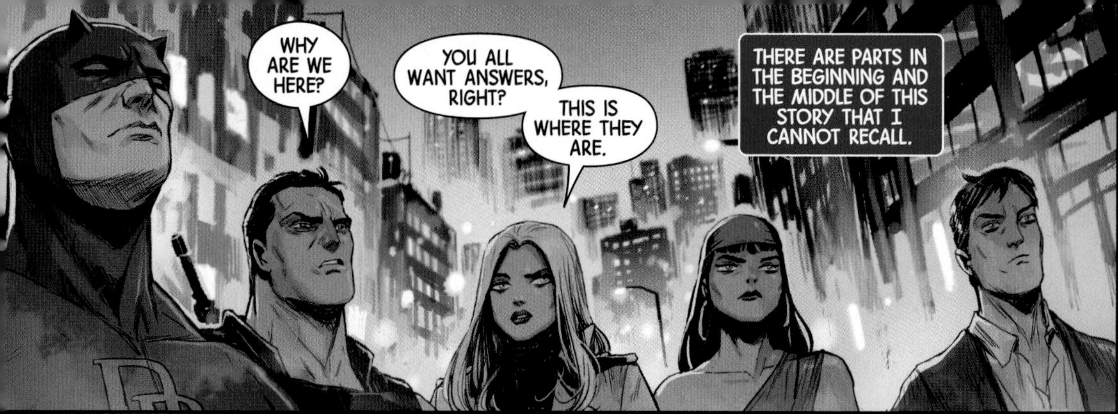
WHY ARE WE HERE?
YOU ALL WANT ANSWERS, RIGHT?
THIS IS WHERE THEY ARE.
THERE ARE PARTS IN THE BEGINNING AND THE MIDDLE OF THIS STORY THAT I CANNOT RECALL.

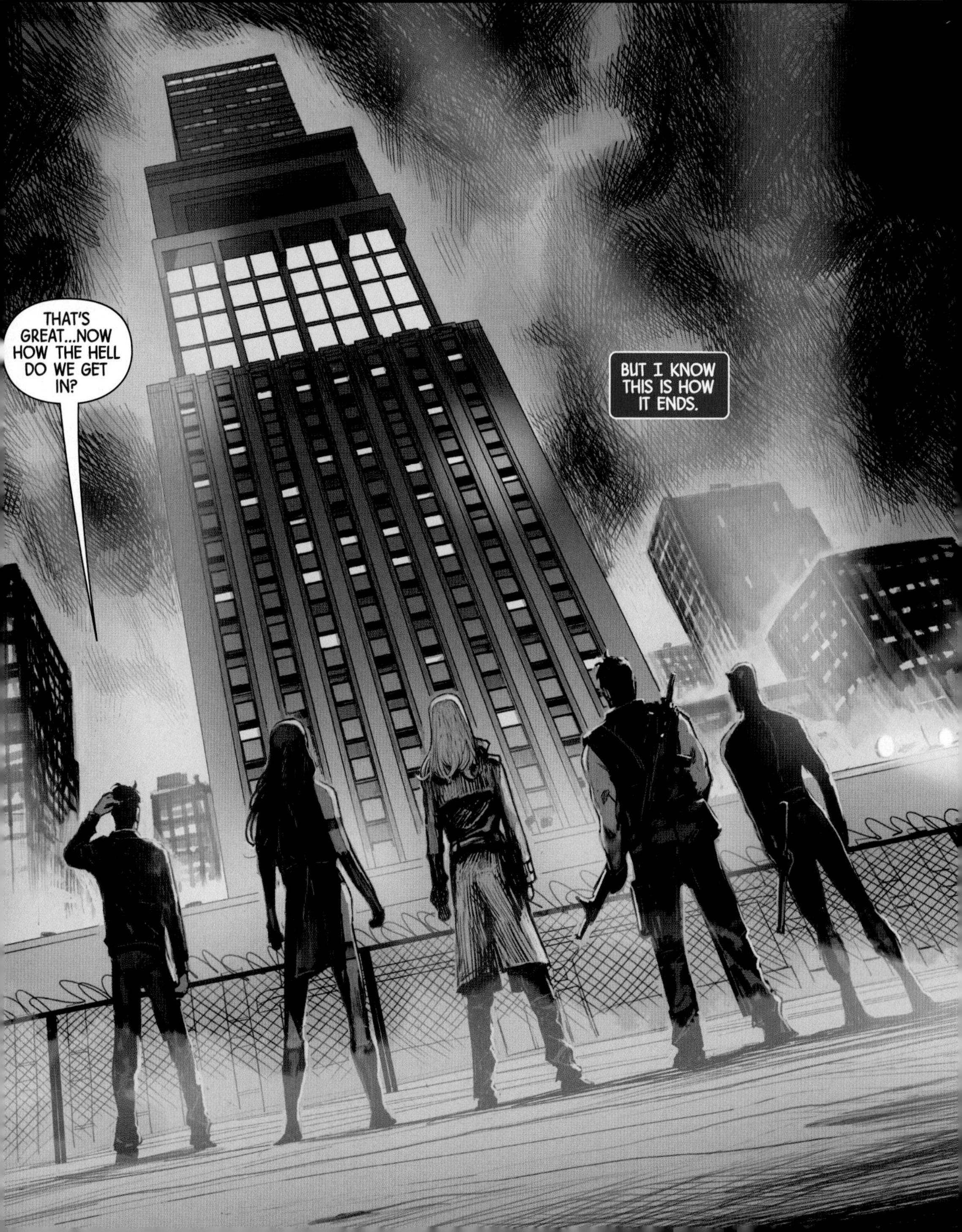
THAT'S GREAT...NOW HOW THE HELL DO WE GET IN?
BUT I KNOW THIS IS HOW IT ENDS.

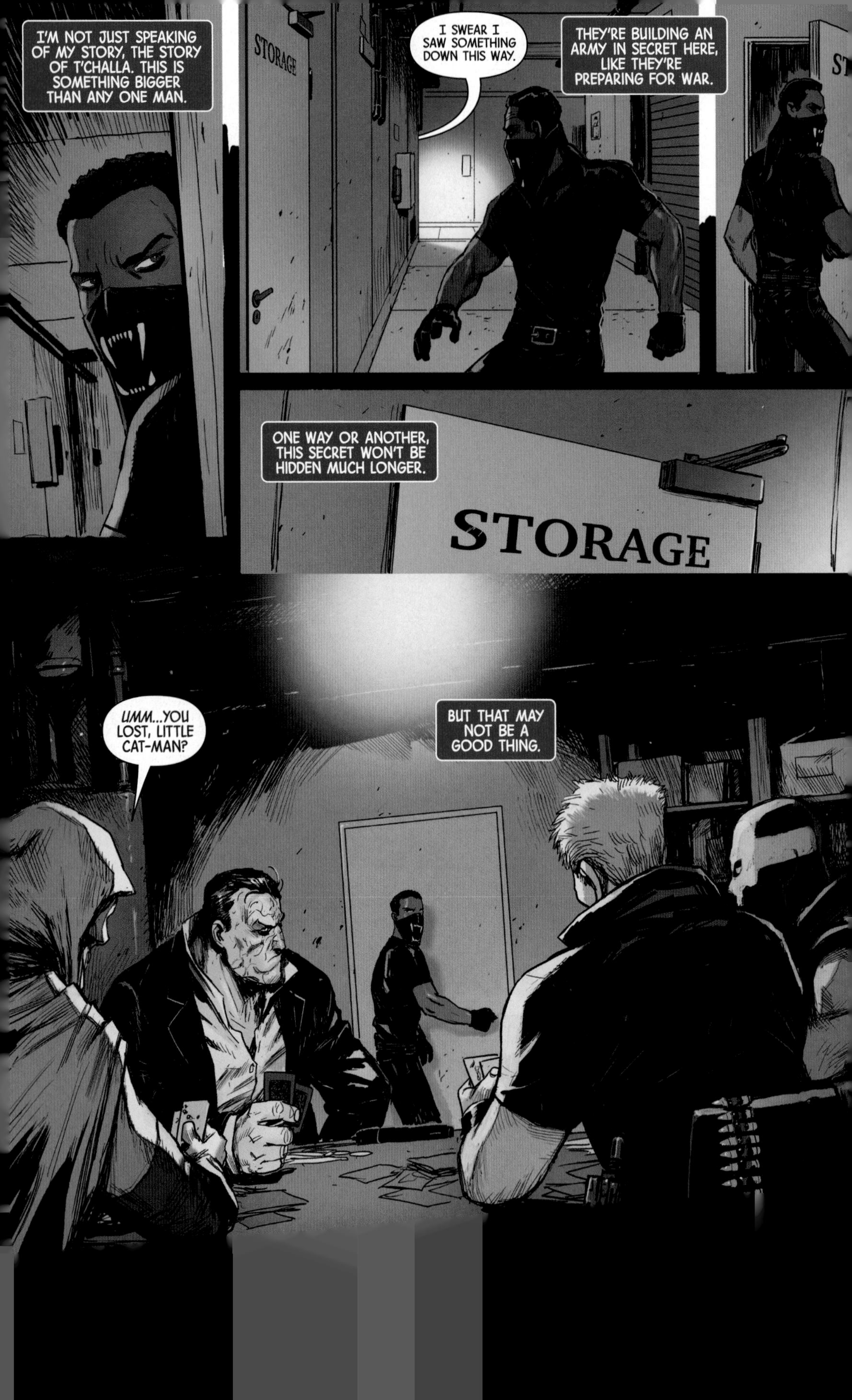
I'M NOT JUST SPEAKING OF MY STORY, THE STORY OF T'CHALLA. THIS IS SOMETHING BIGGER THAN ANY ONE MAN.
STORAGE
I SWEAR I SAW SOMETHING DOWN THIS WAY.
THEY'RE BUILDING AN ARMY IN SECRET HERE, LIKE THEY'RE PREPARING FOR WAR.
ONE WAY OR ANOTHER, THIS SECRET WON'T BE HIDDEN MUCH LONGER.
STORAGE
UMM...YOU LOST, LITTLE CAT-MAN?
BUT THAT MAY NOT BE A GOOD THING.

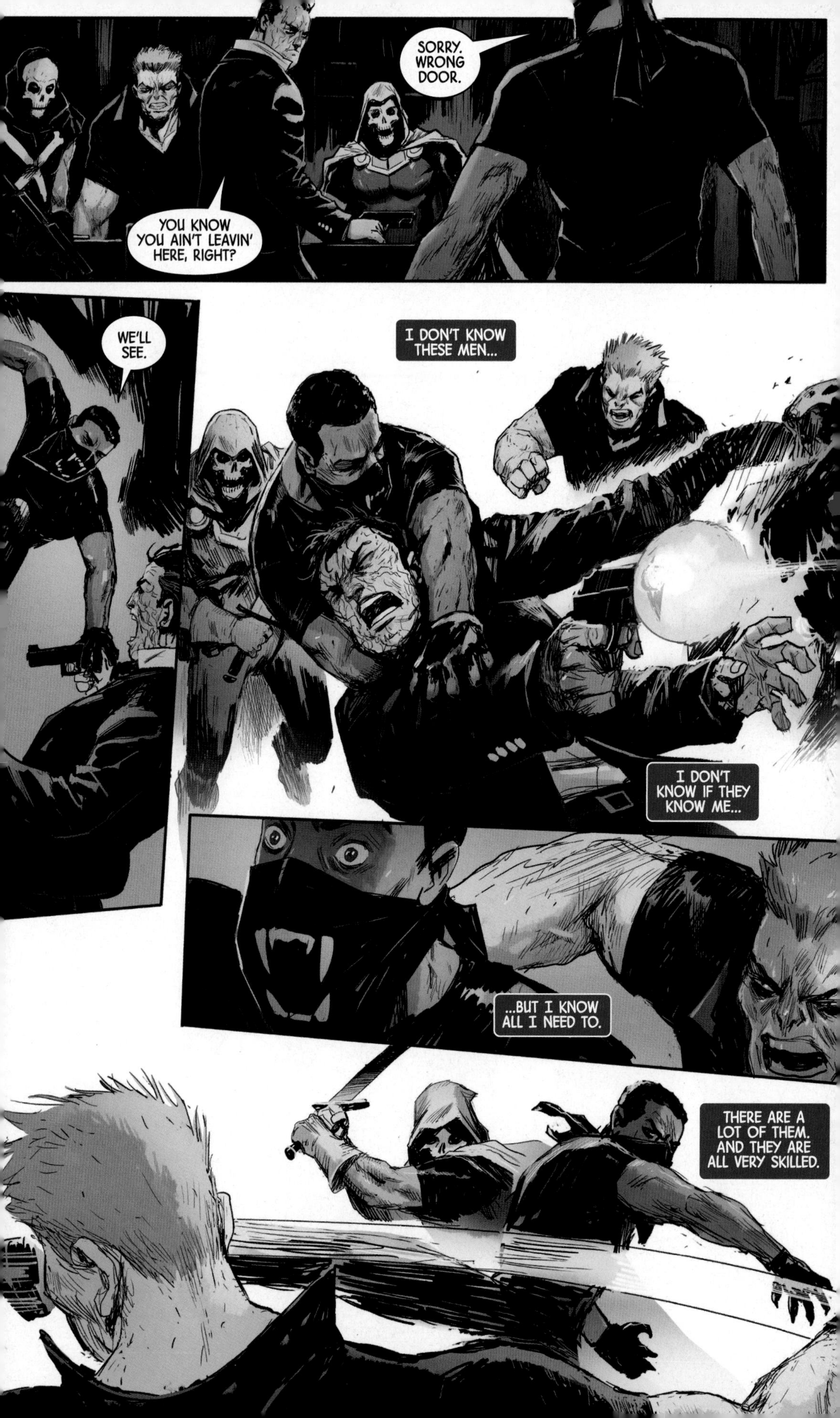
SORRY. WRONG DOOR.
YOU KNOW YOU AIN'T LEAVIN' HERE, RIGHT?
WE'LL SEE.
I DON'T KNOW THESE MEN...
I DON'T KNOW IF THEY KNOW ME...
...BUT I KNOW ALL I NEED TO.
THERE ARE A LOT OF THEM. AND THEY ARE ALL VERY SKILLED.

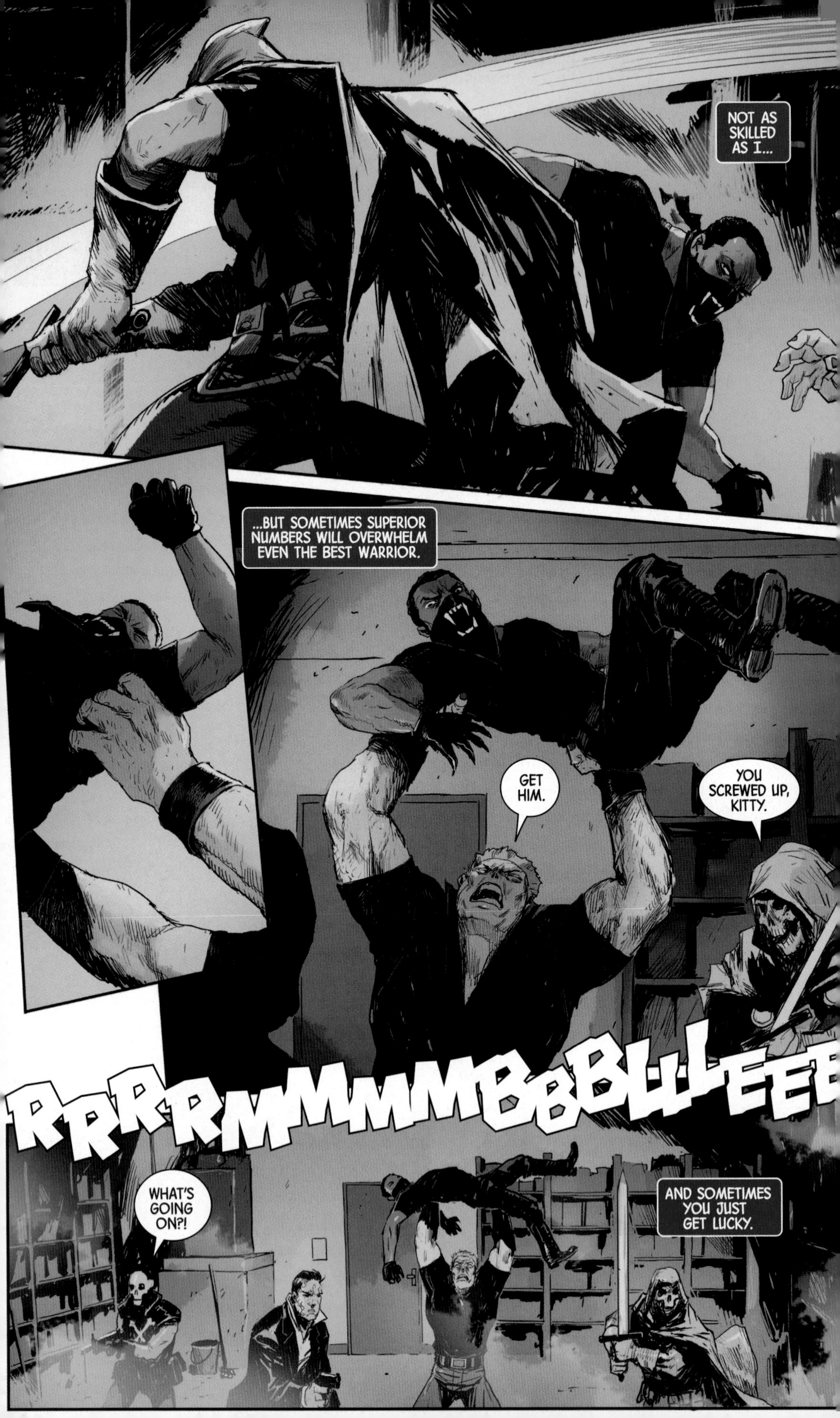
NOT AS SKILLED AS I...
...BUT SOMETIMES SUPERIOR NUMBERS WILL OVERWHELM EVEN THE BEST WARRIOR.
GET HIM.
YOU SCREWED UP, KITTY.
RRRRMMMMMBBBLLLEEE
WHAT'S GOING ON?!
AND SOMETIMES YOU JUST GET LUCKY.

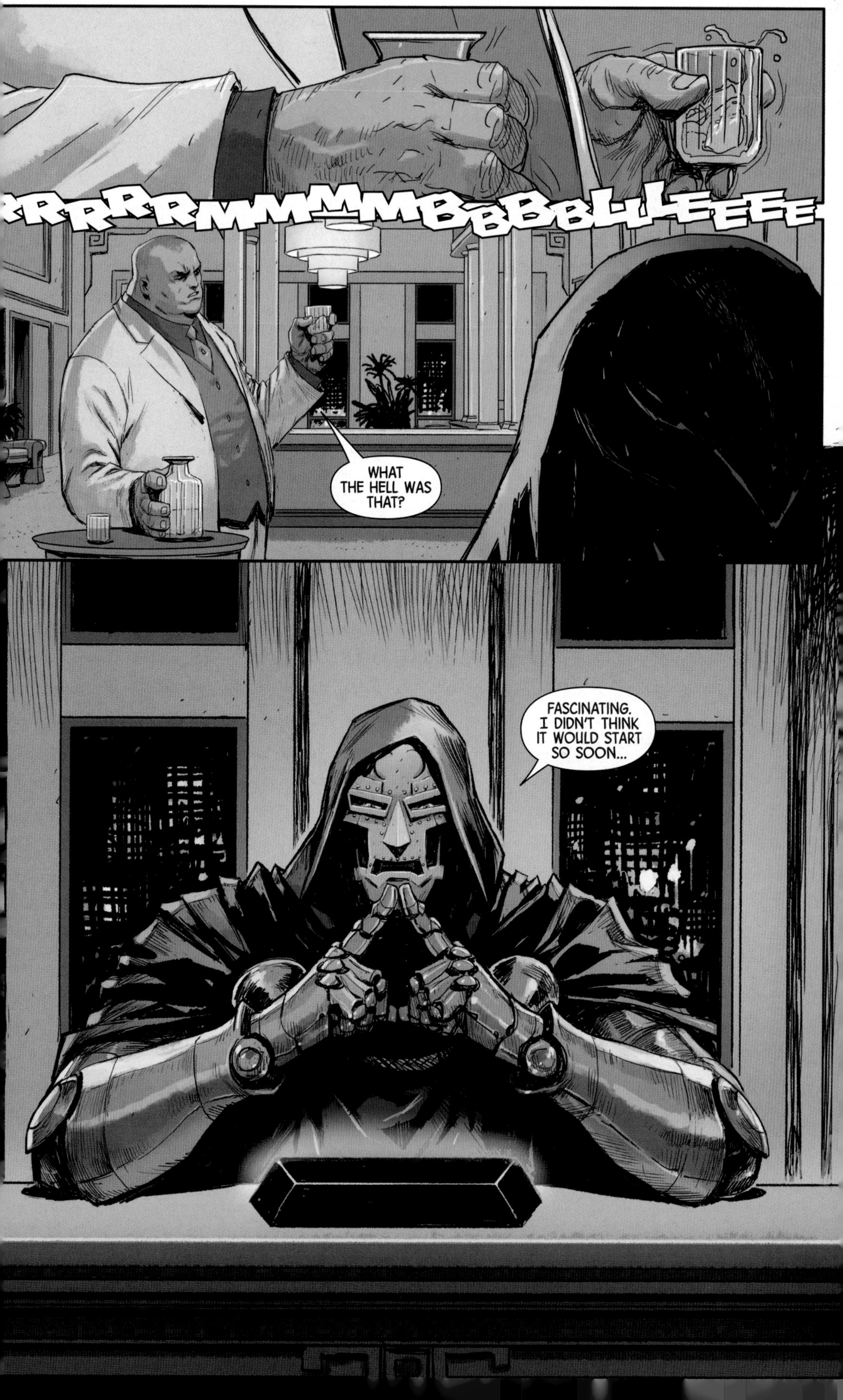

RRRRRMMMMMBBBBBLLLEEEE
WHAT THE HELL WAS THAT?
FASCINATING. I DIDN'T THINK IT WOULD START SO SOON...

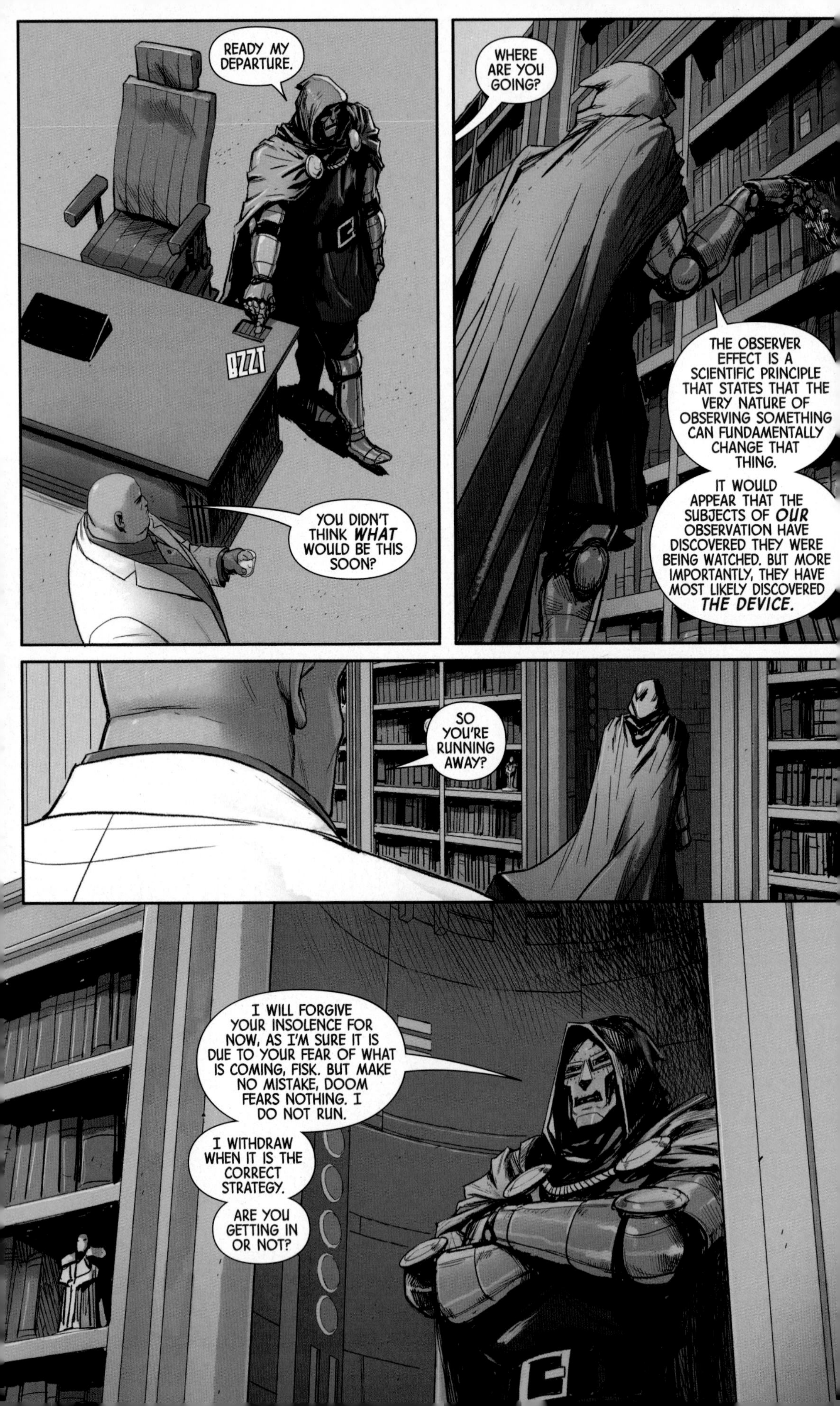
READY MY DEPARTURE.
BZZT
YOU DIDN'T THINK WHAT WOULD BE THIS SOON?
WHERE ARE YOU GOING?
THE OBSERVER EFFECT IS A SCIENTIFIC PRINCIPLE THAT STATES THAT THE VERY NATURE OF OBSERVING SOMETHING CAN FUNDAMENTALLY CHANGE THAT THING.
IT WOULD APPEAR THAT THE SUBJECTS OF OUR OBSERVATION HAVE DISCOVERED THEY WERE BEING WATCHED. BUT MORE IMPORTANTLY, THEY HAVE MOST LIKELY DISCOVERED THE DEVICE.
SO YOU'RE RUNNING AWAY?
I WILL FORGIVE YOUR INSOLENCE FOR NOW, AS I'M SURE IT IS DUE TO YOUR FEAR OF WHAT IS COMING, FISK. BUT MAKE NO MISTAKE, DOOM FEARS NOTHING. I DO NOT RUN.
I WITHDRAW WHEN IT IS THE CORRECT STRATEGY.
ARE YOU GETTING IN OR NOT?

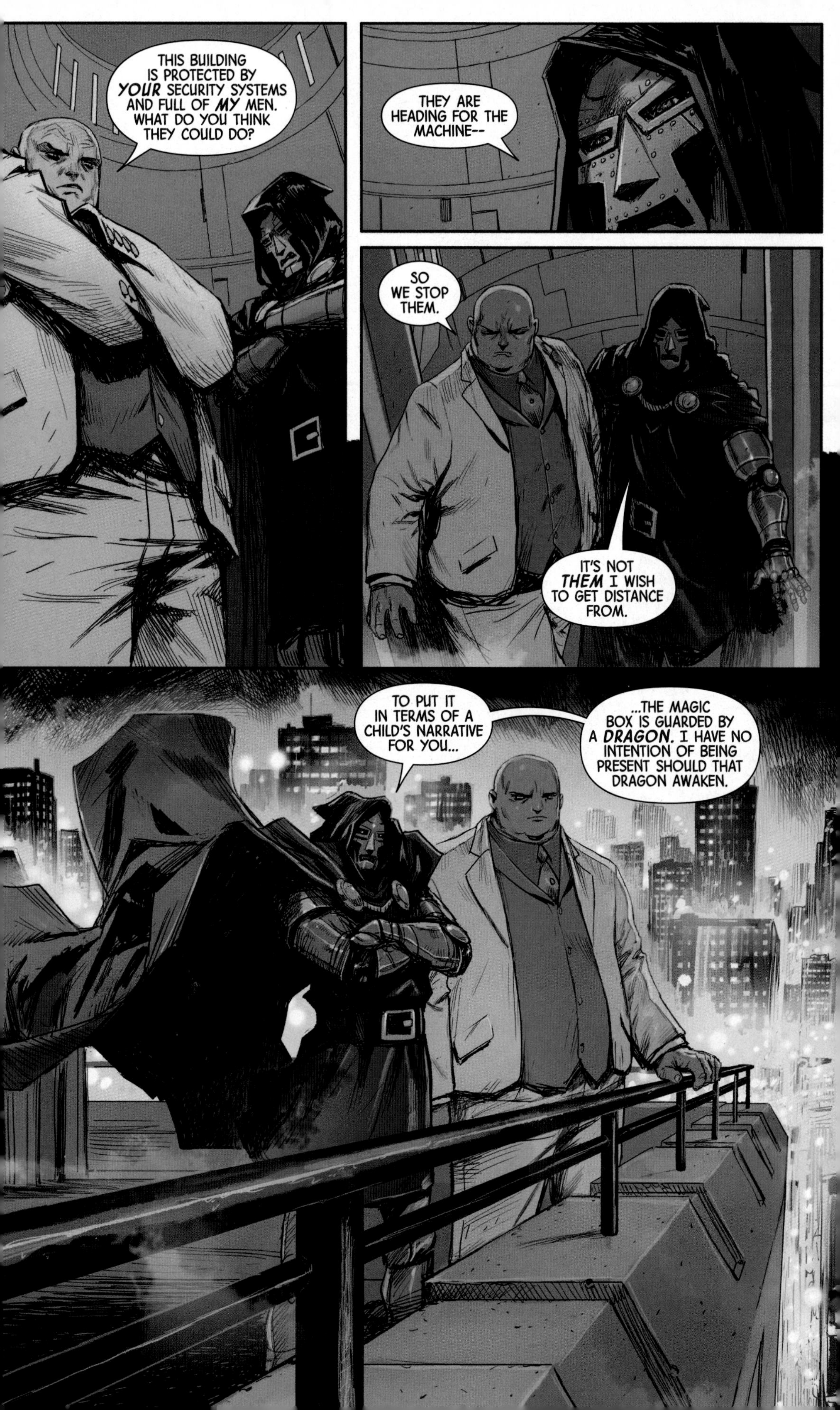
THIS BUILDING IS PROTECTED BY YOUR SECURITY SYSTEMS AND FULL OF MY MEN. WHAT DO YOU THINK THEY COULD DO?
THEY ARE HEADING FOR THE MACHINE--
SO WE STOP THEM.
IT'S NOT THEM I WISH TO GET DISTANCE FROM.
TO PUT IT IN TERMS OF A CHILD'S NARRATIVE FOR YOU...
...THE MAGIC BOX IS GUARDED BY A DRAGON. I HAVE NO INTENTION OF BEING PRESENT SHOULD THAT DRAGON AWAKEN.

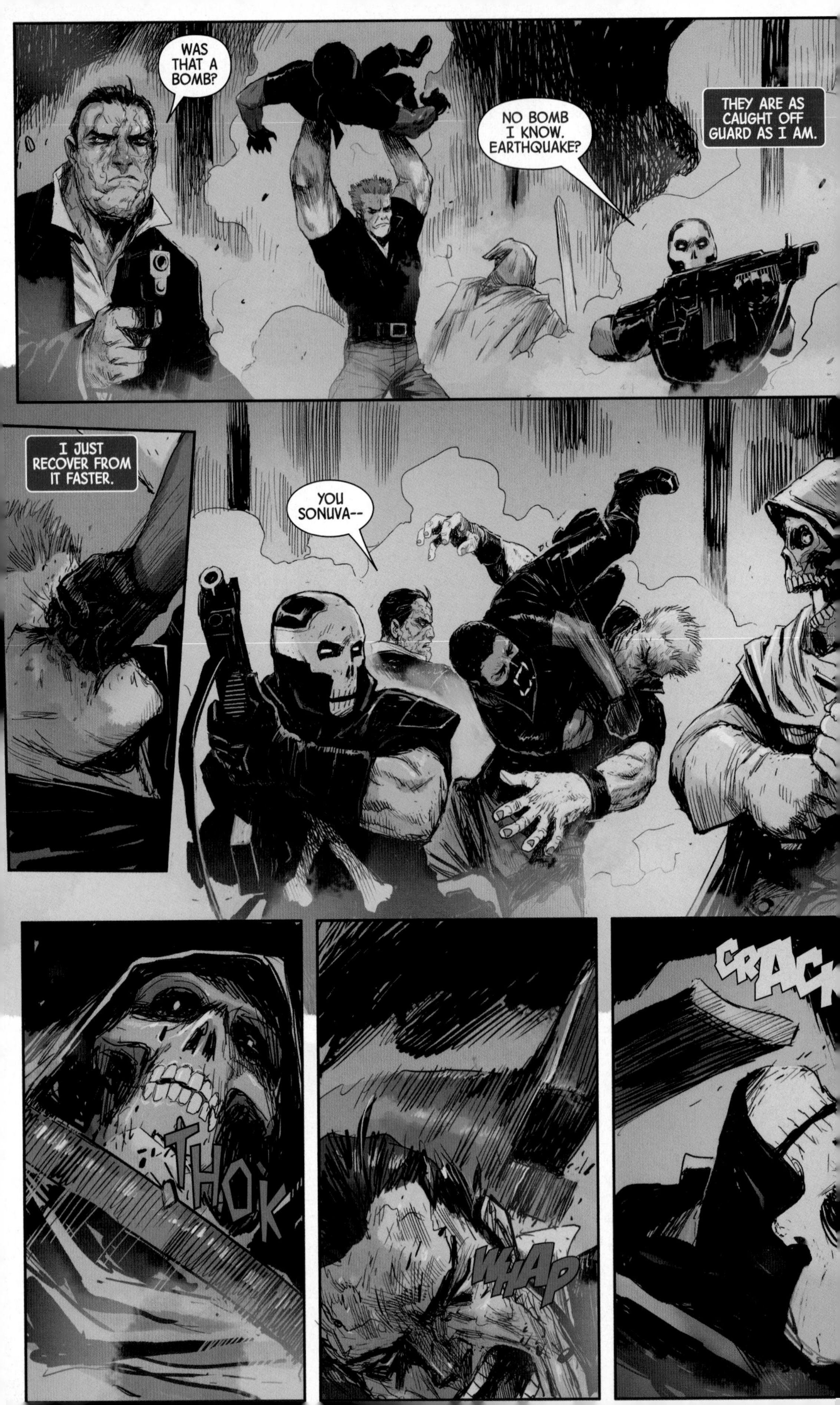

WAS THAT A BOMB?
NO BOMB I KNOW. EARTHQUAKE?
THEY ARE AS CAUGHT OFF GUARD AS I AM.
I JUST RECOVER FROM IT FASTER.
YOU SONUVA--
THOK
WHAP
CRACK

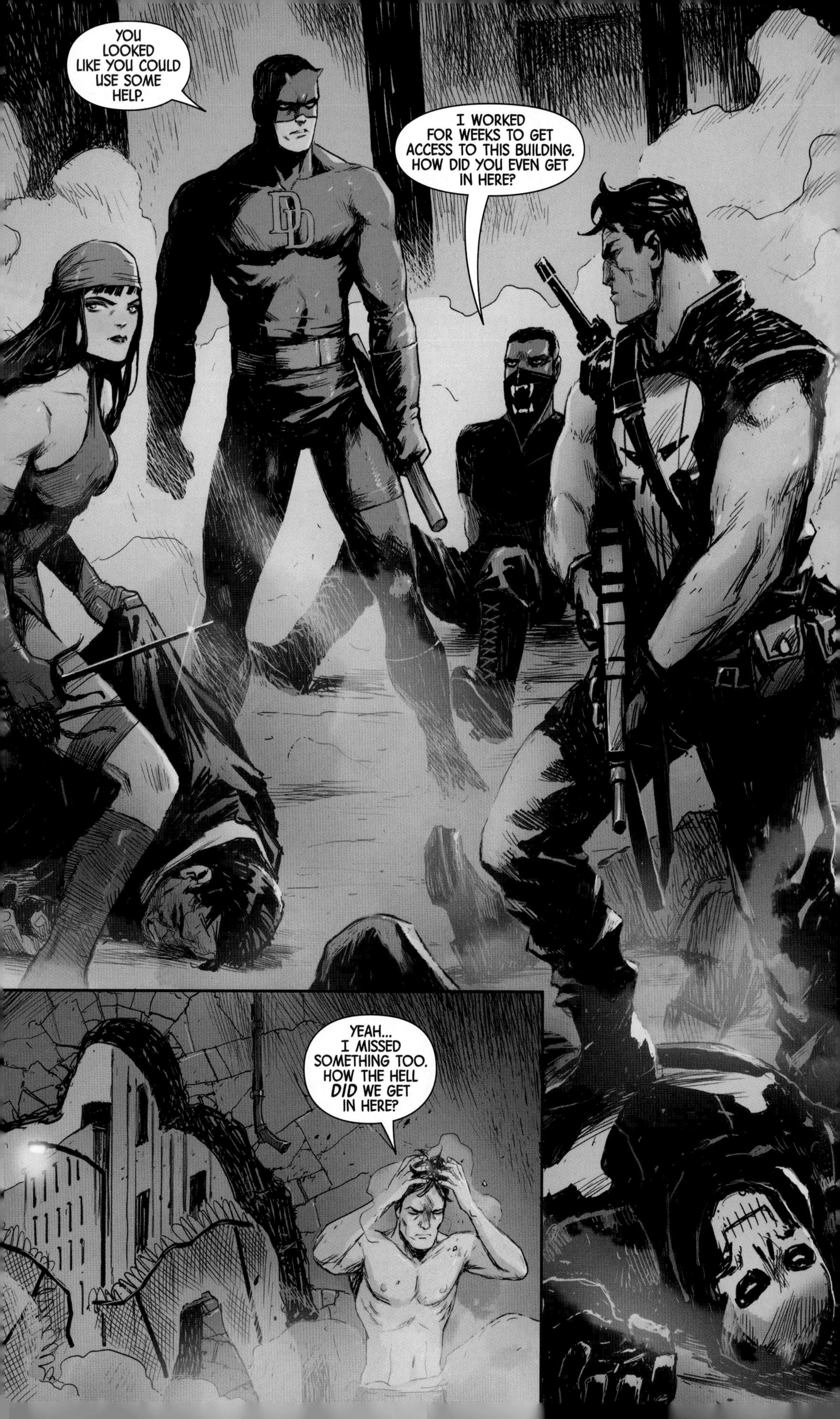
YOU LOOKED LIKE YOU COULD USE SOME HELP.
I WORKED FOR WEEKS TO GET ACCESS TO THIS BUILDING. HOW DID YOU EVEN GET IN HERE?
YEAH... I MISSED SOMETHING TOO. HOW THE HELL *DID* WE GET IN HERE?

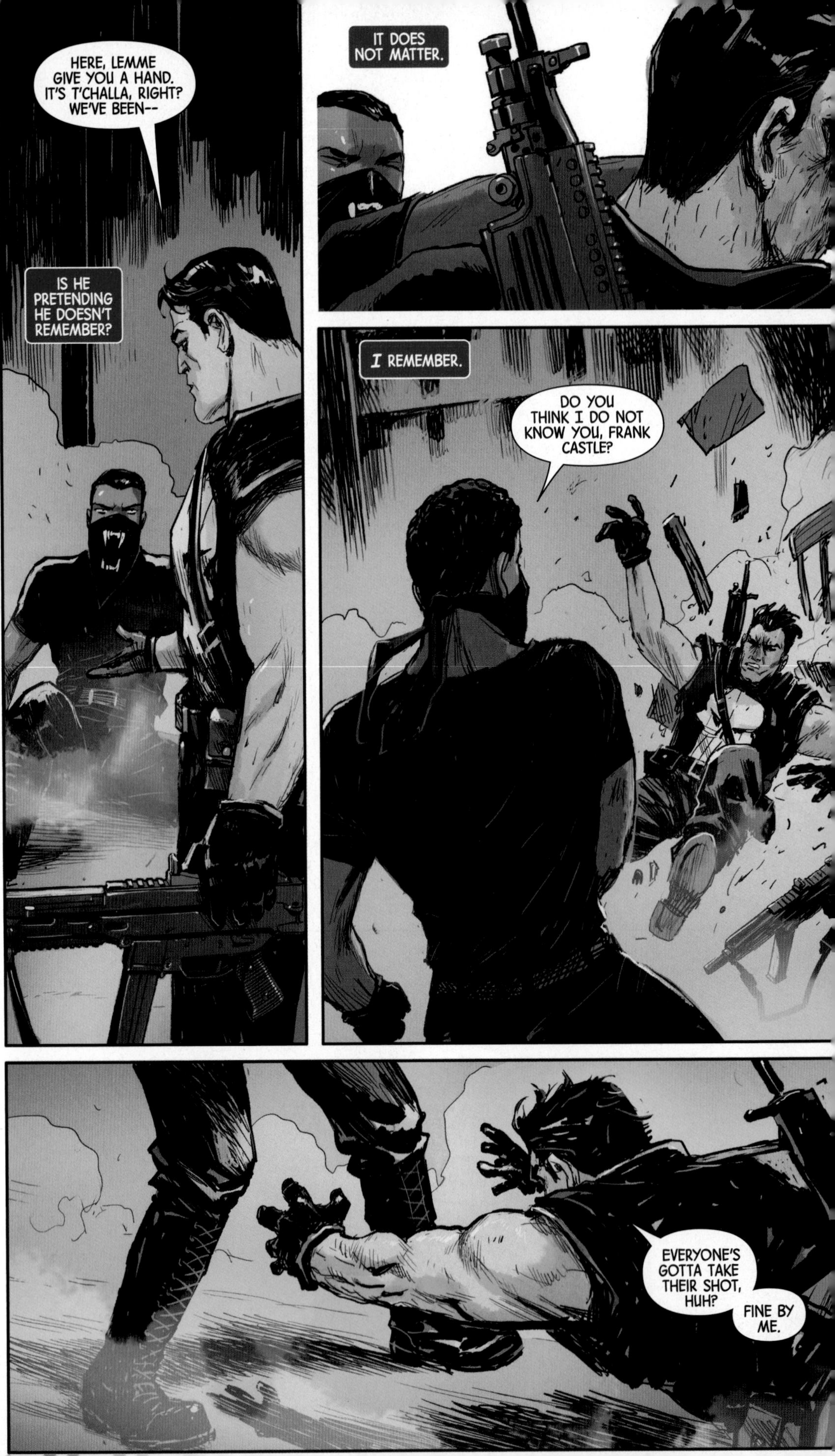
HERE, LEMME GIVE YOU A HAND. IT'S T'CHALLA, RIGHT? WE'VE BEEN--
IS HE PRETENDING HE DOESN'T REMEMBER?
IT DOES NOT MATTER.
I REMEMBER.
DO YOU THINK I DO NOT KNOW YOU, FRANK CASTLE?
EVERYONE'S GOTTA TAKE THEIR SHOT, HUH?
FINE BY ME.

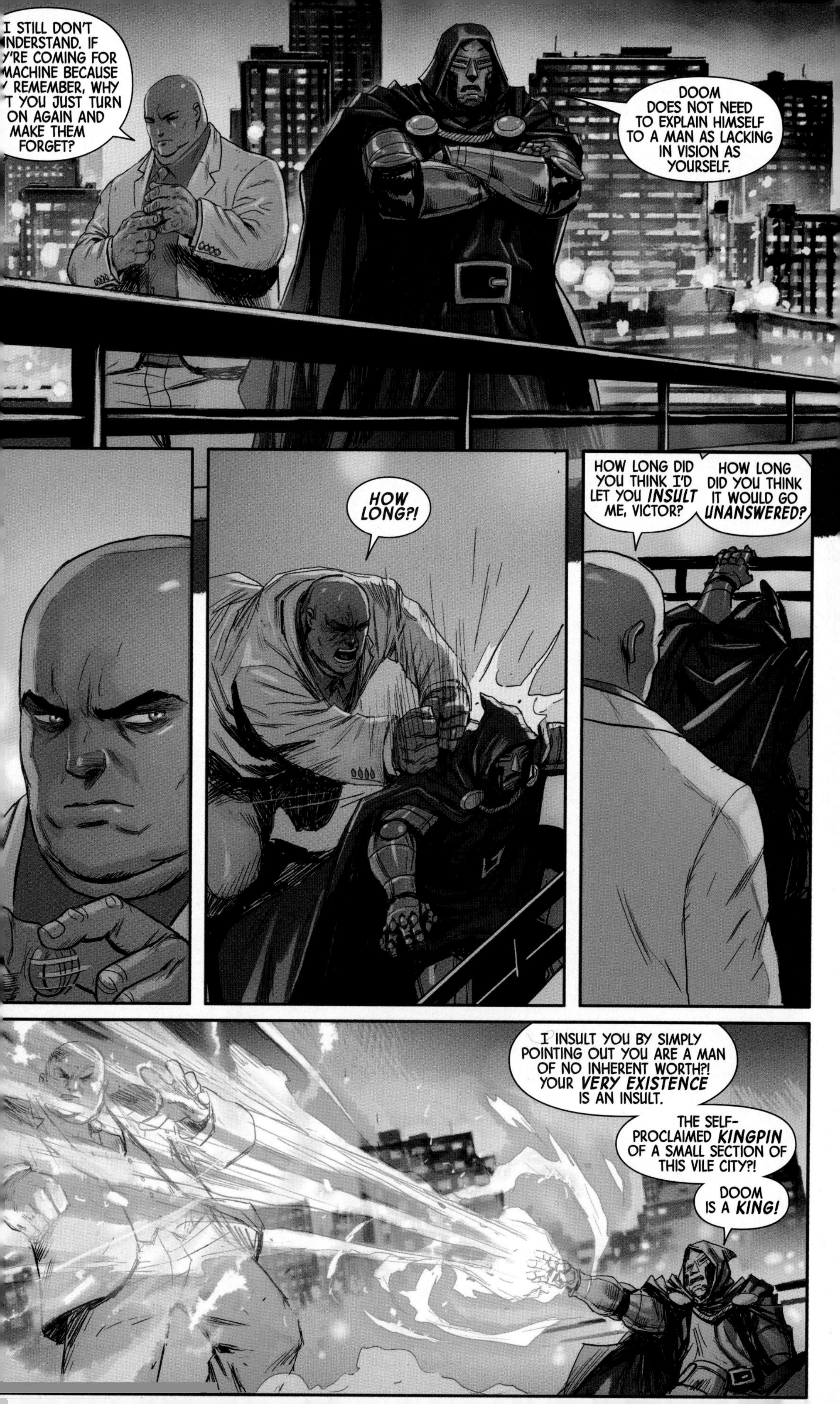

I STILL DON'T NDERSTAND. IF Y'RE COMING FOR MACHINE BECAUSE REMEMBER, WHY T YOU JUST TURN ON AGAIN AND MAKE THEM FORGET?
DOOM DOES NOT NEED TO EXPLAIN HIMSELF TO A MAN AS LACKING IN VISION AS YOURSELF.
HOW LONG?!
HOW LONG DID YOU THINK I'D LET YOU INSULT ME, VICTOR?
HOW LONG DID YOU THINK IT WOULD GO UNANSWERED?
I INSULT YOU BY SIMPLY POINTING OUT YOU ARE A MAN OF NO INHERENT WORTH?! YOUR VERY EXISTENCE IS AN INSULT.
THE SELF-PROCLAIMED KINGPIN OF A SMALL SECTION OF THIS VILE CITY?!
DOOM IS A KING!

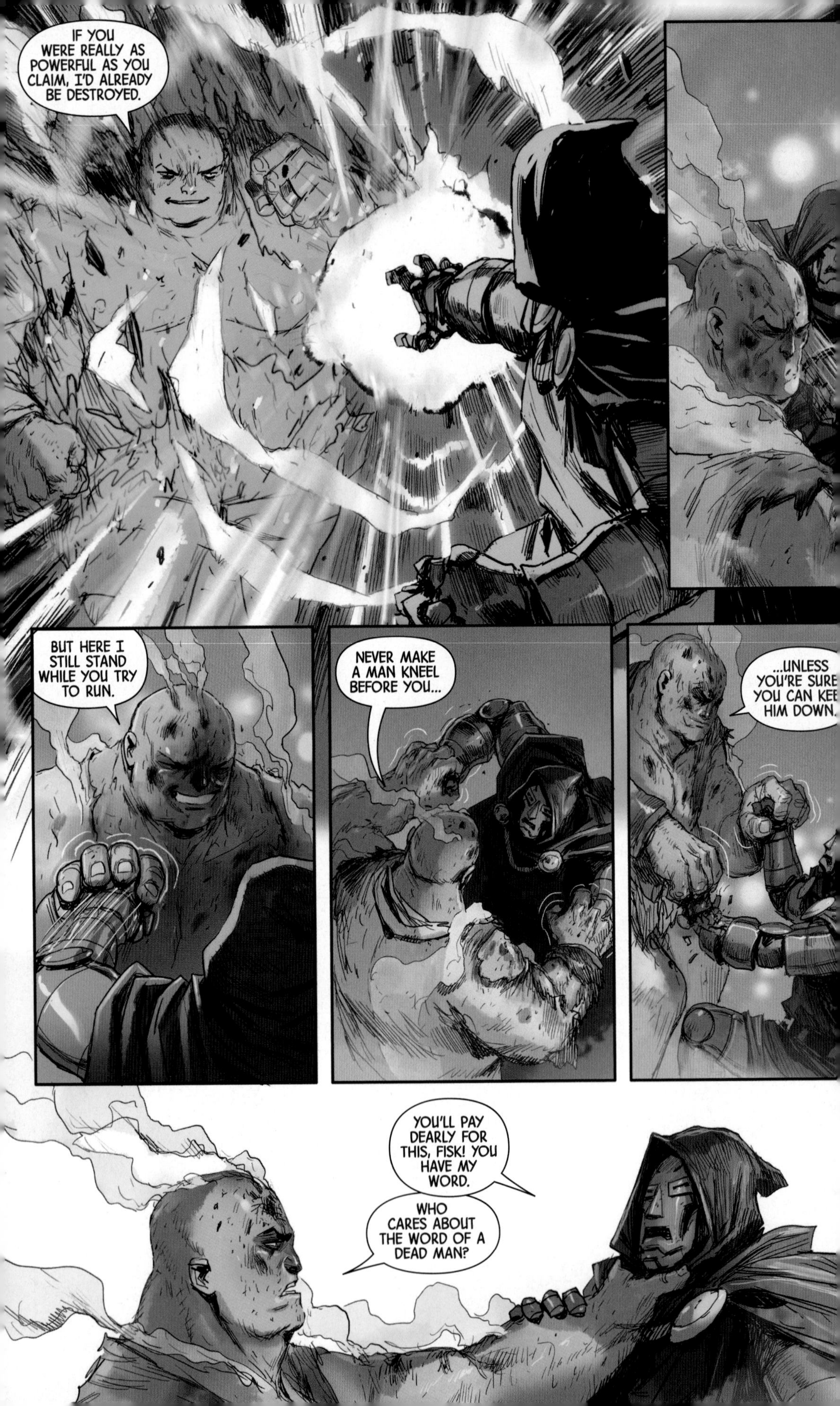

IF YOU WERE REALLY AS POWERFUL AS YOU CLAIM, I'D ALREADY BE DESTROYED.
BUT HERE I STILL STAND WHILE YOU TRY TO RUN.
NEVER MAKE A MAN KNEEL BEFORE YOU...
...UNLESS YOU'RE SURE YOU CAN KEE HIM DOWN.
YOU'LL PAY DEARLY FOR THIS, FISK! YOU HAVE MY WORD.
WHO CARES ABOUT THE WORD OF A DEAD MAN?

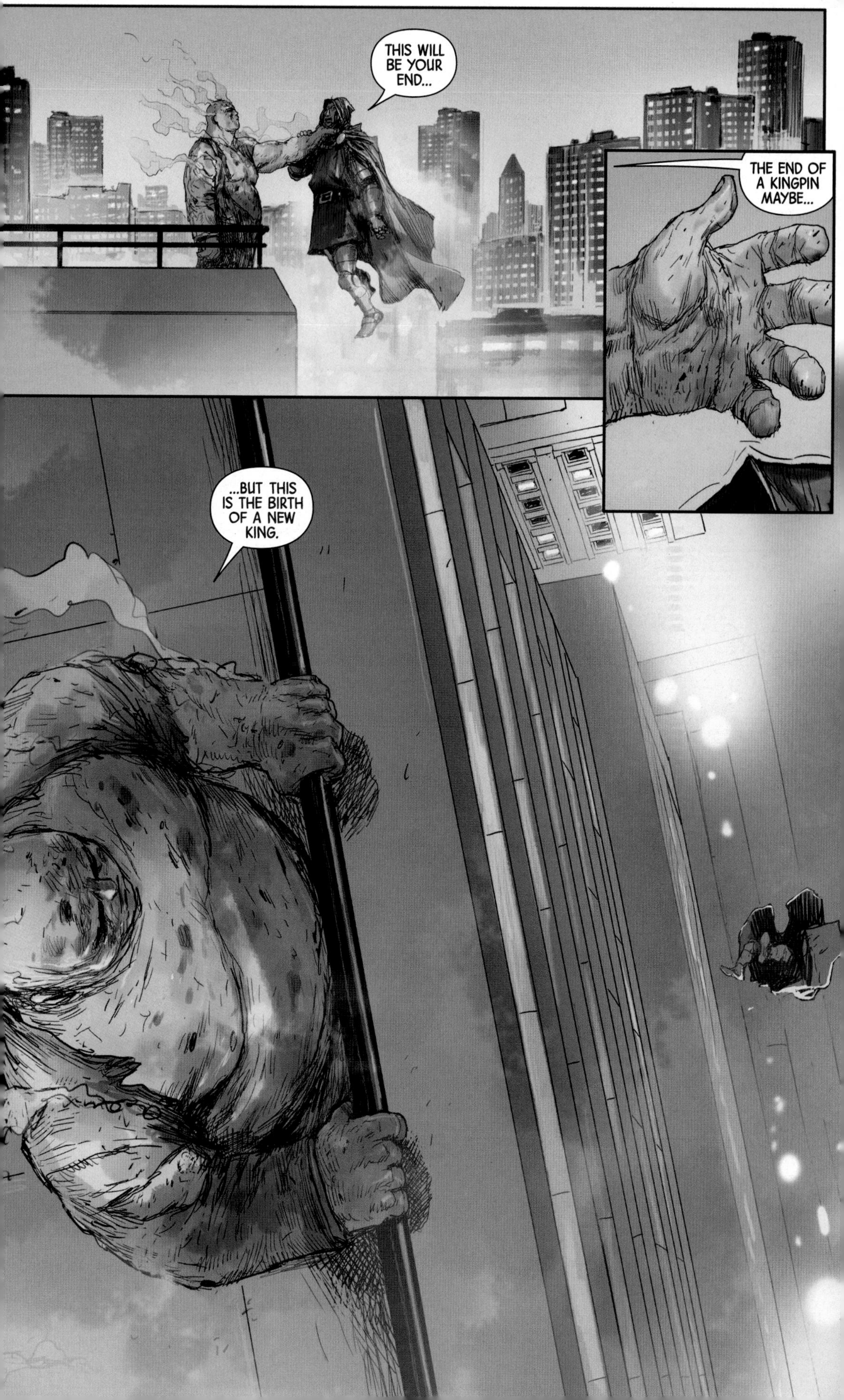
THIS WILL BE YOUR END...
THE END OF A KINGPIN MAYBE...
...BUT THIS IS THE BIRTH OF A NEW KING.

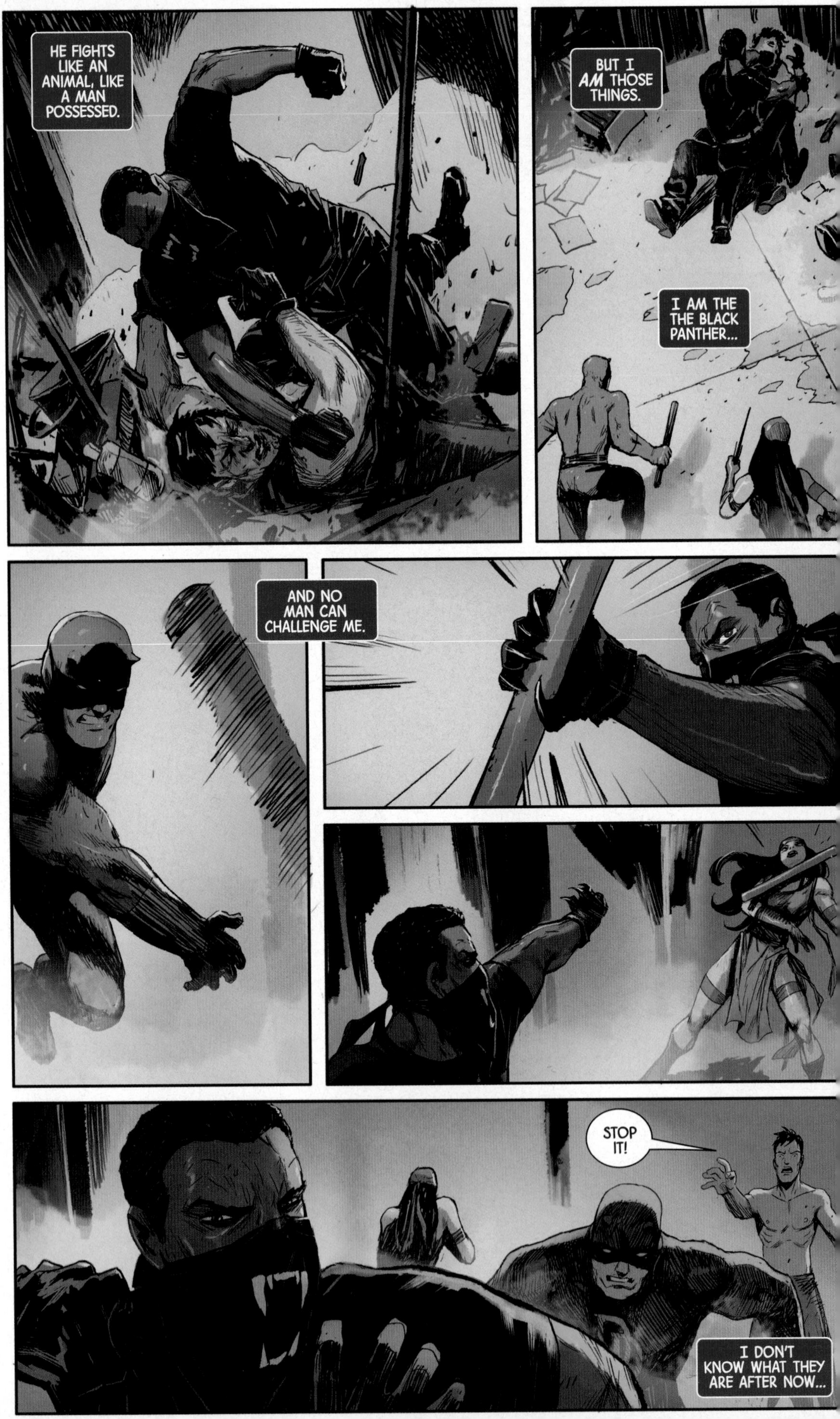
HE FIGHTS LIKE AN ANIMAL, LIKE A MAN POSSESSED.
BUT I AM THOSE THINGS.
I AM THE THE BLACK PANTHER...
AND NO MAN CAN CHALLENGE ME.
STOP IT!
I DON'T KNOW WHAT THEY ARE AFTER NOW...

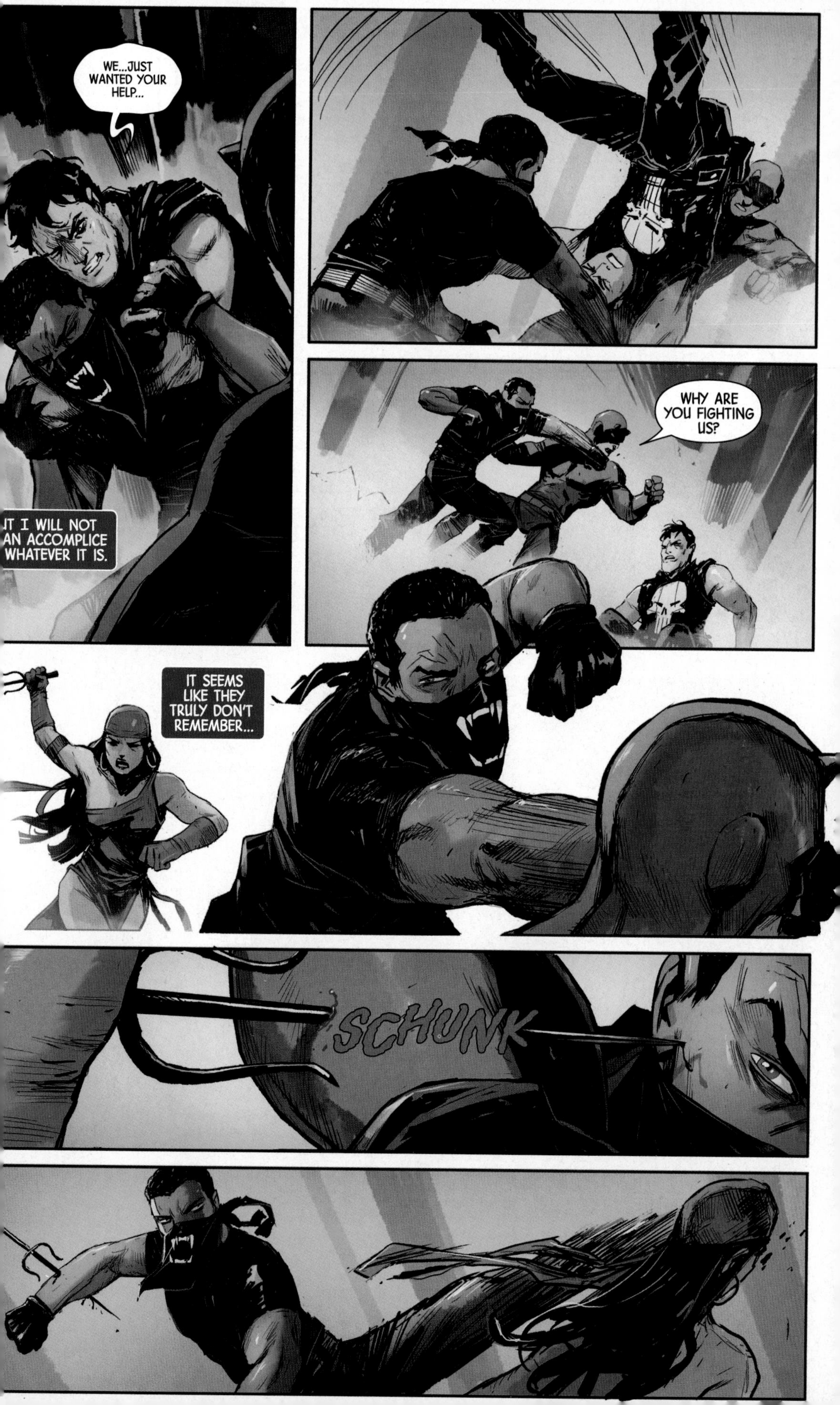
WE...JUST WANTED YOUR HELP...
IT I WILL NOT AN ACCOMPLICE WHATEVER IT IS.
WHY ARE YOU FIGHTING US?
IT SEEMS LIKE THEY TRULY DON'T REMEMBER...
SCHUNK

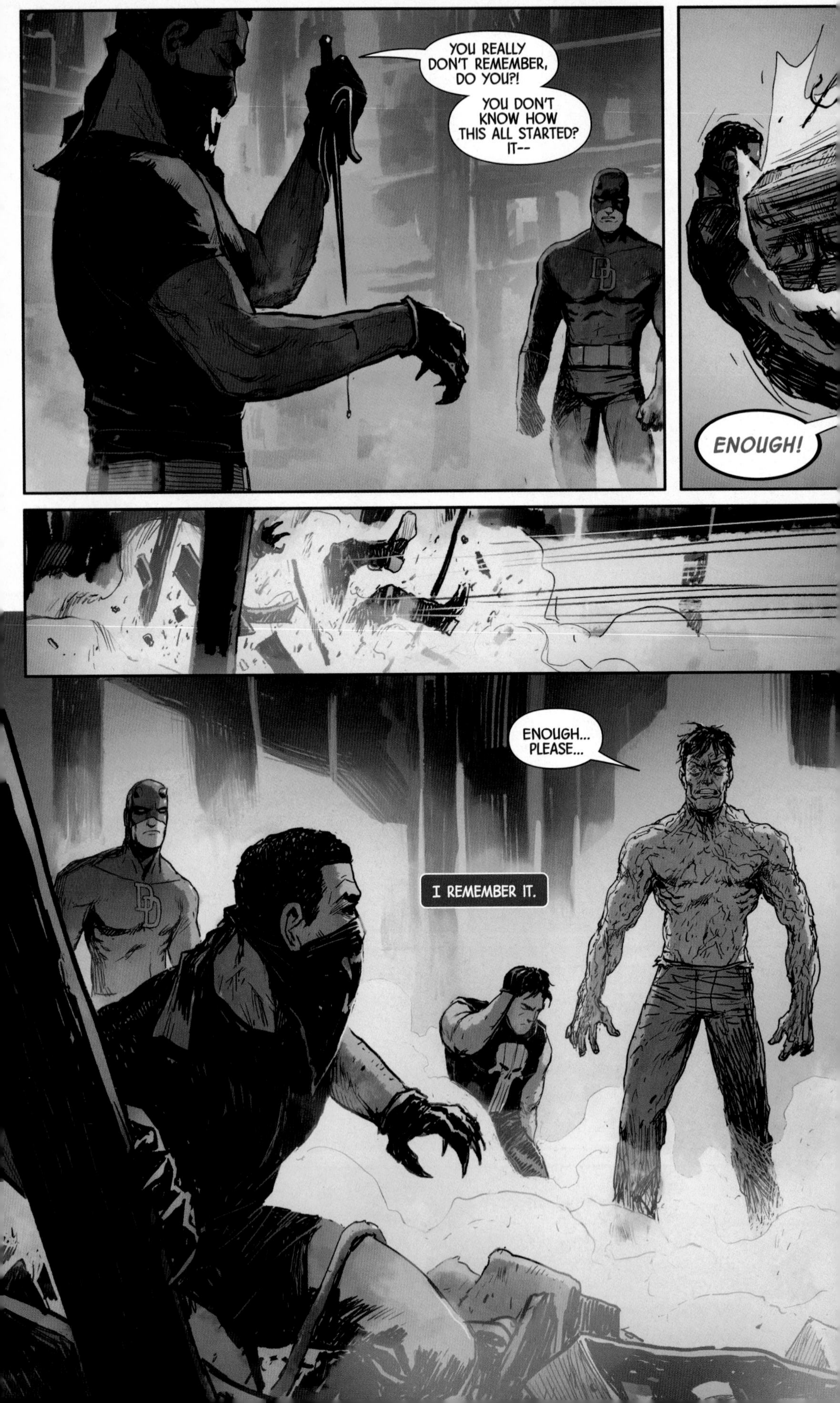
YOU REALLY DON'T REMEMBER, DO YOU?!
YOU DON'T KNOW HOW THIS ALL STARTED? IT--
ENOUGH!
ENOUGH... PLEASE...
I REMEMBER IT.

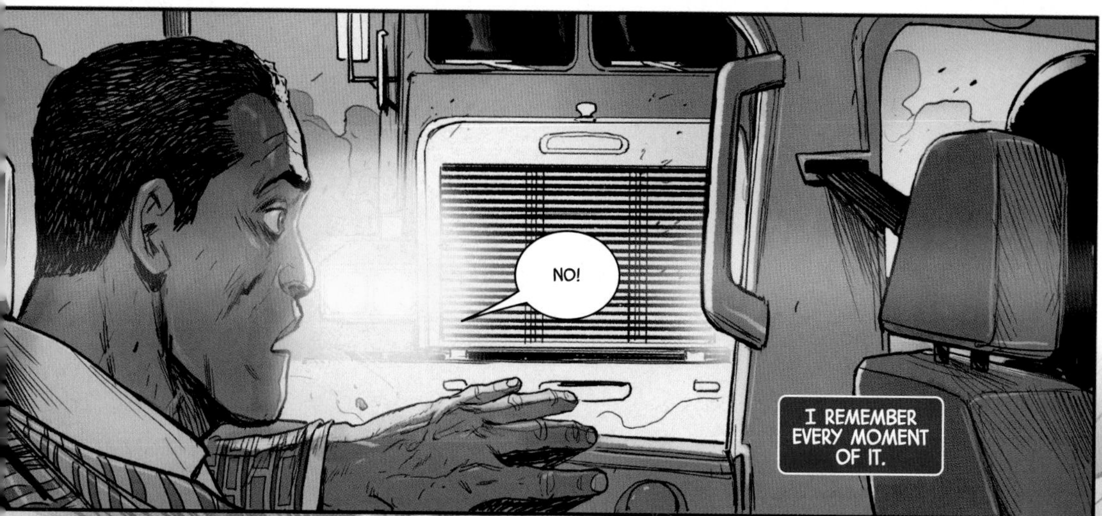
NO!
I REMEMBER EVERY MOMENT OF IT.

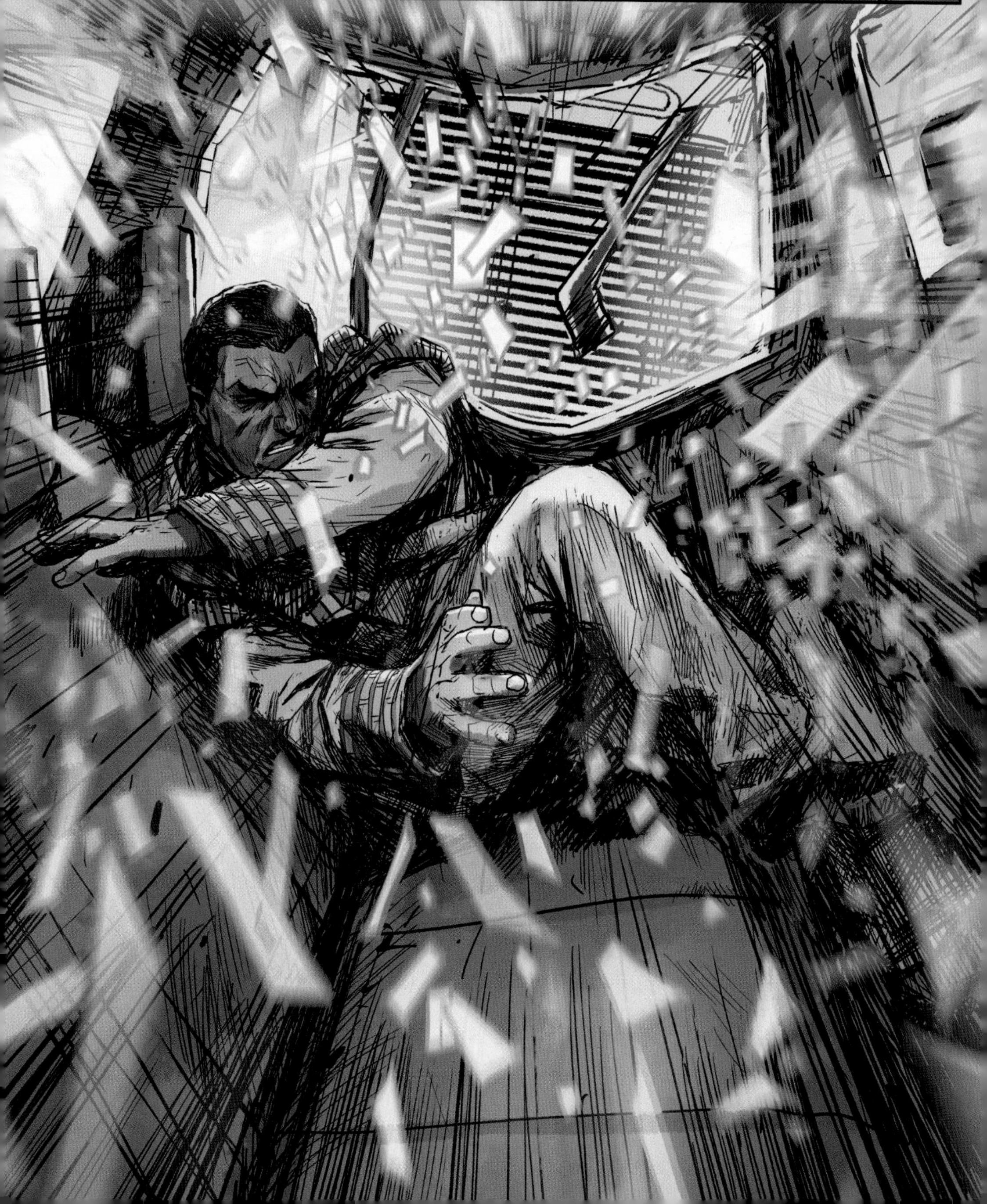

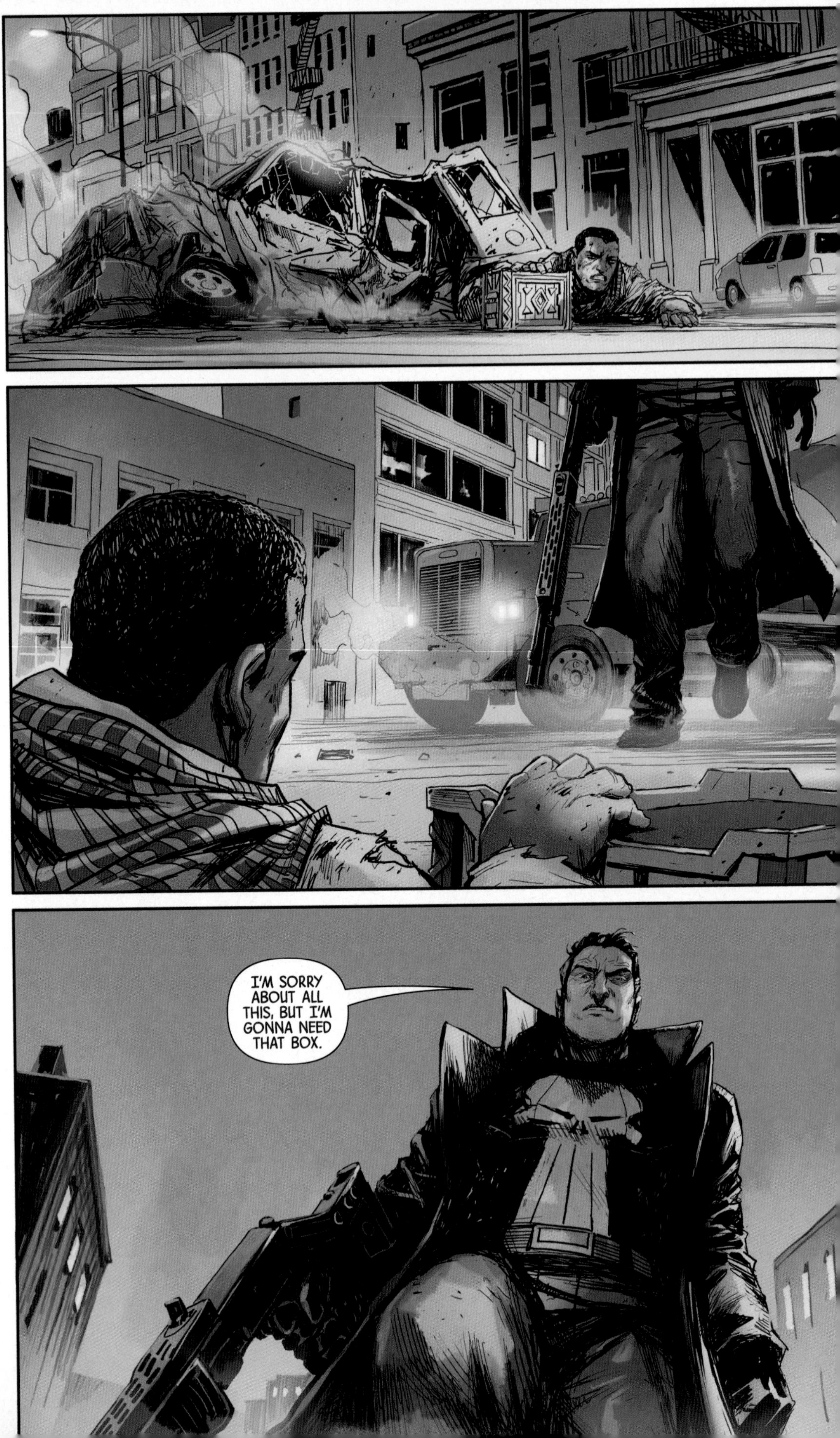
I'M SORRY ABOUT ALL THIS, BUT I'M GONNA NEED THAT BOX.

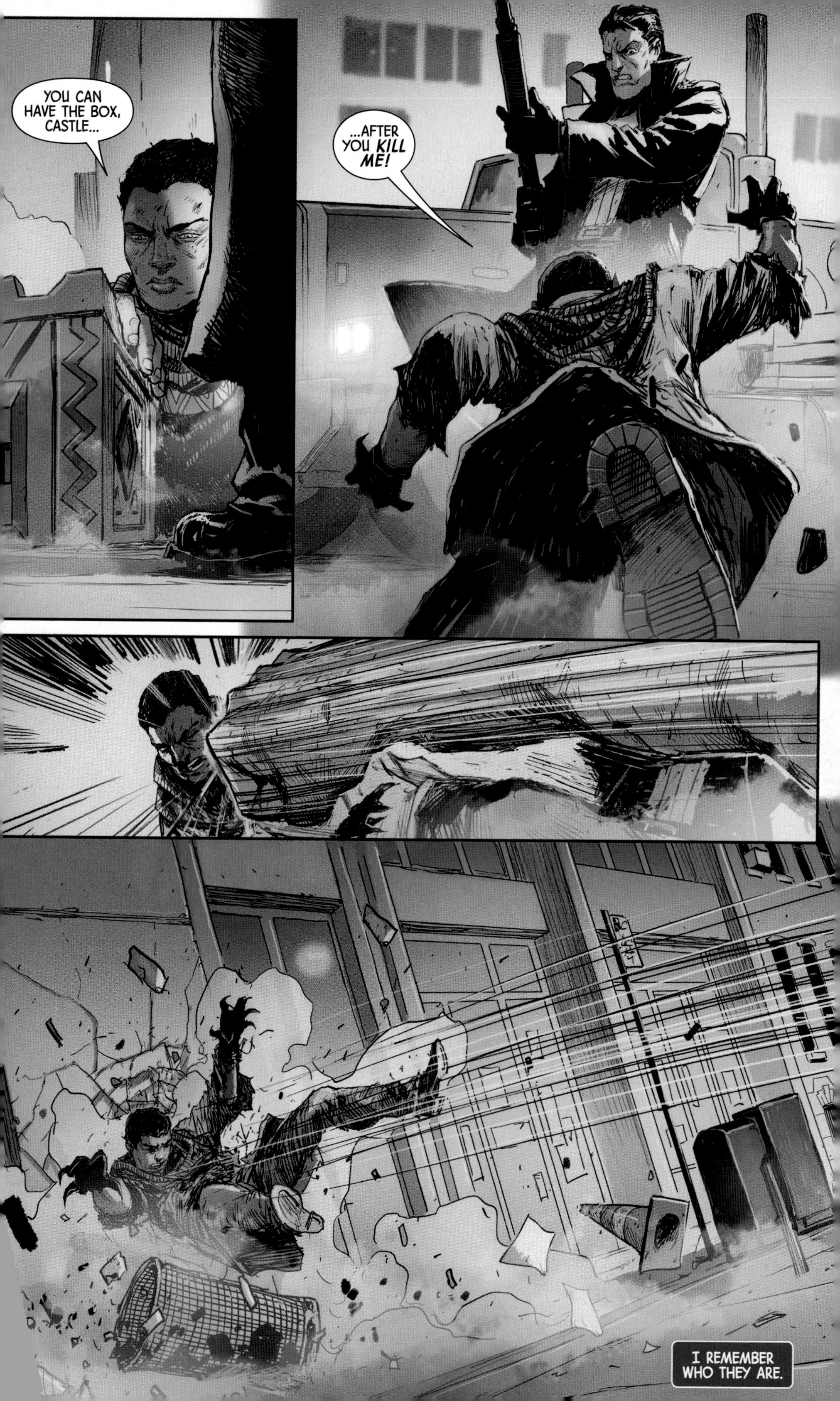
YOU CAN HAVE THE BOX, CASTLE...
...AFTER YOU KILL ME!
I REMEMBER WHO THEY ARE.

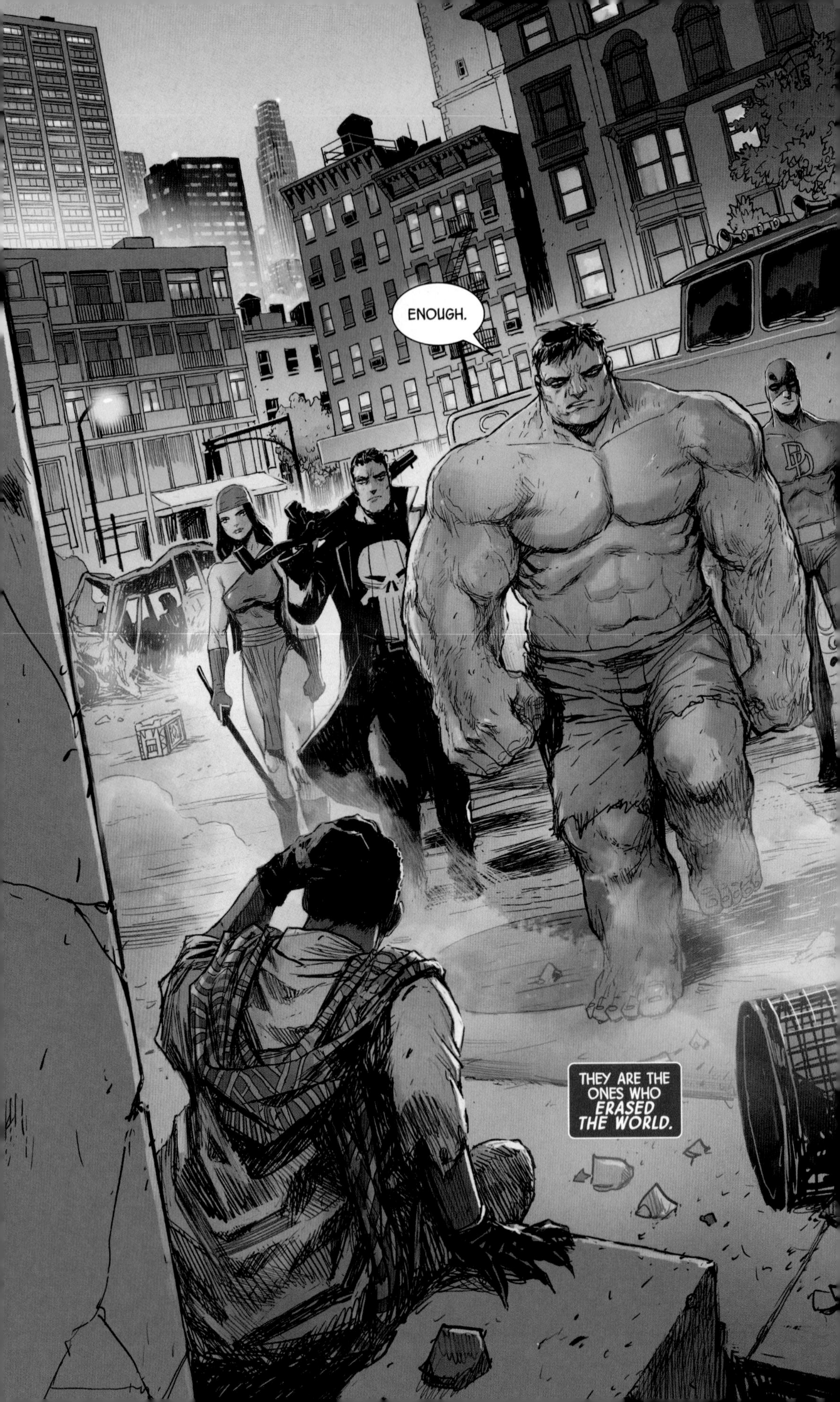
ENOUGH.
THEY ARE THE ONES WHO *ERASED THE WORLD.*

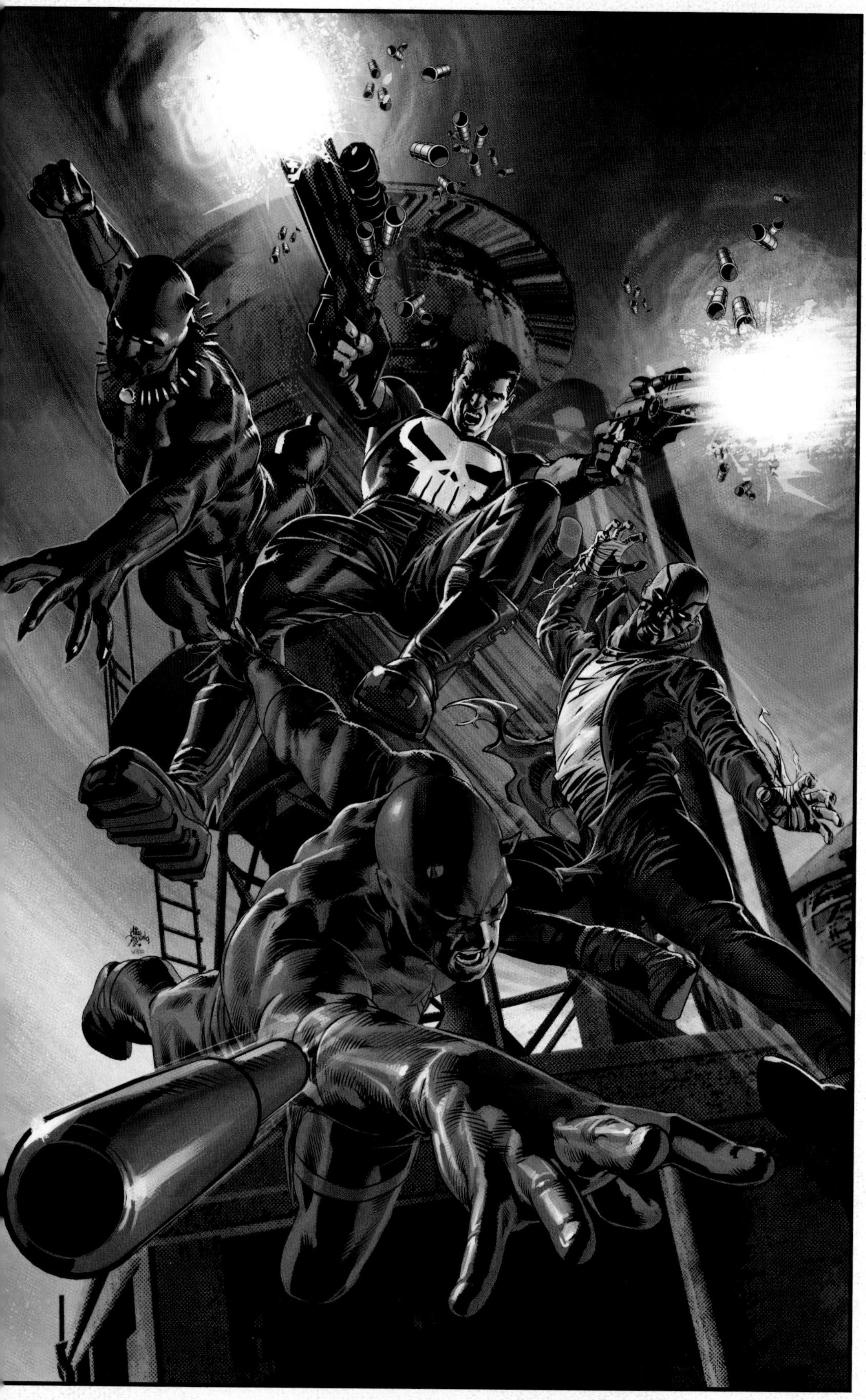

MIKE DEODATO JR. & DEAN WHITE
#1 variant

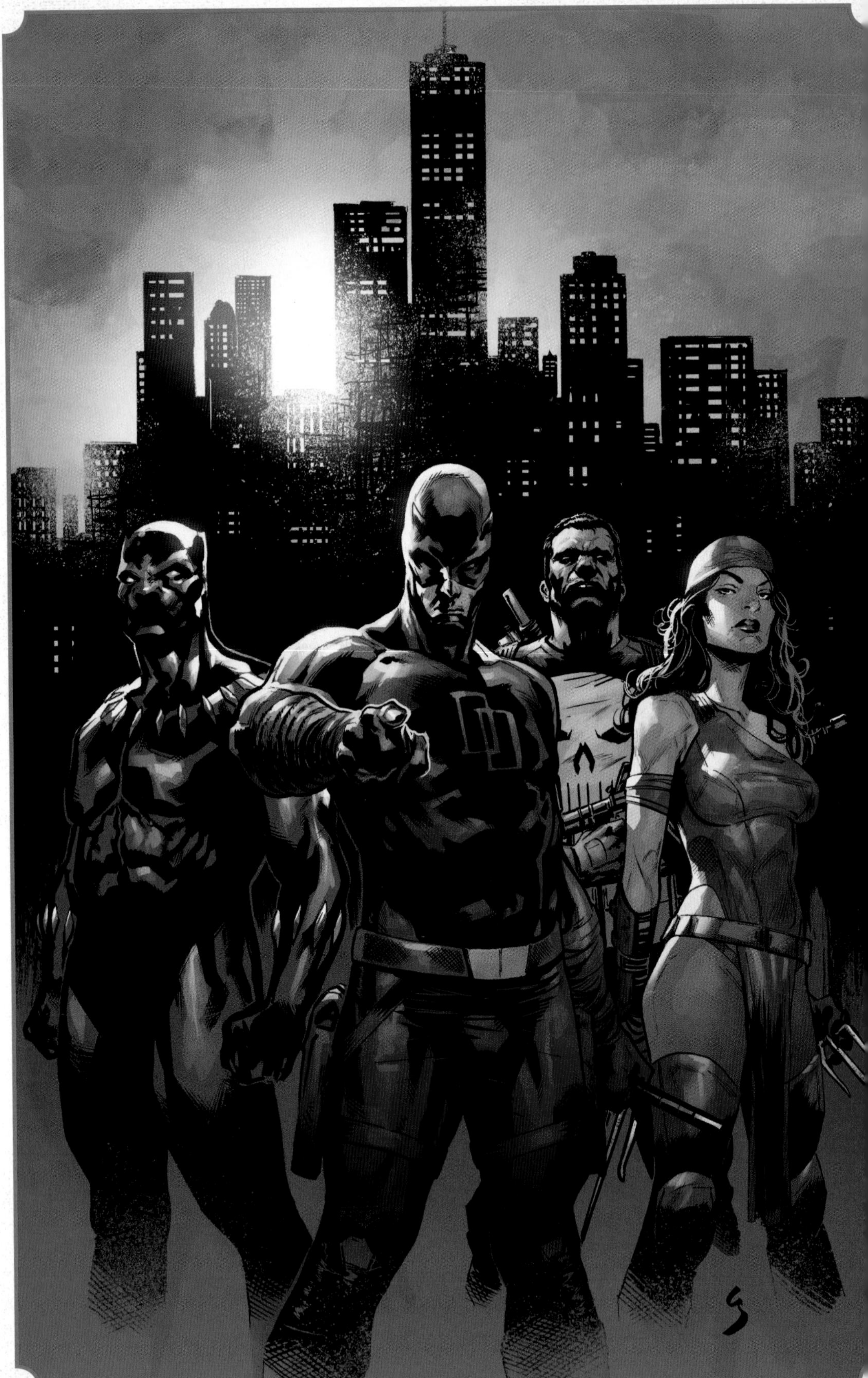

6

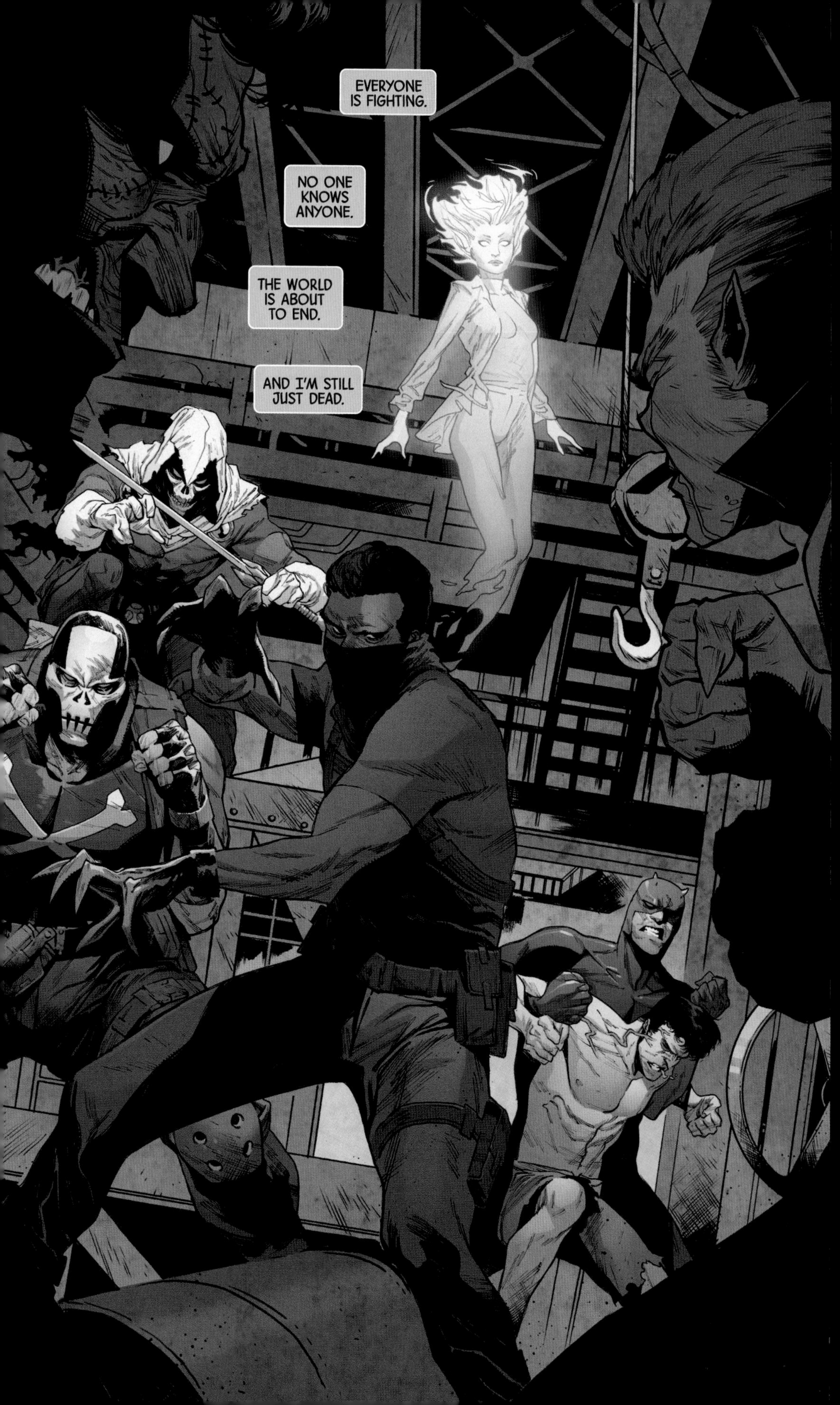
EVERYONE IS FIGHTING.
NO ONE KNOWS ANYONE.
THE WORLD IS ABOUT TO END.
AND I'M STILL JUST DEAD.

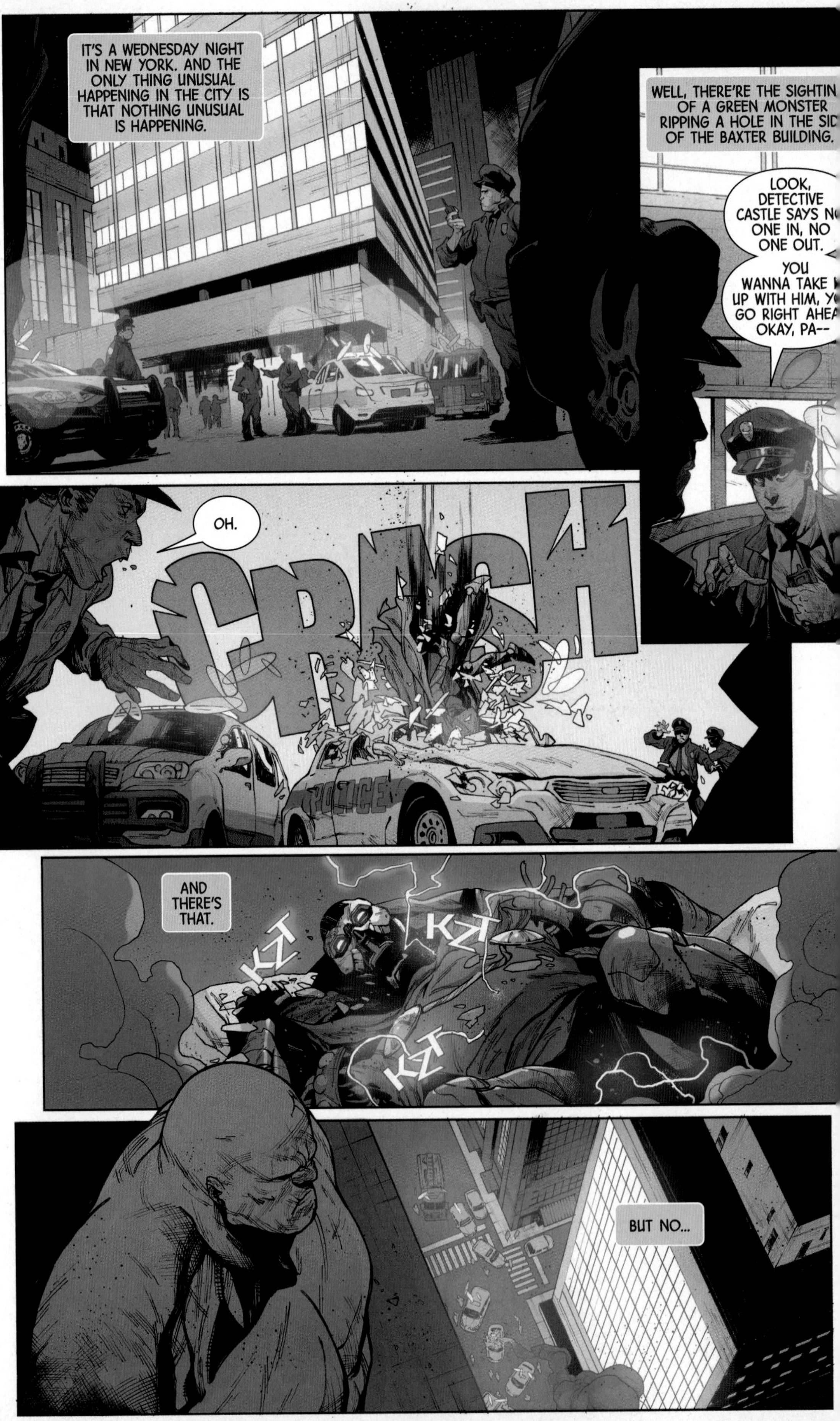
IT'S A WEDNESDAY NIGHT IN NEW YORK. AND THE ONLY THING UNUSUAL HAPPENING IN THE CITY IS THAT NOTHING UNUSUAL IS HAPPENING.
WELL, THERE'RE THE SIGHTIN OF A GREEN MONSTER RIPPING A HOLE IN THE SID OF THE BAXTER BUILDING.
LOOK, DETECTIVE CASTLE SAYS N ONE IN, NO ONE OUT.
YOU WANNA TAKE UP WITH HIM, Y GO RIGHT AHEA OKAY, PA--
OH.
CRASH
AND THERE'S THAT.
KZT
KZT
KZT
BUT NO...

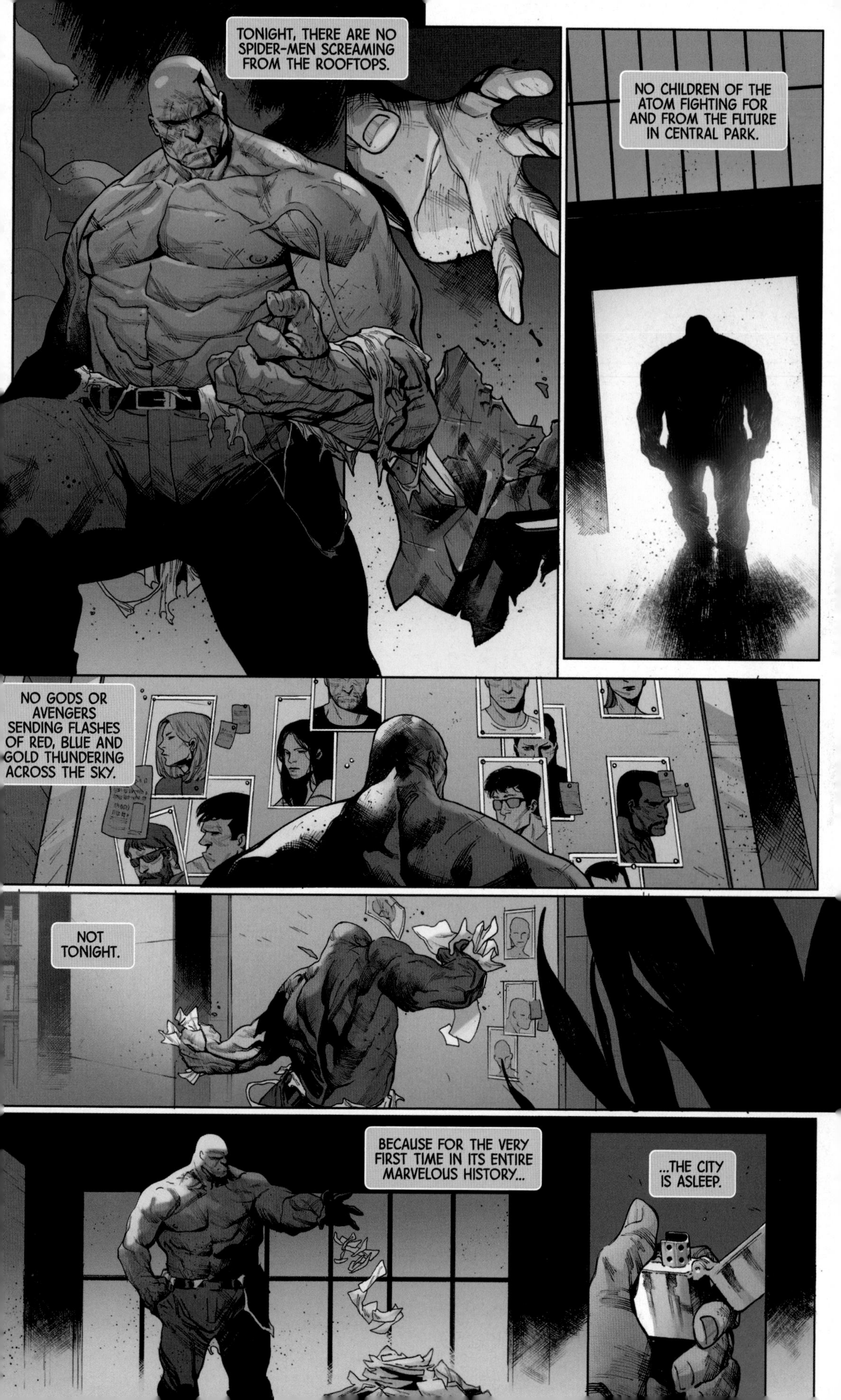
TONIGHT, THERE ARE NO SPIDER-MEN SCREAMING FROM THE ROOFTOPS.
NO CHILDREN OF THE ATOM FIGHTING FOR AND FROM THE FUTURE IN CENTRAL PARK.
NO GODS OR AVENGERS SENDING FLASHES OF RED, BLUE AND GOLD THUNDERING ACROSS THE SKY.
NOT TONIGHT.
BECAUSE FOR THE VERY FIRST TIME IN ITS ENTIRE MARVELOUS HISTORY...
...THE CITY IS ASLEEP.

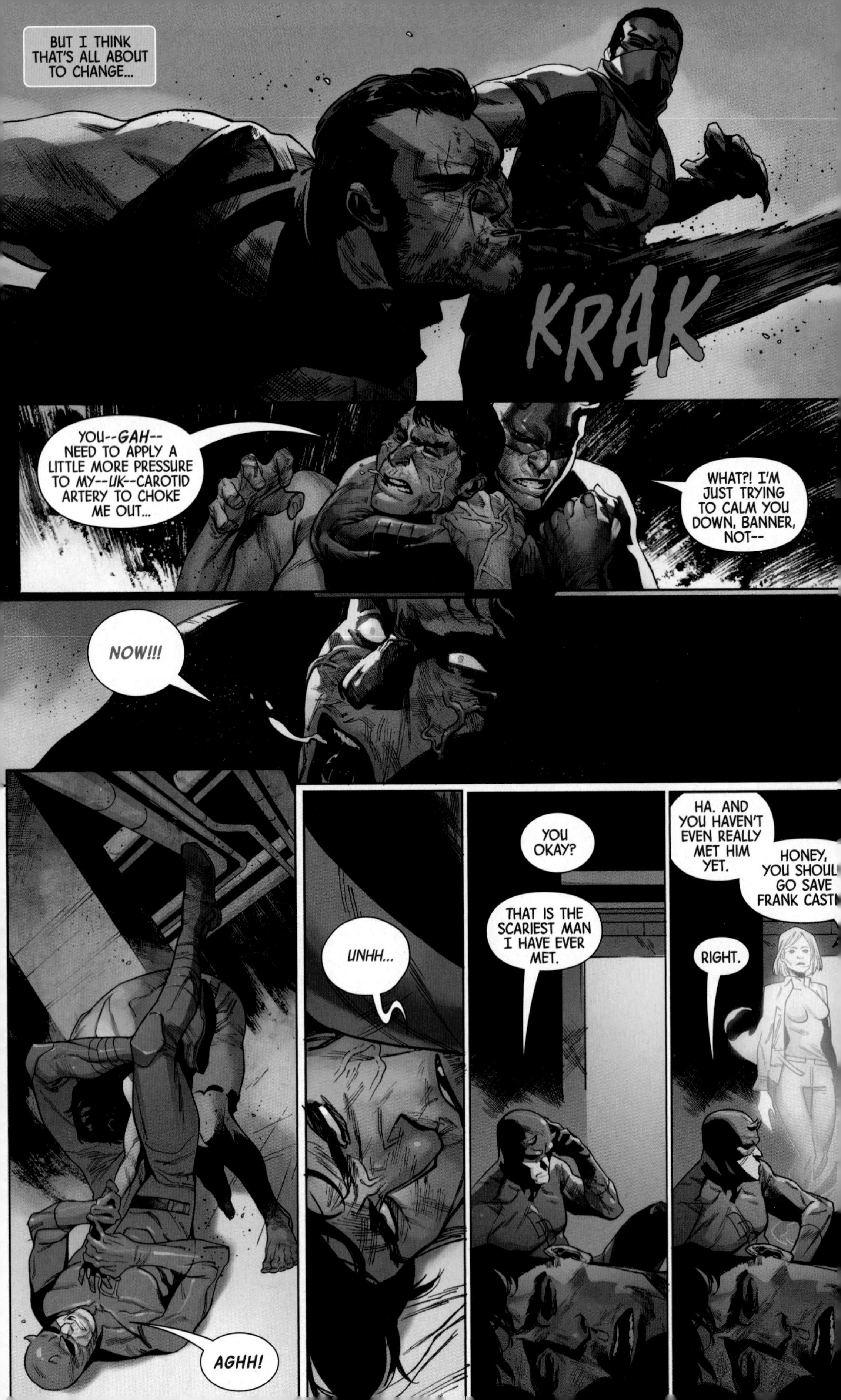
BUT I THINK THAT'S ALL ABOUT TO CHANGE...
KRAK
YOU--GAH--NEED TO APPLY A LITTLE MORE PRESSURE TO MY--UK--CAROTID ARTERY TO CHOKE ME OUT...
WHAT?! I'M JUST TRYING TO CALM YOU DOWN, BANNER, NOT--
NOW!!!
AGHH!
UNHH...
YOU OKAY?
THAT IS THE SCARIEST MAN I HAVE EVER MET.
HA. AND YOU HAVEN'T EVEN REALLY MET HIM YET.
HONEY, YOU SHOUL GO SAVE FRANK CAST
RIGHT.

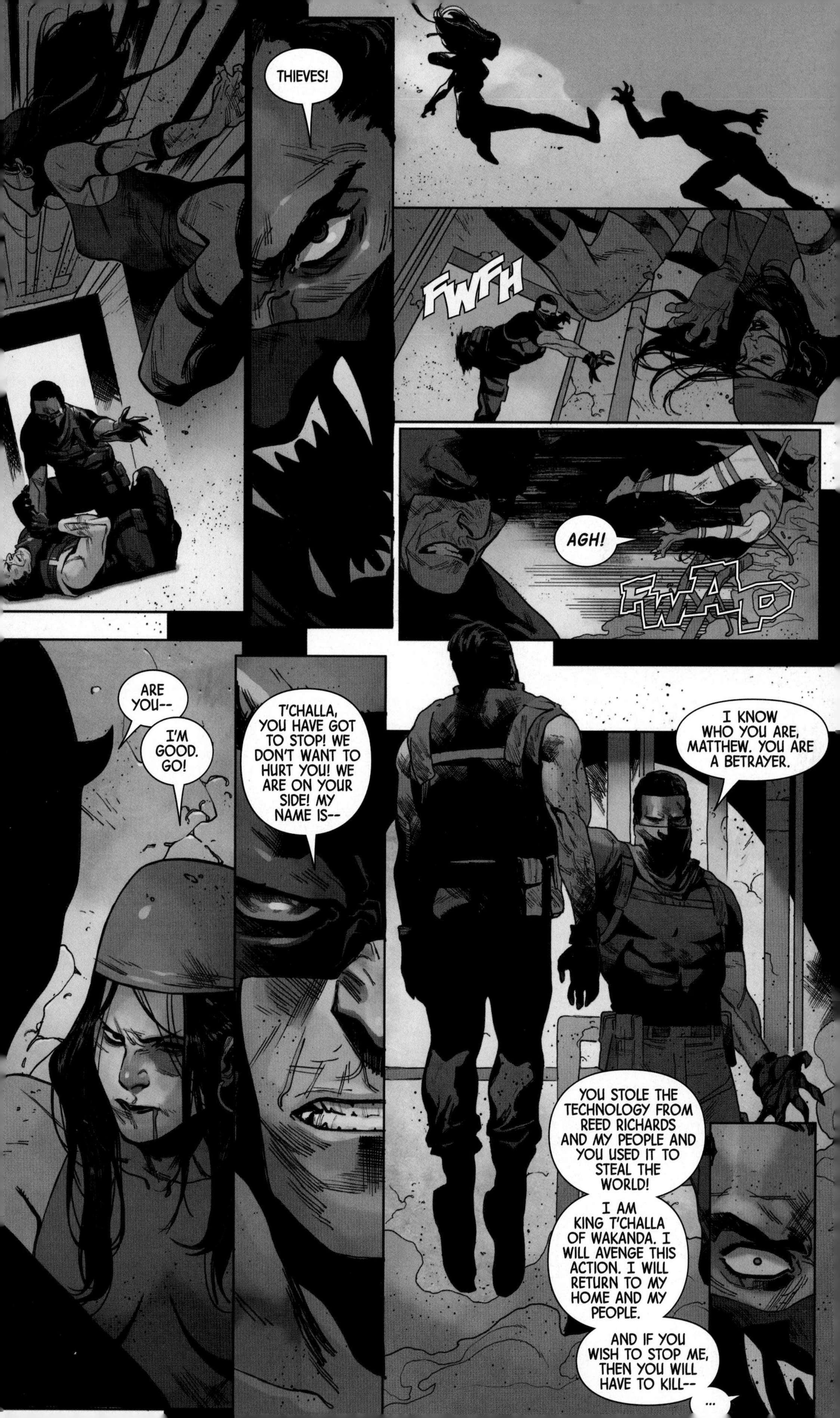
THIEVES!
FWFH
AGH!
FWAP
ARE YOU--
I'M GOOD. GO!
T'CHALLA, YOU HAVE GOT TO STOP! WE DON'T WANT TO HURT YOU! WE ARE ON YOUR SIDE! MY NAME IS--
I KNOW WHO YOU ARE, MATTHEW. YOU ARE A BETRAYER.
YOU STOLE THE TECHNOLOGY FROM REED RICHARDS AND MY PEOPLE AND YOU USED IT TO STEAL THE WORLD!
I AM KING T'CHALLA OF WAKANDA. I WILL AVENGE THIS ACTION. I WILL RETURN TO MY HOME AND MY PEOPLE.
AND IF YOU WISH TO STOP ME, THEN YOU WILL HAVE TO KILL--
...

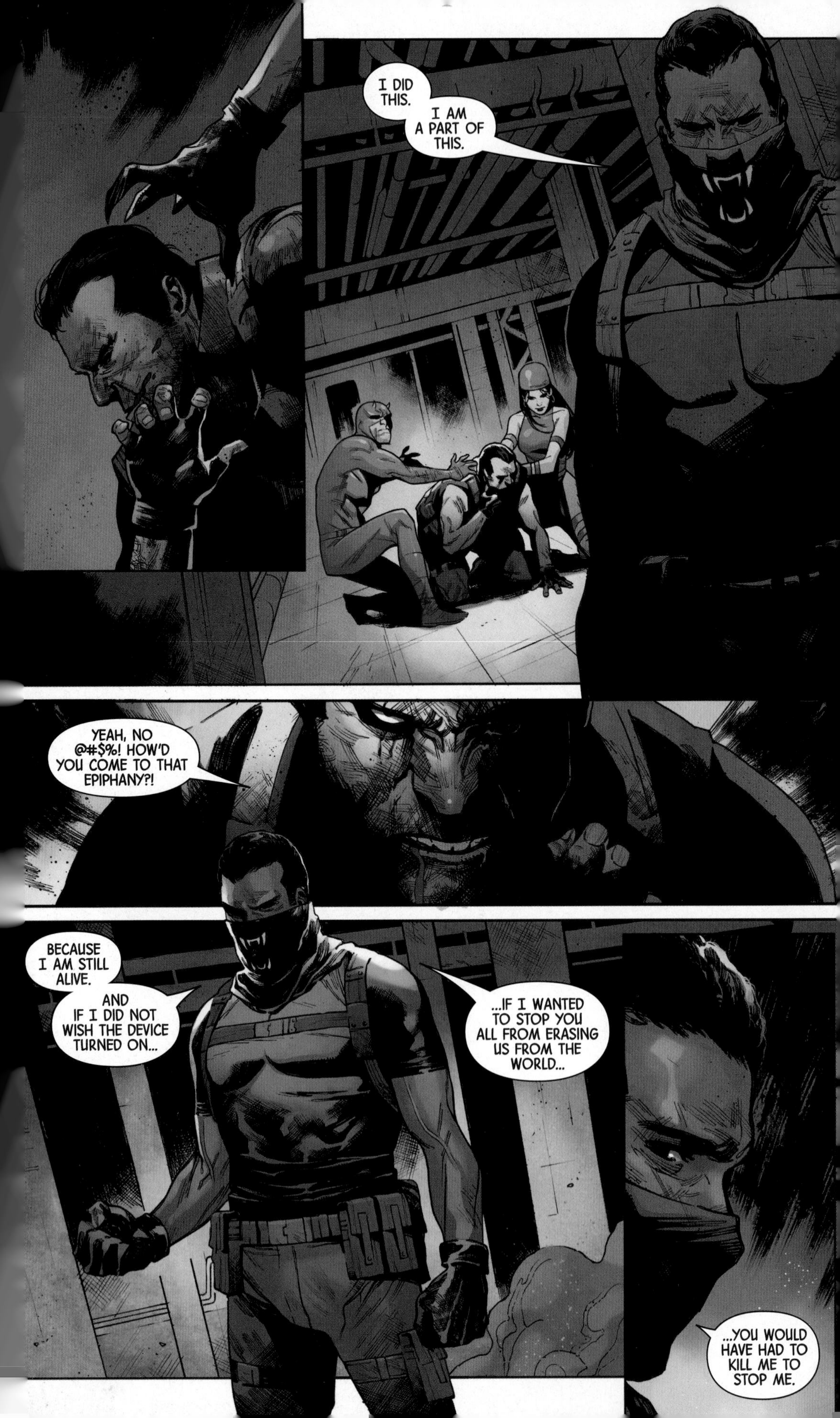
I DID THIS.
I AM A PART OF THIS.
YEAH, NO @#$%! HOW'D YOU COME TO THAT EPIPHANY?!
BECAUSE I AM STILL ALIVE.
AND IF I DID NOT WISH THE DEVICE TURNED ON...
...IF I WANTED TO STOP YOU ALL FROM ERASING US FROM THE WORLD...
...YOU WOULD HAVE HAD TO KILL ME TO STOP ME.

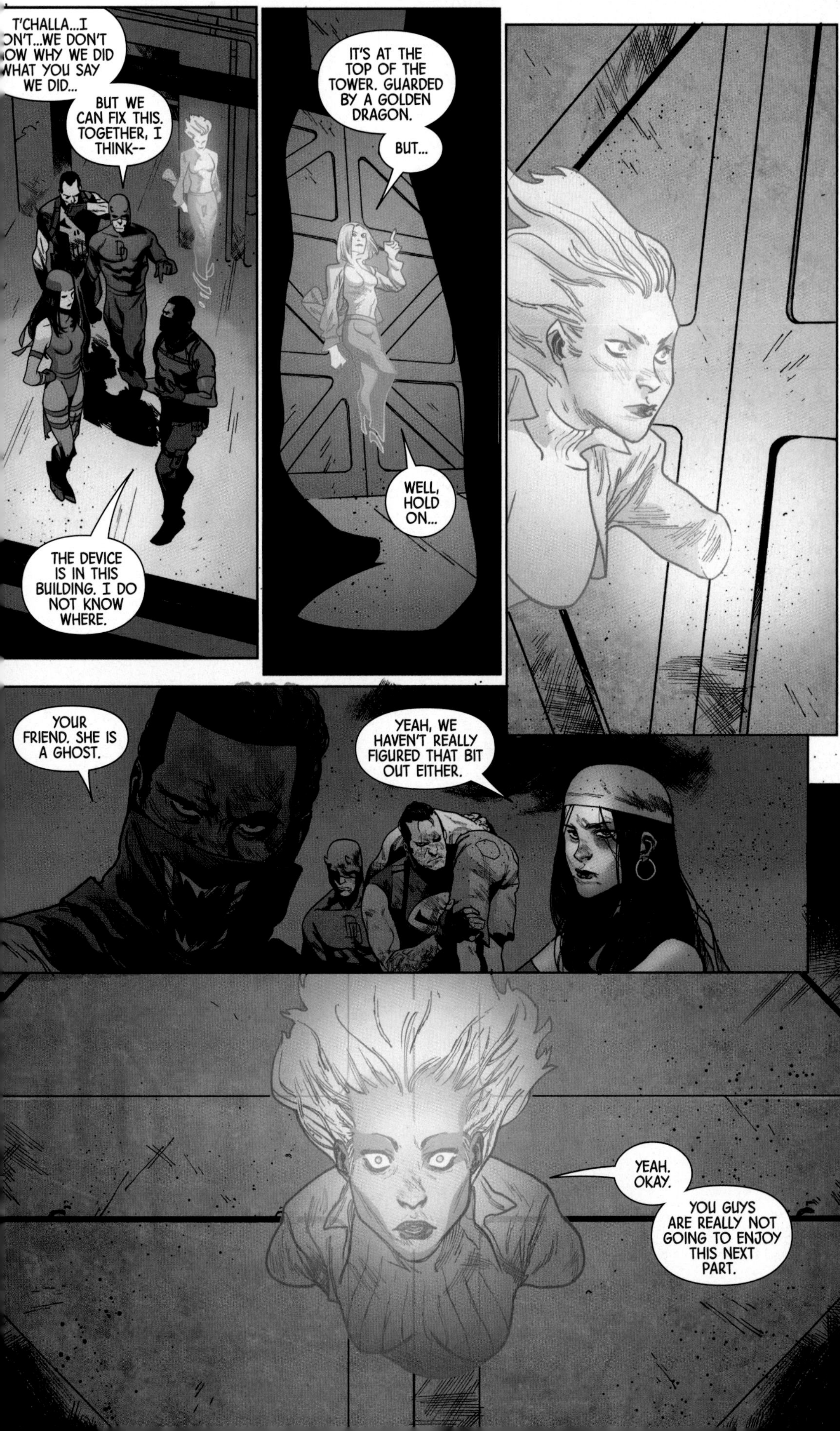
T'CHALLA...I
ON'T...WE DON'T
OW WHY WE DID
WHAT YOU SAY
WE DID...
BUT WE
CAN FIX THIS.
TOGETHER, I
THINK--
THE DEVICE
IS IN THIS
BUILDING. I DO
NOT KNOW
WHERE.
IT'S AT THE
TOP OF THE
TOWER. GUARDED
BY A GOLDEN
DRAGON.
BUT...
WELL,
HOLD
ON...
YOUR
FRIEND. SHE IS
A GHOST.
YEAH, WE
HAVEN'T REALLY
FIGURED THAT BIT
OUT EITHER.
YEAH.
OKAY.
YOU GUYS
ARE REALLY NOT
GOING TO ENJOY
THIS NEXT
PART.

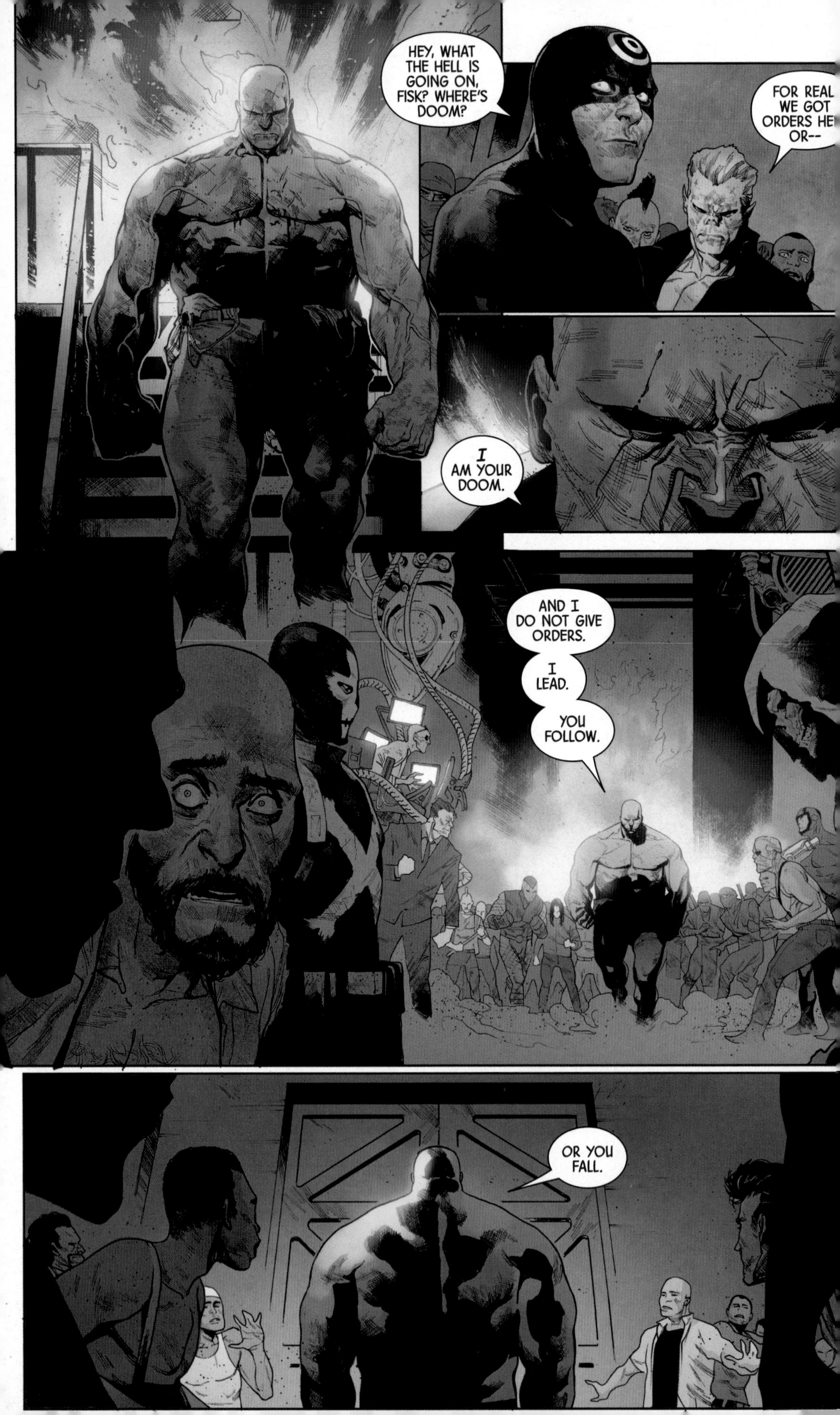
HEY, WHAT THE HELL IS GOING ON, FISK? WHERE'S DOOM?
FOR REAL WE GOT ORDERS HE OR--
I AM YOUR DOOM.
AND I DO NOT GIVE ORDERS.
I LEAD.
YOU FOLLOW.
OR YOU FALL.

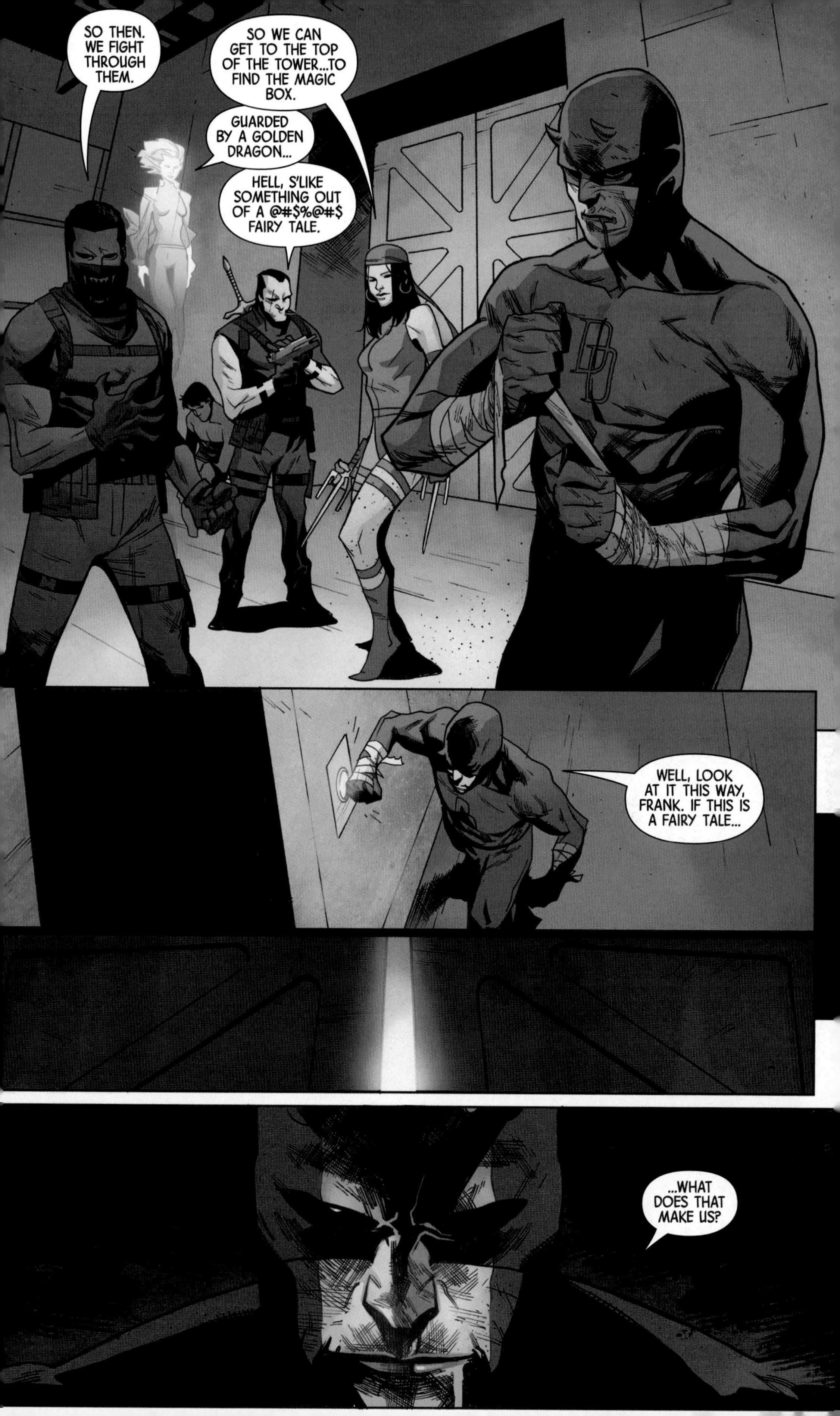
SO THEN. WE FIGHT THROUGH THEM.
SO WE CAN GET TO THE TOP OF THE TOWER...TO FIND THE MAGIC BOX.
GUARDED BY A GOLDEN DRAGON...
HELL, S'LIKE SOMETHING OUT OF A @#$%@#$ FAIRY TALE.
WELL, LOOK AT IT THIS WAY, FRANK. IF THIS IS A FAIRY TALE...
...WHAT DOES THAT MAKE US?

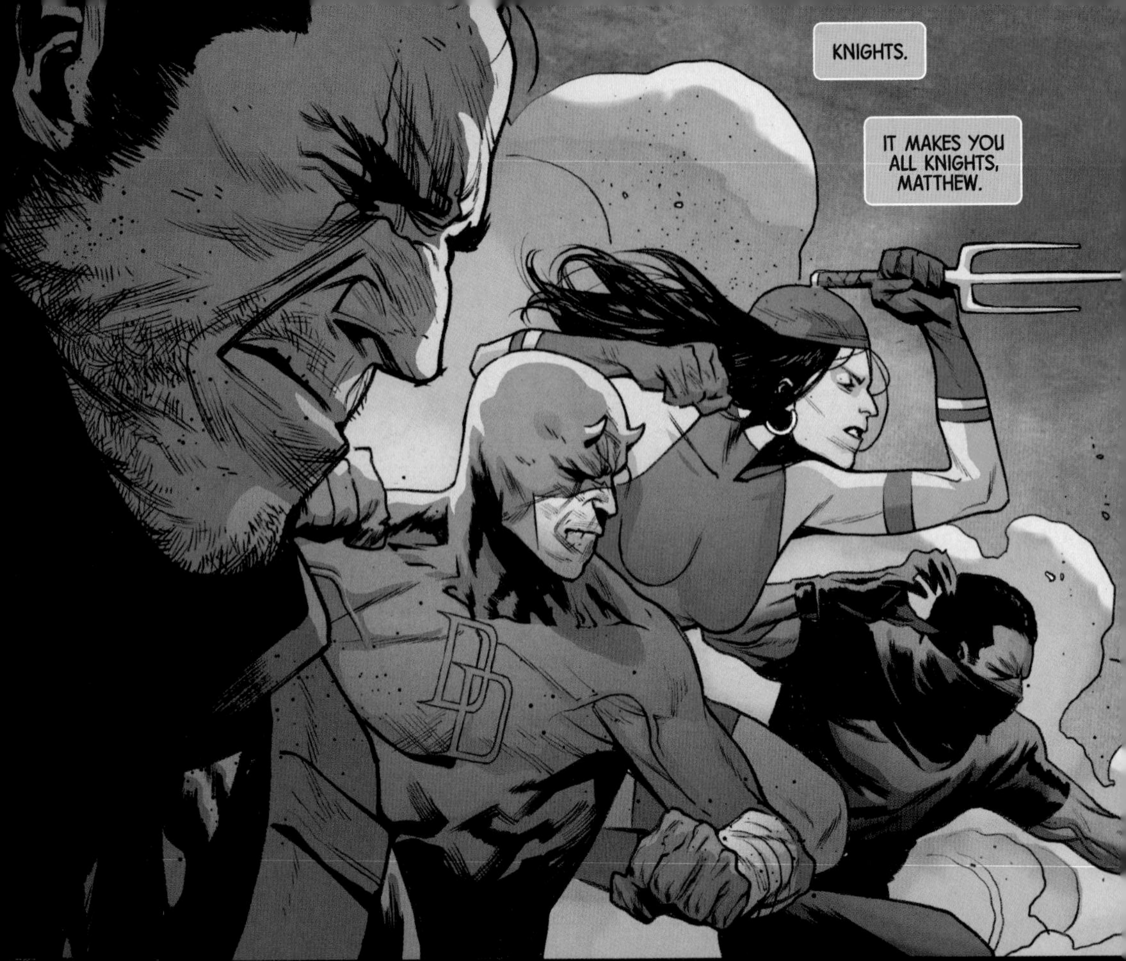
KNIGHTS.
IT MAKES YOU ALL KNIGHTS, MATTHEW.
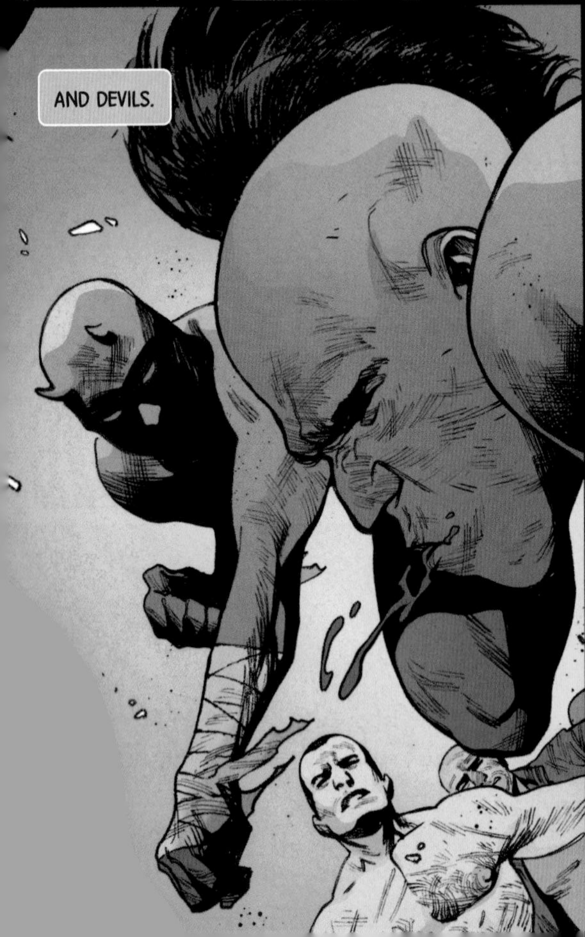
AND DEVILS.
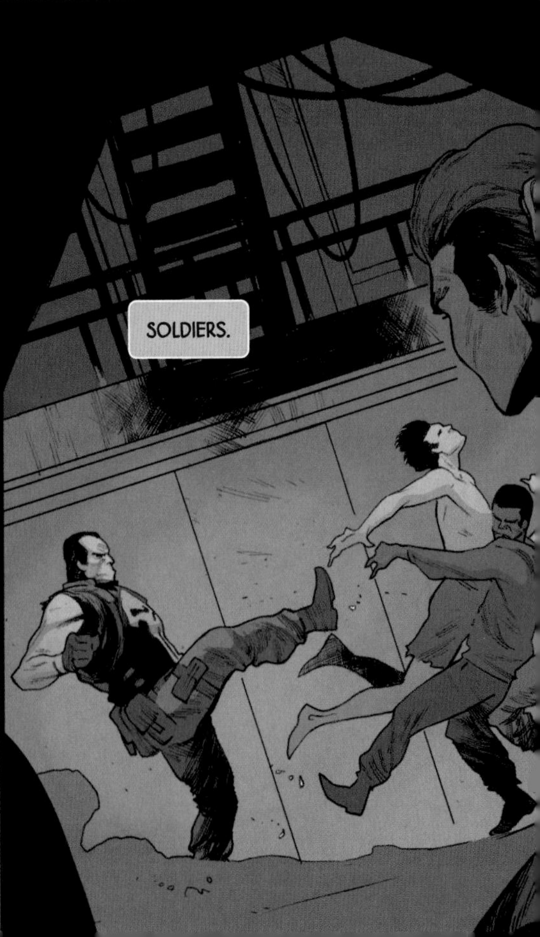
SOLDIERS.

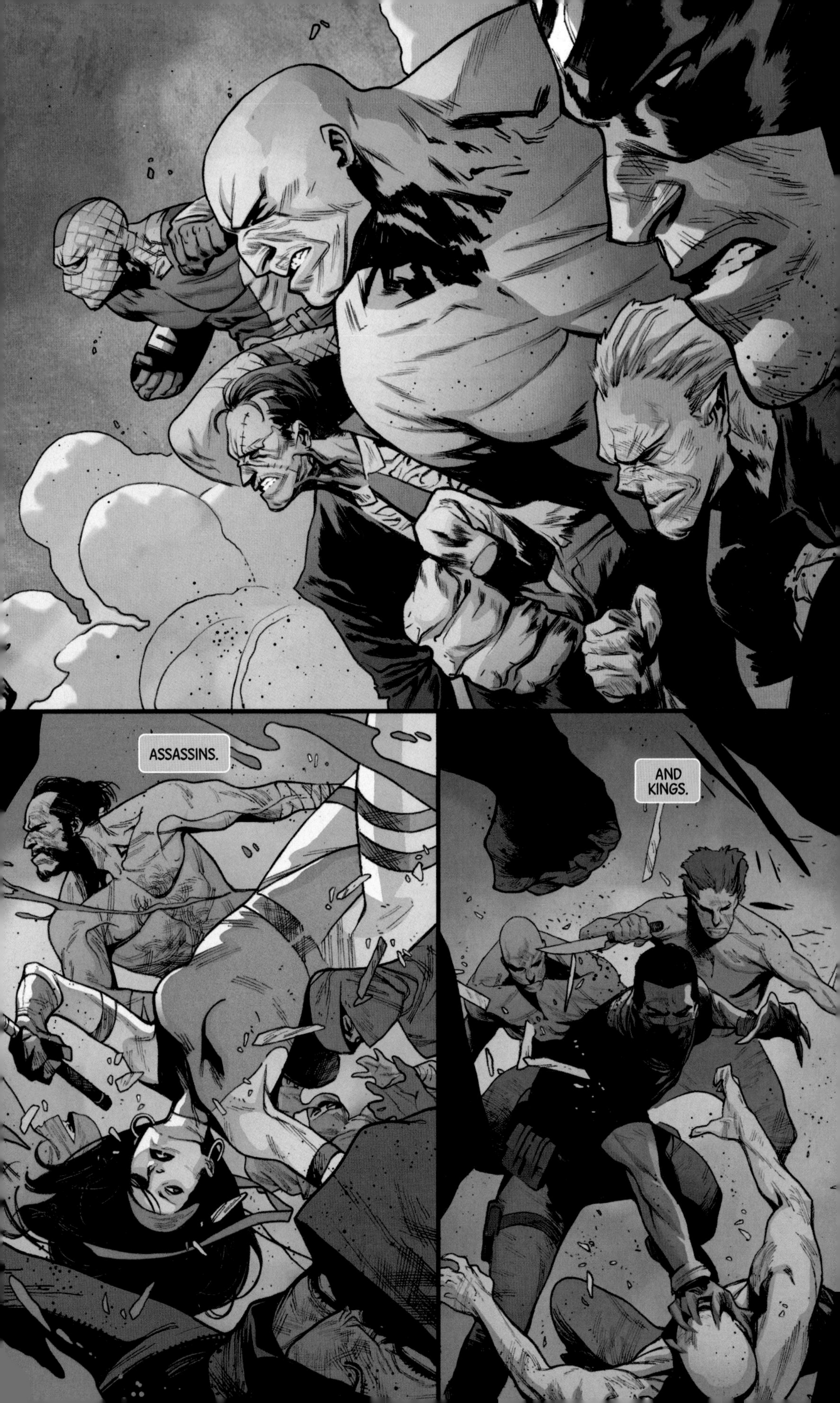
ASSASSINS.
AND KINGS.

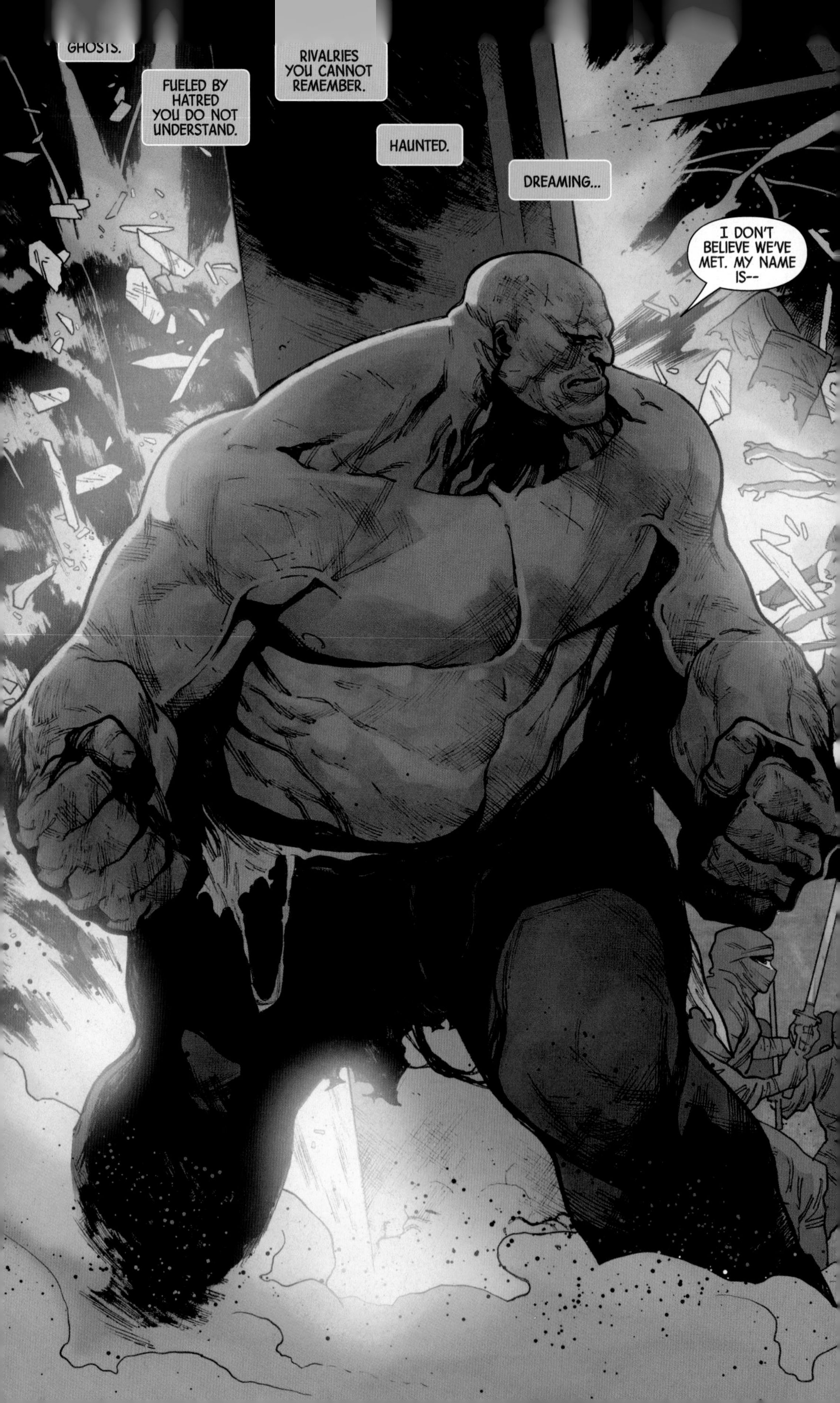
GHOSTS.
FUELED BY HATRED YOU DO NOT UNDERSTAND.
RIVALRIES YOU CANNOT REMEMBER.
HAUNTED.
DREAMING...
I DON'T BELIEVE WE'VE MET. MY NAME IS--

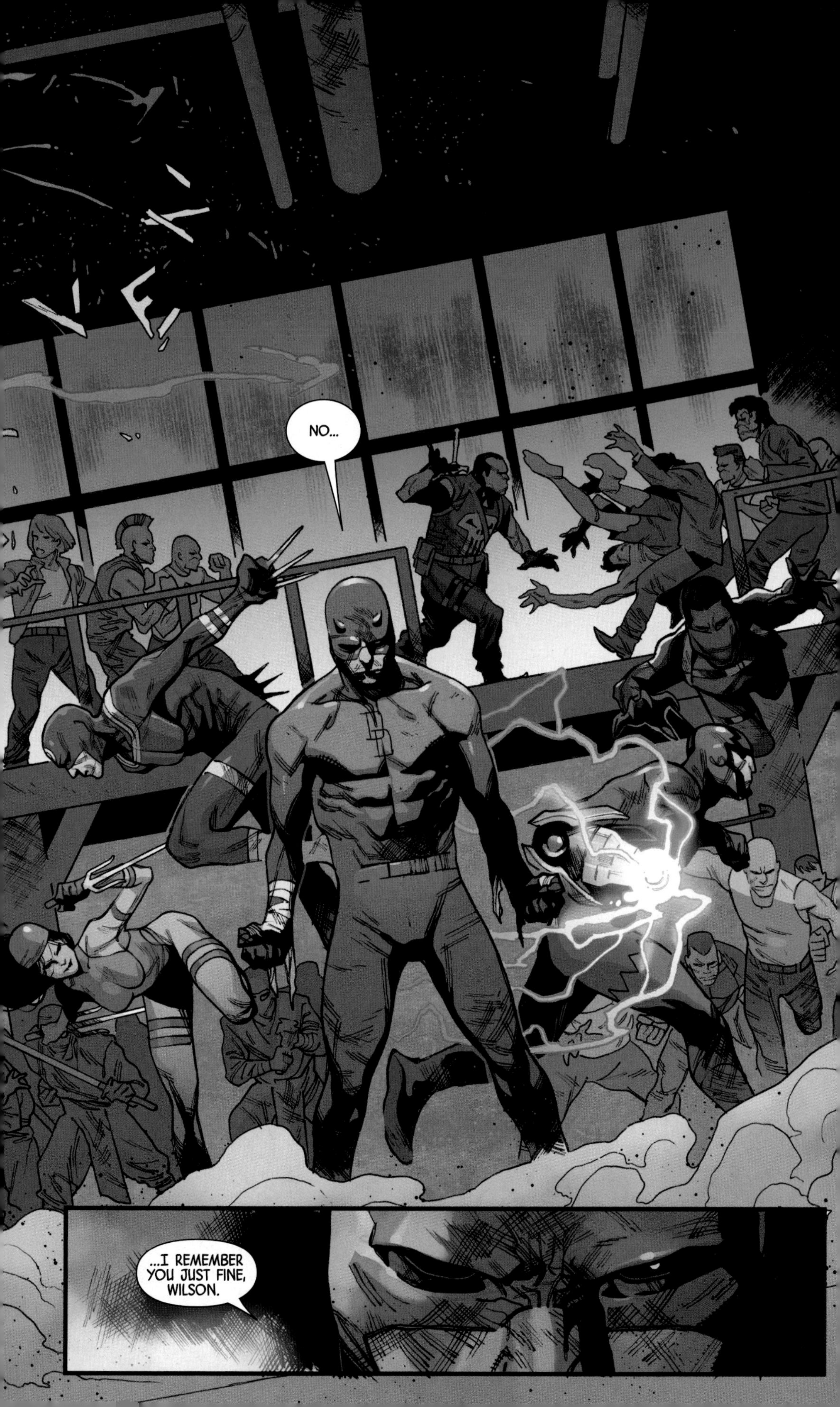
NO...
...I REMEMBER YOU JUST FINE, WILSON.

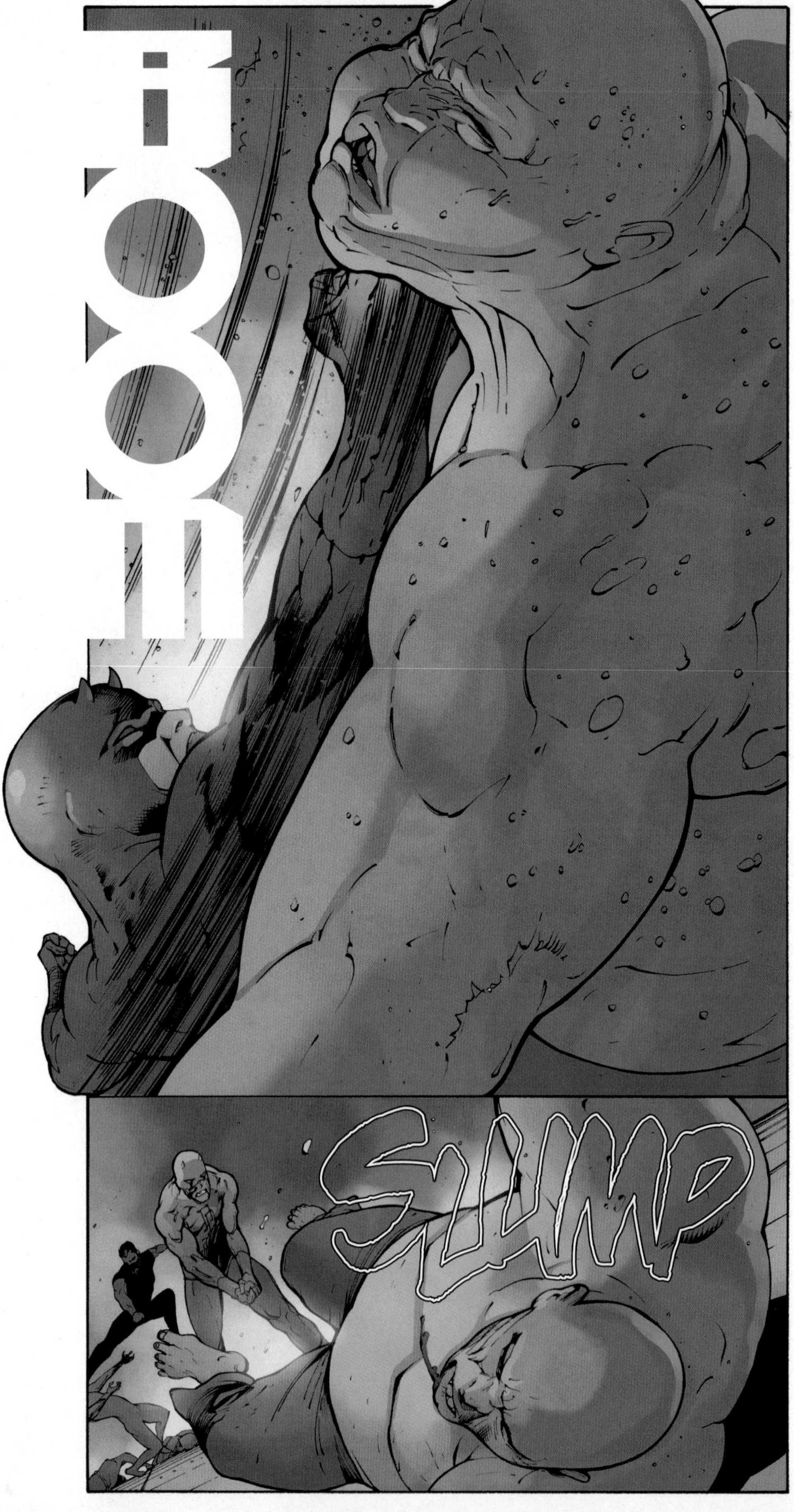
BOOM!
SLUMP

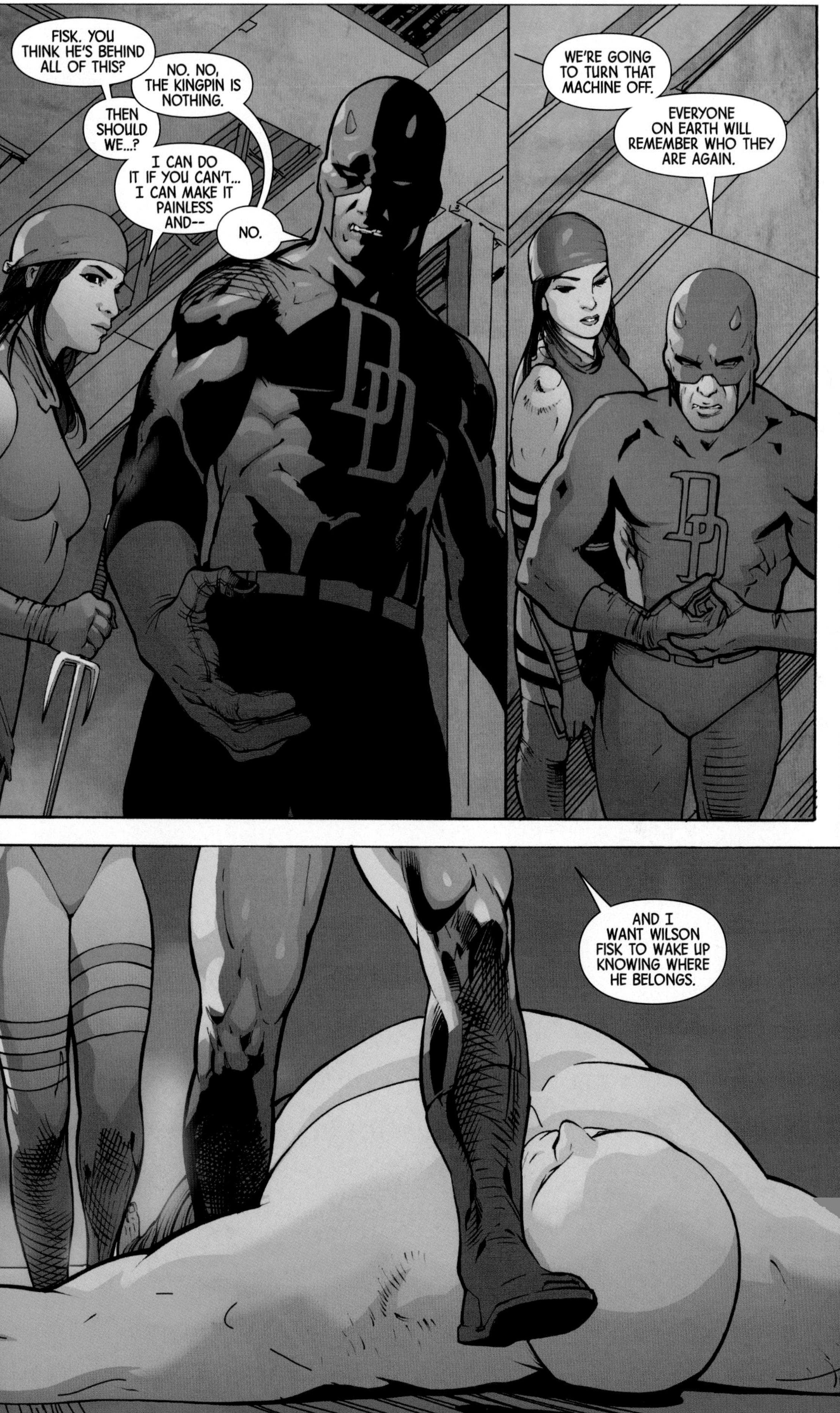
FISK. YOU THINK HE'S BEHIND ALL OF THIS?
NO. NO, THE KINGPIN IS NOTHING.
THEN SHOULD WE...?
I CAN DO IT IF YOU CAN'T... I CAN MAKE IT PAINLESS AND--
NO.
WE'RE GOING TO TURN THAT MACHINE OFF.
EVERYONE ON EARTH WILL REMEMBER WHO THEY ARE AGAIN.
AND I WANT WILSON FISK TO WAKE UP KNOWING WHERE HE BELONGS.

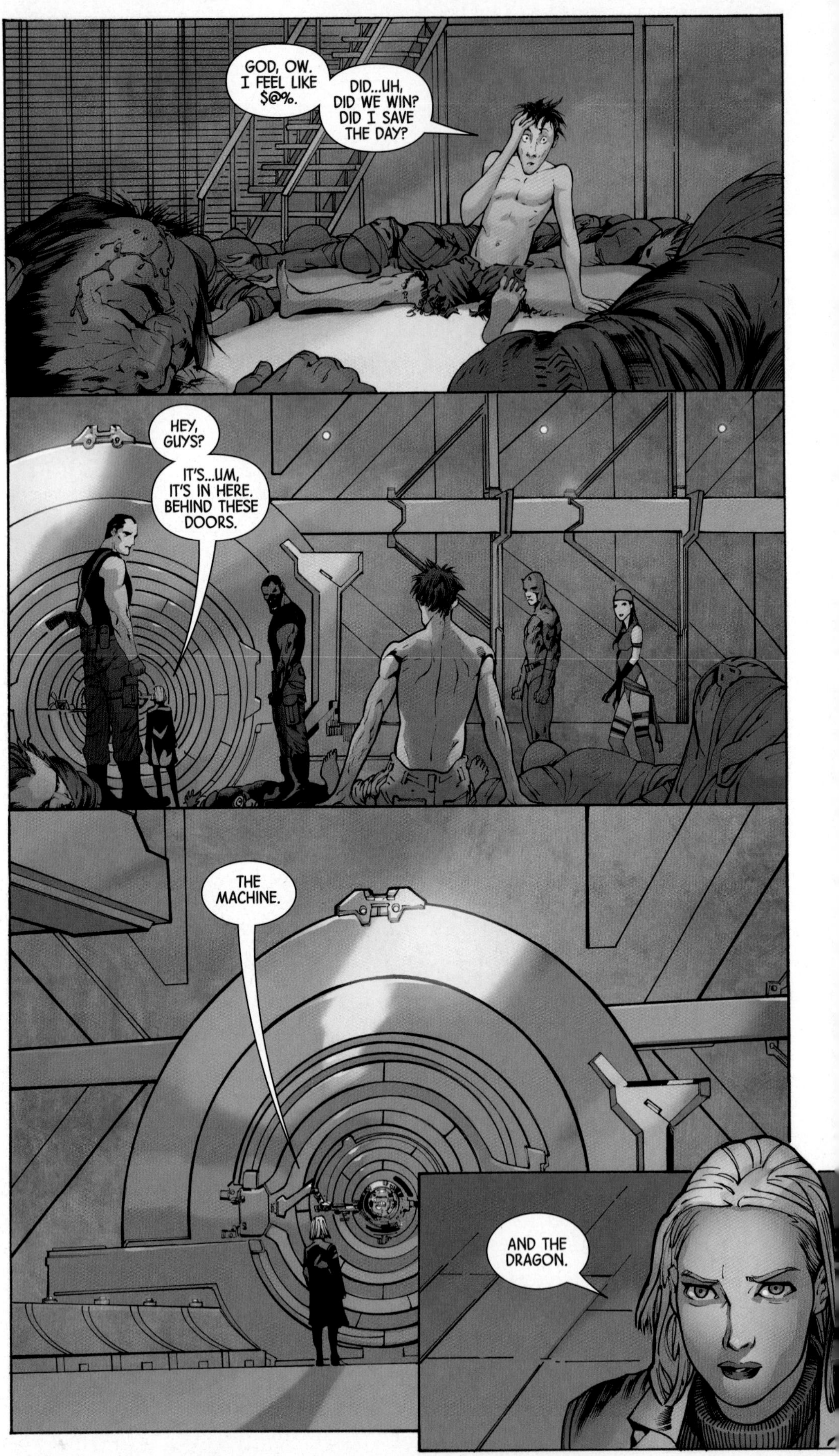
GOD, OW. I FEEL LIKE $@%.
DID...UH, DID WE WIN? DID I SAVE THE DAY?
HEY, GUYS?
IT'S...UM, IT'S IN HERE. BEHIND THESE DOORS.
THE MACHINE.
AND THE DRAGON.

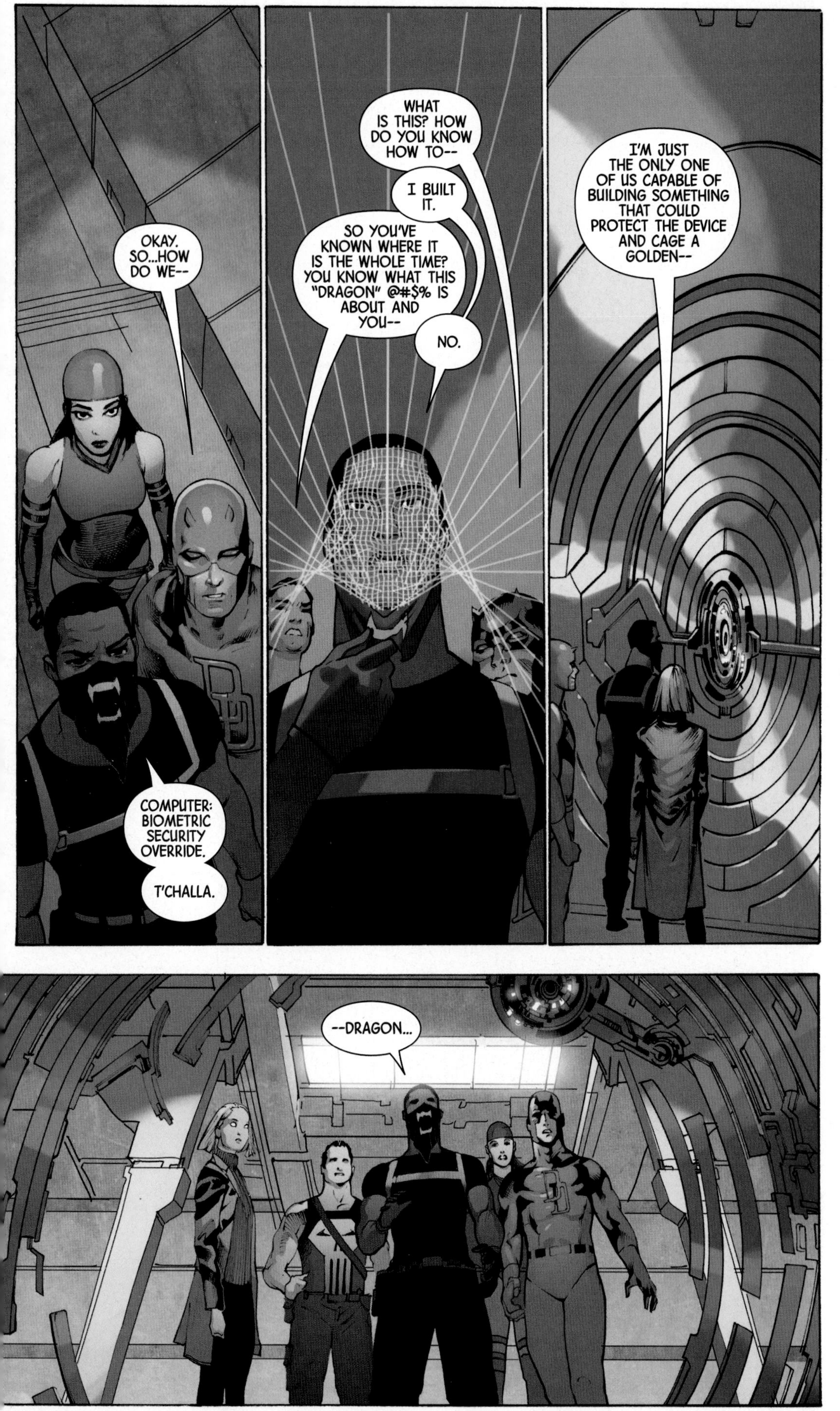
OKAY. SO...HOW DO WE--
COMPUTER: BIOMETRIC SECURITY OVERRIDE.
T'CHALLA.
WHAT IS THIS? HOW DO YOU KNOW HOW TO--
I BUILT IT.
SO YOU'VE KNOWN WHERE IT IS THE WHOLE TIME? YOU KNOW WHAT THIS "DRAGON" @#$% IS ABOUT AND YOU--
NO.
I'M JUST THE ONLY ONE OF US CAPABLE OF BUILDING SOMETHING THAT COULD PROTECT THE DEVICE AND CAGE A GOLDEN--
--DRAGON...

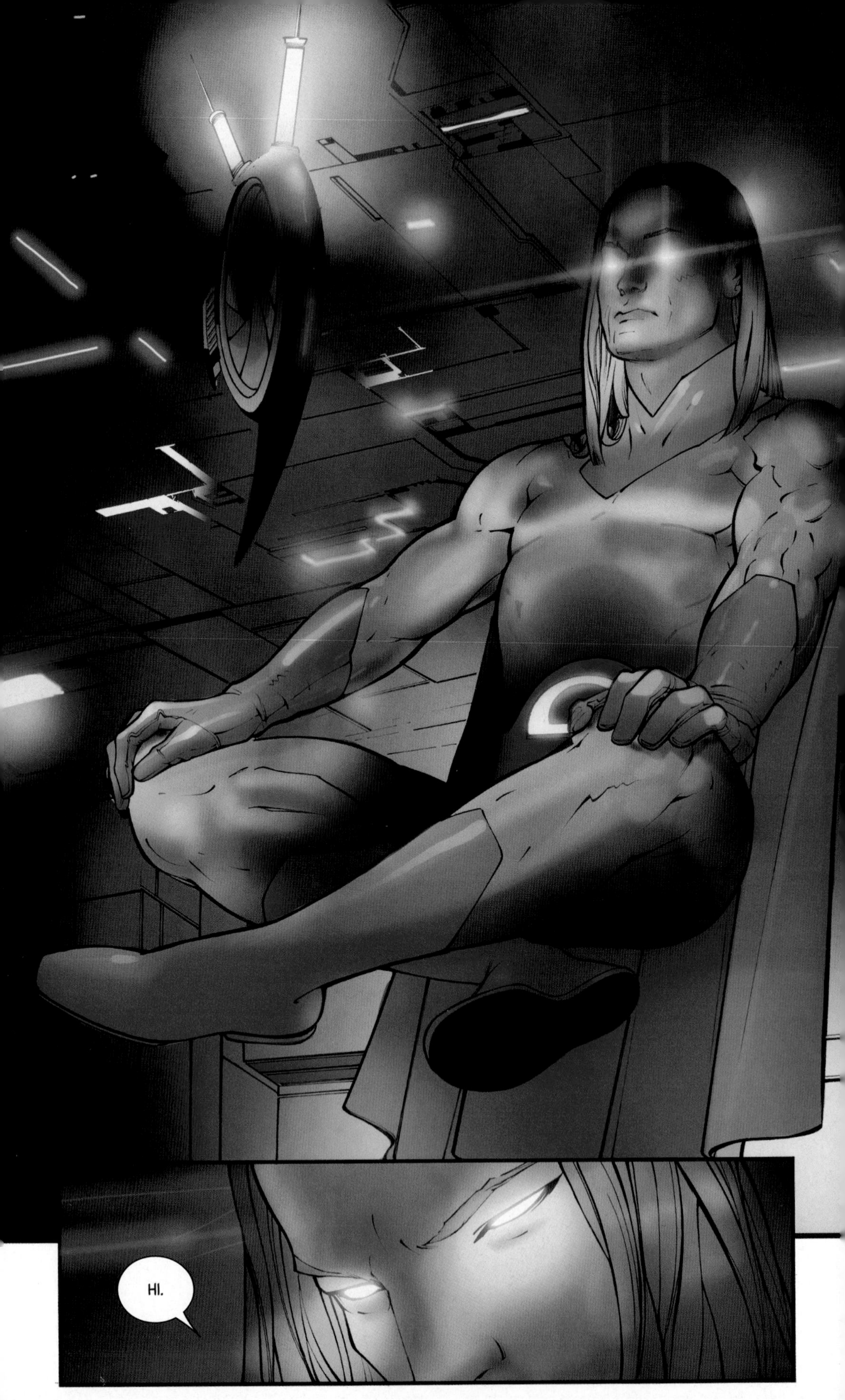
HI.

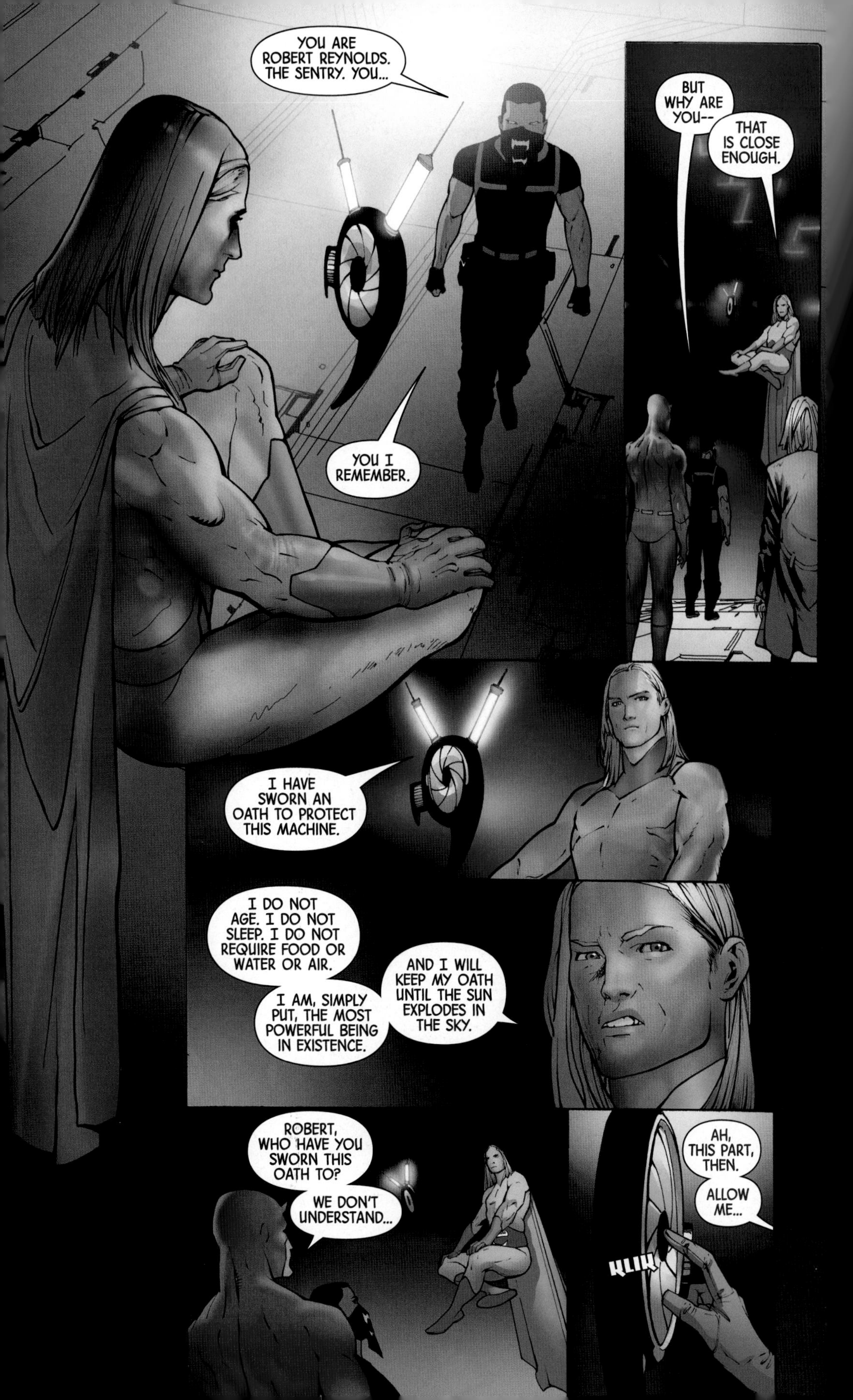
YOU ARE ROBERT REYNOLDS. THE SENTRY. YOU...
YOU I REMEMBER.
BUT WHY ARE YOU--
THAT IS CLOSE ENOUGH.
I HAVE SWORN AN OATH TO PROTECT THIS MACHINE.
I DO NOT AGE. I DO NOT SLEEP. I DO NOT REQUIRE FOOD OR WATER OR AIR.
I AM, SIMPLY PUT, THE MOST POWERFUL BEING IN EXISTENCE.
AND I WILL KEEP MY OATH UNTIL THE SUN EXPLODES IN THE SKY.
ROBERT, WHO HAVE YOU SWORN THIS OATH TO?
WE DON'T UNDERSTAND...
AH, THIS PART, THEN.
ALLOW ME...
KLIK

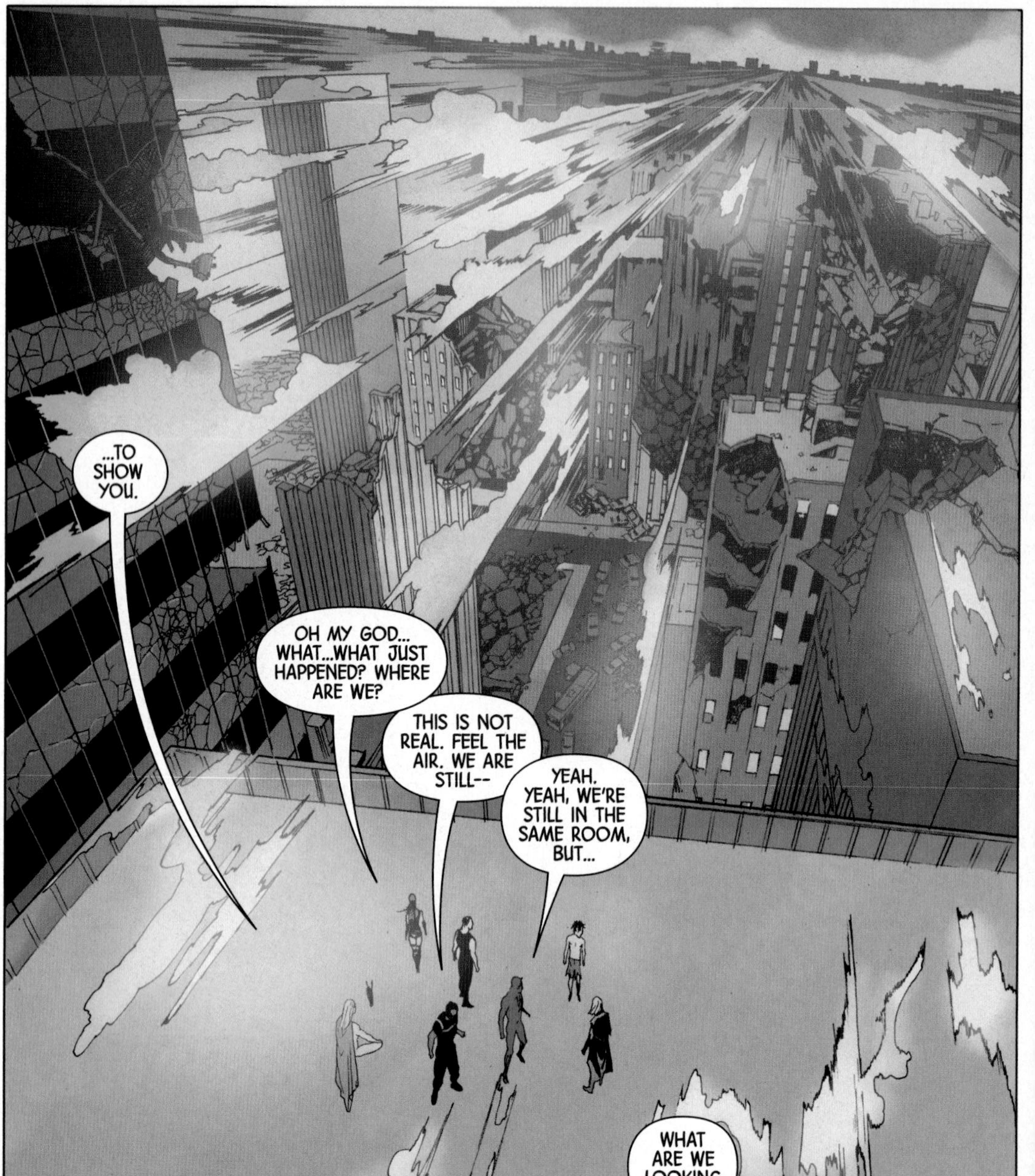
...TO SHOW YOU.
OH MY GOD... WHAT...WHAT JUST HAPPENED? WHERE ARE WE?
THIS IS NOT REAL. FEEL THE AIR. WE ARE STILL--
YEAH. YEAH, WE'RE STILL IN THE SAME ROOM, BUT...
WHAT ARE WE LOOKING AT?

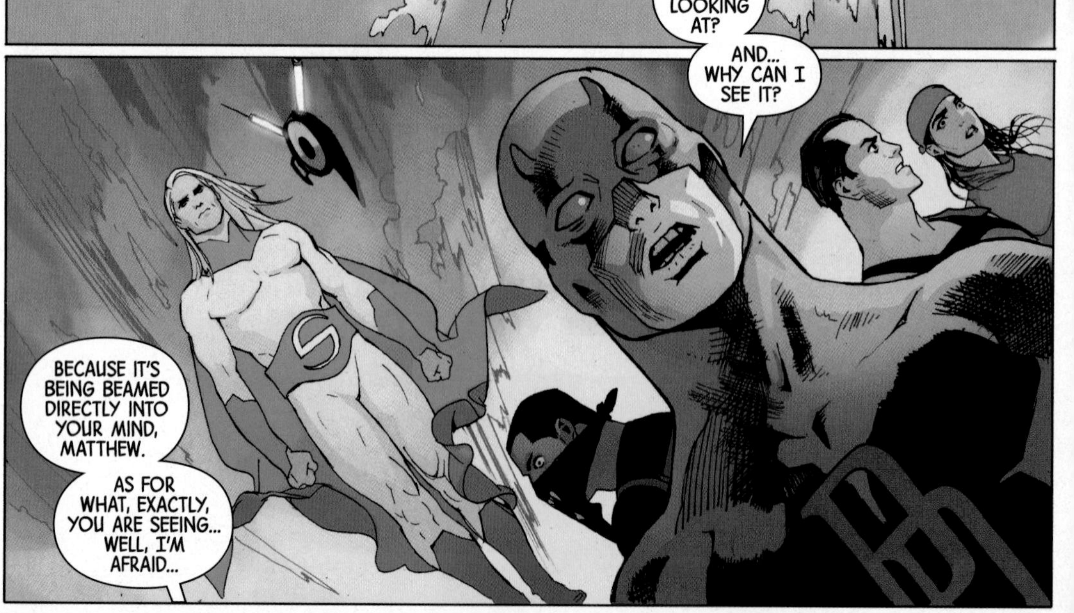
AND... WHY CAN I SEE IT?
BECAUSE IT'S BEING BEAMED DIRECTLY INTO YOUR MIND, MATTHEW.
AS FOR WHAT, EXACTLY, YOU ARE SEEING... WELL, I'M AFRAID...

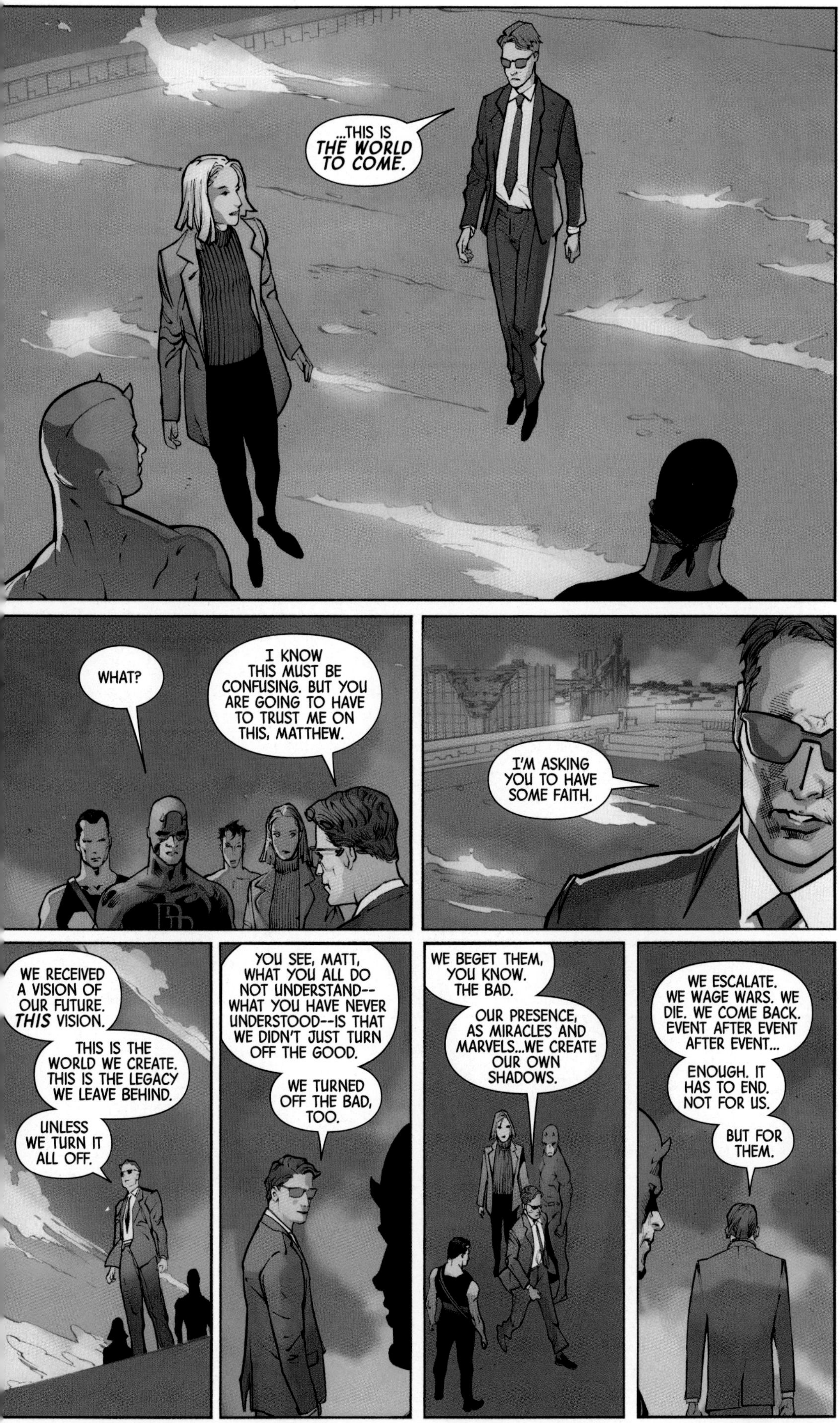
...THIS IS THE WORLD TO COME.
WHAT?
I KNOW THIS MUST BE CONFUSING. BUT YOU ARE GOING TO HAVE TO TRUST ME ON THIS, MATTHEW.
I'M ASKING YOU TO HAVE SOME FAITH.
WE RECEIVED A VISION OF OUR FUTURE. THIS VISION.
THIS IS THE WORLD WE CREATE. THIS IS THE LEGACY WE LEAVE BEHIND.
UNLESS WE TURN IT ALL OFF.
YOU SEE, MATT, WHAT YOU ALL DO NOT UNDERSTAND-- WHAT YOU HAVE NEVER UNDERSTOOD--IS THAT WE DIDN'T JUST TURN OFF THE GOOD.
WE TURNED OFF THE BAD, TOO.
WE BEGET THEM, YOU KNOW. THE BAD.
OUR PRESENCE, AS MIRACLES AND MARVELS...WE CREATE OUR OWN SHADOWS.
WE ESCALATE. WE WAGE WARS. WE DIE. WE COME BACK. EVENT AFTER EVENT AFTER EVENT...
ENOUGH. IT HAS TO END. NOT FOR US.
BUT FOR THEM.

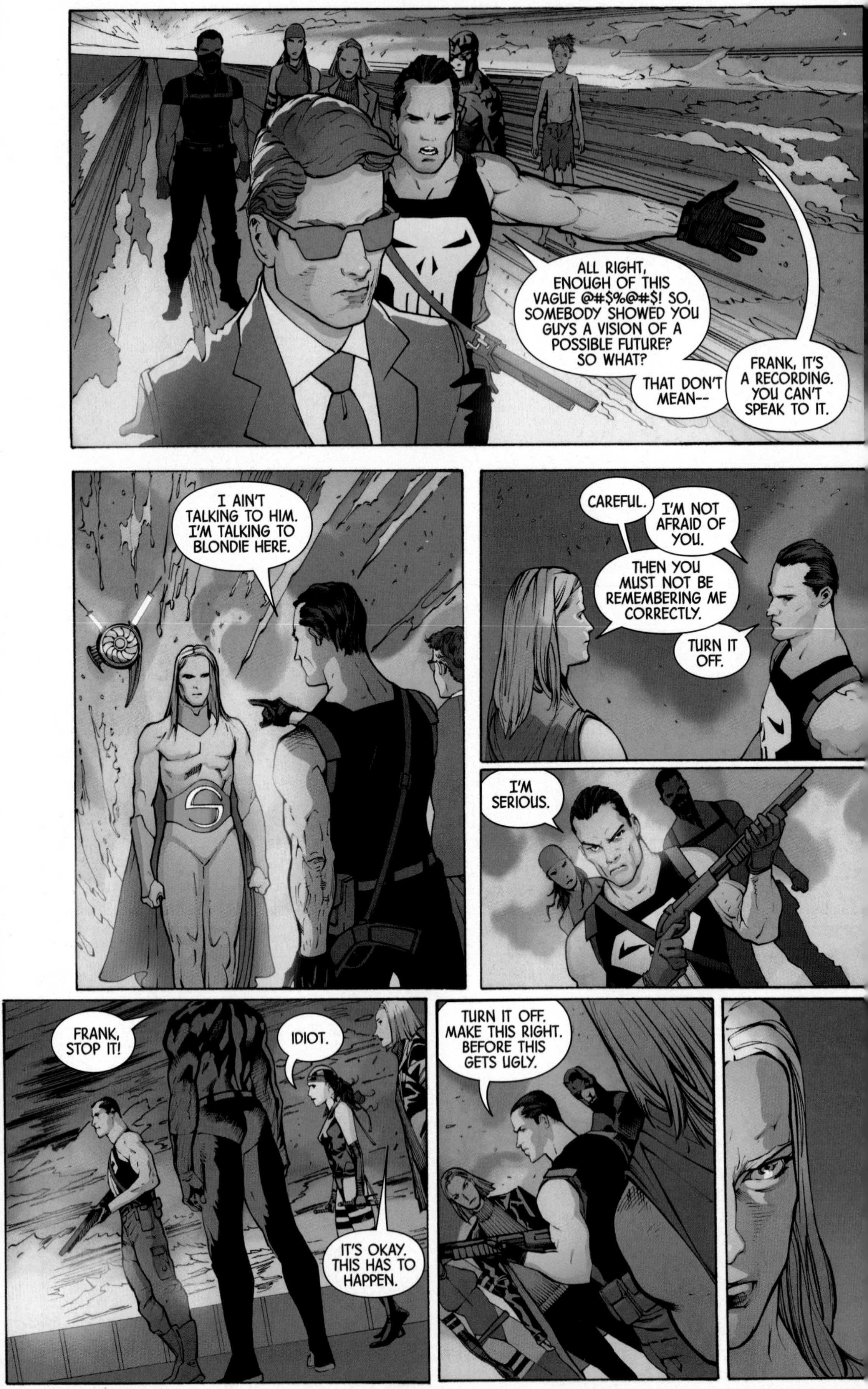
ALL RIGHT, ENOUGH OF THIS VAGUE @#$%@#$! SO, SOMEBODY SHOWED YOU GUYS A VISION OF A POSSIBLE FUTURE? SO WHAT?
THAT DON'T MEAN--
FRANK, IT'S A RECORDING. YOU CAN'T SPEAK TO IT.
I AIN'T TALKING TO HIM. I'M TALKING TO BLONDIE HERE.
CAREFUL.
I'M NOT AFRAID OF YOU.
THEN YOU MUST NOT BE REMEMBERING ME CORRECTLY.
TURN IT OFF.
I'M SERIOUS.
FRANK, STOP IT!
IDIOT.
IT'S OKAY. THIS HAS TO HAPPEN.
TURN IT OFF. MAKE THIS RIGHT. BEFORE THIS GETS UGLY.

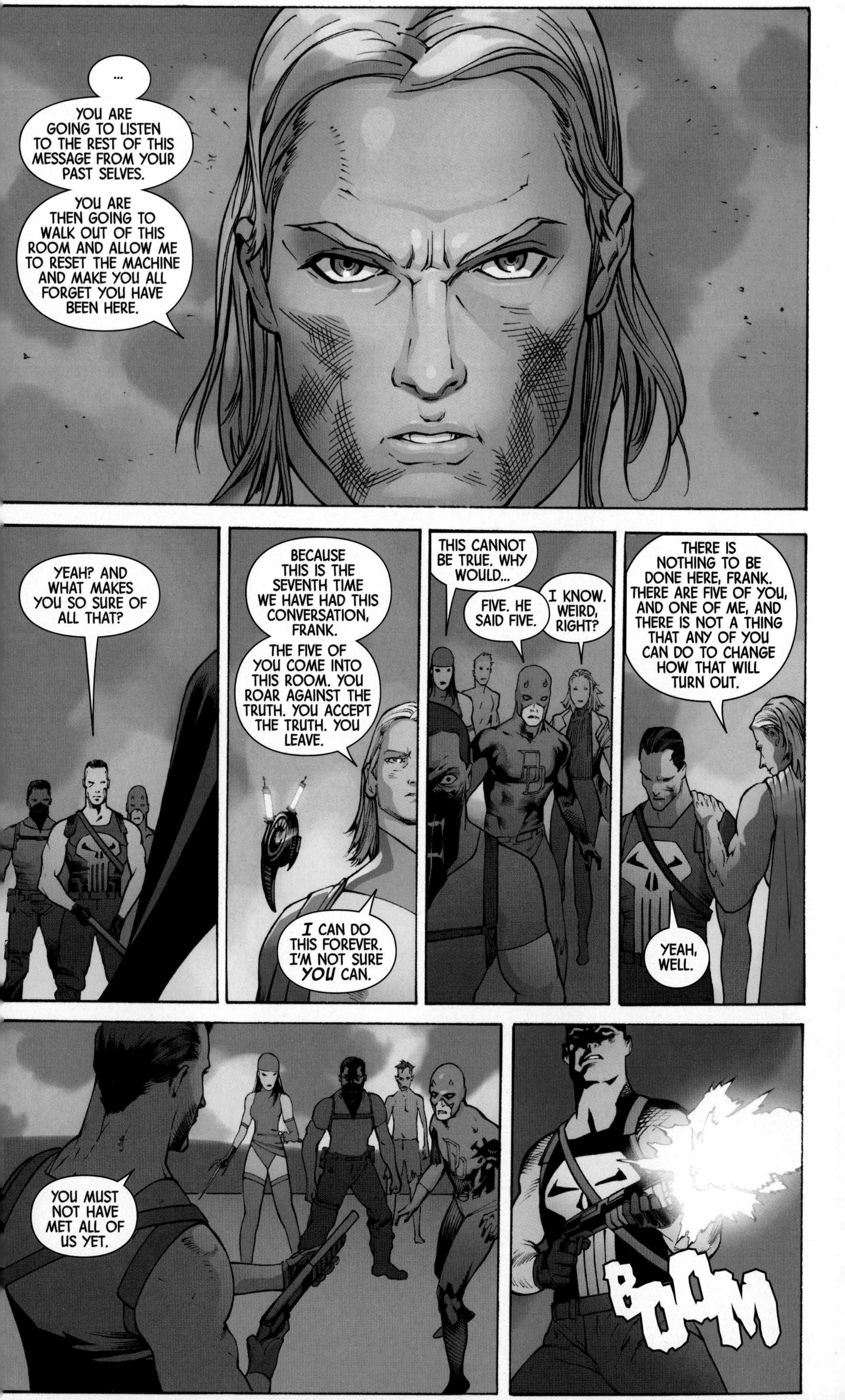
...
YOU ARE GOING TO LISTEN TO THE REST OF THIS MESSAGE FROM YOUR PAST SELVES.
YOU ARE THEN GOING TO WALK OUT OF THIS ROOM AND ALLOW ME TO RESET THE MACHINE AND MAKE YOU ALL FORGET YOU HAVE BEEN HERE.
YEAH? AND WHAT MAKES YOU SO SURE OF ALL THAT?
BECAUSE THIS IS THE SEVENTH TIME WE HAVE HAD THIS CONVERSATION, FRANK.
THE FIVE OF YOU COME INTO THIS ROOM. YOU ROAR AGAINST THE TRUTH. YOU ACCEPT THE TRUTH. YOU LEAVE.
I CAN DO THIS FOREVER. I'M NOT SURE YOU CAN.
THIS CANNOT BE TRUE. WHY WOULD...
FIVE. HE SAID FIVE.
I KNOW. WEIRD, RIGHT?
THERE IS NOTHING TO BE DONE HERE, FRANK. THERE ARE FIVE OF YOU, AND ONE OF ME, AND THERE IS NOT A THING THAT ANY OF YOU CAN DO TO CHANGE HOW THAT WILL TURN OUT.
YEAH, WELL.
YOU MUST NOT HAVE MET ALL OF US YET.
BOOM

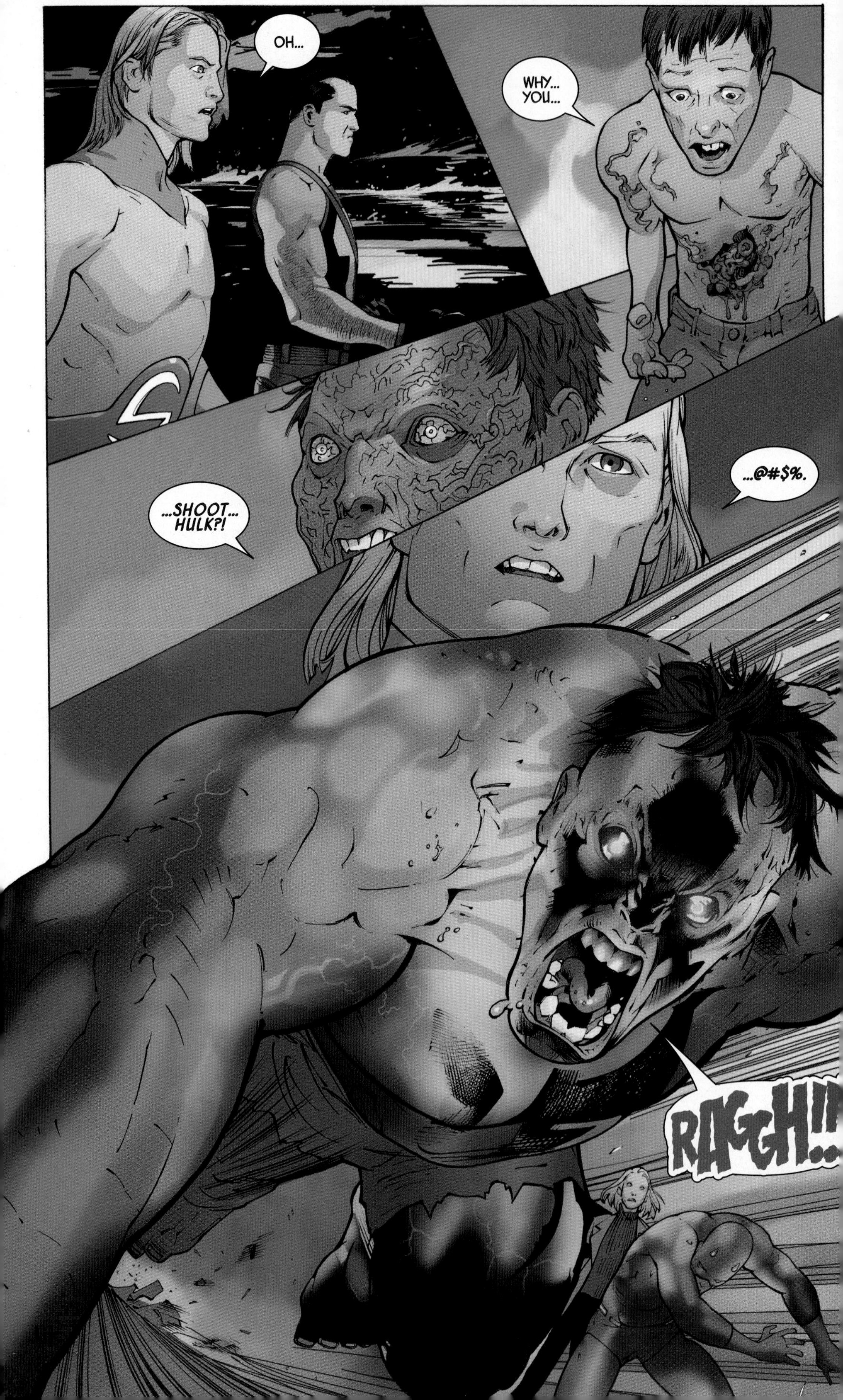
OH...
WHY... YOU...
...SHOOT... HULK?!
...@#$%.
RAGGH!!

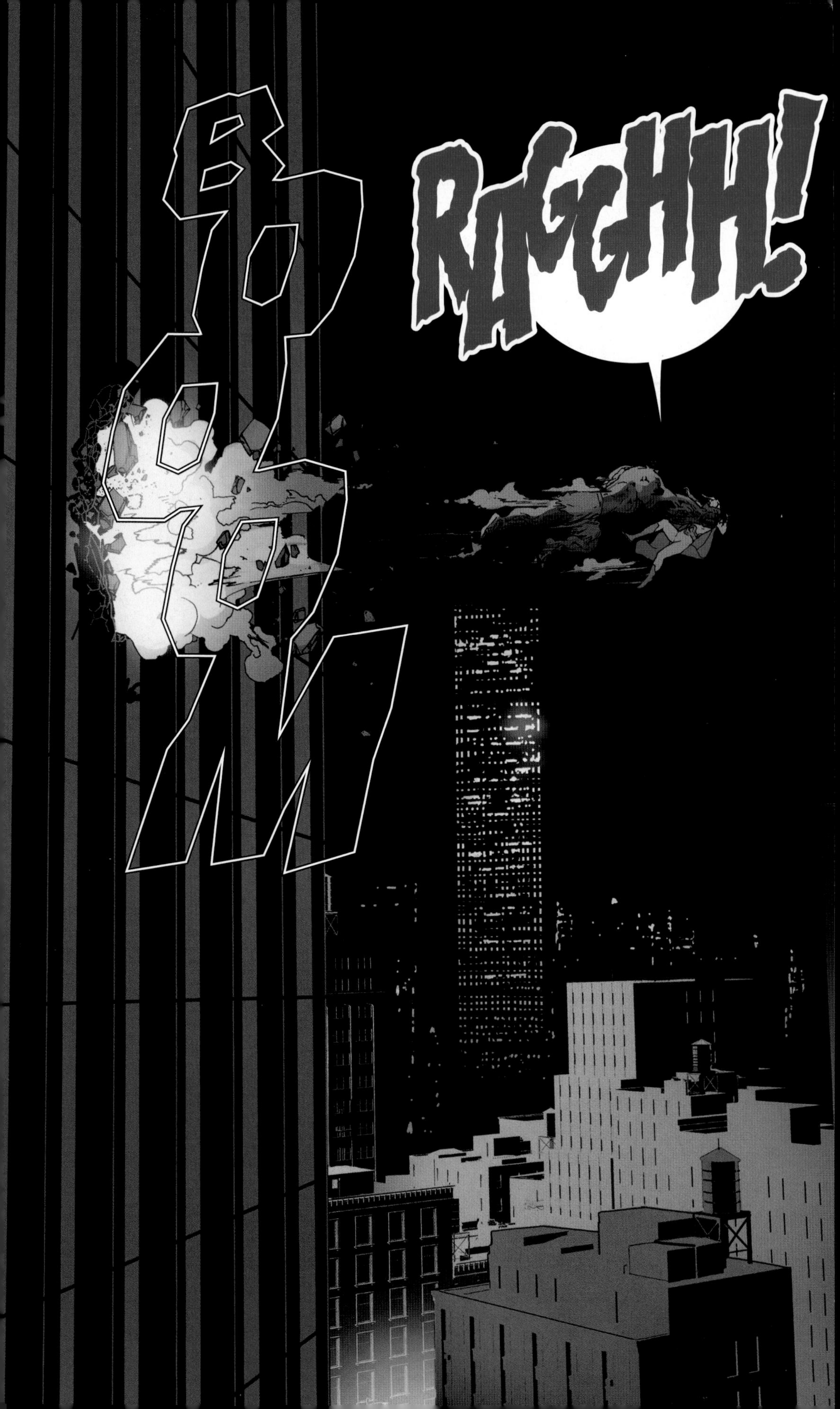
RAGGHH!
BOOOM

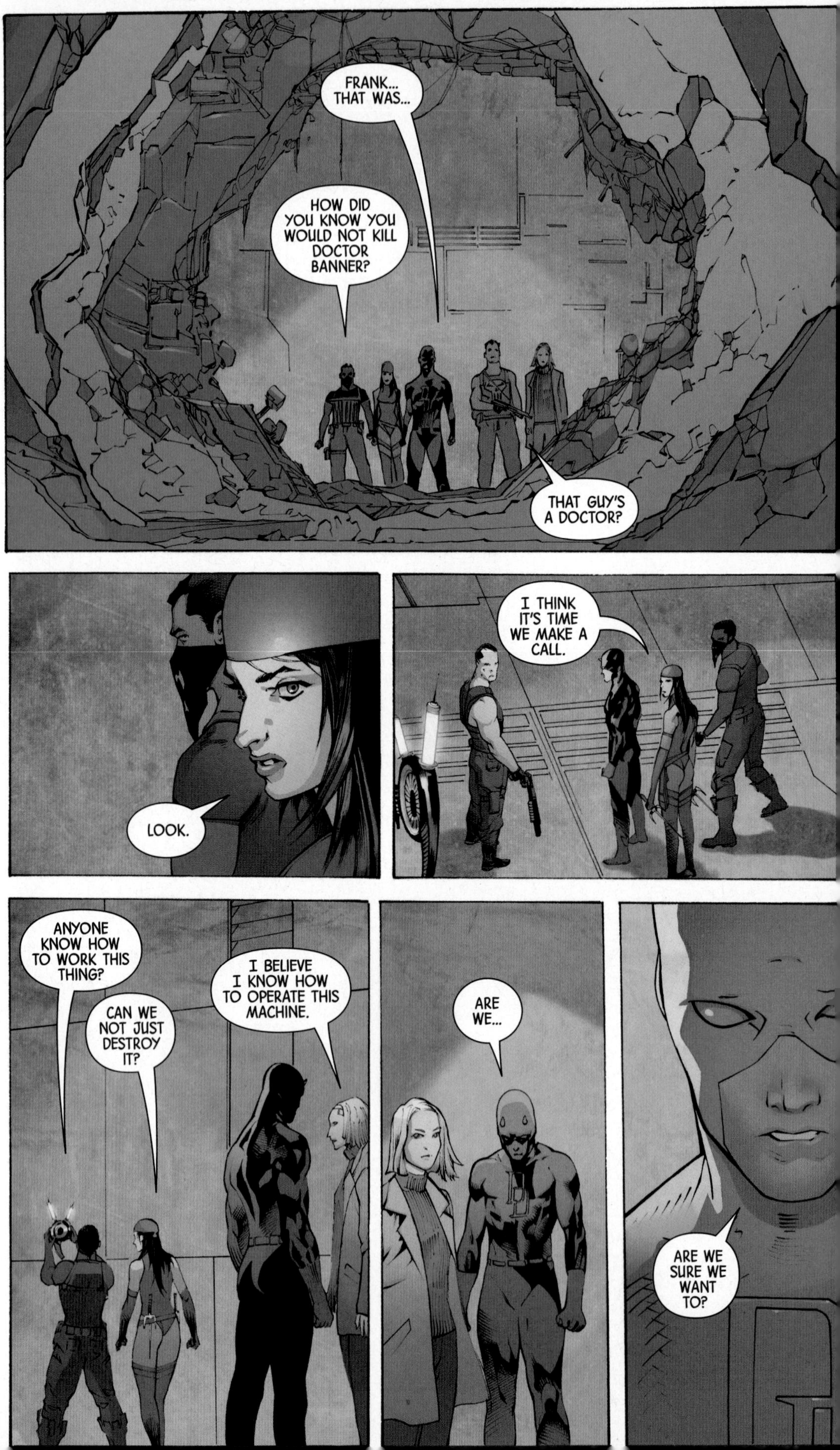
FRANK... THAT WAS...
HOW DID YOU KNOW YOU WOULD NOT KILL DOCTOR BANNER?
THAT GUY'S A DOCTOR?
LOOK.
I THINK IT'S TIME WE MAKE A CALL.
ANYONE KNOW HOW TO WORK THIS THING?
CAN WE NOT JUST DESTROY IT?
I BELIEVE I KNOW HOW TO OPERATE THIS MACHINE.
ARE WE...
ARE WE SURE WE WANT TO?

I MEAN, LOOK AT US. WE'RE THE ONLY THING WRONG IN THIS ENTIRE WORLD.

"WE'RE THE ONLY ONES FIGHTING."

AND ALL FOR WHAT? SO WE CAN HAVE SOMETHING BACK THAT WE MIGHT NOT EVEN WANT?

ELEKTRA... YOU FOUGHT US TOOTH AND NAIL TO STOP THIS. AND NOW...YOU WANT TO JUST TURN IT BACK ON?

YOU WANT TO GO BACK TO THAT LIFE?

IT IS MY LIFE, MATTHEW. NO MATTER HOW AWFUL IT MAY SEEM TO BE.

IT IS MINE. I WILL NOT ALLOW ANYONE TO LAY THEIR HANDS ON WHAT IS MINE.

NOT EVEN YOU.

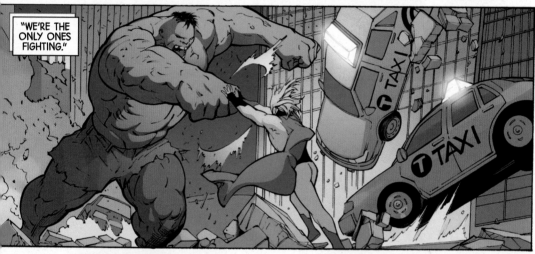

ELEKTRA. CAN WE JUST TAKE A MOMENT? CAN WE JUST STOP TO THINK ABOUT THIS? I MEAN... FOR STARTERS, NONE OF US EVEN KNOWS HOW TO USE THAT THING. HOW CAN WE BE SURE WE'RE EVEN--

I DO.

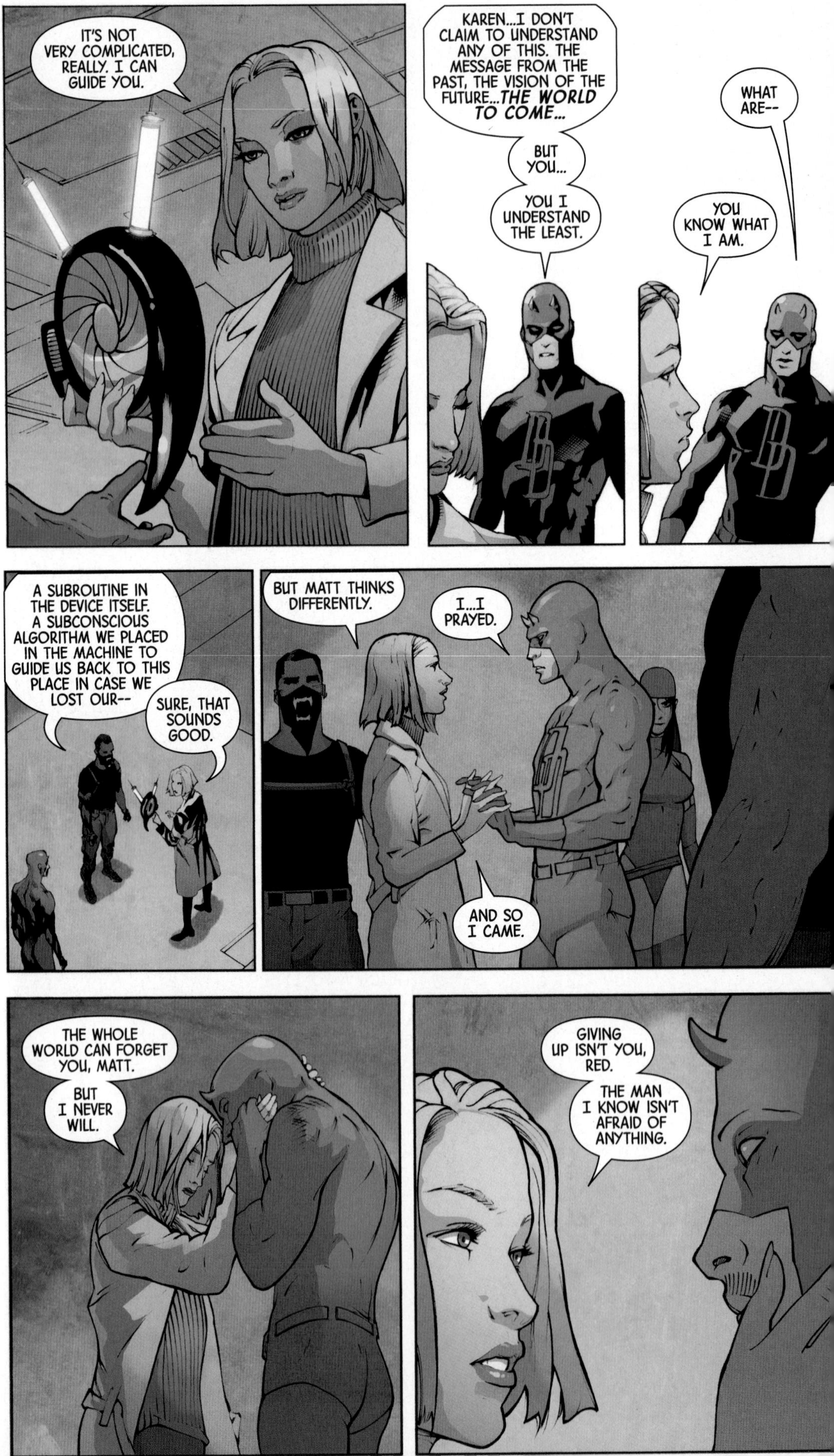
IT'S NOT VERY COMPLICATED, REALLY. I CAN GUIDE YOU.
KAREN...I DON'T CLAIM TO UNDERSTAND ANY OF THIS. THE MESSAGE FROM THE PAST, THE VISION OF THE FUTURE...*THE WORLD TO COME...*
BUT YOU...
YOU I UNDERSTAND THE LEAST.
WHAT ARE--
YOU KNOW WHAT I AM.
A SUBROUTINE IN THE DEVICE ITSELF. A SUBCONSCIOUS ALGORITHM WE PLACED IN THE MACHINE TO GUIDE US BACK TO THIS PLACE IN CASE WE LOST OUR--
SURE, THAT SOUNDS GOOD.
BUT MATT THINKS DIFFERENTLY.
I...I PRAYED.
AND SO I CAME.
THE WHOLE WORLD CAN FORGET YOU, MATT.
BUT I NEVER WILL.
GIVING UP ISN'T YOU, RED.
THE MAN I KNOW ISN'T AFRAID OF ANYTHING.

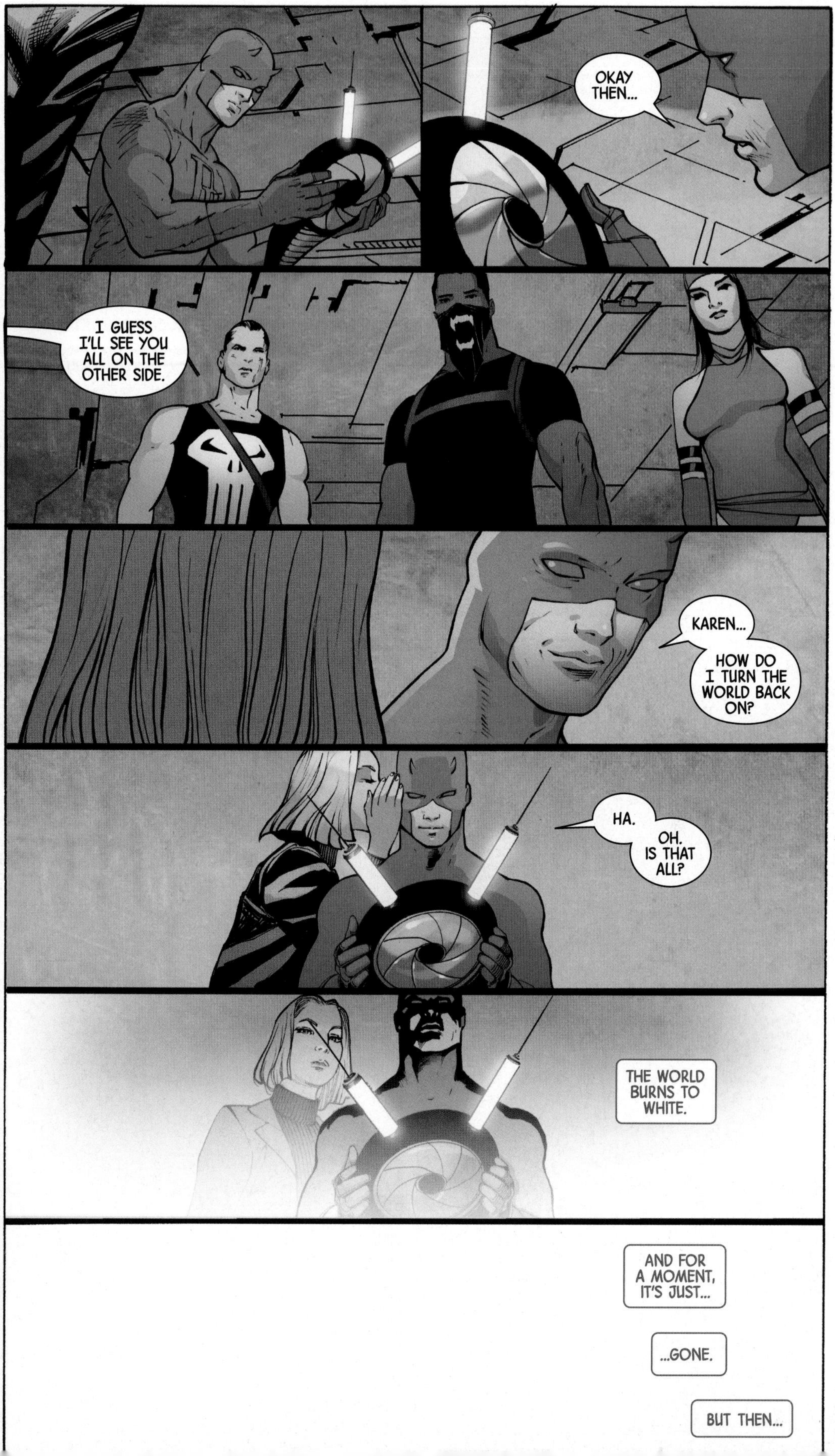
OKAY THEN...
I GUESS I'LL SEE YOU ALL ON THE OTHER SIDE.
KAREN...
HOW DO I TURN THE WORLD BACK ON?
HA.
OH. IS THAT ALL?
THE WORLD BURNS TO WHITE.
AND FOR A MOMENT, IT'S JUST...
...GONE.
BUT THEN...

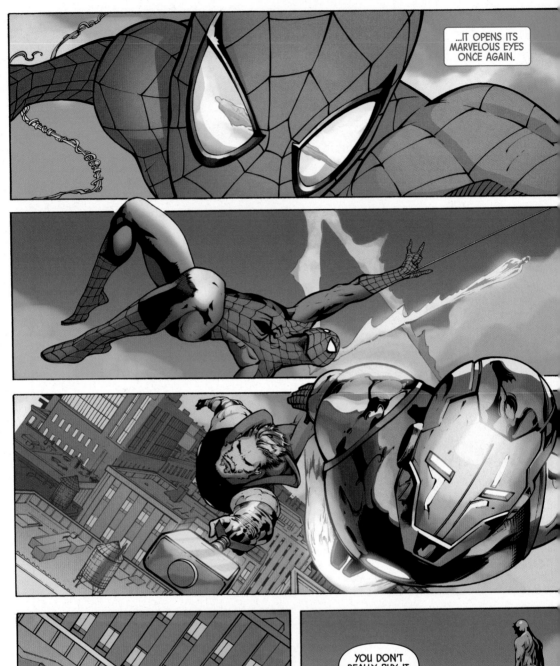

...IT OPENS ITS MARVELOUS EYES ONCE AGAIN.

YOU DON'T REALLY BUY IT, DO YOU?

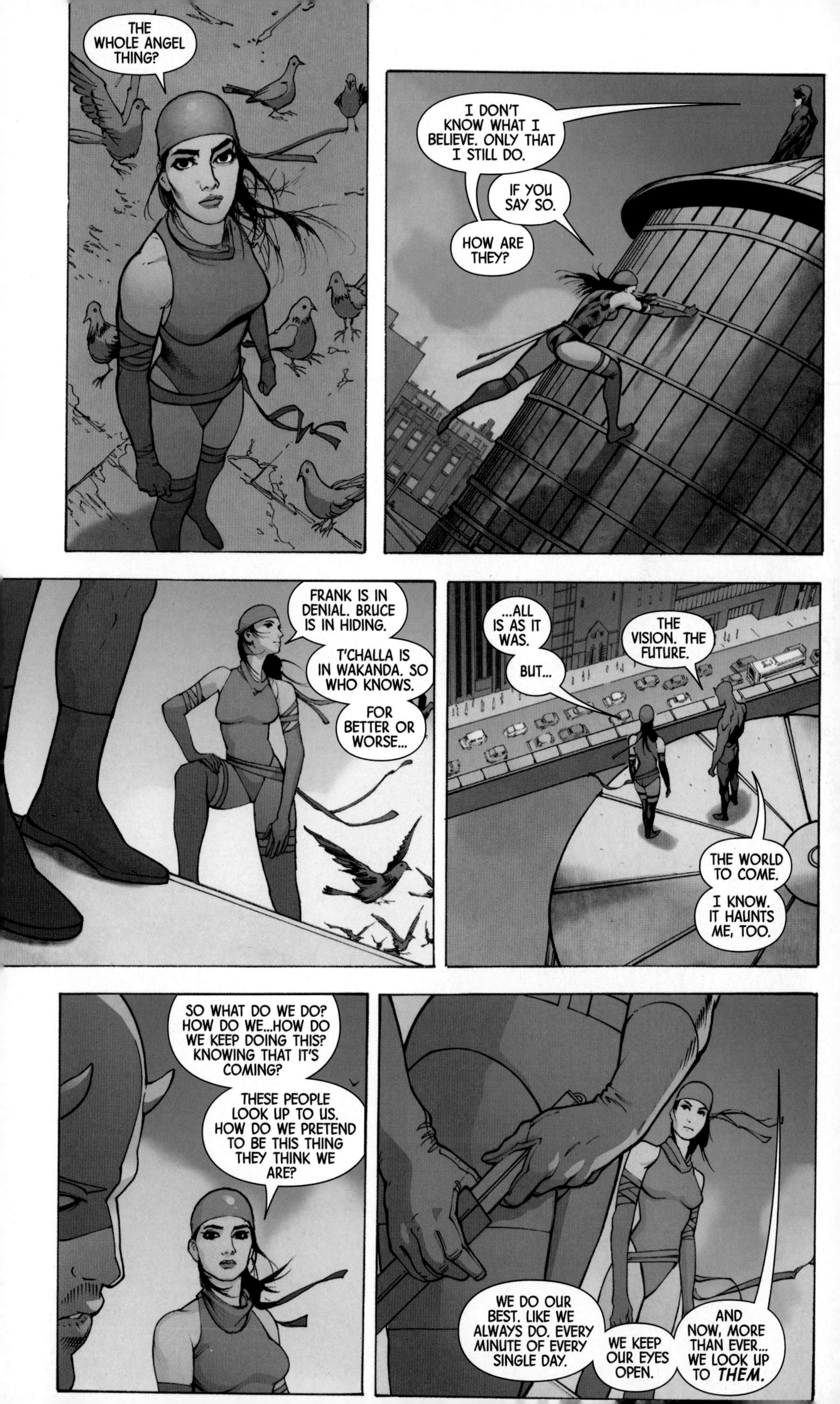
THE WHOLE ANGEL THING?
I DON'T KNOW WHAT I BELIEVE. ONLY THAT I STILL DO.
IF YOU SAY SO.
HOW ARE THEY?
FRANK IS IN DENIAL. BRUCE IS IN HIDING.
T'CHALLA IS IN WAKANDA. SO WHO KNOWS.
FOR BETTER OR WORSE...
...ALL IS AS IT WAS.
BUT...
THE VISION. THE FUTURE.
THE WORLD TO COME.
I KNOW. IT HAUNTS ME, TOO.
SO WHAT DO WE DO? HOW DO WE...HOW DO WE KEEP DOING THIS? KNOWING THAT IT'S COMING?
THESE PEOPLE LOOK UP TO US. HOW DO WE PRETEND TO BE THIS THING THEY THINK WE ARE?
WE DO OUR BEST. LIKE WE ALWAYS DO. EVERY MINUTE OF EVERY SINGLE DAY.
WE KEEP OUR EYES OPEN.
AND NOW, MORE THAN EVER... WE LOOK UP TO *THEM*.

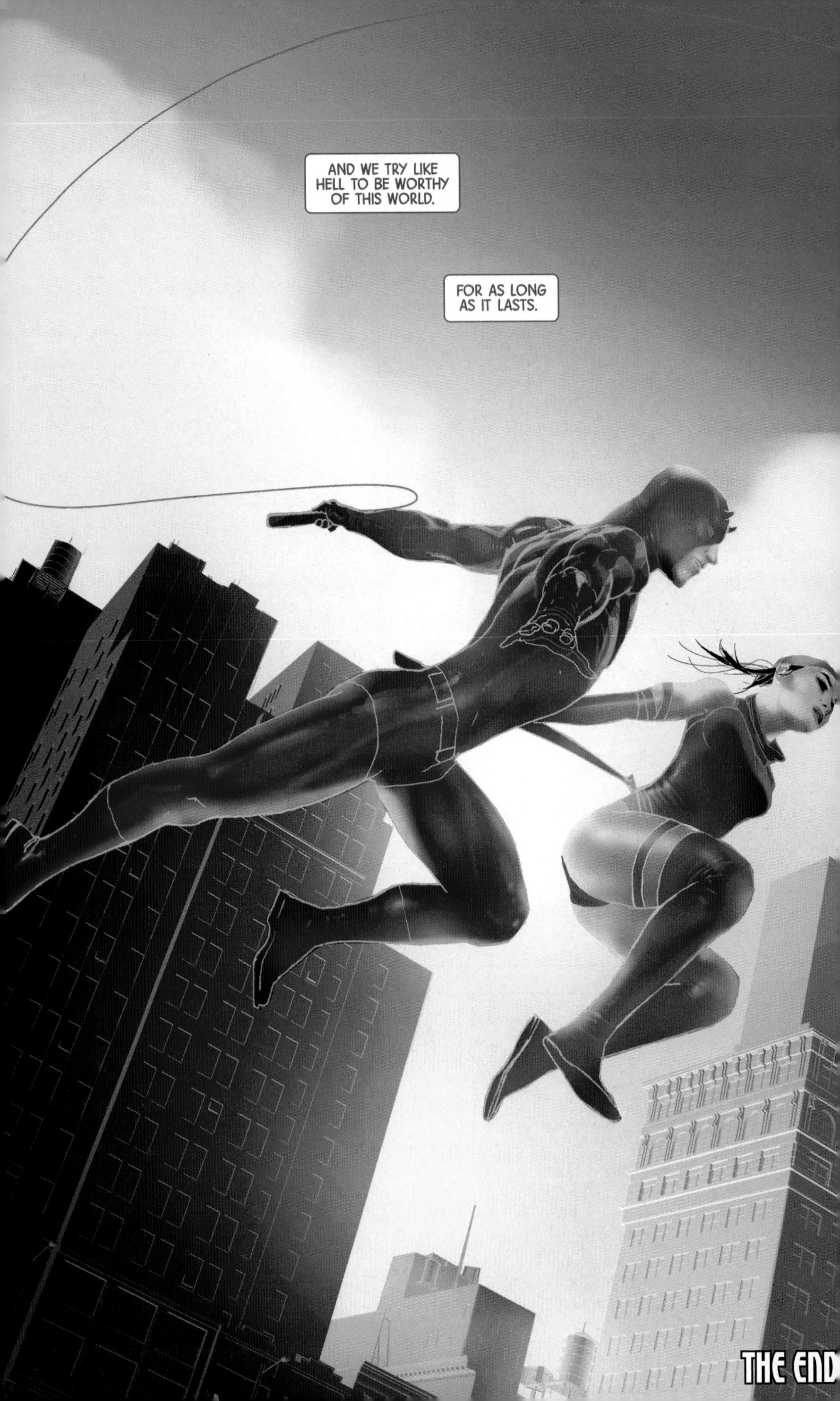
AND WE TRY LIKE HELL TO BE WORTHY OF THIS WORLD.
FOR AS LONG AS IT LASTS.
THE END

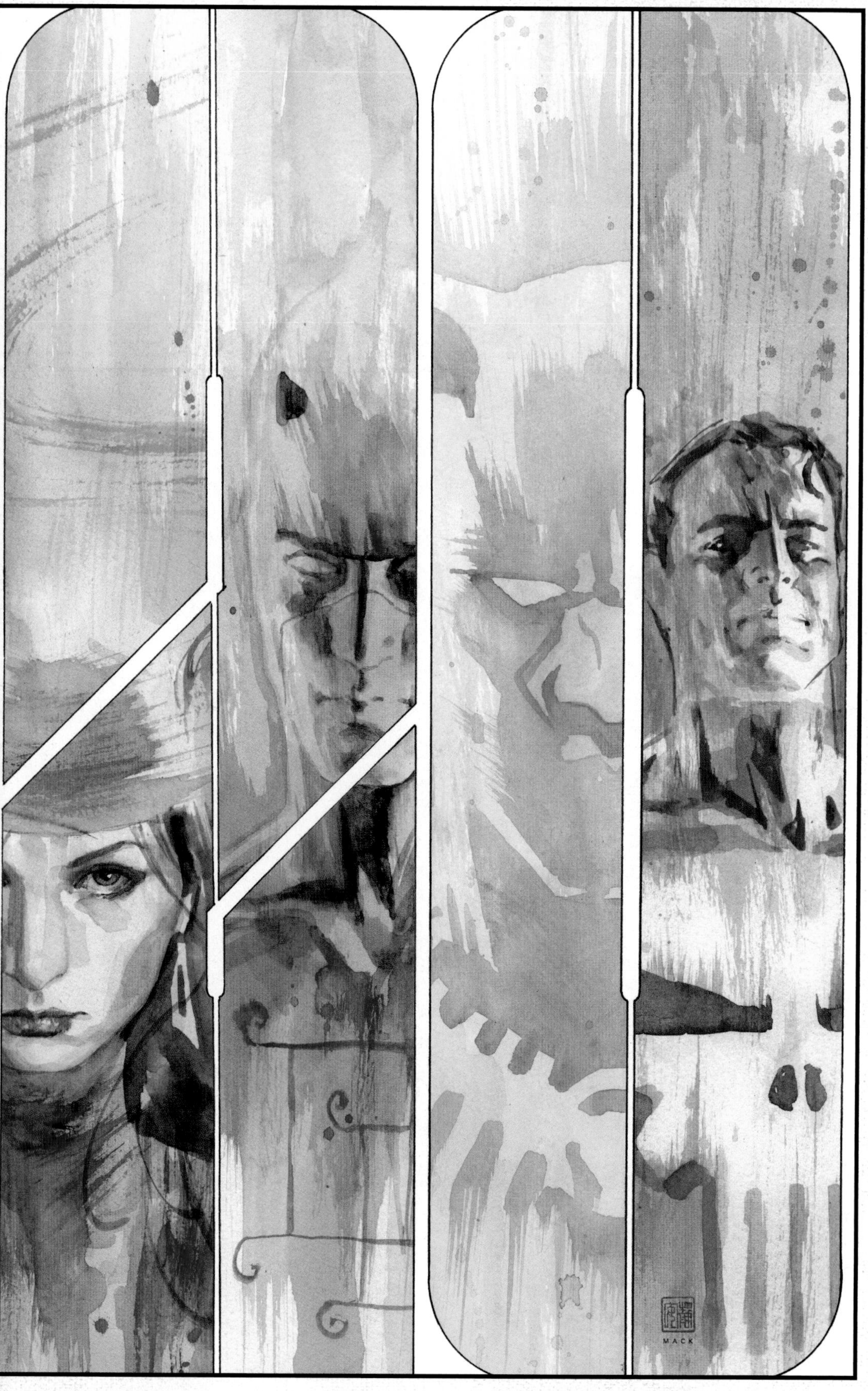
MACK

DAVID MACK
#1 variant

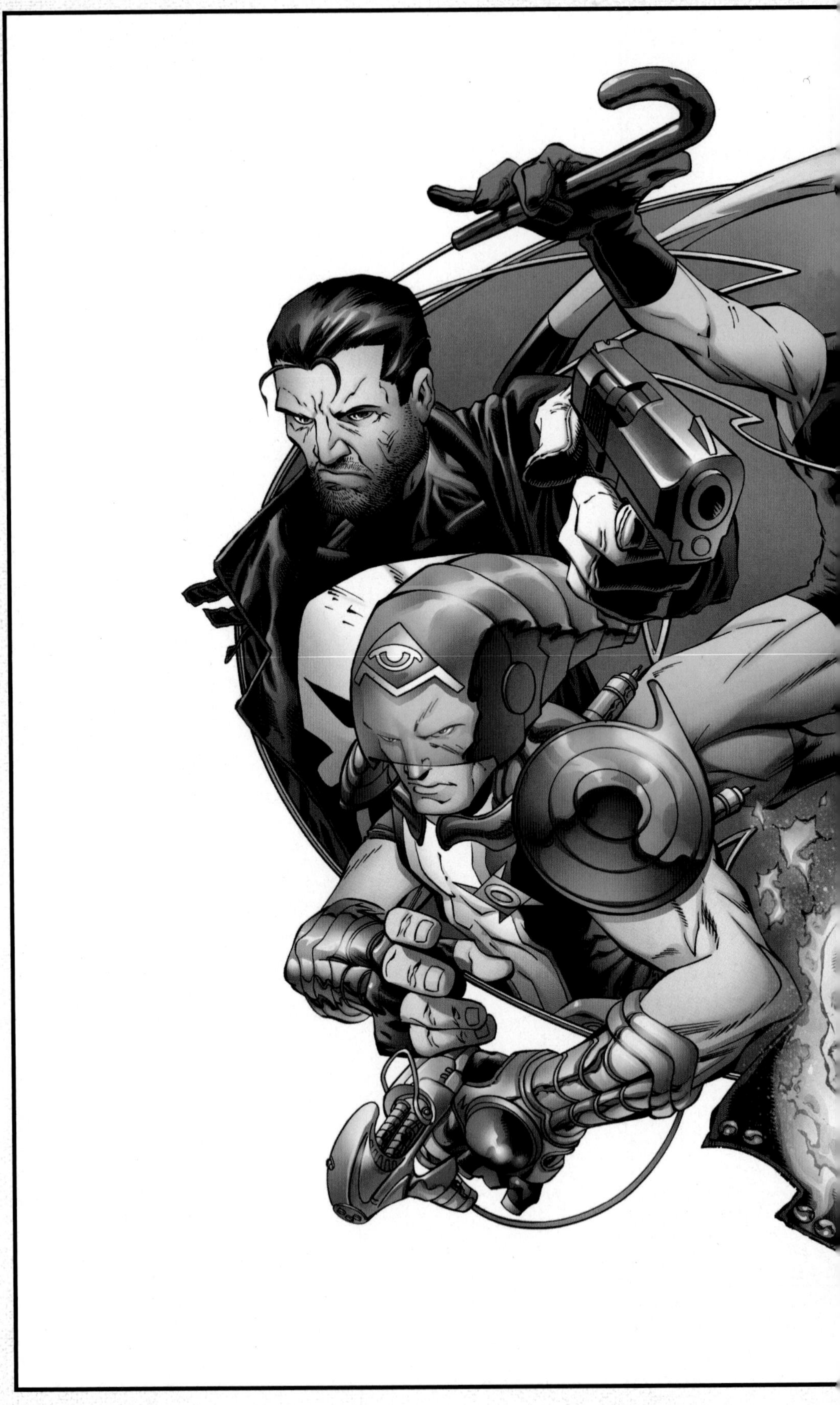

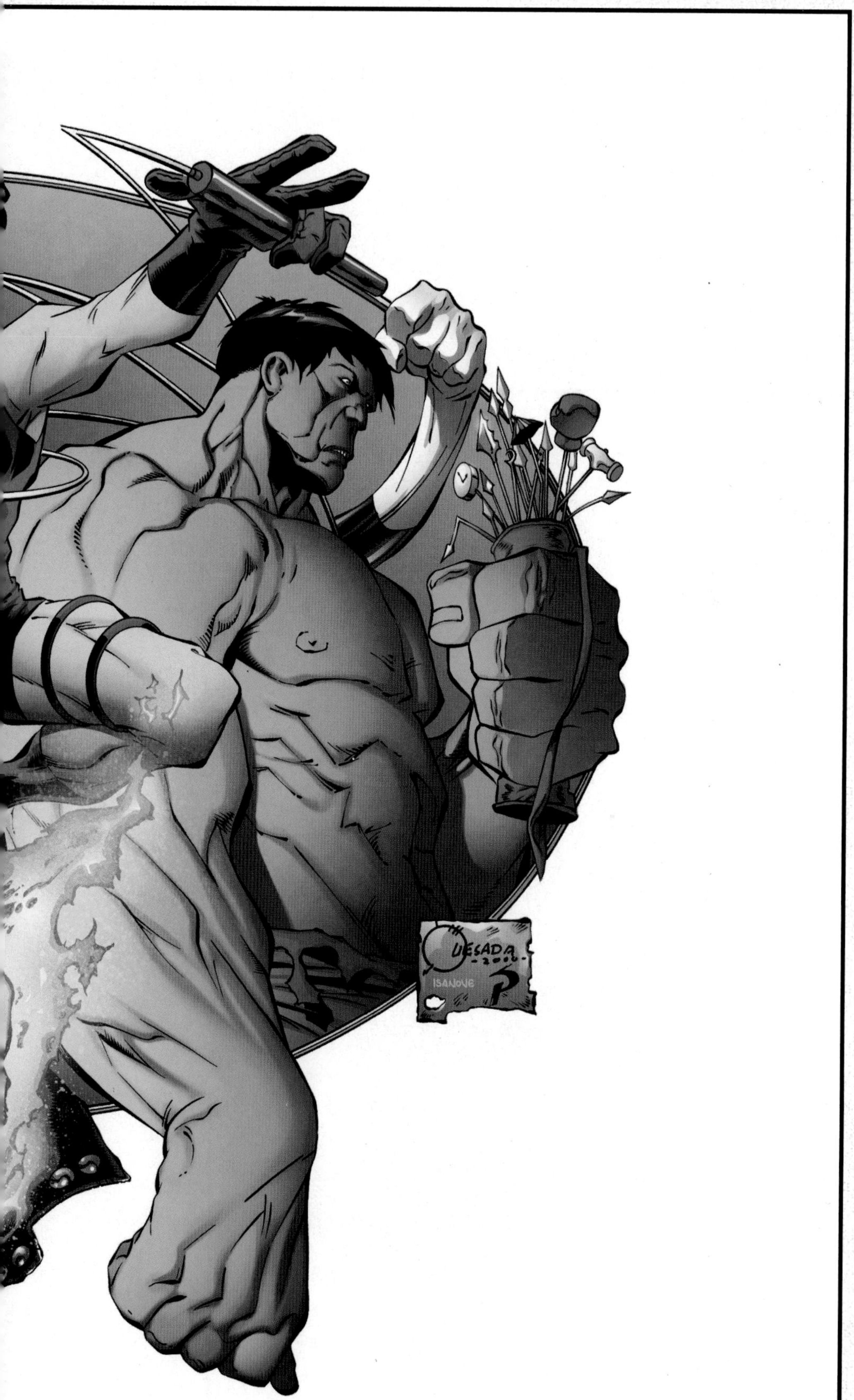
QUESADA
ISANOVE

JOE QUESADA & RICHARD ISANOVE

#1 variant

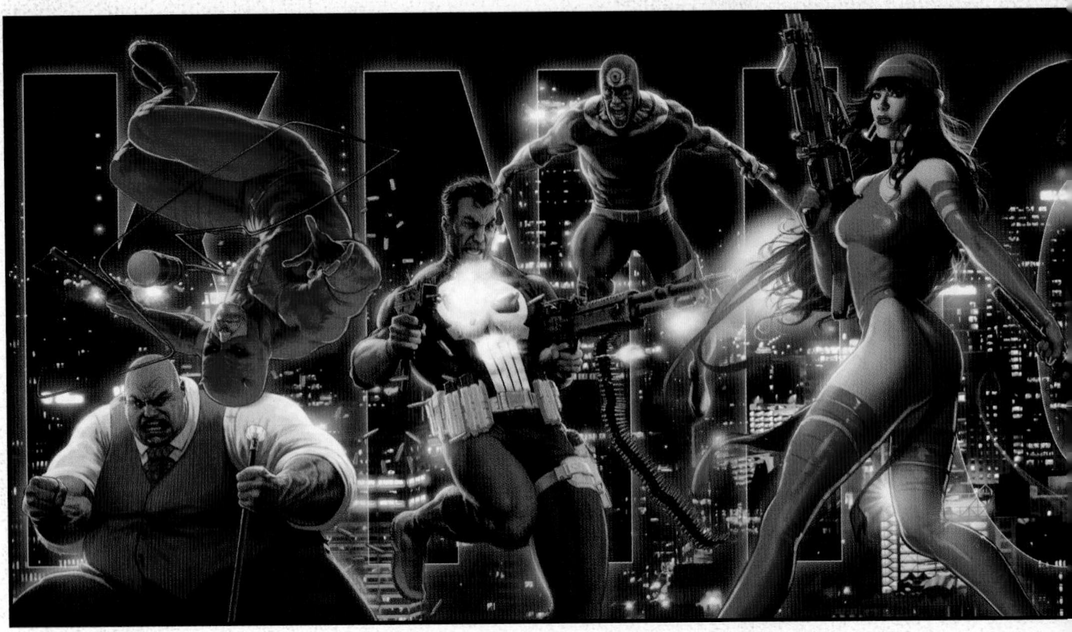

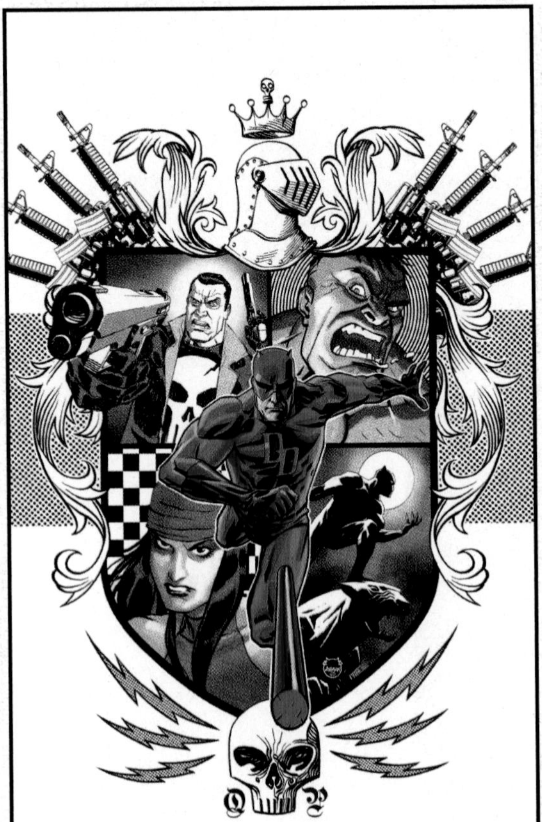

DAVE JOHNSON
#2 variant

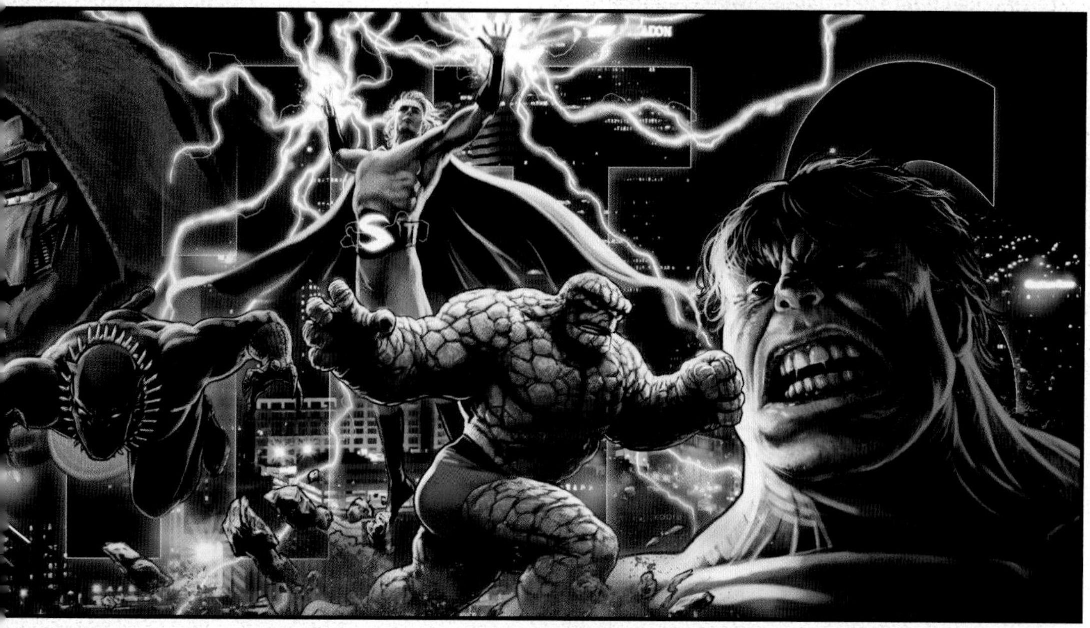

KAARE ANDREWS
#1-6 connecting variants

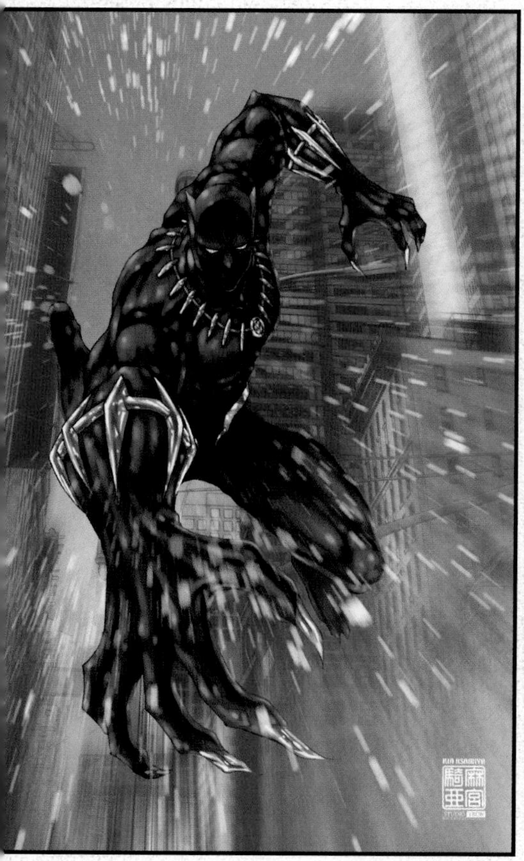

KIA ASAMIYA
#4 variant

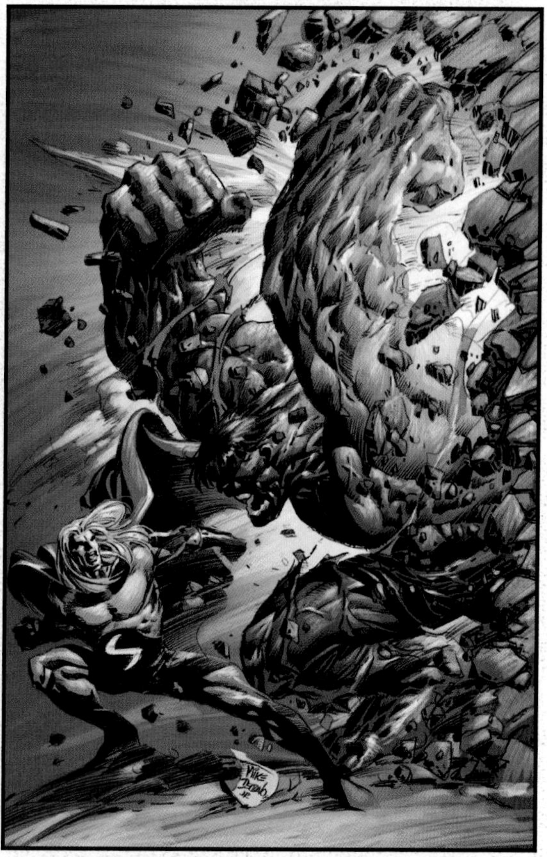

MIKE DEODATO JR. & RAIN BEREDO
#6 variant

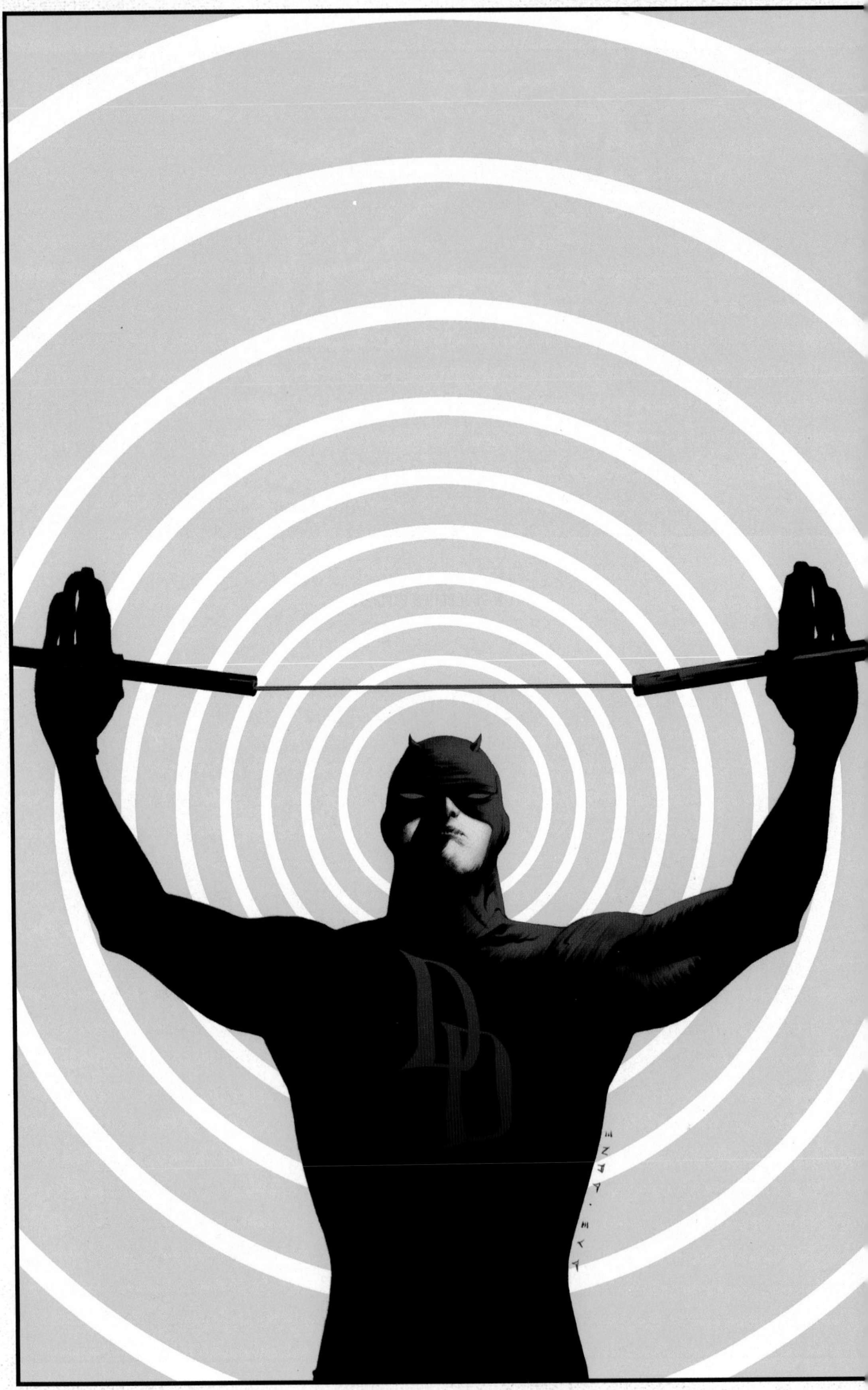

JAE LEE & JUNE CHUNG
#1 variant

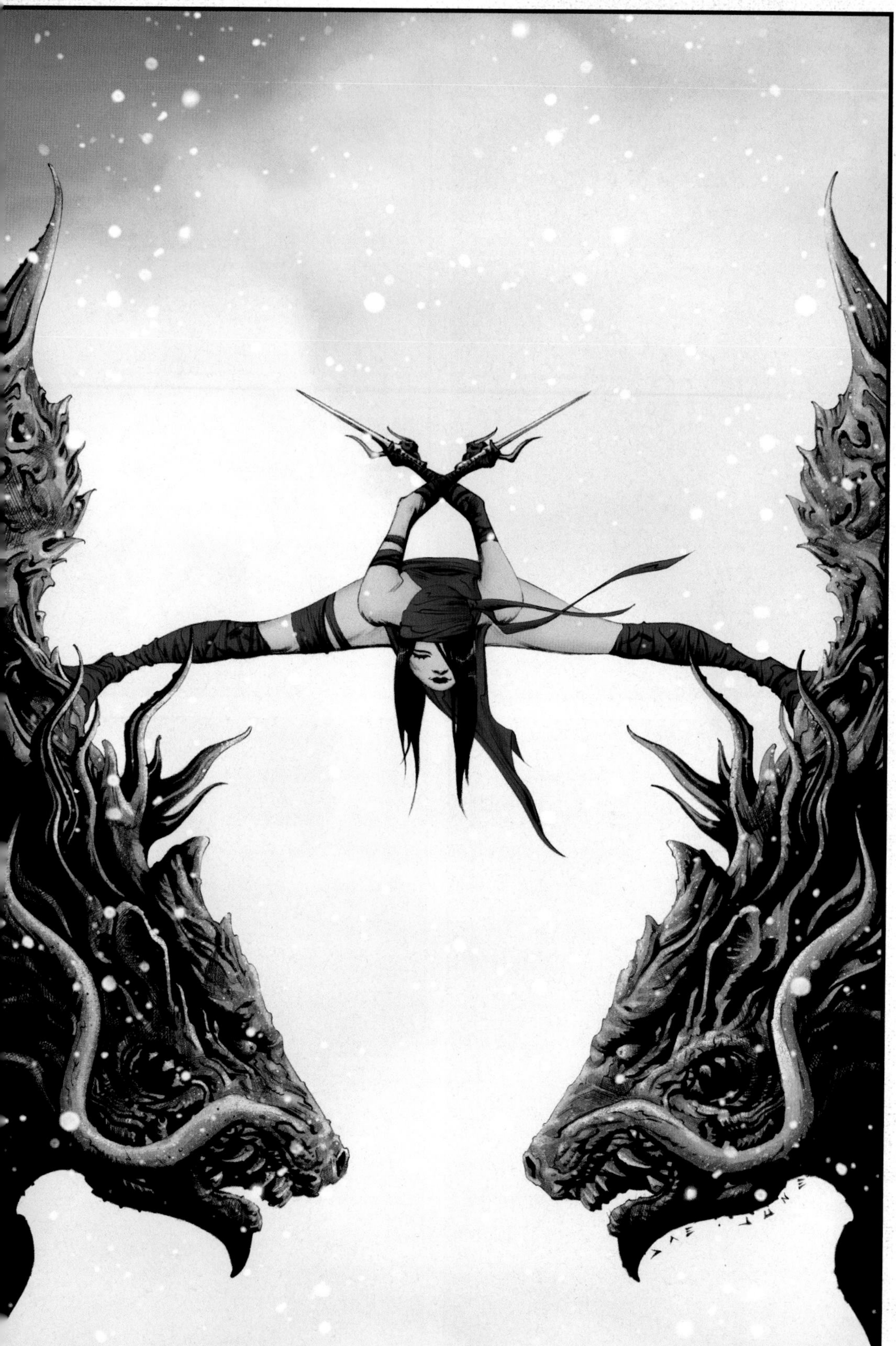

JAE LEE & JUNE CHUNG
#2 variant

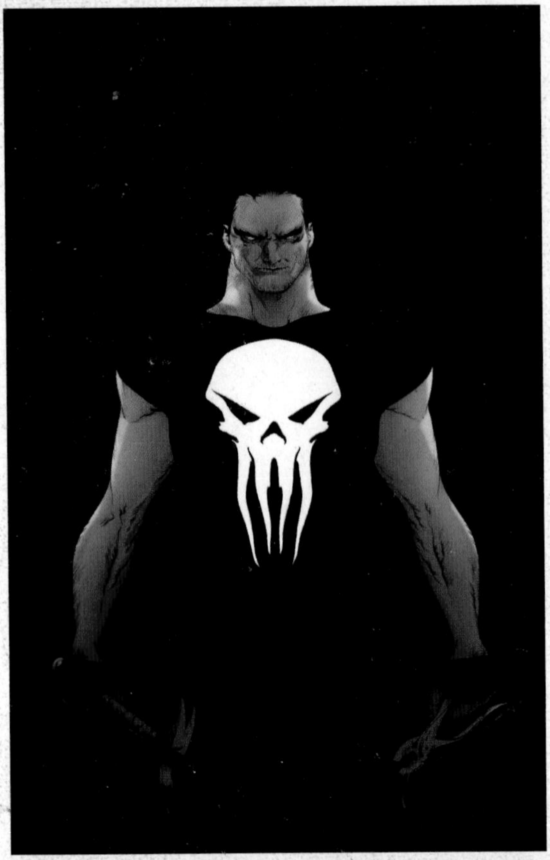
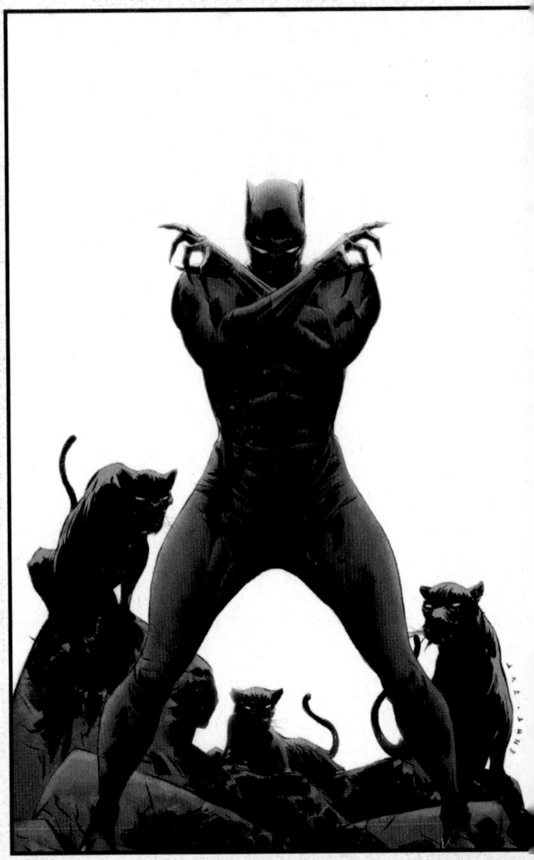
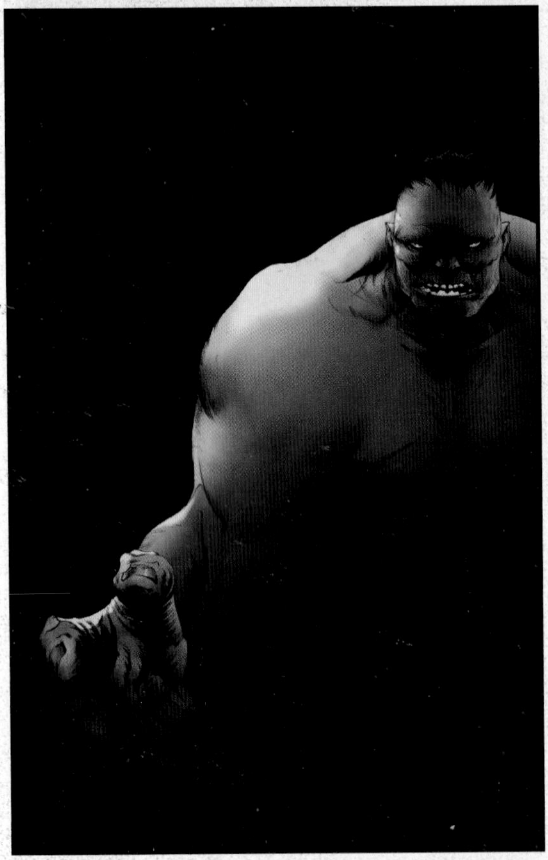
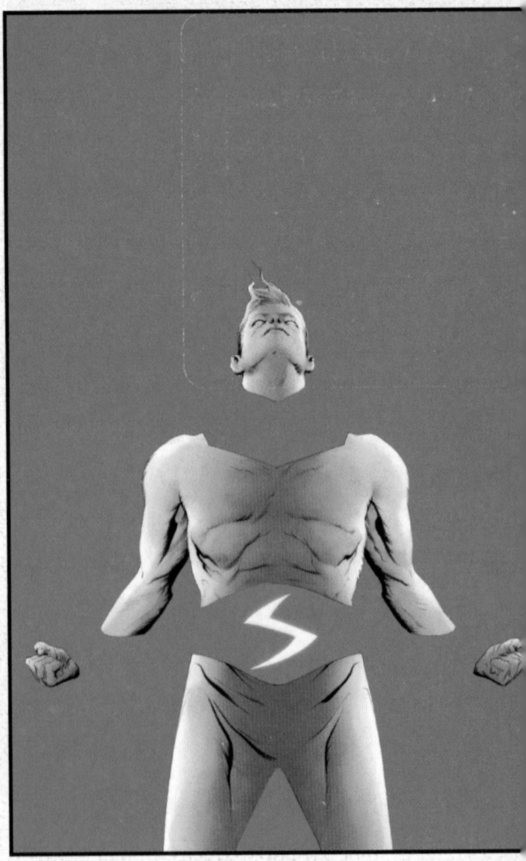

JAE LEE & JUNE CHUNG

#3-6 variants